Jc

D 21

Apartheid South Africa and African States

Apartheid South Africa and African States: from Pariah to Middle Power, 1961-1994

ROGER PFISTER

TAURIS ACADEMIC STUDIES
LONDON • NEW YORK

Published in 2005 by Tauris Academic Studies,
an imprint of I.B. Tauris & Co. Ltd
6 Salem Road, London W2 4BU
175 Fifth Avenue, New York NY 10010
www.ibtauris.com

In the United States of America and in Canada distributed by
St Martin's Press, 175 Fifth Avenue, New York NY 10010

International Library of African Studies (Vol. 14)
ISBN 1 85043 625 8
EAN: 978 1 85043 625 6

A full CIP record for this book is available from the British Library
A full CIP record for this book is available from the Library of Congress

Library of Congress catalog card: available

Printed and bound in Great Britain by TJ International Ltd, Padstow, Cornwall
camera-ready copy edited and supplied by the author

Contents

Map of Africa

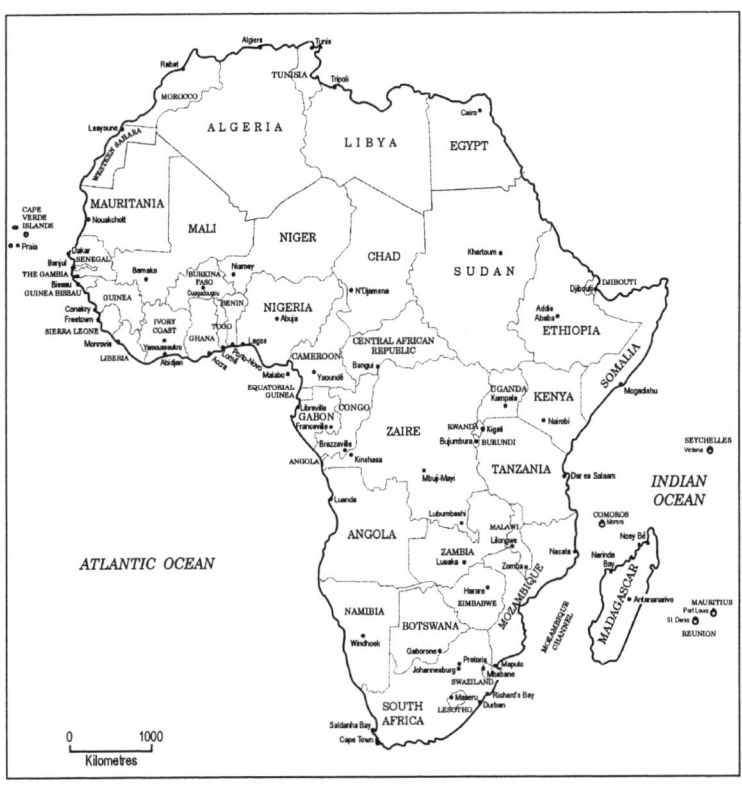

List of Tables and Illustrations

Abbreviations

ABDG	African Business Development Group
AHI	Afrikaanse Handelsinstituut
ANC	African National Congress
APLA	Azania People's Liberation Army
ARB	Africa Research Bulletin
ARCA	Archive for Contemporary Affairs
ARMSCOR	Armaments Development and Manufacturing Corporation
ATS	Department of Agricultural Technical Services
BDC	Bantu Development Corporation
BIS	Bureau interafricain pour la conservation de la terre et l'utilisation du sol (Inter-African Bureau of Soil Conservation and Land Utilisation)
BOSS	Bureau for State Security
BP	British Petroleum
Britmond	British Zaire Diamond Distributors
C.A.R.	Central African Republic
CCTA	Commission pour la coopération technique en Afrique (Commission for Technical Co-operation in Africa)
CDG	Campaign for Democracy in Ghana
CGIC	Credit Guarantee Insurance Corporation
CIA	Central Intelligence Agency
CODESA	Convention for a Democratic South Africa
CSA	Conseil scientifique pour l'Afrique (Scientific Council for Africa)
CSO	Central Selling Organisation
DFA	Department of Foreign Affairs
DGSE	Direction générale de la sécurité extérieure (General Directorate for External Security)
DMI	Directorate of Military Intelligence
DoD	Department of Defence
DP	Democratic Party
ECA	Economic Commission for Africa
EDF	European Development Fund

Eskom	Electricity Supply Commission
FAMA	Fondation pour l'assistance mutuelle en Afrique au sud du Sahara (Foundation for Mutual Assistance in Africa South of the Sahara)
FAO	Food and Agriculture Organisation
FNLA	Front national de libération de l'Angola / Frente Nacional de Libertação de Angola (National Front for the Liberation of Angola)
FRELIMO	Frente de Libertação de Moçambique (Mozambique Liberation Front)
Frolinat	Front national de libération du Tchad (National Liberation Front of Chad)
Gécamines	Générale des carrières et des mines
Habitat	United Nations Centre for Human Settlements
HNP	Herstigte Nasionale Party
ICJ	International Court of Justice
IDASA	Institute for a Democratic Alternative for South Africa
IDC	Industrial Development Corporation
ILO	International Labour Organisation
IMF	International Monetary Fund
IR	International Relations
Iscor	Iron and Steel Corporation
MIBA	Société Minière de Bakwanga
MK	Umkhonto we Sizwe
MPLA	Movimento Popular de Libertação de Angola (Popular Movement for the Liberation of Angola)
NAT.ARC.	National Archives of South Africa
NIS	National Intelligence Service
NP	National Party
OAU	Organisation of African Unity
OCAMM	Organisation commune africaine, malgache et mauricienne
OGAPROV	Office gabonaise d'amélioration et de production de viande (Gabonese Office for the Improvement and Production of Meat)
OPEC	Organisation of the Petroleum Exporting Countries
PAC	Pan-Africanist Congress
PFP	Progressive Federal Party
PP	Progressive Party
PRP	Progressive Reform Party
RENAMO	Resistencia Nacional Moçambicana (Mozambican National Resistance)
RI	Republican Intelligence
RSA	Republic of South Africa
SAA	South African Airways
SAAF	South African Air Force
SACOB	South African Chamber of Business
SACP	South African Communist Party

SADC	Southern African Development Community
SADCC	Southern African Development Co-ordination Conference
SADF	South African Defence Force
Safmarine	South African Marine Corporation
SAFTO	South African Foreign Trade Organisation

SAPA	Société Africaine des Produits Alimentaires
SDECE	Service de documentation extérieure et de contre-espionnage (Department for Foreign Information and Counterespionage)
SMTF	Société Minière de Tenke Fungurume
SNH	Société Nationale d'Habitat
Soekor	Southern Oil Exploration Corporation

SSC	State Security Council
S.W.A.	South West Africa
SWAPO	South West Africa People's Organisation
TRC	Truth and Reconciliation Commission
UAL	Union Acceptances Limited

UMHK	Union Minière du Haut Katanga
UN	United Nations
UNITA	União Nacional para a Independência Total de Angola (National Union for the Total Independence of Angola)
UNOMSA	United Nations Observer Mission in South Africa
USSALEP	United States-South African Leadership Exchange Program

| USSR | Union of Soviet Socialist Republics |
| UTA | Union des Transports Aériennes |

Preface

Research for this study began in 1998 at the Institute for Political Science of the University of Zurich whilst working simultaneously with Professor Jürg Gabriel as a Research Assistant at the Center for International Studies (CIS) in Zurich. He was then concurrently supervising my thesis. I thank him for facilitating and partly financing a four-month research stay in South Africa in early 1999. In this context, acknowledgement is most gratefully made to the Swiss Agency for Development and Cooperation (SDC) for providing the major part of the financial assistance. I also sincerely thank Professor Marie Muller, then Head of the Department of Political Science at the University of Pretoria, for allowing me the use of an office and of the infrastructure at the Department during the three months I was based in Pretoria.

In July 2001, I transferred my PhD registration to the Department of Political Studies at Rhodes University in Grahamstown, South Africa, for the final preparation of the study. The minimal supervision I received originally was partly compensated by the viewpoints given by Doctor Ivor Sarakinsky from this Department. During many late afternoon walks, we exchanged insights on a number of issues. Academic input also came from Professors James Barber, Research Associate at the South African Institute of International Affairs in Johannesburg and Affiliated Lecturer of the Centre of International Studies at Cambridge University, and Deon Geldenhuys at the Department of Political Studies of Rand Afrikaans University in Johannesburg. I thank them for their time and comments on earlier drafts.

The most relevant and crucial contribution to this study, however, came from Professor Peter Vale, whom I thank most sincerely for his excellent assistance as the supervisor of my thesis during the revision process after August 2002. He took over the supervision after accepting the appointment as the Nelson Mandela Professor of Politics at Rhodes University from 2003. I hold in high esteem his significant and valuable input.

The academic aspect aside, I received great assistance from several archivists and librarians. The study is based on primary documents from the Department of Foreign Affairs in Pretoria, and I am foremost indebted to the extensive help given by Neels Muller from their archive. Among the librarians, Sue Ogterop from the University of Cape Town's African Studies Library, Amanda Wortman at the Africa Institute in Pretoria and Esta Jones from the Archive for Contemporary Affairs in Bloemfontein deserve special mention. Their support was always speedy and is acknowledged with many thanks.

While an intellectual exercise, this study also became a great personal challenge.

My stay in South Africa in early 1999 halted abruptly, when I became the victim of a car accident in Fort Beaufort, Eastern Cape, on 25 April. I sustained serious injuries that resulted in great hardship and made me aware of the finality of one's existence. At the same time, the traumatic event changed the future course of my life in the most positive way. I will never forget the presence of my parents, Peter and Agnes, in those most difficult of times. Thanks are also due to the members of staff of the three rehabilitation clinics where I spent several months for their caring help, and in particular Doctor Peter Zangger from the SUVA Clinic in Bellikon, Switzerland.

Last, but not least, I wish to extend hearty thanks to several friends. Foremost, I deeply appreciate Jackie's caring help, constant encouragement and companionship. Her exceptional assistance in Johannesburg in many ways merits a special accolade. Thanks are also due to Gina and Robert for their kind hospitality while in Bloemfontein during January 1999.

Since 2002, the author of this study has been a Visiting Research Fellow at the Centre for International and Comparative Politics at the University of Stellenbosch.

1

Introduction

Aim and Scope

This study examines South Africa's foreign relations with the black African countries beyond southern Africa, primarily guided by information derived from research in the Department of Foreign Affairs (DFA) archive in Pretoria and thus viewed from a South African perspective. These relations were determined by the inherent conflict between Pretoria's apartheid ideology and its ambition to be accepted as a fellow African state on the one hand, and African continental rejection of its race discrimination policies and the consequent exclusion from the community of African states on the other. As African diplomatic activities against apartheid significantly contributed to South Africa's international isolation, it was generally recognised that the road to international acceptance was contingent on the normalisation of relations with Africa.[1]

The geographic area of interest encompasses the 39 African countries and islands between southern and North Africa. The South African approach to this region differed significantly from that towards the other two. Due to their geographical proximity and economic dependence, and once independent, Angola, Botswana, Lesotho, Mozambique, Namibia,[2] Swaziland, Zambia and Zimbabwe, the former Rhodesia, effectively constituted South Africa's backyard;[3] military maps of the mid-1970s show these countries also lay within reach of its airforce.[4] Malawi, to which not all factors applied, is not considered as part of southern Africa in this study. Following the DFA's organigrams, the North African countries Algeria, Egypt, Libya, Morocco, Tunisia and the Western Sahara are excluded from this study.[5]

The study begins in 1961, when South Africa attained the status of a Republic, independent from the British Commonwealth. Concurrently, a wave of independence was sweeping across the continent. In 1963, the newly independent African states formed the Organisation of African Unity (OAU). With the OAU equating the struggle for decolonisation with that against apartheid,[6] African states mobilised international opposition against South Africa through the OAU and at the United Nations (UN). Support was also given to South Africa's principal liberation movements, the African National Congress (ANC) and the Pan-Africanist

Congress (PAC). The first democratic elections in April 1994 mark the end of the study, as this historical event finally removed the divisive issue between South Africa and African states. However, following the political reforms initiated by President Frederik Willem de Klerk four years earlier, Pretoria no longer aimed at finding their acceptance as a white African state, but rather at obtaining recognition for the reforms that had been instituted. Yet, a massacre on the night of 17/18 June 1992 in the township of Boipatong, south of Johannesburg, undermined the government's strategy. The ANC accused Pretoria of being the main culprit for the massacre. At its request, the OAU called on the UN Security Council to discuss the political crisis. The subsequent deployment of a UN and other observer missions to South Africa ended Pretoria's ambitions. We argue the African dimension at that moment in South Africa's political transition has been neglected.

Chapter 2 on South Africa's Foreign Policy System, a term derived from Deon Geldenhuys' standard work on South Africa's apartheid foreign policy,[7] presents the state and non-state actors relevant to this work, placing an emphasis on the personalities involved. The years reviewed in this study saw the rule of four South African executives, each of whom left his specific imprint on Pretoria's foreign policy towards Africa. The country's foreign relations with those states are therefore organised in four chapters following these periods. Appendix A contains biographies of key DFA officials.

Conceptual Framework

Our study is interdisciplinary, encompassing aspects from the academic disciplines of History, Political Science and International Relations (IR). While the differences between them are usually emphasised, voices from all sides propagate a conversation across the demarcations, arguing this would add value to their research.[8] The present work is an example of such "cross-fertilization",[9] allowing us to categorise it as Diplomatic History. Claimed by both historians and international relations scholars to be a sub-field of their discipline,[10] we understand it in broad terms, as set out in the journal of the same name devoted to the study of Washington's foreign relations: "*Diplomatic History* should be a forum for discussion of many aspects of the diplomatic, economic, intellectual, and cultural relations of the United States".[11] We now turn to the various disciplinary components and their contribution to our investigation.

This study is a historical one, entailing the principal components of what historians are said to do, namely to uncover "an objectively knowable past" and to describe a particular event rather than classes of events in a "narrative-based rather than theory-based" way by using archival sources.[12] The single most innovative aspect resulting from their approach is a revisionist assessment of IR and Political Science hypotheses:

"At the very least political scientists could learn a great deal about the validity of their own models if historians would use them and offer critical assessments of their strengths and limitations".[13] A finding in this study, for example, vitiates the claim South Africa's foreign relations with all African states were an expression of the country's political economy. At the same time, historians tend to be suspicious towards IR and Political Science theories. Noting in 1982 "[e]ven the best of the older diplomatic histories tended to be descriptive rather than analytical", the President of the American Historical Association urged those interested in the study of international relations to cross boundaries: "we may gain in analytical sophistication if we overcome our congenital distrust of theory".[14] We attempt to do precisely this, using IR and Political Science concepts to give this study a conceptual framework. Regarding the former's input, International Relations has been circumscribed as a "generic concept for a vast array of activities, ideas and goods that do or can cross national boundaries", embracing "social, cultural, economic, and political exchanges".[15] During the Cold War, the discipline tried "to explain the relationships between power, stability and order", in the context of which the term hegemony was coined.[16] Being a contested concept, it has been altered and enlarged; the idea of preponderance, of which political scientist Bull distinguishes three sub-forms, is useful for our purposes:

> *Dominance*: "characterised by the habitual use of force by a great power against the lesser states comprising its hinterland"
> *Hegemony*: "The great power prefers to rely upon instruments other than the direct use or threat of force, and will employ the latter only in situations of extremity"
> *Primacy/Leadership*: "The position of primacy or leadership which the great power enjoys is freely conceded by the lesser states within the group concerned"[17]

This study views sub-Saharan Africa as a "sub-system" in international relations,[18] with South Africa as the most powerful nation in terms of economic development, technological superiority and military capacity. Following the above categorisation, dominance suitably describes Pretoria's behaviour in the immediate neighbourhood, while its approach beyond varied between hegemony and primacy. If a country was prepared to accept South Africa's predominant position, the relationship was closer to primacy, but nearer to hegemony in the other cases. Pretoria always presented itself as a leader on the continent, stressing "it desired 'leadership through service' in its relations with Africa",[19] offering various forms of assistance, and it had difficulty understanding that, because of its apartheid policy, the majority of African countries was unwilling to become appreciative followers. In contrast, post-Second World War, the United States provided war-torn Europe with material and normative, or moral, resources; its international relations value system of a world order "that stressed openness, nondiscrimination, and greater prospects for joint gains" found followers among European states.[20] As this did not apply to South Africa's position in Africa, clashing with the moral and political objective of pan-Africanism, Pretoria could not become a member of transnational bodies, such as the OAU and the Southern African Development Co-ordination Conference (SADCC). Consequently, South Africa interacted with the states of interest on a bilateral basis, offering economic and politico-military incentives for them to deviate from their anti-apartheid stance.

We also draw on Political Science, particularly the study of foreign policy, applying the definition whereby it is "the sum of official external relations conducted by an independent actor (usually a state) in international relations".[21] The only reservation relates to "official", as much of South Africa's foreign policy of interest here was conducted in secrecy. In Chapter 2, presenting the state and non-state actors involved, we make the case for a bureaucratic politics model, arguing the state is not a homogeneous unit. We further subscribe to an understanding of foreign policy being determined by domestic and external factors,[22] the latter comprising a regional, continental and international dimension (Figure 1). Regarding the domestic factor, and acknowledging foreign policy is conducted in pursuit of a country's national interest, there is agreement the survival of apartheid was the cornerstone of South Africa's foreign policy.[23] The developments in its immediate neighbourhood are understood as the regional environment, which significantly impacted on the country's foreign relations with the countries further north. The continental factor comprised, first, Africa's struggle against apartheid. Second, with the African sub-system comprising politically and economically weak states,[24] Pretoria's bargaining chips stood some chance of achieving the desired results. Third, dealing with African states involved taking into account certain characteristics relevant to their foreign policy making, particularly the dominant role played by a country's executive.[25] This was important to the extent that advantages resulting from economic co-operation with South Africa were thought to persuade them to take Pretoria's side. South Africa's foreign relations of interest here were also influenced by developments in international politics. First, the African community of states used the United Nations to pressure Pretoria into abandoning apartheid. Second, in its undertakings in the former French colonies, the Pretoria government had to acknowledge the continuously strong influence of Paris. Third, the Cold War between the US and the Soviet Union was relevant.

In the context of South Africa's foreign policy toward Africa, we need to discuss the thesis that it had been the expression of the country's political economy. The study of political economy is concerned with the "interaction of the state and the market as the embodiment of politics and economics in the modern world".[26] Of the three fundamentally dif-

ferent perspectives – liberalism, nationalism, Marxism – the Marxist view
interests us. Without going into all its details, it stressed "the primacy of
economics, seeing all else as derivative, as epiphenomena, the superstruc-
ture upon an economic base".[27] Arguing the capitalist economy had a
tendency to overproduce goods due to insufficient domestic demand, and
taking into account the uneven development among nations, it proposed
capitalist economies were forced to look for new markets, thus explaining
colonialism and imperialism: "The acquisition of colonies had enabled
the capitalist economies to dispose of their unconsumed goods, to ac-
quire cheap resources, and to vent their surplus capital".[28] Political scientists Timothy 'Tim' Shaw and Roger Southall used this view of political
economy to explain South Africa's drive into Africa in the early 1970s,
basing their argument on the country's economic development in the
1960s. Throughout this decade, its domestic economy had significantly
expanded, with growth rates of more than 7 per cent on average, resulting in increased import while export stagnated. Pretoria subsequently
propagated an import substitution policy and established a commission
of inquiry. In 1972, the report of the so-called Reynders Commission
highlighted the need for export promotion,[29] recommendations leading to
the formation of the Private Sector Export Advisory Committee in the
same year and the Interdepartmental Committee for Exports in 1974.[30]
Prior to this, Pretoria had been served solely by the Export Trade Advisory Committee until 1967 and its successor, the Export Promotion
Council. In the second half of the 1960s, Pretoria fostered plans for a
'Greater South Africa' and a 'Southern African Common Market', aimed
at consolidating and extending Pretoria's powerful economic position in
the immediate neighbourhood. Against this background, Shaw and
Southall argued Pretoria's drive into Africa was "an expression of the
dynamics of South African political economy".[31] Even though not deny-
ing its Outward-Looking Policy had "major political-diplomatic and
military-strategic objectives", they emphasised the "underlying material
basis in the requirement of South African-based capital for increased
resources, larger markets, expanding spheres for investment and maintenance of the existing supply of foreign migrant labour".[32]

The accuracy of their interpretation can now be assessed, by analysing hitherto unavailable statistical evidence on South Africa's trade with
sub-Saharan Africa. In 1962, the Department of Customs and Excise
ceased publishing these figures on a country-to-country basis,[33] probably
to prevent unnecessary embarrassment for those countries trading with
the Republic despite their verbal anti-apartheid stance. In 1995, the Cabinet decided to still treat these figures as confidential,[34] suggesting the
post-apartheid government was guided by similar considerations. This
situation notwithstanding, files in the DFA archive contained that data,
evidently provided by its sister department. Appendixes B and C present
a comprehensive picture of South Africa's trade with all black African

countries. Although the absolute accuracy of the figures cannot be guaranteed due to "backdoor trade" through third-party countries, double-invoicing, clandestine trade and other factors,[35] we can draw two important conclusions. First, the countries in South Africa's immediate neighbourhood constituted its main trading area; the trade volume with the countries further north was insignificant.[36] Second, all sub-Saharan African countries maintained trade relations, though some at a very low level, with Pretoria usually exporting more than importing.

In conclusion, we validate Shaw's and Southall's view of the Outward-Looking Policy towards southern Africa as having been motivated primarily by economic considerations. However, we disagree with their thesis that Pretoria pursued the same goals further north, "an attempt to divide the continent's opponents of apartheid by establishing cooperative relations with willing black African states".[37] Rather, our statistical evidence confirms what political scientist Guelke suggested in 1974:

> I am not arguing that she has no economic ambitions outside Southern Africa (...). But outside Southern Africa at least, the Republic's political objectives – notably, the neutralisation of African-sponsored campaigns in the U.N. against *apartheid* – clearly enjoy the highest priority in the formation of her outward-looking policy.[38]

Organised business and private enterprises were part of Pretoria's Outward-Looking Policy in Africa, but trade and other economic activities were merely levers to lure African countries into contact.

Sources and Literature

The prime motivation for this study lay in the fact that our topic has been neglected in the secondary literature. In an attempt to fill this gap, we conducted research in 1999 and 2000 in South African archives considered to house relevant documentation. We had unrestricted access to two non-governmental archives, the Archive for Contemporary Affairs (ARCA) at the then University of the Orange Free State in Bloemfontein[39] and the ANC Archive at the University of Fort Hare in Alice, Eastern Cape.[40] The former houses, *inter alia*, collections from politicians, foreign service officials, economists and cultural and economic bodies. The consulted documents were somewhat meagre, but provided especially relevant information on the organised Afrikaner business association Afrikaanse Handelsinstituut. The ANC Archive, open to the public since 1996, stores documents from a number of the ANC Exile Missions. The material yielded meagre results for the purposes of this study, but has been included in our recent article on the ANC's exile diplomacy in Africa.[41] These two archives aside, no other 'private body' opened its doors. The archive of the multinational Anglo American Corporation, in particular, would undoubtedly have provided a mine of information. However, as other researchers experienced,[42] it is practically inaccessible, quite likely because the company aims to prevent embarrassing information regarding collaboration with the apartheid regime being exposed. At the time of our research, there was no obligation for the private sector to lay bare the past. Due to the post-1994 political dispensation, a different situation prevailed with regard to the use of government archives. Most importantly, the National Archives Act (No 43 of 1996), enacted in January 1997, reduced the closed access period from the previous 30 to 20 years. During our stay in South Africa in 1999, we therefore had the right to access material up to and including 1979. Despite this liberal legislation, the state of affairs of archival management necessitates critical comments relating to the substance of and the practical access to the material. Both questions are of great significance to a study such as this, relying on primary sources, and we now deal with the four government archives we used.

Although mandated to act as custodian over the archives of central and regional government offices, the National Archives[43] did not have much power to enforce its brief. Several government departments refused to subject their records to appraisal or transfer them, amongst them the Departments of Foreign Affairs and Defence and the national intelligence agency. The accessible collections of potential interest for this study came from the Private Secretary to the Minister of Information and the Department of Information. This dearth in material can be explained by referring to South African archivist Verne Harris, who rightly suggested secrecy and an authoritarian management ethos were the government's modus operandi, with serious implications for the collection and preservation of archival documentation.[44] This statement most clearly applies to the security apparatus, as we will see. In contrast, we gained the impression the DFA was different. Its lower-ranking civil servants appear to have followed a rather legalistic policy regarding the collection of records; the Truth and Reconciliation Commission (TRC)[45] only mentions one case of record destruction in this department prior to the 1994 elections.[46] However, one qualification regarding their files' comprehensiveness needs to be made. André Jaquet, who held various diplomatic posts in the period under review, described to us the working ethos of Roelof Frederik 'Pik' Botha, the Minister of Foreign Affairs (1977-94), and two senior officials of importance in this study, namely Bernardus Gerhardus 'Brand' Fourie and Peter Rae Killen: "both the Minister and Brand Fourie had their own extensive files. (..) Rae Killen had three safes and a few filing cabinets in his office which were crammed full of files, some of which eventually went to Registry and most of which were probably shredded. (...) I believe that Pik Botha also took a large number of files to his smallholding in Pretoria North when he left office".[47] The organisation of the files greatly facilitated our research in the Union Buildings.

The collections consulted were substantial, sometimes containing documents from other government agencies and newspaper cuttings. Access was not arbitrary, as was seemingly the case during apartheid.[48] Prior to our arrival, we had established contact with the person in charge, Neels Muller, and his assistance proved to be incredibly helpful. For reasons unclear to date, he originally granted access to the files up to April 1994. However, after some six weeks of research, the situation was suddenly reversed; access was curtailed as provided for in the Archives Act. Henceforth, our access to the files became limited to 1979 in the case of 16 countries, as opposed to access up to or beyond 1991 for 15 countries.[49] Nonetheless, there is enough justification for defining the time framework until 1994. Crucially, the files on Nigeria and Uganda, key countries post-1990, were open for the entire period under review.

Regarding the national intelligence agency and the Department of Defence, both were involved in human rights violations, and therefore had a keen interest in purging their records. In its findings, the TRC concluded: "By May 1994, a massive deletion of state documentary memory within the security establishment had been achieved". National intelligence apparently destroyed its records on a regular basis since 1982.[50] The few noteworthy documents we obtained from the Minister's Office are referenced in this work, but not listed in the bibliography. In principle, the Department of Defence, with its own archival repository, staffed by military personnel, granted access subject to the National Archives Act regulations, but most of the documents we could consult date from the early 1960s. There seems to be no desire on the part of this department to disclose its apartheid activities, as underlined by a personal anecdote. Having requested photocopies of material contained in a box dated 1970, we were summoned by military intelligence staff. During the course of the interview, it became clear this box had been erroneously declassified. Furthermore, staff members mentioned higher-ranking military officials had removed large amounts of archival material prior to the 1994 elections and the TRC hearings, as confirmed in the TRC's final report.[51]

To supplement the primary and secondary sources, we interviewed and corresponded with former DFA officials, military staff, politicians, academics and representatives from private and state companies. However, Brand Fourie declined to make any statements. Leo Henry 'Rusty' Evans, Deputy-Director General and Director-General (1990-92, 1992-97), did not respond to our attempts of establishing contact. We unsuccessfully pursued different avenues to access Lukas Daniël 'Niël' Barnard, who headed national intelligence during the 1980s. Also, several people of importance, such as Prime Minister Balthazar Johannes 'John' Vorster, Cornelius Petrus 'Connie' Mulder and Eschel Mostert Rhoodie from the Department of Information, the DFA's Rae Killen, or Niël Barnard's predecessor, Hendrik Johannes van den Bergh, are no longer alive.

2

South Africa's Foreign Policy System

Introduction

Since this study is also about Pretoria's foreign policy towards the African states beyond southern Africa, this chapter provides the setting necessary to the understanding of the players. In doing so, we distinguish between state and non-state actors, acknowledging "states are definitely not the only significant actors in international relations".[1] While pursuing individual goals, a "policy coalition"[2] existed between the different actors to advance the minority's interests. Private and official links are significant in this study and we refer to the Policy Network approach, a loose politico-sociological description for such contacts in pursuit of powerful interests.[3] In beginning with the state as a foreign policy actor, we do not consider it as a homogeneous entity, referring to the "agency-based perspective". While recognising a country's executive "is formally the key figure in all foreign policy decisions",[4] this approach emphasises the role of bureaucracy and its public servants.[5] Within this perspective, the "bureaucratic politics model" and the "psychological model" are relevant. The former stipulates "the foreign policy decisions and actions of a government do not represent the intent of any one figure, but rather are the unintended result of bargaining, pulling, hauling, and tugging by bureaucratic competition in their ceaseless quest for more funds, resources, and influence".[6] The model's confrontational aspect is usually emphasised, but it has rightly been suggested that it can also be about "doing 'deals' with their bureaucratic opponents".[7] As this also applied to Pretoria's foreign policy making, South African scholars used the description of a "village council running a foreign policy",[8] leading to "haphazard"[9] policy formulation, and aptly rejected the idea of it being "concerted, well-organised, well-thought out, unified, homogenous, linear-directional".[10] The psychological approach stresses the role played by the individual public servant.[11] Adhering to this view, we put a relatively strong emphasis on the personalities of the relevant officials.

In view of the above, we first present the state actors. For easy reference, Table 1 contains the names of the executives, the ministers and administrative heads in the DFA, and indicates the rival government entities with the relevant officials.

Figure 1: *Environments of South African Foreign Policy Making*

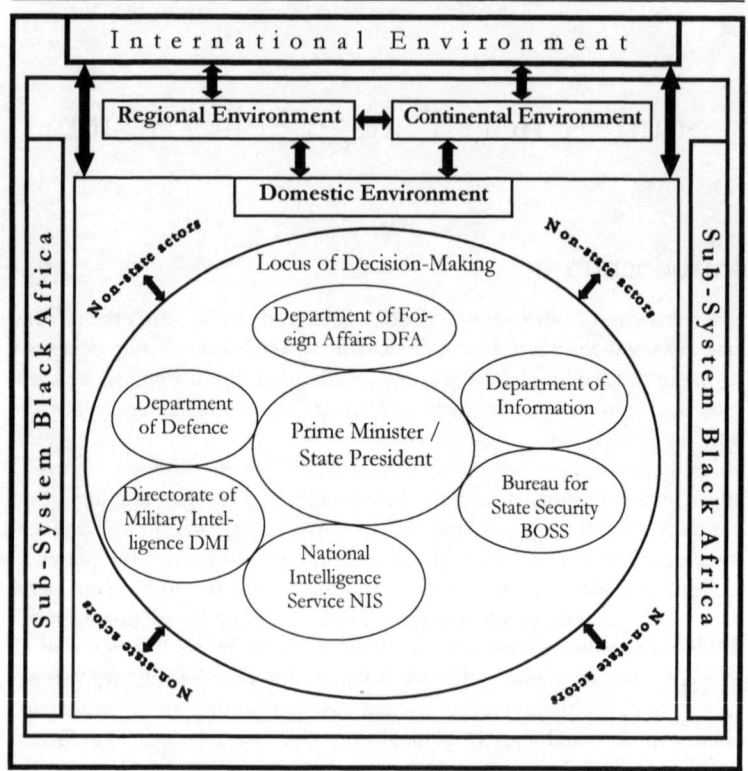

Prime Ministers and State Presidents

At the beginning of Hendrik Verwoerd's Premiership, British Prime Minister Harold Macmillan delivered his Wind of Change speech in Cape Town in February 1960, heralding Great Britain's departure from Africa, a contributory factor to Pretoria's withdrawal from the Commonwealth in March 1961. That decision was supplemented by Verwoerd's domestic policies as a stalwart of the ruling National Party (NP), wanting to "maintain white supremacy for all time to come".[12] His stance reflected the *laager* mentality of the Afrikaner community, describing a defensive and isolationist frame of mind originating from the closed defensive circle into which the Afrikaner settler ox-wagons moved when threatened by attacks from the blacks. It was further defined by the hostilities fanned by the Anglo-Boer War (1899-1902).[13] As Verwoerd had no practical foreign policy making experience, he initially tended to rely on his Minister of External/Foreign Affairs.

Table 1: State Actors in Pretoria's Foreign Policy Making

	Prime Minister / State President	Department of Foreign Affairs		Other Government Agencies
		Minister	Secretary / Director-General	
1961	Hendrik **Verwoerd** (September 1958 – September 1966)	Eric **Louw** (January 1955 – December 1963)	Gerhardt **Jooste** (August 1956 – June 1966)	
1966 1971 1976	John **Vorster** (September 1966 – September 1978)	Hilgard **Muller** (January 1964 – March 1977)	Brand **Fourie** (July 1966 – April 1982)	**Department of Defence** P.W. Botha **Military Intelligence** Fritz Loots, Neels' van Tonder **Bureau for State Security BOSS** Hendrik van den Bergh **Department of Information** Connie Mulder, Eschel Rhoodie
1981 1986	Pieter Willem **Botha** (September 1978 – August 1989)	Pik **Botha** (April 1977 – April 1994)	Hans **van Dalsen** (May 1982 – March 1985) Rae **Killen** (April 1985 – March 1987)	**Department of Defence** Magnus Malan **Military Intelligence** P.W. van der Westhuizen, Daan Hamman **National Intelligence Service NIS** Niël Barnard
1991 1994	Frederik Willem **de Klerk** (September 1989 – May 1994)		Neil **van Heerden** (April 1987 – September 1992) Rusty **Evans** (October 1992 –)	**National Intelligence Service NIS** Niël Barnard

On 13 September 1966, John Vorster became Prime Minister. Compared to Verwoerd, who had been stabbed to death on 6 September, his leadership was more relaxed and pragmatic, permitting a degree of racial interaction in sport and, in 1971, Malawi replaced its white ambassador in Pretoria with a black one. His pragmatism had repercussions on Pretoria's foreign policy, which became known as Outward-Looking Policy

and was "marked by secrecy, *ad hoc* arrangements, and over-dependence on close confidants".[14] As a result, his premiership experienced serious inter-departmental fights over the leading role in this field. Indeed, it can be argued Vorster stumbled over his "serious lack of decisive leadership".[15] During 1977, South African newspapers brought to light some of the clandestine activities the Department of Information and the national intelligence agency, the Bureau for State Security (BOSS), backed by Vorster, had pursued since 1972, resulting in the 'Information Scandal'.[16] Due to the mounting political pressure, Vorster resigned in September 1978. However, the scandal served as a smokescreen to hide a power struggle that had developed during the 1970s for the leadership of the country.[17] The military strongly resented both the Department of Information's and BOSS's dominant position within Vorster's ambit; divergent policy approaches were at the centre of the conflict. Once Vorster had resigned, the race for the premiership began. The main competitors were the Ministers of Information and Defence, Mulder and P.W. Botha. The bitterly contested election took place on 28 September 1978, while the Information Scandal helped tip the balance in favour of Botha.

P.W. Botha, a National Party man, was already the party's national campaign organiser at a relatively youthful 30. During his steady rise through the ranks he was a Member of Parliament, Deputy Minister and Minister in various departments, becoming the NP's leader in the Cape Province during 1966 and, in April of that year, the Minister of Defence, a post he held until October 1980.[18] Botha was thus experienced in domestic and foreign policy making,[19] both dominated by a realist worldview whereby the "wise and efficient use of power by a state in pursuit of its national interest is (..) the main ingredient of a successful foreign policy"[20]. The change in leadership from Vorster to Botha therefore "brought dramatic changes in personality, style and substance in the policy-making process".[21] Crucially, Botha established "the political dominance of the military (...) in key decision-making";[22] the State Security Council (SSC), established in 1972, but seldom used under Vorster, emerged "as the primary overall planning and decision-making body".[23] Botha also streamlined the bureaucratic apparatus and initiated a constitutional reform whereby, after 1984, the country's executive was no longer referred to as Prime Minister, but as State President; the formerly symbolic position of State President was abolished.[24] Botha's tough and uncompromising policy ended in August 1989, forced to resign due to illness and allegations of erratic behaviour.

With F.W. de Klerk succeeding, pragmatism returned to Pretoria. Born to a politically renowned family, he entered politics in 1978, subsequently holding a variety of ministerial portfolios. Parallel to his ascendancy in government, de Klerk rose within the NP ranks, becoming the party's Transvaal and national leader in 1982 and 1989 respectively.[25] Not known as a reformer during his ministerial days, de Klerk's speech at the opening of Parliament in February 1990 was particularly surprising. He lifted the 30-year ban on the ANC and other black liberation movements, and announced Nelson Mandela's release from prison that materialised nine days later.[26] When assessing whether de Klerk's initiatives were born of personal conviction or political necessity we subscribe to the view of South African political scientists Geldenhuys and Kotzé who suggested he did not come to question the philosophy behind apartheid, but found its practical application impossible to maintain.[27] In foreign policy matters, de Klerk was not experienced, and, in stark contrast to his predecessor, none of his ministerial portfolios had dealt directly with security matters. As a result, the foreign service officials held a predominant position, although sometimes competing with national intelligence.

Department of Foreign Affairs

Established in 1927 as the Department of External Affairs, the foreign affairs ministry only enjoyed influence after its separation from the Prime Minister's Office in 1955 and its renaming as Department of Foreign Affairs in 1960.[28] The majority of the foreign service officials in this study were guided by idealist or liberal worldviews, with a belief in democratic principles and the rule of law,[29] rather than the use of force as the elements of interaction between states; the non-interference in the domestic matters of another state and the restriction to civilian aspects, even if they had knowledge of military activities, were central to the DFA's approach. Pik Botha described the DFA's attitude toward military endeavours: "Do what you need to do, but don't let us know about it".[30]

The Africa Division as the bureaucratic section was instrumental in formulating and implementing the DFA's Africa policy. Established in 1955 as Africa and International Organisations, it changed its name to Africa Division (1957-78), to International Organisations, Central and North Africa (1979-80), to Africa Directorate (1981-87) and finally to the Africa Branch (1988-94);[31] for practical purposes, we will refer to Africa Division throughout. In 1954, the foreign affairs ministry launched the idea of an Interdepartmental Committee on African Affairs,[32] but this never became functional.[33] The superiors of the civil servants in the Africa Division were the Minister and the Secretary, Director-General after 1984. Prime Minister Johannes Gerhardus Strijdom (1954-58) valued and appreciated the diplomatic experience of Eric Hendrik Louw and made him the Minister of External Affairs in 1955.[34] Louw also became Verwoerd's trusted man in the field, making his influence felt in 1960 by insisting on renaming the Department of External Affairs to that of Foreign Affairs.[35] Louw had already been instrumental in creating the Department's first geographical division, the Africa Division.[36] Verwoerd's foreign policy self-assurance increased over the years, however, and Louw's influence waned accordingly,[37] also contingent on the strong personality of Secretary Gerhardt Jooste (1956-66). He had an impressive diplomatic record,[38] but it was his firm National Party commitment that facilitated a close relationship with Verwoerd. Consequently, Verwoerd either ignored Louw's advice in favour of Jooste's or decided himself.[39]

Jooste's power base also curtailed the influence of Hilgard Muller, Louw's successor. Characterised as quiet, cautious, having little drive and being an implementer rather than an initiator, he carried little weight and played a fairly subordinate role under Verwoerd.[40] Muller rose in status under Vorster, but was increasingly by-passed by Brand Fourie, who succeeded Jooste in 1966, such as suggested by Donald Sole, a career DFA official.[41] Fourie, a hard-working official with immense knowledge of international affairs and a long record as a foreign service officer, became a dominant figure during the next 16 years. He was particularly close to Vorster, who consequently ignored Muller's advice on various occasions. The personalities of Fourie and Muller significantly impacted on Pretoria's relations with African countries until the early 1970s. Benefiting from South Africa's status as the economically and technologically most advanced African nation, they promoted the provision of technical assistance, technological know-how and financing for projects to win over African leaders. In implementing their policies, Fourie and Muller were assisted by, *inter alia*, Under-Secretary Albertus 'Albie' Burger, who later carried a particularly heavy weight as Ambassador to Paris (1969-74), the co-ordination centre for Pretoria's activities in Francophone Africa, the former French colonial territories. French political scientist Bach described Burger as "one of the principal artisans of [South Africa's] opening towards the outside world".[42]

Pik Botha succeeded Minister Muller in April 1977. Having started his DFA career at the age of 21, he held the prestigious position as a member of Pretoria's legal team in the S.W.A./Namibia case at the International Court of Justice (ICJ) (1963-66). He then made his way further up the ranks, becoming Ambassador to the US and Permanent Representative to the UN (1974-77). In stark contrast to his predecessor, Pik Botha's character has been described as assertive, ambitious, flamboyant and ebullient, pursuing a style admired by his colleagues. In politics, he demonstrated a more liberal attitude than many of his staunchly conservative colleagues. Most importantly, the S.W.A./Namibia issue was not a non-negotiable theme, with Pik Botha being key to bringing about Namibia's eventual independence in 1990, greatly improving Pretoria's relations with Africa. This was facilitated by Pik Botha's personality, described as an Africanist, who felt at ease in private discussions with African counterparts.[43] Two senior DFA officials commented: "his chemistry with them (...) was excellent", "they walked arm in arm" and "he had a way of dealing with the black people which made them believe that he was absolutely not a racist. The colour of his skin didn't matter".[44]

Pik Botha had the assistance of three consecutive administrative departmental heads. Following Brand Fourie, Hans van Dalsen (1982-85) did not have his predecessor's high profile; there is no reference to him in the literature and his name occurs in comparatively few primary documents. In contrast, Director-General Rae Killen (1985-87) was a far more established and respected personality with significant influence. He had a particular interest in Africa, having headed the Africa Division (1982-84); Donald Sole suggests Killen's laid "the groundwork for the improvement of relations with other African states".[45] Among the civil servants in the Africa Division who supported their work, Glenn Babb played an influential role as Deputy Director, Director and eventually Deputy Director-General. He pursued an assertive foreign policy style, not afraid to deal with military and national intelligence issues. Fellow official Paul Runge described him as an "extremely enthusiastic person", "very collaborative (...), the bridge for everything; wherever there was action, he would talk to whoever to achieve the objective. He had a lot of relations with national intelligence".[46] Rusty Evans was of significance as Minister Plenipotentiary[47] at the London Embassy and as Head of the West Africa Section, before becoming Deputy Director-General for Africa. Finally, French-speaking Runge worked on Francophone Africa at the Paris Embassy, prior to becoming Project Liaison Officer in Gabon and then Senior Officer in the West Africa Directorate.

While the DFA's role as prime foreign policy actor suffered under P.W. Botha, it again rose to prominence after the late 1980s. A momentum of importance was the strong team of Pik Botha and Director-General Neil van Heerden, whom Pik Botha had favoured when they served in Washington, subsequently working together in the Namibia negotiations.[48] Interviewed in 1999, van Heerden emphasised his interest in Africa: "There was no other Division in the Department which was more enthusiastic than the Africa Division. (...) There were no other Divisions that worked under lousier conditions (...), [but people] were driven with a passion".[49]

We now introduce the state actors that challenged the DFA's presupposed dominant foreign policy making position.

Military

The military's influence on Pretoria's foreign policy making towards the countries of interest was significant during two periods, both times related to P.W. Botha: the late 1960s, during his early days as Defence Minister, and the 1980s, when he was the country's executive. The men from, what is referred to as, the Directorate of Military Intelligence (DMI) were relevant in both phases. Established in 1961, it became the predominant intelligence-gathering agency from the late 1970s. The following of its heads – called Directors of Military Intelligence until 1974,

Chiefs of Staff: Intelligence thereafter – are important to our study: Pierre Marais Retief (1961-66), Frederik Wilhelm 'Fritz' Loots (1966-71), Heinrich de Villefort 'Hein' du Toit (1971-77) and Pieter Willem van der Westhuizen (1978-85).[50] Loots,[51] a Broderbond member,[52] an organisation introduced later, deserves special mention, as he played a crucial role in directing South Africa's engagement in the Nigerian Civil War (1967-70). In that context, Cornelius Jacobus 'Neels' van Tonder was of equal significance. Officially accredited as a member of the diplomatic corps at the South African Embassy in Paris,[53] van Tonder oversaw Franco-South African co-operation in Francophone Africa. He impressed officials even outside the military sphere, such as former DFA Director-General van Heerden who spoke with the highest regards about him:

> [the military] started to develop a breed of military officers that were (...) quite excellent. They were enormously well trained (...) and they needed no sloppy diplomats to tell them what to do. (...) They were all can-do people, and Neels van Tonder was one of the prime examples of that. (...) Neels was one hell of an operator. (...) Speaks French like a Frenchman, understands the culture and goes anywhere.[54]

Reflecting the close relationship with van Tonder, P.W. Botha later put him in command of the Directorate of Special Tasks (1975-84), responsible for the military destabilisation of southern African countries.[55]

When the military again relegated the foreign affairs ministry to the background during the 1980s, Defence Minister Magnus Malan (1980-91) played an important role. As the Commander-in-Chief of the South African Defence Force (SADF) (1976-80), he developed close ties with P.W. Botha, whose political and strategic views he shared. His rise in the military has been explained by his senior position in the secretive Broederbond.[56] Daniel Smith 'Daan' Hamman, also a Broederbond member,[57] was of importance as DMI Brigadier during the first half of the 1980s.

In the late 1960s and during the 1980s, in line with its realist worldview, the military relied on power politics, involving military co-operation with France and mercenaries and armament sales. Geldenhuys therefore rightly suggested they "would typically be less concerned than the diplomats about potential international diplomatic repercussions flowing from the use of the military instrument of foreign policy".[58]

Department of Information

The Department of Information, assisted by the Bureau for State Security, challenged the DFA's primacy in the early 1970s, a development facilitated by Minister Muller's relatively weak personality traits[59] and

Prime Minister Vorster's personal connections with senior Department of Information and BOSS officials. The former's approach was somewhere between the military's realist and the foreign service officer's idealist/liberal stance, whose policy style it judged as being too mild to successfully alleviate South Africa's international isolation.[60] Those attempting to render Pretoria's foreign policy both more assertive and successful were Connie Mulder, Minister of Information since 1968, Eschel Rhoodie, Secretary from 1972, and Lourens Erasmus Smit 'Les' de Villiers, Deputy Secretary from 1973. Broederbond member Mulder had been active in local and national politics and had led the NP's countrywide information campaign. Rhoodie had served, between 1957 and 1971, as Press Attaché and Information Officer at the missions in Canberra, Washington, New York and The Hague, prior to becoming Deputy Editor of the Department of Information's secretly funded magazine *To the Point*. Les de Villiers, also a Broederbonder, had been active in South African journalism and was later involved in the Information section at the missions in Ottawa (1963-66) and New York (1967-72).[61] The bureaucratic vehicle used to impact on Pretoria's foreign policy was the Department of Information, an integral part of the foreign affairs ministry since 1955, only becoming a separate department in 1972.[62] In Rhoodie's and de Villiers' view, it had previously operated "more like a glorified post office or a tourist agency". Together with Minister Mulder, they upgraded it and subsequently "embarked on a large-scale secret propaganda offensive", also in Africa;[63] Rhoodie's autobiography reads: "I believed, intensely, that acceptance by the moderate states in Africa was the key to acceptance by the rest of the world".[64]

These ventures came to an end with the Information Scandal; Vorster resigned, Mulder became Minister for Plural Relations and Development and Rhoodie's and de Villiers' careers ended in 1977. In 1980, under Prime Minister P.W. Botha, the department was reintegrated into the foreign affairs ministry. A vital element in its activities had been national intelligence support.

National Intelligence

The Republican Intelligence (RI), launched in 1963 as the "clandestine extension of the Security Police",[65] was South Africa's first national intelligence agency, but its existence only became public knowledge in 1969, when it was succeeded by the Bureau for State Security, headed by Hendrik van den Bergh. His membership of the Broederbond and the Ossewabrandwag (Ox-wagon Guard), a right-wing movement congruent with Hitler's ideas on racial purity, led to his internment during the Second World War, in the same camp as John Vorster, a leading Ossewabrandwag figure.[66] As a result, a strong bond of friendship developed between them, causing Vorster, then Minister of Justice (1961-66), to promote van den Bergh to head the RI.[67] A primary source issued by Vorster confirms BOSS became Pretoria's prime intelligence gathering body, intruding even the military intelligence domain, and van den Bergh had "unrestricted access" to the Prime Minister.[68] Van den Bergh also maintained a close relationship with Eschel Rhoodie,[69] with Deon Geldenhuys referring to the "Mulder-Rhoodie-Van den Bergh triumvirate".[70] Consequently, the men from the Department of Information enjoyed direct access to and protection from the Prime Minister. On the administrative side, BOSS facilitated the clandestine transfer of money to this Department. After 1974, funds were first channelled through the Department of Defence, whose accounts could not be discussed in Parliament, and then transferred to BOSS, acting as "bankers for Information".[71] This strained the relationship between BOSS and Defence, with Les de Villiers citing Mulder and Rhoodie as having made the remark: "P W Botha was unhappy about his department being used to breast-feed Secret Information".[72] On a personal level, sharp clashes characterised van den Bergh's relationship with P.W. Botha.[73] Van den Bergh apart, Albertus 'Albie' Geldenhuys is an important figure in our study, especially related to Pretoria's contact with Francophone Africa in the first half of the 1970s. Figuring as a Technical Adviser at the Paris Embassy on the DFA's *Foreign Affairs List*, he was a BOSS agent in reality. He reached this position more than likely because he spoke fluent French and because his father, Michael 'Mike' Geldenhuys, was van den Bergh's personal friend and number four at BOSS headquarters in Pretoria during the 1970s.[74]

The Information Scandal also put an end to BOSS's existence; van den Bergh resigned on the very day P.W. Botha was elected Prime Minister. During the next two years, the military brought the national intelligence agency under control to prevent clashes where the two state actors' briefs overlapped. Crucially, parallel to holding the premiership and remaining the Minister of Defence, P.W. Botha, in November 1978, took over the ministerial portfolio in what now became the Department of National Security.[75] Furthermore, he made Hendrick Jacobus 'Kobie' Coetsee the Deputy Minister in both the Departments of Defence and of National Security. Coetsee had studied Law at the University of the Orange Free State, was a NP Member of Parliament for Bloemfontein West from 1968, the party's leader in the Orange Free State and chaired the NP's Study Group on Defence from 1978.[76] P.W. Botha and Coetsee cemented their grip on the national intelligence by making Alec van Wyk the administrative head; he did not have van den Bergh's assertive profile, the secondary literature barely mentioning him.[77]

In November 1979, P.W. Botha appointed the 30 year old Political Science Professor Niël Barnard from the University of the Orange Free State to head the Department of National Security.[78] In June 1980, Barnard assumed his post in what was now the National Intelligence Service (NIS). Barnard's appointment clearly bore Kobie Coetsee's handwriting, given his political power base in the Orange Free State and close links as an Alumnus of the local university.[79] At the same time, Barnard's academic profile favoured P.W. Botha's choice. Barnard's doctoral thesis on *The Power Factor in International Relations* and other publications[80] were testimony "to a close correspondence between his views and those of Prime Minister P W Botha on the need for a comprehensive strategy for securing South Africa's interests in an alien environment".[81] Reflecting the powerful position it built up during the 1980s, the NIS retained its importance in Pretoria's foreign policy making even under de Klerk. However, in February 1992, de Klerk made Barnard the Director-General of Constitutional Development Services, removing him from the foreign policy making scene.

Following our presentation of the state actors, we will now discuss the relevant non-state actors (Table 2), particularly their position vis-à-vis what Figure 1 depicted as the locus of decision-making.

Progressive Party

The Progressive Party was the only significant opposition to the ruling National Party. Formed in 1959 and relying largely on financial support from Harry Oppenheimer of the Anglo American Corporation, it changed its name to Progressive Reform Party (PRP, 1974), to Progressive Federal Party (PFP, 1977) and to Democratic Party (DP, 1989).[82] Three of its politicians, Colin Wells Eglin, Helen Suzman and Frederik van Zyl Slabbert, paid visits to several African countries beyond southern Africa. Eglin's prolific leadership (1971-78) contributed to the party's parliamentary breakthrough in the 1974 elections, and during his tenure the party was particularly active in Africa. He briefly held this post again from 1986 to 1988. Suzman, a well-respected political figure and one of the earliest female parliamentarians, held the party's seat in Parliament from 1961.[83] Slabbert, having a strong academic background, never became a party-man.[84] In 1986, in a move of great surprise to white South Africans, Slabbert resigned as PFP Leader and from Parliament because, as he put it: "I had a very real sense of 'having had enough', especially as 'things' had worsened and not improved".[85] Slabbert then established the Institute for a Democratic Alternative for South Africa (IDASA).[86]

Broederbond

Established in 1918, the Broederbond (Brotherhood union) "played a crucial role in creating, legitimising and maintaining the system of apartheid".[87] There were, however, splits between the *verligte* (enlightened) and *verkrampte* (constricted) elements, a contributory factor to factional strug-

Table 2: *Non-State Actors in South Africa's Foreign Relations with Africa*

	Political Parties	Progressive Party
	Civil Society	Broederbond
	Think Tanks	Africa Institute, South African Institute of International Affairs
	Media	Rand Daily Mail
	Organised Business	Afrikaanse Handelsinstituut, Durban Chamber of Commerce, South Africa Foundation; South African Foreign Trade Organisation
Companies	Parastatal	Industrial Development Corporation
	Private	Anglo American Corporation, Bessemer Steel Construction, Brian Colquhoun Hugh O'Donnell and Partners, Credit Guarantee Insurance Corporation, LTA, Roberts Construction, Safair, Southern Sun

gles within the National Party, exemplified by the formation of the Herstigte Nasionale Party (HNP, Reconstituted National Party) in 1969 and the Information Scandal.[88] In the period under consideration, only two Cabinet Ministers were not Broederbond members, notably Eric Louw, probably due to his non-political attitude,[89] and this study will identify several other men of importance as Broederbond members. The secretive union thus effectively constituted the National Party's unofficial decision-making centre: "The Broederbond does not dictate as such to the various bodies in government (...). There is, rather, direct interaction between the Bond and these bodies (...). The key people with whom the Broederbond discusses matters of the day are all Broeders anyway".[90] We argue the Broederbond's belief system became imprinted on Pretoria's foreign policy. In particular, the idea that the Afrikaners were a chosen people with the right and mission to civilise Africa and keep communism out, formed the underlying basis of its policy toward Africa for much of the period under consideration.

Think Tanks

In apartheid South Africa, the Africa Institute in Pretoria and the South African Institute of International Affairs in Johannesburg corresponded to the notion of think tanks: "relatively autonomous organizations engaged in the research and analysis of contemporary issues independently of government, political parties, and pressure groups".[91]

The former was established in 1960, financed by the government through the Department of National Education. Yet, it was not Pretoria's front organisation; the secondary literature agrees that the Africa Institute's work was primarily "fact-producing and not policy-making".[92] In particular, mention must be made of their journals *South African Journal of African Affairs*, continued by *Africa Insight*, and *Africa Institue Bulletin*, as well as a wide range of monographs, many of which we reference. Having said this, though, we will reveal Joseph Hulme Moolman and Gerhard Max Erich Leistner, simply referred to as Erich, became drawn into Pretoria's Africa ventures as the Africa Institute's Director (1971-77) and Deputy Director (1973-77) respectively.

Founded in 1934, the South African Institute of International Affairs was completely different in nature. Its ideological and social base has been characterised as "upper-class, English-oriented and liberal",[93] as funding came primarily from the English-speaking business community. Crucially, Anglo American's Harry Oppenheimer was its National Chairman from 1980 to 1990. The Institute was well-respected, due mostly to its publications and its high public profile in the form of conferences and media presence.[94] Former foreign service officer Charles John Adkinson Barratt, simply referred to as John,[95] significantly boosted the Institute's stature as its Director (1967-94).[96] While he suggested the Institute should "provide a link or bridge between the academic world and those in politics and government",[97] it was relatively removed from the Afrikaner dominated foreign policy making circles;[98] it was a matter of formality that the Minister of Foreign Affairs was one of its honorary presidents.

Rand Daily Mail

This white English-speaking newspaper was significantly critical of Pretoria's apartheid policy. Established in 1902 in Johannesburg, its reporting was acceptable to the government initially, but this changed when the National Party came to power in 1948. Over time, the daily took a more radical, in South African terms, political stance in response to the increasing limits upon the press freedom and began to side with the Progressive Party. This change also related to the personality of Laurence Gandar, Editor from 1957 and Editor-in-Chief after 1966, who had previously worked as Harry Oppenheimer's public relations adviser.[99] Some of its more prominent journalists, such as Allister Sparks, sustained the paper's liberal position. Sparks had joined the *Rand Daily Mail* in 1958, holding the Editorship from 1977 to 1981. In 1966, whilst he was the political correspondent, the daily won a World Press Achievement Reward for its exposure of apartheid injustices and the maltreatment of prisoners, especially blacks. Two other journalists of note were Benjamin Pogrund and Anton Harber. Pogrund worked with the paper from 1958, covering the ANC's and the PAC's activities; its leaders, Mandela and Robert Sobukwe, became his lifelong friends. He eventually became the paper's Deputy Editor, a position he held until 1985.[100] During these days, the *Rand Daily Mail* revelations led to the Information Scandal. The paper proved to be a thorn in the flesh of the next government and this led to its closure in 1985.[101] Harber, with the paper since 1981 and then political reporter, launched *The Weekly Mail* to uphold a critical voice against Pretoria. It became an integral part of the 'alternative press', "the only significant media voices not controlled by either the government or big capital".[102] Given its co-operation with the British daily *The Guardian*, it was renamed *Weekly Mail & Guardian* (1993) and *Mail & Guardian* (1995).[103]

Organised Business

Before detailing the organised business entities, as well as the private and parastatal companies – the latter being a firm "at least 50 per cent owned by the state"[104] – a few remarks are necessary concerning the relationship between the business sector and apartheid politics, as well as the division between Afrikaner and English-speaking business. These issues help us analyse the business sector's role in South Africa's relations with Africa.

Business activity during the apartheid period became a matter of academic controversy from the 1970s, the central question being whether business was against or supportive of the racist system.[105] The significance of this issue was highlighted by the Carlton Conference in Johannesburg (1979) and the Good Hope Conference in Cape Town (1981), when Prime Minister P.W. Botha attempted to form a partnership between politics and business.[106] On both occasions, "the list of names from the private sector read like a Who's Who of South African business".[107] In a nutshell, the viewpoints of the two main schools of thought, the liberal and the Marxist/revisionist, have been summarised as follows: "the revisionists emphasise the compatibility of apartheid with capitalism whereas the liberals view apartheid as alien to it".[108] The domestic South African context has usually been the focus of investigation. In this study, the pivotal question is whether business activities coincided with, maybe even supported, Pretoria's foreign policy towards Africa, or whether they were in conflict with one another.

Regarding the disjuncture between Afrikaner and English-speaking business, traditionally, Afrikaner economic activity was largely restricted to farming, while British capital was strong in the mining and industrial sector.[109] In geographic terms, Pretoria was associated with Afrikanerdom and political power, while Johannesburg represented economic influence by a predominantly English-speaking upmarket social class, the latter being personified by Harry Oppenheimer of the Anglo American Corporation. Notable exceptions among Afrikaner business were Jan S. Marais, whom we will discuss at a later stage, and Anton Rupert, whose Rembrandt Group, a tobacco empire, was involved in different economic sectors.[110] The government's early attempt to promote Afrikaner economic activity was, in 1940, the establishment of the Industrial Development Corporation (IDC), referred to as a "bulwark against the Anglo-American Corporation".[111] After assuming political power in 1948, the NP's initiatives intensified with the creation of state-owned industries and nationalised services, such as the Iron and Steel Corporation (Iscor) and the Electricity Supply Commission (Eskom).[112] Over time, the disjuncture between Afrikaner and English-speaking business eroded.[113] So much so, that P.W. Botha attempted to co-ordinate industrial policies and integrate Afrikaner and English-speaking business, for example, at the 1979 Carlton Conference – symbolically held in Johannesburg – with representation from both camps, such as Oppenheimer and Rupert.[114]

Turning to the organised business sector, the Afrikaanse Handelsinstituut (AHI), the Durban Chamber of Commerce, the South Africa Foundation and the South African Foreign Trade Organisation (SAFTO) are relevant and are now examined in alphabetical order.

The *Afrikaanse Handelsinstituut* (Afrikaner Commercial Institute) was established in 1942 with the purpose of "promoting the Afrikaner's economic interests and establishing the Afrikaner in the business world".[115] It was an early expression of Pretoria's intention of challenging the dominance of the organised English-speaking business community. Its organisational and ideological links with government and its influence on the country's economic policy were manifold: the Broederbond was crucial in establishing the Handelsinstituut; after 1948, Pretoria recognised the AHI as the official representative of Afrikaner business interests; in 1960, the AHI helped lay the foundations for the establishment of and was subsequently well represented on the Prime Minister's Economic Advisory Council; it was on both the government's Export Trade Advisory Committee and the Export Promotion Council;[116] finally, the AHI chose Pretoria, and not Johannesburg, as its base.[117] Reflecting all this, the DFA established a special file for correspondence with the AHI,[118] something it did not do for its English-speaking counterpart, SAFTO. Similar to the process of South Africa's foreign policy formulation, a relatively small number of individuals were influential in the AHI. Frederick François de Wit Stockenström, a Broederbonder[119] and Economic Advisory Council member during the 1970s,[120] dominated the AHI's activities as its Executive Director (1966-84). Paul Kruger Hoogendyk, referred to as a "successful independent businessman",[121] was AHI Board Member (1961-68), Vice-President (1969-72) and President (1973-74). He was also director of the parastatals IDC and Iscor and the private companies Bessemer Steel Construction and South African Breweries, SAFTO Vice-Chairman and Chairman (1977-81, 1982-85), South Africa Foundation Trustee (1974-92) and member of the Economic Advisory Board in the 1970s.[122] Ideologically, he appears to have been close to Pretoria's apartheid policies, being a Broederbond member[123] and Chairman of the Xhosa Development Corporation (1972-77),[124] an institution established in 1965 as part of Pretoria's homelands policy to promote the economic development of both the Transkei and Ciskei.[125] The third man of relevance in the Afrikaanse Handelsinstituut was Jan Marais, who rose from Deputy Chairman (1961) to President (1967/68). He was also on the IDC Board of Directors (1968-77), a member of the Economic Advisory Council (1967-68) and NP Member of Parliament (1977-81).[126] The AHI involved itself in trade promotion during the end of the 1960s, with trade missions to Europe, the Far and Middle East. In Africa, the focus was on southern Africa, the drive further north limited to Malawi.

The *Durban Chamber of Commerce* was South Africa's largest chamber of commerce. According to its Chief Executive Geoffrey Winston Tyler (1985-99), it was active world-wide, mounting economic missions around the globe.[127] On the African continent, missions were despatched to southern Africa and beyond, with an emphasis on Malawi and the western Indian Ocean islands.[128]

In 1959, against the background of the potential imposition of economic sanctions against South Africa, Anglo American Chairman Harry Oppenheimer, together with Anton Rupert, established the *South Africa Foundation* to make the interests of organised business heard. Its main purpose was "to sponsor visits to this country by important and influential businessmen and opinion makers"[129] to improve South Africa's image overseas and thereby prevent punitive measures.[130] Mirroring their little economic interaction with South Africa, African countries were not prominent target areas. The Foundation's input into Pretoria's foreign policy making came "not so much from the Foundation as an organisation, but rather from prominent individuals associated with it".[131] For much of the period under consideration, a President and Director General were the key executive organs. Making the Foundation an economic heavyweight, it comprised between 24 and 34 Executive Trustees – called the Council after 1972 –, as well as Trustees, ranging in number from 185 in 1967 to a peak of 320 in 1981.[132] Foundation Director General James de Lacy 'Peter' Sorour (1973-87) explained their role to us:

> [they] were invited to join the Board of Trustees because of their status. Only active politicians were excluded. Naturally each would have his or her own political views which they were free to express where and how they wished – but not as "representatives" of the Foundation. The purpose of the Board was to lend prestige to the Foundation (...). An individual Trustee could only represent the Foundation if specifically delegated to do so in a special case by the President or the DG [Director General].[133]

Christian Neethling 'Chris' Barnard and Jack Penn are of relevance in our study as Trustees from 1970 and 1972 respectively.[134] Barnard was a Professor at Cape Town's Groote Schuur Hospital, becoming internationally famous for performing the world's first heart transplant in 1967.[135] Penn was a renowned plastic surgeon.[136] Probably the most prestigious Trustee (1967-92) was Harry Oppenheimer. A Foundation executive of importance was Basil Edward Hersov.[137] As Chairman and Managing Director of Anglovaal (1972-2000), a very large company involved in mining, financial and industrial enterprises, he could be rated as one of South Africa's most important business representatives, second only to Harry Oppenheimer.[138] Two other relevant executives were Peter Sorour,[139] and Jan Marais.[140] Marais' links with Afrikaner business aside, he had laid the foundation for his business career in 1955 by forming the important Trust Bank.[141]

Established in 1963 and composed almost exclusively of English-speaking companies, the Johannesburg-based *South African Foreign Trade Organisation* was engaged in trade promotion.[142] In 1984, Chief Executive Willem Bernard 'Wim' Holtes (1963-92),[143] described its *raison d'être*: "We have always seen our role as making the SA businessman more aware of his export potential and the need for him to become more internationally orientated in his outlook. The rest of the world is a large, untapped market and he should be looking to establish his place there".[144] SAFTO provided its membership, rising from 130 companies in 1963 to peak at 1,443 in 1987/88,[145] *inter alia*, with an information database, export focused publications, the provision of SAFTO executives for specific assignments such as market surveys and export workshops. From the late 1970s, so-called special "area services" or "business groups" with a geographical focus were established.[146] SAFTO's relations with Pretoria can be described as co-operative. It was represented on the Export Trade Advisory Committee and the Export Promotion Council[147] and, although nominally a private sector organisation, received financial support from the government, ranging between 12 and 18 per cent of SAFTO's revenue.[148] In 1963, SAFTO declared in what could be called its White Paper: "It will be an important part of SAFTO's work to maintain close liaison with the Government."[149] On an official level, in 1965 and 1968, for instance, the Minister of Mines and Planning (1964-67) and of Economic Affairs (1967-70), Jan Friedrich Wilhelm Haak, addressed SAFTO.[150] During his Chairmanship (1981-86), Paul Hoogendyk established a particularly close link; Wim Holtes commented he "was a great supporter of government, that's for sure".[151] Until the mid-1980s, southern Africa enjoyed preference in SAFTO's activities.[152] Outside this area, it restricted itself to Malawi and the western Indian Ocean islands. Trade opportunities further north, acknowledged with caution initially,[153] were only pursued from the second half of the 1980s

Parastatal and Private Companies

Technical assistance aside, one of Pretoria's levers to achieve its ambitions in Africa was to provide capital goods for construction, transportation and other projects. While this could be considered as development aid, this support was not provided without self-interest, the projects being financed and executed by a South African parastatal and several private enterprises whose primary interest is economic profit. This section provides background information on the companies involved, beginning with the former and presenting the latter in alphabetical order.

The general objective of the parastatal *Industrial Development Corporation* was "to promote industrial development, by assisting the private sector in the financing of new industries or schemes for the expansion or rationalisation of industries, by initiating development projects preferably in partnership with either local or overseas interests".[154] In 1960, the IDC launched a scheme to finance the export of capital goods and services,[155] providing credits for periods from two to ten years at attractive interest rates, contingent on export credit insurance cover from South Africa's Credit Guarantee Insurance Corporation (CGIC). According to its own presentation, the IDC "operates on normal commercial considerations". However, and although its Directors came, and still come, from the private sector, they were nonetheless government-appointed,[156] and this inevitably impacted on its business practice. The personality factor again played an important role, with the names of Managing Directors and Chairmen revealing the influence of Afrikanerdom. Notably, Paul Hoogendyk and Jan Marais, both well-established Afrikaner businessmen and ideologically close to Pretoria's policies, were members of the Board of Directors (1958-68; 1968-77).[157] According to Wim Holtes, the IDC was "very active" in terms of financing the export of capital goods to African countries.[158] In southern Africa alone, the IDC financed two massive projects with major political implications, namely the Cahora Bassa Hydroelectric Scheme in Mozambique and the Cunene River Dam on the Angola-Namibia border.[159]

Among the private companies, the *Anglo American Corporation* was undoubtedly the largest, the most powerful and influential. The activities we have mentioned already represent only a fragment of its many facets. Industrial sociologist Innes aptly suggested: "the Anglo American Group of companies is a major force in the economic, political and social life in South Africa".[160] Among its network of more than 150 different holding and operating companies, the leading global diamond producer De Beers Consolidated Mines, was the most important.[161] Founded in 1917 by Ernest Oppenheimer, Anglo American soon expanded its activities throughout southern Africa, and world-wide. It became a typical Multinational Corporation, "privately owned business enterprises organised in one society with activities in another growing out of direct investment" that, in order to secure their investments, "have an interest in both economic and political stability".[162] In the period under review, the Oppenheimer family controlled Anglo American through a highly complicated labyrinth of cross-holdings in the persons of Chairmen Ernest Oppenheimer (1917-57), his son Harry (1957-82), Gavin Walter Hamilton Relly (1983-90) and Julian Ogilvie Thompson (1990-2002).[163] Besides being the

"octogenarian patriarch of South African business",[164] Harry Oppenheimer was active in domestic politics as a Member of Parliament for the
United Party – the then opposition to the ruling NP – immediately after
the Second World War, and later as the financier of the opposing Progressive Party. While Michael Spicer, Anglo American Executive Director, suggested to us there was "overt hostility" between the multinational
and the government in the 1960s,[165] we agree with the secondary literature: "there can scarcely be constant war between Anglo American and
the government. Their economic embrace may be devoid of love, but is
nonetheless muscular".[166] In the mid-1970s, for example, Harry Oppenheimer openly supported Pretoria's Détente in southern Africa,[167] and at
the 1979 Carlton Conference he spoke of "the beginning of a new relationship between the state and private business in South Africa".[168]

In 1952, Afrikaner businessman Hoogendyk established the pri-
vately-owned and non-registered company *Bessemer Steel Construction*, serv-
ing the agricultural industry by designing, manufacturing and erecting
steel silos for the storage of bulk grain.[169] The US, South Africa's homelands and southern Africa were the main markets,[170] but some activity
also took place in African countries further afield.

The engineering company *Brian Colquhoun Hugh O'Donnell and Partners*, established in Rhodesia in 1948 as a regional practice of Brian Colquhoun and Partners, Consulting Engineers, London, offered a comprehensive consultancy service for building and civil engineering projects in
Africa. It provided expertise in housing, hotels, airports, mining, bridges,
railways and other projects. Its core area of interest in Africa was southern Africa, with offices in Botswana, South Africa, Swaziland, Zambia
and Zimbabwe.[171]

In 1956, South Africa's leading insurers and financial institutions
established the *Credit Guarantee Insurance Corporation*, the result of a discussion during the 1950s whereby there was a "growing feeling among South
African exporters [that they] were at a definite competitive disadvantage,
because they didn't feel secure in offering long-term credit facilities".[172]
Credit Guarantee's objective, therefore, was to provide insurance for the
export of capital goods, namely cover against the risk of non-payment by
a foreign buyer. Any contract submitted for its consideration had to have
at least a 70 per cent local content, spent on South African goods and
services. In 1958, the government entered into a long-term contract with
Credit Guarantee, according to which it provided the firm with reinsur-
ance cover, particularly for political risks not normally covered by the
private insurance market.[173] It was common practice for the IDC to finance a long-term contract and act as an "export bank", with Credit
Guarantee acting as insurer.[174] Over the years, Credit Guarantee gained in
importance, growing from an insured value of $294 million in 1966 to
$6.7 billion in 1991.[175] African countries beyond southern Africa did not
feature prominently. In our correspondence, Credit Guarantee Managing

Director Christoph Leisewitz referred to the business involving these countries as being "of minor importance".[176] Regarding the company's executives, General Manager Klaus Oppenheimer (1956-65) represented the company on the Export Trade Advisory Committee and the Export Promotion Council.[177] Prior to joining the CGIC in 1959, eventually becoming Managing Director (1982-88), Johannes Jeremia 'Jan' Bouwer had worked for Pretoria's Department of Commerce and Industries. While with the CGIC, he was also on SAFTO's Board of Directors (1974-88), becoming its Vice-Chairman (1987-88).[178] This flirtation with English-speaking organised business notwithstanding, Wim Holtes described him as a "firm Afrikaner".[179] Further, in 1989, President P.W. Botha awarded him with the Order for Meritorious Services.[180] Finally, German-born Christoph Leisewitz joined the firm in 1965, rising to Senior General Manager (1982-86), Executive Director (1986-88) and Managing Director (1988-2002). Underlining his significance, he was also on SAFTO's Board of Directors from 1989 to 1995.[181]

The construction company *LTA* came into existence in 1965, following the merger of three companies in the building, contracting and civil engineering sectors, among them Anglo American Corporation Construction, Anglo American's civil engineering branch. Anglo American's stranglehold of LTA, in terms of financial structure and the company's management,[182] only came to an end in 2000, when the company was acquired by the construction group Aveng.[183] Together with Murray & Roberts Ltd, LTA dominated South Africa's construction sector in the period under review. It was involved in some key infrastructure installations in South and southern Africa, including the Orange Fish River Tunnel, the Groote Schuur Hospital, the Koeberg nuclear power station near Cape Town and the Cahora Bassa Hydroelectric Scheme.[184] Regarding the company's relationship with Pretoria, we corresponded with Spencer Roland Whiting, with LTA from 1965 to 1983, according to whom "contact between LTA, the CGIC and DFA was quite exceptional and co-operation was excellent. We fronted for CGIC and DFA on several occasions".[185]

The *Roberts Construction Co Ltd* was part of the civil engineering and building construction firm Murray & Roberts Ltd. The holding company Murray & Roberts came into being in 1967, as a result of the merger of Murray & Stewart (Pty) Ltd in Cape Town and Roberts Construction in Johannesburg. Following an agreement between the owners at the time of the merger, Murray & Stewart concentrated on the Cape Province and Namibia, while Roberts Construction serviced South Africa's three remaining provinces[186] and the African countries. Its interest in the latter was significant throughout the period under review. In 1976, Murray & Roberts' Managing Director John Edgar Dale 'Bill' Bramwell declared: "we are also doing a fair amount of work in what used to be called French Africa. (...) We think this whole area has great prospects for us".[187] Further, the firm's 1991 Annual Report reads: "Murray & Roberts' heart is in Africa".[188] In this context, the ties to the DFA were especially close. According to Paul Runge, "there was a lot of interaction. I would, at Foreign Affairs, receive Murray & Roberts and people like that".[189] We originally assumed this was based on the personality factor, as so often in this study, notably by the kinship between Stephen Alexander 'Steve' and Jan George Boyazoglu. The former, Jan's cousin,[190] was with Murray & Roberts from 1954, most importantly as Deputy Managing Director (1970-79).[191] Employed by the Department of Agricultural Technical Services (ATS), Broederbond member Jan Boyazoglu was Agricultural Counsellor at the Paris Embassy (1965-82), also accredited to other European countries.[192] He "played a remarkable role in facilitating contact between the South African Government and the French speaking African Governments", Donald Sole, who knew him while Ambassador to Germany (1969-77), wrote to us.[193] However, in our correspondence, Jan Boyazoglu strongly rejected our assumption that a link existed between his work and the activities of Murray & Roberts in Francophone Africa: "I know nothing of Murray and Roberts' involvement and interests in Africa in general and in the Gabon in particular. In fact, my relationship with my cousin Steve Boyazoglu has always been distant and at best superficial. In the years since I left South Africa for Paris until his death in the early 2000s, we probably only met five to six times".[194]

Safair has aptly been profiled as "an airline with strong governmental connection", "one of the world's busiest all-cargo fleets and an essential link in South Africa's "Africa connection", the semi-secret (…) trade with (…) black African nations".[195] The company came into existence in 1969 as a subsidiary of the South African Marine Corporation (Safmarine), established by the multinational Anglo American, the IDC, Eskom and Iscor, in recognition of the need for an ocean freight company.[196] Safair co-ordinated and rationalised Safmarine's interests in the airline companies Air Cape, Namib Air, Trek Airways, Luxavia and Aviation Technical and Terminal Services. Significantly, Luxavia flew between Johannesburg and Luxembourg. Although a South African-financed firm, its Luxembourg registration allowed it to fly there directly, across the African continent,[197] thus avoiding the air sanctions imposed against the national airline South African Airways (SAA). Safair's specialisation was technical maintenance to other airlines and transport of all kinds of cargo;[198] this study focuses on the latter. For that purpose, Safair utilised its Lockheed-built Hercules fleet of L100 aircraft. They formed the basis of what Safair Managing Director Braam Loots (1981-93) called "our total Africa strategy. (…) These aircraft are ideal for remote areas. They can move bulk and require little ground infrastructure".[199] Jacobus Pieter van Aswegen, Loots' successor until 1999, referred to them as "Land Rovers of the sky". He further explained to us that, not being allowed to offer scheduled freight service and to compete with South Africa's national airline, Safair leased out its planes. The South African Defence Force became its most important client. To avoid the unnecessary wear and tear on its planes after the 1977 mandatory UN arms embargo, following which the SADF no longer received spare parts for its own Lockheed-built C-130 aircraft, it leased Safair's civilian planes. Still according to van Aswegen, business with the SADF formed the "backbone" of the company, and "if it were not for them, it would have been difficult". The DFA was also a customer, but of comparatively little significance.[200]

One of South Africa's leading hotel resort chains, *Southern Sun*, was established in 1969. The impetus came from South African Breweries, a leading brewery partly owned by Anglo American.[201] Solomon 'Sol' Kerzner, another major Breweries shareholder, became Southern Sun Chairman and influenced the fate of this and other related companies in the following two decades. From the 1970s, Southern Sun began to hold a dominant position in South Africa's hotel trade, subsequently expanding abroad. Thus, Kerzner participated in two companies that became involved on the Comoros and Mauritius. A few words are necessary about Sol Kerzner and his interaction with the Pretoria government. Born in 1935 in Johannesburg as the son of a Jewish-Russian immigrant family, he worked his way up to become "one of the most successful entrepreneurs in the entertainment business".[202] Described as "flamboyant"[203] and as a "man who achieves what he sets out to do",[204] his importance in the business community was reflected in him being a South Africa Foundation Trustee (1980-92).[205] However, since the 1994 elections, newspaper reports have suggested Kerzner used financial means to garner political support for his business plans. In 1996, he was alleged to have financed both the ANC and the NP 1994 election campaigns. The ANC initially rejected the media reports, but Mandela later confirmed their validity; the NP neither confirmed nor rejected the claim.[206] In 1999, Kerzner was accused of having bribed the prime minister of the Transkei to obtain gambling rights in the former homeland.[207] Finally, in 1997 and again in 2002, his lawyers succeeded in preventing the sale of the book entitled *Kerzner Unauthorised*, written by journalist Allan Greenblo.[208] This action certainly did not help in silencing those who accused him of being a businessman with shady dealings.

This chapter introduced the relevant state and non-state actors, background necessary to contextualise their role in our study.

3

Wind of Change:
H.F. Verwoerd, 1958-66

African Independence

Hendrik Verwoerd's premiership coincided with the wave of independence that swept across the African continent, closely tied to which was Macmillan's Wind of Change speech in 1960, heralding Britain's departure from Africa. The newly independent states declared the eradication of colonialism as their primary goal; South Africa became their target due to its domestic apartheid policy, its occupation of South West Africa/Namibia and its support for the white regime in Rhodesia. This struggle took place at the UN, co-ordinated through the 'African Group'. Initiatives at the Security Council were generally met with resistance by the Western permanent members, but stood a better chance in the General Assembly due to Africa's numerical majority.[1] In 1960, the African Group was exposed to its first test after South Africa's police killed 69 blacks during protests in the Sharpeville township on 21 March. Eight African and 21 Asian states demanded a Security Council meeting and drafted a resolution declaring the situation in South Africa, if it continued, to be "one that might endanger international peace and security". While not providing for the imposition of mandatory sanctions, what became Resolution 134 on 1 April sent a warning this might be an option. Three years later, African pressure resulted in Resolution 181, imposing a voluntary arms embargo.[2]

Appeasement[3]

White South Africa was relatively unprepared for these developments unthinkable hitherto. Not only did it "not at first realise the full impact of the changing political climate",[4] but the wave of African independence must have been a "traumatic event".[5] In 1959, Foreign Minister Eric Louw referred to Africa's moves towards independence as "disturbing, and indeed, alarming events";[6] according to Louw, this should only come about in the far distant future, if at all. Yet, the new political dispensation now required a strategy for deflecting the disquieting and ever-increasing African attacks on South Africa.

As indicated in Chapter 2, Minister Louw and Secretary Jooste strongly influenced Verwoerd's foreign policy making, and actively pursued their proposal of providing African states with technical and other forms of assistance.[7] Since their establishment in the early 1950s, Pretoria had been a member of four organisations concerned with such co-operation: the Inter-African Bureau of Soil Conservation and Land Utilisation (BIS), the Commission for Technical Co-operation in Africa (CCTA), the Scientific Council for Africa (CSA) and the Foundation for Mutual Assistance in Africa (FAMA). After African independence, Pretoria's motivation to assist African nations through these agencies was to present itself as a trustworthy partner, hoping to appease those seeking its international isolation. However, appeasement was not successful, because Pretoria "seriously underestimated African hostility towards apartheid";[8] by 1963, it was excluded from the OAU, CCTA, CSA, BIS and FAMA, and African pressure resulted in its expulsion from the International Labour Organisation (ILO), the Food and Agriculture Organisation (FAO) and the UN Economic Commission for Africa (ECA).[9] South Africa's diplomatic representation on the continent was also severely affected; by 1964, it was limited to those countries still under colonial rule, Angola, Mauritius, Mozambique and Rhodesia.[10]

Apartheid's intricacies made the establishment of equitable relations with African states impossible in any case; the presence of a black ambassador in South Africa would have meant his exposure to the apartheid legislation applied to any black South African, which was obviously in conflict with the international conventions on diplomatic immunity. In attempting to find a solution to the problem, diplomatic suburbs for black ambassadors were planned outside Cape Town and Pretoria, but this did not eventuate as Verwoerd probably found that too risky.[11] Alternatively, he proposed nominating a "roving ambassador", a white ambassador touring Africa's capitals, thus avoiding the posting of black ambassadors to South Africa; this was only introduced on an *ad hoc* basis, with the Head of the Africa Division usually acting in this capacity.[12] However, the construction of a multiracial hotel at Johannesburg's then Jan Smuts Airport, where diplomats could meet, was pursued,[13] although this was only built in the early 1970s,[14] reflecting the sensitivity of the matter. In the same context, it was only in 1967, under Prime Minister Vorster, that Malawi became the first African state to establish a diplomatic mission in Pretoria. While *The Star* hailed this as the "start of a new era in South Africa's foreign relations",[15] the government did not dare to take it to its full conclusion; the appointed ambassador was white. It took another four years for Malawi to appoint a black ambassador.[16]

Congo

We will now separately examine the military's reaction, differing significantly from that of the foreign affairs ministry, to African independence. It became involved in the Republic of Congo, where the political situation deteriorated within a week of independence from Belgium in June 1960; an army mutiny threw the country into turmoil, causing Brussels to send troops to its former colony, subsequently replaced by a UN peace force.[17] Yet, neither the UN force nor the armed forces, led by Joseph-Désiré Mobutu, could prevent Moïse Tshombe, with strong mercenary assistance, from declaring the Katanga province as independent in July. In August, Albert Kalonji followed this example with the diamond-rich Kasai province. The following month, the central government collapsed and Prime Minister Patrice Lumumba resigned. After Lumumba's death in detention in January 1961, under suspicious circumstances,[18] Mobutu's army intervened and subsequently administered the country. Despite the deployment, in February, of a UN task force to terminate Katanga's secession, this only materialised in January 1963 when Tshombe went into exile. Yet, as rebellions continued throughout 1964, and given his success during Katanga's secession, Tshombe was invited home in July 1964 to bring stability to the country. Upon his return, becoming Prime Minister until October 1965, he formed a new government and renamed the country the Democratic Republic of Congo. While relying on mercenary help, Tshombe also called on Belgium and the US for assistance.[19]

Given the nature of these developments, the military fashioned Pretoria's response, contextualised in its position during the colonial period, when Pretoria equalled its status on the continent to that of the colonial powers; the Africa Charter of 1949, conceived by Prime Minister Daniel Francois Malan (1948-54), proposed co-operation with the colonial powers to prolong Western control over Africa. Pretoria intended becoming the bridgehead of Western civilisation in Africa, defending the continent against communism and the Indian influence and keeping it non-militarised.[20] In line with this stance, the military took part in the conferences in Nairobi (1951) and Dakar (1954), bringing together the colonial powers to discuss the issue of "African Defence".[21] On the occasion of the Dakar conference, Defence Minister Francois Christiaan Erasmus (1948-59) indicated: "South Africa's participation in any defense of Africa would be with only limited manpower. (...) Her chief contribution would have to consist of war material and general supplies".[22] In its reaction to the Congo crisis, the military's room for manoeuvring was apparently not much greater; it was only in 1963 that it became directly involved, although Defence Minister Jacobus Johannes 'Jim' Fouché (1959-66) shared the Africa Charter principles.[23]

After pro-Western Tshombe had declared Katanga's independence, we can safely assume Pretoria sided with him for ideological reasons, with

Verwoerd presenting South Africa as "a bastion in Africa for Christianity and the Western world".[24] In any event, two Katanga ministers visited the Republic in August and September 1961 to obtain assistance.[25] The issue of armaments supplies to Tshombe was discussed at the highest level in the SADF during 1962,[26] but there is no indication he was provided with such assistance in this phase. However, while direct military intervention is improbable, Pretoria chose something of a middle road by approving of South African mercenaries fighting for Tshombe. As co-operation with mercenaries was an important element in South Africa's foreign relations with Africa at this time and later, we introduce relevant personalities and aspects necessary to understand this aspect.

A mercenary can be defined as a "hired professional soldier who fights for any state or nation".[27] Two mercenaries play a meaningful role in our study, namely Frenchman Pierre Robert 'Bob' Denard and the South African-based 'Mad' Mike Hoare. In the 1960s, the use of mercenaries was an accepted international trend and their use was not hindered under South African law either. On reading article 121A of the Defence Act (No 44 of 1957), relevant in the period under review, it becomes clear "being a mercenary is not per se an offence in terms of South African law";[28] any South African who was not a member of either the SADF or the Reserve could become a mercenary. Denard and Hoare were amongst the Katanga mercenaries,[29] but only Hoare's role is of relevance here, with no evidence of contact between Pretoria and Denard on this occasion. While we presently describe Hoare, Denard will be introduced in Chapter 4. Born in India as the son of Irish parents and educated in Ireland and Britain, Hoare served the British Army in India and Burma. After the Second World War, he immigrated to South Africa, settling in Pietermaritzburg, near Durban, started a safari business and travelled extensively in Africa.[30] His nationality defied final clarification,[31] although this is an important aspect to understand Pretoria's reaction to his mercenary activities. Circumstantial evidence suggests he adopted South African citizenship, reinforced by the fact Britain did not demand his extradition after the Seychelles coup in 1981 and a South African court sentenced him to prison.

Returning to the Congo crisis, DFA documents suggest Pretoria knew of Hoare and about 16 South African mercenaries supporting Tshombe. Despite the lack of clear evidence on direct collaboration with Pretoria's military, there is little doubt their activities found tacit approval, at the least, because the mercenaries with South African nationality had to be given leave, either from the SADF or the Reserve, to prevent legal action against them upon their return. Whereas the military did nothing to stop South African mercenaries fighting in Katanga, Brand Fourie, Permanent Representative to the UN at the time, warned Jooste this might further worsen the country's international image, advising the government to stop mercenary involvement. With Louw certainly and

Jooste possibly supporting Fourie's view, Pretoria subsequently threatened all mercenaries with the loss of their passports.[32] Whether the military translated this into actual action remains unclear.

Still in the period 1960-63 and related to South African military involvement in the Congo, two Kasai representatives came to South Africa to ask for such support. They had a meeting with Anglo American's Harry Oppenheimer in September 1960 to obtain mining and military assistance. Their specific choice was no coincidence, because the Republic of Congo was probably Anglo American's largest mining involvement in Africa beyond southern Africa. Dating from the 1920s, its diamond subsidiary, De Beers had considerable interests in Mbuji-Mayi, capital of the central Kasai-Oriental province.[33] Although Oppenheimer supported Kalonji's cause, he does not appear to have been in a position to assist. However, he described the meeting in a written report to Prime Minister Verwoerd, linking both Anglo American's economic and the government's political interests in the province:

> They told me that their object (...) was to obtain a supply of arms for use against the troops of Lumumba who are invading the Kasai Province (...). I expressed sympathy with them in their opposition to Lumumba but explained that it was naturally quite impossible for any private individual in South Africa to obtain arms for them. (...) I felt it desirable that I should at once inform you of what had taken place.[34]

According to Verwoerd's instant reply, the two men subsequently had a discussion with a DFA official on that matter: "He informed them that having regard to all the circumstances, it would not be possible to supply them with military equipment, but like any other buyer they would be able to purchase non-military equipment from private sources if they so desired".[35] We can explain this by referring to the above-stated reasons dissuading Pretoria from becoming directly involved in the Congo crisis.

During Tshombe's premiership until October 1965, Pretoria became comparatively more engaged militarily, this time to keep Tshombe in power. The press reported on the presence of South African mercenaries on Tshombe's side,[36] euphemistically referred to as "white volunteers" in DFA documents.[37] Among them was Hoare, leading the 5 Commando with an education camp for some 350 to 400 mercenaries based in northern Katanga.[38] Compared to his earlier position, Verwoerd now openly approved South African mercenary activity. At the opening of the Cape Nationalist Congress in August 1964, he argued: "We will not interfere if a legitimate government goes about this matter legitimately".[39] Seven days later, possibly after the foreign service officials intervened, Verwoerd tried to dissimulate this pronouncement in a press statement: "When I said (...) the Government of the Republic (...) did not intend at the moment to interfere if there were people in South Africa who went to the Congo as volunteers to assist a legal and internationally recognised government, it was of course with the understanding that it would not affect South Africa's interests". However, the reasons given for this attitude were not political or legal, but economic in nature. In Verwoerd's view, the departure of mercenaries might "disrupt the labour market", therefore adding to the "manpower shortage which has to be filled at considerable cost by means of State aided immigration".[40] Thus, Pretoria almost certainly failed to intervene, particularly as the military did not object to mercenary action. According to diplomatic historian Gleijeses, Lawrence Raymond 'Larry' Devlin, the Station Chief of the US Central Intelligence Agency (CIA) in the Congo, reported to Washington: "many of the mercenaries arriving at Kamina are actually South African Army regulars placed on leave status for six months". In August 1964, Gleijeses further states, Pretoria's military despatched a C-130 plane "with what is obviously military equipment" to Tshombe. However, Gleijeses indicates Pretoria did not send military forces, although it had apparently been asked for them.[41]

The above suggests the military, compared to the first phase of the Congo crisis, had gained in influence on Verwoerd vis-à-vis the foreign service corps for three reasons. First, its strongly increased capacity since 1961, with France as main armaments supplier. Second, Verwoerd's above-cited statement in August indicates he felt greater confidence because the US also supported Tshombe. Referring to Malan's 1949 Africa Charter, this may have raised hopes of South Africa achieving an equal footing with important nations intervening in Africa, even though Washington preferred not to be associated with Pretoria.[42] Third, South Africa had an economic interest in the political stability of the Republic of Congo. In particular, the hope was for its inclusion in a "Greater South Africa", an idea proposed by Verwoerd and Jan Haak, then Deputy Minister of Planning, Economic Affairs and Mines (1961-64), and comprising the plan for a "Southern African Common Market", enlarging Pretoria's economic influence in this area .With South Africa as the core country, it would have embraced Northern and Southern Rhodesia (Zambia, Zimbabwe), Nyasaland (Malawi), the Portuguese territories Angola and Mozambique, the High Commission Territories Bechuanaland (Botswana), Basutoland (Lesotho) and Swaziland and the independent Congo.[43] Yet, the stability brought about by Tshombe was not long-lasting; Mobutu and his troops intervened in November 1965, ruling the country with an iron fist until 1997. He renamed the country Republic of Zaire in 1971 and himself Mobutu Sese Seko in 1972. In 1973, Africa Division Counsellor Johan Frederick Pretorius described Mobutu's "attitude towards the Republic" as "unfriendly".[44] With Tshombe, Pretoria had lost a partner in a country with economic potential.

Isolation

Toward the mid-1960s, South Africa found itself completely isolated on the African continent and increasingly so within the international community. The DFA's approach of winning over those African states amenable to contact with Pretoria by providing technical assistance did not result in any tangible results, and the military's Congo excursion equally fell short of establishing a stable situation. These developments were an important factor for the Afrikaner community to retreat into the *laager*. Petrus Johannes 'Piet' Cillié, Editor of the Afrikaans daily *Die Burger* (1954-77), close to the National Party, and a Broederbond member,[45] described the prevailing sentiments:

> We have scarcely had time to digest these radical changes in our destiny; but we certainly are groping our way to a new sense of purpose (...) the events of 1960 and its aftermath threw South Africa into a fiercely patriotic and defensive mood which to a large extent still persists (...). The early sixties, then, were dominated by a defensive, an often aggressively defensive mentality and a sense of isolation.[46]

Though isolation dominated, this was not the complete picture. According to the mainstream secondary literature, Pretoria's Outward-Looking Policy toward Africa only began under Vorster in 1967, with Lesotho and Malawi as the initial successes. Yet, cognisance is not taken of the fact that several developments in this direction had already taken place under Verwoerd, leading Geldenhuys to attribute to him "a commendable degree of flexibility in foreign policy matters".[47] In particular, reference is made to Verwoerd's meeting with Leabua Jonathan, the Prime Minister of soon-to-be independent Lesotho, in September 1966 in Pretoria. Being the first open encounter between the South African executive and a foreign black leader, it was a great diplomatic success for Pretoria, even though the meeting took place in complete secrecy for fear of repercussions among the conservative elements.[48] Already in April of that year, and as revealed in the following chapter, the Malawi Labour Representative in Johannesburg, who represented the country's mine workers, had approached DFA Deputy Secretary Burger, resulting in him leading a group of three men to Malawi in July. We therefore argue Muller's Department of Foreign Affairs was responsible for Verwoerd's openness and flexibility. While not intending to stretch the importance of personalities and make undue connections between historical dates, it is significant to note Verwoerd's meeting with Jonathan took place roughly two months after the resignation of Secretary Jooste, said to be a staunchly committed NP follower in comparison to his successor, Louw.

We have now outlined how the foreign affairs ministry and the military tried to come to terms with African independence. However, African anti-apartheid activity continued, leaving South Africa increasingly isolated internationally. The following chapter examines the developments of that situation during John Vorster's premiership.

4

What Relations with Africa?
B.J. Vorster, 1966-78

Outward-Looking Policy

The term Outward-Looking originated in a contribution in the September 1965 issue of the magazine *News/Check*, edited by an Afrikaans journalist and "forerunner of *verligte* thought",[1] entitled "The Choice before South Africa: Look Inwards or Look Outwards".[2] The term subsequently entered South Africa's political vocabulary.[3] The Outward-Looking Policy was based on Pretoria's regained confidence in the political, economic and military spheres. In particular, in 1966, the International Court of Justice found Ethiopia and Liberia did not possess the *locus standi* in the S.W.A./Namibia case to challenge South Africa's occupation and South Africa experienced an economic boom.[4] The policy's principal aim was to bring about a *modus vivendi* with African states, responsible for South Africa's isolation.[5] However, Vorster's foreign policy making towards Africa became dominated by inter-departmental rivalry. While sometimes interrelated and running parallel, and based on the insights gained from our research, we can broadly categorise the conflicting strategies into four phases: Outward Movement, describing the DFA's activities towards African states beyond southern Africa after 1967; Dialogue, interaction initiated by the military around 1966 with Francophone countries in West Africa; Secret Diplomacy, practised by the Department of Information from 1972; and Détente, relating to Pretoria's attempts to deal with the new situation in southern Africa from 1974/75. We will now analyse these phases in turn.

Outward Movement

In pursuing his Africa policy, Vorster initially followed in Verwoerd's footsteps by meeting with Lesotho's Prime Minister, Jonathan, in January 1967, probably on Minister Muller's advice, who held a relatively influential position at that time. Given Lesotho's almost complete dependence on its all-surrounding neighbour, the final communiqué emphasised the importance of Pretoria's assistance.[6] The DFA equally provided technical assistance and expertise and finance for development/investment projects to impress African countries further north. The former had its roots in the 1950s, when Pretoria was still a member of the BIS, CCTA, CSA and FAMA. After exclusion from these transnational bodies, the DFA offered the same kind of assistance on a bilateral basis.[7] Regarding the development/investment projects, it co-operated with private and parastatal companies. It usually supported projects or provided technical assistance in areas meaningful to the leaders of target states, hoping to alter their anti-apartheid stance, evidenced in Deputy Secretary Carl von Hirschberg's report of December 1979 related to the Comoros: "projects which are closest to the heart of the President and therefore likely to appeal to him. This is politically important".[8] These considerations also surfaced in the DFA's activities in Malawi and Madagascar.

Malawi

It seems likely Pretoria targeted this former British colony primarily due to its propinquity to South Africa's borders. Furthermore, President Hastings Kamuzu Banda's conservative and western-oriented politico-ideological style made him a promising partner, and Malawi was strongly dependent on South Africa in terms of trade, investment and employment for migrant mine workers.[9] The migrant workers issue resulted in close contact between the two countries. In April 1966, the Malawi Labour Representative in Johannesburg invited Under-Secretary Albie Burger to attend Malawi's July independence celebrations. In accepting the offer, Burger was accompanied by a member of the Board of Trade and Industries and the SADF's Chief, Werndly Renaut van der Riet.[10] The latter's presence substantiates suggestions in the secondary literature that Pretoria gave Banda military support for his South Africa-friendly position.[11] This initial contact was fruitful, as Burger, in December, led a trade mission to Malawi.[12] In the following decade, more than a dozen official delegations, mainly composed of government representatives involved in trade, finance, commerce, industry and development, paid reciprocal visits, of which only the most significant ones are mentioned now.[13]

In March 1967, three Malawi Ministers visited South Africa to sign a trade agreement,[14] following which, in September, diplomatic relations on an ambassadorial level were established. Further substantiating indications of military support for Banda, a Military Attaché was accredited at South Africa's Mission.[15] In August 1968, Minister Muller met Banda in Malawi, leading to Vorster's follow-up visit in May 1970, accompanied by Muller and Petrus Solomon 'Lang Piet' Rautenbach, his Planning Adviser. Vorster was confident enough to undertake such a step, possibly reassured by the inroads Pretoria had simultaneously made into more distant and more important African countries, as we will see in the following section. As the first visit of a South African executive to an independent African state, the country's press hailed it as an "historic breakthrough",[16] credit for which is not to be attributed to the Department of Foreign Affairs alone. In particular, Rautenbach was an important figure and key in arranging Vorster's visit.[17] Given his parallel involvement in Pretoria's contact with Madagascar, as we shall see, we now provide some background on Rautenbach.

Though Rautenbach passed away in 1998, we were able to correspond with his daughter, Renée Conradie; we also used newspaper reports.[18] Rautenbach's academic background in both economics and planning, coupled with government departmental stints from the late 1950s, made him an ideal component of the Malawi projects.[19] However, and clearly of greater importance, he was close to the Prime Minister, as we learnt from former Africa Institute Director Erich Leistner (1978-99), of whose Council Rautenbach was a member (1984-92).[20] Renée Conradie indicated his friendship with Vorster developed from 1966, due to interaction in planning matters, recalling Vorster "trusted his opinion" and the two "often played golf together",[21] Vorster's sports passion. Henceforth, Rautenbach held positions of great political relevance, even beyond Vorster's Premiership.[22] Additionally, Rautenbach had been an influential Broederbond member from the early 1950s.[23] Leistner summed up the reasons for Rautenbach's role in Pretoria's Africa policy: "Vorster's detente [sic] efforts were not universally popular within the ranks of his party (many supporters were scandalized by Vorster sitting "between the two *meide*[24]" when he visited Malawi). Hence the need for a trustworthy contact person".[25] While Renée Conradie recalled her father had been a "close, old friend" of Hilgard Muller,[26] this indicates the Foreign Affairs Minister's increasingly weak position at the time. Vorster's meeting with Banda was reciprocated by Banda's visit to South Africa in August 1971. As a result, both countries upgraded their missions to embassies, while Fouché and Muller returned Banda's visit in March 1972. These political ties were strengthened by the involvement of South African companies in the construction of a new capital and the railway link from Malawi to a Mozambican seaport, now discussed in some detail.

At independence, the southern town of Zomba served as Malawi's capital. Banda argued that, to attract investment so far focused on Blantyre, south of Zomba, the capital should be situated in the country's centre. However, it has been convincingly suggested his personal interest in bringing the centre of political power closer to his home terrain was equally important.[27] After Banda's approach to the British to finance the building of the new capital at Lilongwe, 200 km north of Zomba, had failed, he turned to South Africa for support, utilising Pretoria's willingness to provide assistance for political gain. Under-Secretary Burger expressed some caution regarding the project's viability, causing Banda to complain to Minister Muller,[28] while a DFA report of 1979 described it a "prestige project".[29] Nevertheless, South African firms, together with Pretoria's financial support, participated in the so-called Lilongwe Capital Project, possibly because Rautenbach's favourable position towards the project found Pretoria's support. In fact, during his 1968 parliamentary speech, Banda hailed Rautenbach's engagement in having led a "team on physical planning" to Malawi in 1967.[30] Already in October 1966, the Malawi Development Corporation had signed an agreement with the Johannesburg-based company Imex, which became responsible for planning and designing the new capital.[31] Imex had only been established one month prior to this agreement, with Anglo American, the IDC and Union Acceptances Ltd (UAL), Anglo American's private merchant bank,[32] as main shareholders, and Klaus Oppenheimer, related to the Anglo American Oppenheimer family and former Credit Guarantee General Manager, as Managing Director.[33] Contrary to the latter's claim of having kept a distance from the Oppenheimers,[34] his involvement suggests a family strategy to further diversify its economic activities. In any case, it appears the IDC provided the Malawi government with the necessary loan, insured by Credit Guarantee, to engage Imex. After the completion of the planning process, construction work began, again with South African participation. In May 1968, Pretoria granted a loan of $11.1 million at the interest rate of 4 per cent;[35] it is likely the IDC provided the finances, insured by Credit Guarantee. Regarding the participation of South African firms, a note in the loan contract stated it was "expressly tied to the condition that maximum use was made of South African contractors".[36] However, we could only ascertain the identity of one company, the Johannesburg-based firm Dominion Earth Works that won the contract worth $1.9 million for the construction of some 50 km of road from Zomba to Lilongwe.[37] Malawi's new capital was inaugurated in 1975.[38]

The second development/investment project, the railway line to Nacala, was to provide Liwonde, near Blantyre, with rail access to the sea for import and export. Of the entire 700 km distance to be covered, Banda had already secured some financing from the Japanese for the Malawi section to the border. For the rest, he expressed the hope to Minister Muller in September 1967 "anything (...) you can do to assist us in this too I should naturally very greatly appreciate".[39] Banda again counted on Pretoria's preparedness to assist with the purpose of making political inroads into Africa. His calculations proved correct again; only three days after the announcement of the Lilongwe Capital Project loan, the IDC granted a credit of $15.2 million. The construction of the railway line, the provision of rolling stock and locomotives was awarded to the Malawi Railway Construction Company, partly owned by South Africa's engineering firm Roberts Construction. The IDC acted as the financier and Credit Guarantee as the insurer with the provision that 60 per cent of the material, and not 70 per cent as stipulated in its business guidelines, be bought from South Africa.[40] This is a good example of Pretoria and the country's business sector co-operating to the benefit of the host country and each other. It helped the DFA to fulfil its political ambitions, while Roberts Construction landed a profitable and risk free order. The above developments activated South Africa's trade organisations, reinforcing Pretoria's political ambitions. In September 1968, the Durban Chamber of Commerce undertook a Business and Goodwill Mission to Malawi,[41] while Hoogendyk and Stockenström led an Afrikaanse Handelsinstituut delegation there in August 1969.[42] The former, the first such venture by South African organised business to independent Africa, was a direct result of the 1967 trade agreement, reflecting its initial enthusiasm in tapping the unexplored markets. The mission's final report summarised: "exporters should not underestimate the value of the Malawi market. (...) it has significant potential for the future and is as well a bridge over which South Africa can reach adjacent markets".[43] Yet, the Chamber's second mission in November 1973 concluded trade had not taken off, while also stating: "Malawi certainly holds promise for the future (...) South African exporters should seriously consider this market".[44] However, its third mission in April/May 1979 pointed out "that Malawi is not a captive market".[45] The Chamber's decision to have sent three missions, despite Malawi's low rating, was probably linked to Kenneth William Hobson, the Chamber's long-time General Manager (1965-84). He had good connections with and knowledge of Malawi, having been a civil servant in the Finance Ministry in the Government of the Federation of Rhodesia and Nyasaland prior to becoming General Manager of that Federation's Association of Chambers of Commerce.[46] Regarding its excursions, the Afrikaanse Handelsinstituut saw them as an economic supplement to Pretoria's Outward Movement, as reflected in the press statement on the trade mission's departure to Malawi:

> the A.H.I. is fully aware of the fact that the Republic of
> South Africa is part and parcel of the continent. We be-
> lieve that we must develop means so that the people on
> this continent, and particularly on the sub-continent, can
> assist each other and help develop one another. For that
> reason, we are prepared to share our business acumen,
> technological knowledge and ingenuity.[47]

Yet, this remained the AHI's only activity in Africa beyond southern Africa for reasons provided in the report on the Malawi visit: "There is no doubt that the country has possibilities for sound and profitable capital investment, and also opportunities for profitable development. It should be pointed out, however, that investment possibilities in the Republic of South Africa are probably greater and more promising".[48]

Although access to the DFA's Malawi files was restricted to the end of 1979, with Banda Pretoria had won a reliable partner in Africa and there is no indication the relations between the two countries suffered any serious setback in the remaining period under review.

Madagascar

The second country of importance in the Outward Movement was presided over by Philibert Tsiranana since independence from France in 1960. Compared to Malawi, the reasons for Pretoria to establish contact with this country are less evident, as the factor of economic dependence was less important. In October 1965, Tsiranana made the first step by inviting a mission to survey the country's chrome, graphite, bauxite and gold deposits, and to make suggestions for their exploitation. Seeing a possibility to make relatively easy inroads into another independent African country, the DFA approved, deploying a mission comprising representatives of the IDC, the state-financed Southern Oil Exploration Corporation (Soekor),[49] the Afrikaner investment and mining company General Mining and Finance Corporation[50] and the Chamber of Mines. While the DFA files record no follow-up initiatives to this mission, economic interaction between the two countries entered a new phase when Albie Burger led a mission, mainly consisting of representatives from the Departments of Tourism, Commerce and Industries, to Madagascar in July 1967.[51] Presumably as a result, the number of flights between the two countries increased from one to two per week.[52] Anglo American also showed an interest in Madagascar. In March 1968, a five-man delegation went there on an exploratory mission, facilitated by its Paris representative, Serge Combard. After the mission's return, President Tsiranana's Technical Adviser and Combard called on Albie Burger to inform him "about the investment plans of Anglo-American in Madagascar, and to enquire whether, in principle, the South African Government approved". The Under-Secretary's report further reveals Anglo American's interest in nickel, bauxite and uranium mining.[53] The secondary literature suggests the company mined the nickel deposits in the mid-1970s,[54] but Anglo American Executive Director, Spicer, argued in 1999 nothing came off the ground because of the government's "nationalistic policies",[55] referring to the Marxist orientation of Tsiranana's successor after 1972.

Further, in November 1968, four businessmen from the Afrikaner insurance, investment and mining companies Sanlam, Federale Volksbeleggings and the General Mining and Finance Corporation[56] visited the island. They briefed officials from the Departments of Foreign Affairs, Finance and Commerce before and after the mission, suggesting the "political climate (...) is most favourable to South Africa, but could receive a severe setback if no action follows our visit".[57] Vorster took this up by sending Planning Adviser Rautenbach and another Department of

Planning official to Madagascar from 27 February to 12 March 1969.
They considered the development of Nosy Be in the northern tip of
Madagascar "a good investment", as by "concentrating on that island,
tourism, commerce and other activities will combine to give a maximum
return",[58] and recommended deploying an official mission for further
investigation. Led by Deputy Secretary Robert John Montgomery, that
mission took place in November 1969, concluding a hotel project would
be viable.[59] Probably as a result of the Anglo American mission to Madagascar in 1968, which had investigated various "investment plans", the
hotel chain Southern Sun became involved in this. Despite Anglo American's focus on mining, tourism was "also involved", as Burger reported
after meeting Combard and Tsiranana's Technical Adviser.[60] We argue
the multinational's interest in this sector was motivated by its participation in South African Breweries, the major shareholder in Southern Sun,
although Anglo American's Spicer unconvincingly argued this had always
been "a minority indirect position" and "it simply wouldn't register on
our radar screen" how South African Breweries "handles its business".[61]
In fact, only six months after Anglo American's mission, South African
Breweries engaged itself in the project by presenting its "preliminary
thinking" to the DFA, asking Pretoria "to provide 70% of the capital
costs of the hotel at an interest rate of 7% per annum", while Anglo
American was going to "provide the remaining 30% (...) in the form of
equity capital". Repayment would start after ten years and over a period
of 15 years, while Pretoria was again "asked to guarantee the entire hotel
project against nationalisation by the Malagasy Government".[62] The DFA
adopted that proposal, giving it even closer access to Madagascar.

During the discussions with a Malagasy delegation that visited the
Republic in June 1970, Pretoria proposed a "low-interest loan" of $2.8
million "for the development of the Nossi Bé infrastructure", "dependent
upon the satisfactory conclusion of detailed negotiations to be entered
into by S.A. Breweries/Southern Sun Hotel Corporation group (..) with
the Malagasy Government". Pretoria further offered South African
Breweries a loan at even softer conditions than originally requested by
them. The estimated cost of $3.1 million was to be shared, as South Afri-
can Breweries suggested, with the IDC providing and Credit Guarantee
insuring a $2.1 million loan at an interest rate of only 6 per cent and for
repayment in six-monthly instalments over ten years after the project's
completion.[63] In August, the proposal was further discussed between a
visiting Malagasy delegation and, *inter alia*, Brand Fourie, two DFA Africa
Division officials, Planning Adviser Rautenbach, an IDC representative
and Credit Guarantee's Jan Bouwer.[64] The hotel deal was finalised in the
following months and signed by Minister Muller during a visit to Antananarivo in November 1970. On this occasion, he was accompanied by
Fourie, Counsellor Jeremy Shearar, Rautenbach, his Private Secretary,
two IDC representatives, the South African Breweries Chairman and

Managing Director, as well as Southern Sun Chairman Sol Kerzner and Managing Director John Howell Ward.[65] The agreement detailed the government-to-government loan of $3.2 million at an interest rate of 4 per cent to be repaid in six-monthly instalments only 12 years after completion of the project and over a period of ten years. This loan, insured by Credit Guarantee, was to be used for the improvement and upgrading of the infrastructure at Nosy Be.[66] In a separate agreement, the IDC granted Antananarivo a credit of $2.1 million to build the hotel. An interest rate of 6 per cent, credit repayment in six-monthly instalments after February 1983 over a period of ten years applied, with Credit Guarantee insuring the deal.[67] Compared with Credit Guarantee's and the IDC's normal business practices, the terms and conditions of the two agreements were particularly soft for the credit taker.

South Africa's initiative in upgrading the island's tourist infrastructure also received impetus from Malawi's President, Pretoria's reliable and supportive partner. During Tsiranana's visit to Malawi in April 1969, Banda proposed the idea to him,[68] both agreeing tourism should be developed in southern Africa, including South Africa. In this context, Frenchman Pierre Jérome Ullmann organised a tourism seminar that took place in Antananarivo in June 1969. He was the director of Bedeaux Africa in Johannesburg, a management and industrial consulting firm, and Inter-Afrique Services in Madagascar, an import-export agency,[69] explaining why Ullmann became Pretoria's middleman with Antananarivo, interesting the South Africans in the construction of a dry dock in Madagascar. The sea route around the Cape and through the Mozambique Channel was of strategic significance after the closure of the Suez Canal in 1967 resulted in increased oil traffic from the Persian Gulf to Europe and North America. As shipyards and dry docks to accommodate the tankers were non-existent along most of the route, Narinda Bay in north-western Madagascar was considered to counter this lack. A French firm presented a preliminary study in 1970.[70] Muller was informed of this project during his visit to Madagascar in November, while Ullmann updated Muller and Fourie in March 1971. However, Pretoria faced a dilemma; it had to decide between extending the facilities in South Africa to permit oil tankers to dock, thereby assisting the country's economy, and supporting Narinda Bay to win an African state. The rising financial implications complicated participation in the latter.[71]

After Ullmann's meeting with Muller and Fourie, the DFA propagated the Narinda Bay project to bolster its Outward Movement, with several delegations paying reciprocal visits to discuss Pretoria's participation.[72] In June 1971, Ullmann met Deputy Secretary Montgomery, Under-Secretary Best and Counsellor Shearar to report the results of his contacts with South Africa's business sector since the March meeting. According to him, the IDC clearly preferred upgrading Cape Town harbour, and Basil Hersov from Anglovaal was equally uninterested.[73] The IDC's stance as a parastatal is understandable, while Hersov's negative attitude was motivated by his company's interest in coal exports through Richards Bay.[74] Given these sobering responses, Ullmann stressed to the DFA officials "the political importance" Antananarivo attaches to Narinda Bay and its abandonment "could seriously affect the climate of relations between the two countries".[75] Given that its files do not record further activity, the DFA's standpoint evidently could not compete with South Africa's economic interests. In any case, the projects in Madagascar were halted in June 1972, when Didier Ratsiraka ousted Tsiranana in a coup d'état. Given his Marxist stance, Antananarivo's position vis-à-vis Pretoria changed completely. Ratsiraka declared "the Malagasy government will take control of the realisation of the hotel at Nossi-Bé [sic]",[76] what Southern Sun's Kerzner described as "a great blow".[77] After bilateral discussions, the Malagasy government was prepared to honour the agreements, repaying both loans by March 1973.[78] In contrast, Ratsiraka did not intend forcing the South Africans to withdraw from Narinda Bay.[79] However, pursuing its own economic interests, Pretoria disengaged, and the IDC financed the construction of a dry dock in Saldanha Bay, north of Cape Town.[80]

Lusaka Manifesto

The DFA's Outward Movement initiatives only produced one tangible result, the establishment of diplomatic relations with Malawi. However, given Malawi's economic dependence on South Africa and its little significance in continental matters, it was only a relative success. Nonetheless, it had some impact on Africa's unified anti-apartheid position in that Malawi abstained when the UN General Assembly voted on the Lusaka Manifesto in November 1969,[81] a document 13 African states[82] adopted at the Fifth Summit of Eastern and Central African States in the Zambian capital in April, and the OAU in September that year. This major assessment of African policy towards South Africa was a compromise between those fundamentally rejecting apartheid and those interpreting it as allowing contact with Pretoria.[83] Yet, when comparing the Manifesto's pragmatic approach with Pretoria's task of winning African states so they would refrain from attacking South Africa, the DFA's strategy of utilising economic levers fell short of achieving this aim.

In addition to its policy not having achieved the desired results, the contentious issue of black ambassadors in South Africa was a factor in the struggle between the *verligte* and *verkrampte*, eventually leading to a split within the ruling National Party in 1969.[84] Pretoria had persistently tried to avoid this by mooting the idea of diplomatic suburbs for African ambassadors, by allowing Malawi only to send a white ambassador, by trying to assure the electorate relations would only be established with well-disposed African states and by emphasising "nothing will be done that is not to South

Africa's advantage".[85] However, the *verkrampte* understood Vorster's mixed sports policy and the Outward Movement as perceptible moves towards the dismantling of apartheid, breaking away from the NP and forming the Herstigte Nasionale Party. Although not generating a large following, the divisions within Afrikanerdom required consideration in the formulation of Pretoria's foreign policy toward Africa. Any move that could be construed as undermining the privileged status of these whites might have domestic repercussions.[86] The military, which conducted none of its operations in public, was not limited in its Africa approach and successfully brokered what became the Dialogue policy. Whereas the DFA's more public initiatives suffered under the pressures of Afrikanerdom.

Dialogue

The military was the principal actor in Pretoria's Dialogue with Africa, at least initially. Originating in Malan's Africa Charter, it sought to play a continental role alongside the colonial powers. While originally disposing of relatively limited capacities for such activities, the arrival of arms, from France in particular, enhanced its arsenal from the mid-1960s and gave it the confidence to now play such a role. The different approaches towards Africa led to friction and inter-departmental jealousy. In particular, Minister Muller later claimed Dialogue had resulted from the DFA's endeavours,[87] even though it had been initiated by the military. Given the latter's co-operation with France over Dialogue, we now examine the framework in which this took place.

Although decolonisation removed its direct political control over its many former African colonies, France successfully managed to institutionalise and cement the political, economic, military and cultural ties. Particularly close relations were retained with the Ivory Coast, Gabon, the Central African Republic (C.A.R.), all of which concluded post-independence defence and military assistance agreements.[88] Yet, the relations between Francophone African countries and Paris were interdependent. While needing French military support and economic assistance, most Francophone African leaders accepted being part of the French system, according them a certain grandeur. For France, on the other hand, the wielding of power in Francophone Africa was central to its ambition of playing an important role in world politics, a situation that gave its former colonies some form of leverage.[89] Similar to Pretoria's foreign policy making, a small number of officials influenced France's foreign relations with African states. The personalities we will introduce are essential in understanding the *modus operandi* of the Paris-Pretoria alliance in Francophone Africa from the late 1960s. Jacques Foccart's dominant influence stemmed from an elaborate network of personal connections to Africa's political elite, the French military and intelligence, with one author suggesting: "little went on in Francophone Africa that

Foccart was not quickly made aware of".[90] Foccart laid the foundation for his "bureaucratic predominance in all things African"[91] with the work in his family's import-export company that primarily traded with the African colonies prior to the Second World War. In France, Foccart's close contact with the politico-military and intelligence establishment was rooted in his involvement in the French Résistance during the Second World War, becoming General Charles de Gaulle's confidant. In 1961, two years after assuming the presidency, de Gaulle made Foccart Secretary General in the Presidency of the Republic for African and Malagasy Affairs,[92] the key vehicle in formulating French Africa policy during de Gaulle's presidency (1959-69). Consequently, Foccart "was at the elbow of his own president and in constant touch with African presidents and their important ministers".[93] Furthermore, Foccart was a "close friend"[94] of Michel Debré, minister in several important departments since 1958 and Defence Minister from June 1969.[95] Foccart's Résistance involvement also provided him with direct access to the Department for Foreign Information and Counterespionage (SDECE).[96] In particular, he put Maurice Robert, Colonel in the Résistance, in charge of SDECE's Africa operations (1960-73).[97] Jean Mauricheau-Beaupré was another, rather mysterious, figure in Foccart's network. To cite Péan's journalistic work on the French secret services: "From 1960, «Monsieur Jean» finds himself involved in all jolts on the black continent. Wherever France hesitates to intervene officially, or the SDECE is too detectable, we can see appear the profile of Mauricheau-Beaupré".[98] Foccart referred to him as an "indefatigable militant of reconciliation between black Africa and South Africa".[99] Due to his Résistance involvement, Mauricheau-Beaupré was very close to Jacques Foccart, Michel Debré and Maurice Robert.[100] Finally, he was adviser to presidents Felix Houphouët-Boigny of the Ivory Coast, Albert Bernard – Omar from 1973 – Bongo of Gabon and François Tombalbaye of Chad.[101]

The close bilateral Franco-South African relations further provides the framework to understand co-operation between the two countries in Africa. The French representative abstained when the UN Security Council adopted the 1963 voluntary arms embargo and France subsequently became a principal armaments supplier to South Africa until the mid-1970s.[102] Pik Botha described the importance of these deliveries: "All these helicopters and the aircraft, coming from France, at a time in our history when we were totally isolated; you must not forget the impact of that; it is tremendous. If you are alone on the ocean, and your boat is about to sink, then another ship goes along; that is quite something".[103] Military exchange intensified after P.W. Botha became the Minister of Defence in 1966, keen to obtain French armaments to strengthen the military's standing and to have the support of an important international political actor. Between 1969 and 1971 alone, he paid four official visits to France, during which he also met both Debré and Foccart.[104] In return,

South Africa provided France with uranium, furthering France's goal of playing an important role in world politics, and, until 1974, French personnel made use of a space tracking station near Pretoria to monitor French satellites launched from Kourou, Guyana.[105] After the mid-1970s, however, Franco-South African relations became more "banal";[106] Foccart departed from office in May 1974, and Pretoria's military involvement in Angola and Mozambique made it increasingly difficult for Paris to explain its South Africa links to its Francophone African partners.[107]

Alden and Daloz appropriately summarise the geopolitical convergence of the French and South African interests in Africa until the mid-1970s: "Each state, aspiring to play a significant role in international politics through the projection of power on the African continent, has based its claim to this status on the combination of military wherewithal and economic pre-eminence".[108] We now examine the implications.

Chad

The first available evidence of Franco-South Africa co-operation in Africa we found relates to the former French colony Chad, which shared the northern border with Moscow-allied Libya, making it a potentially interesting listening post for the military intelligence community. It appears the Director of Military Intelligence, Brigadier Pierre Retief, established contact when he met President Tombalbaye in October 1965 in Chad, facilitated through Foccart's and Mauricheau-Beaupré's services. In a letter of May 1970 to P.W. Botha over Nigerian Civil War issues, Retief's successor, Fritz Loots states: "Up to now, they have gone out of their way to be helpful to make contact in Africa. So, for example, we have to thank them for our contact with (...) Chad".[109] During their encounter, Tombalbaye and Retief agreed communism posed a threat to Africa and closer co-operation should therefore be established between the two countries. As a first step, Retief proposed geological assistance to explore Chad's mineral resources, motivating Tombalbaye to make such a request to Vorster.[110] After their mission in October 1966, the two geologists suggested Pretoria should provide the relevant authorities in Chad with equipment for further explorations,[111] following which, in March 1967, Vorster offered Tombalbaye two Land Rovers, a rock cutting machine, a diamond driller and the deployment of further geologists.[112] After Tombalbaye accepted the offer, Muller promised to deliver as soon as possible.[113] Yet, according to the DFA files, Tombalbaye only resumed contact with Muller on that matter in 1970, informing him all material had arrived and it was in good working order. Tombalbaye explained his silence with domestic problems, referring to the military attacks from the Libya-supported National Liberation Front of Chad (Frolinat), the politically underrepresented northern community.[114] At the same time, Tom-

Tombalbaye's behaviour also lay in rivalry between the DFA and the military regarding relations with Chad.

Apart from assisting Pretoria's military intelligence, Mauricheau-Beaupré served as the link between Vorster, Muller and Tombalbaye, delivering letters, ensuring the transport of the above geological equipment and allowing his house outside Paris to be used as a meeting place,[115] causing Muller to refer to him as "our mutual friend".[116] However, what van Tonder later termed "the cotton affair"[117] mirrored the policy differences between the military and the foreign affairs ministry. The incident originated in Tombalbaye's letter to Vorster in March 1967, asking Pretoria to buy cotton,[118] Chad's major agricultural product. Subsequently, van Tonder discussed the issue with Tombalbaye, informing him: "the Government itself normally does not buy cotton, and that the requirements for this season have already been bought".[119] Evidently not satisfied, Tombalbaye, during his visit to Paris in May, discussed the issue with Ambassador Burger,[120] who wrote to Pretoria he supported Tombalbaye's approach. Following that lead, Muller wrote to Tombalbaye: "My Government has accepted Mr. Burger's recommendation that we should buy, if the quality is acceptable, some of your cotton at a special premium above world prices. My Government does not normally act as buyer of cotton, but we are prepared to do so in this instance in an endeavour to assist you".[121] This divergence caused significant friction between the two state actors. In July 1969, during a discussion with Muller, van Tonder used the incident to exemplify the dispute over respective areas of responsibility: "I recalled the episode when I newly arrived here [in Paris] and when the Ambassador [Burger] warned me not to cross wires with him. (You know the story of the telegram that was sent about the cotton affair in Chad.) I sometimes have the impression that people work more for themselves than for anything else".[122] After the defeat of the Franco-South African military alliance in the Nigerian Civil War in January 1970, the DFA reasserted itself over the military, possibly motivating Tombalbaye to resume contact with them. While assuring Muller his foreign minister would in future refrain from launching verbal attacks against Pretoria, such as during the 1969 UN General Assembly,[123] the main aim of his letter was to again request Pretoria to buy cotton.[124] However, Muller only replied more than two months later, merely stating he had taken note of the offer and making it clear the geological assistance offer had to be reconsidered. To that end, he enquired about a possible meeting with one of Tombalbaye's ministers in June 1970 in Europe,[125] but the DFA files do not contain any follow-up details.

Nigerian Civil War

The differences between the foreign service corps and the military over the cotton affair in Chad were insignificant compared to those related to

Pretoria's involvement in Nigerian Civil War. This war began in 1967, when the south-eastern province of Biafra declared its independence from Nigeria, a move the federal government – with the support of the Soviet Union and Great Britain – opposed.[126] In Africa, only Gabon, the Ivory Coast, Tanzania and Zambia recognised Biafra as a sovereign state,[127] deviating from the OAU's position to safeguard the territorial integrity of African states. While the reasons for Tanzania's and Zambia's stance are not our interest, the Gabonese and Ivorian presidents, vociferously anticommunist, considered a Soviet-supported Nigeria a threat to West Africa's security. Consequently, Bongo and Houphouët-Boigny offered their countries as transit areas for the channelling of weapons to the Biafra secessionists, co-ordinated by Mauricheau-Beaupré and Maurice Delauney, France's Ambassador in Libreville from 1965.[128] French journalist Péan refers to Mauricheau-Beaupré as the "chief conductor of the clandestine French support to the Biafra secessionists".[129]

Paris supported the secessionists for several reasons. First, given their privileged status among the Francophone African nations, President Bongo and especially Houphouët-Boigny successfully pressured de Gaulle into supporting Biafra to secure their stability.[130] Second, Nigeria's hegemonic position in West Africa posed a potential threat to the French sphere of interest in the region. According to Foccart's memoirs, de Gaulle considered a "break-up of Nigeria" desirable.[131] Further, Paris attempted forging closer links with Ghana, a former British colony surrounded by the former French colonies Ivory Coast, Burkina Faso and Togo, to counterbalance Nigeria's influence. In 1972, Counsellor Johan Pretorius wrote: "Foccart's organisation, and Mr. Beaupré [sic] in particular, became involved in (...) Biafra and Ghana in the framework of France's attempts to "infiltrate" the English-speaking countries in Africa".[132] This needs to be seen against the overall picture of French-British rivalry in Africa, accentuated by de Gaulle's dislike of the British, resulting from London's unhelpful attitude towards the Résistance during the Second World War.[133] The importance of anti-British feelings as a factor for France to support Biafra is confirmed in a letter from Mauricheau-Beaupré to P.W. Botha in November 1970: "We know the subject well, we who were a moral colony of the Anglo-Saxons until de Gaulle returned". In the same correspondence, he speaks of "Anglo-Saxon hypocrisy" on two occasions, referring to the inconsistent British policy towards de Gaulle during the Second World War.[134] A final dimension of France's role in the Nigerian Civil War relates to the French petroleum group, Elf Aquitaine, as admitted by Foccart and confirmed in a report by van Tonder to Ambassador Burger.[135] Elf Aquitaine was a pillar of French influence in Africa, deploying a policy "that was in symbiosis with [that of] Jacques Foccart".[136] Having some oil rights in Biafra, it aimed at controlling all reserves, consequently financing weapons and arms deliveries to the secessionists by using the income generated from selling Biafran oil.[137] While France, Gabon and the Ivory Coast had supported Biafra from the early days of the Nigerian Civil War, Pretoria's military only became involved during the second half of 1969, rooted in P.W. Botha's contact with Houphouët-Boigny, most certainly initiated by Mauricheau-Beaupré. That link was subsequently maintained through the services of Fritz Loots.[138] Botha's first recorded meeting with Houphouët-Boigny took place in March 1969 in Paris, their discussions being dominated by the shared pre-occupation with the communist influence in Africa.[139] As Ivorian political scientist Daddieh remarks: "Houphouët-Boigny detested communism and saw in Pretoria the much needed bulwark against this menace to the continent".[140] Within a month, Houphouët-Boigny met Loots in Paris, subsequently inviting P.W. Botha and Loots to come to Abidjan.[141] Later correspondence and events suggest Loots, on behalf of P.W. Botha, had offered military assistance to Biafra and a loan of $1.4 million to the Ivory Coast.[142] The primary documents do not reveal the purpose of this loan and van Tonder did not divulge any information to us. Foccart's memoirs suggest Houphouët-Boigny then pushed for closer contact, through Mauricheau-Beaupré's mediation,[143] regarding a joint military operation in support of Biafra. In fact, in his report to Fritz Loots on a meeting with Minister Muller, van Tonder states Houphouët-Boigny sought contact with Pretoria due to "profound conviction", and not because of French pressure.[144] Another letter from van Tonder to Loots further underlines that president's influence on Paris and Pretoria regarding support for Biafra:

> The Minister [Muller] also reported on the importance that we attach to the policy that the French government pursues regarding indirect as well as direct help to Biafra. HB responded by saying that he would see [French President] Pompidou on 16 July [1969] and that he would inform us what the results of the discussion were. He added that the indirect help actually goes through the Ivory Coast and therefore was more a matter between him and France rather than Biafra and France.[145]

In July 1969, P.W. Botha decided to provide Biafra with "more or less 200 tons", for which time period is not recorded, of unspecified "weapons of ammunition". This did not, however, correspond to the 250 t Mauricheau-Beaupré had requested on behalf of Houphouët-Boigny;[146] this difference may have been a compromise between the military's interest in promoting contact with Houphouët-Boigny and the caution of launching itself into an uncertain adventure with no guarantee of the Biafran cause to succeed. Within the rectangular network of co-operation between France, Gabon, the Ivory Coast and South Africa in this context, Portugal played a supportive role. During talks with his Portuguese counterpart in June 1969, Hilgard Muller was asked to give assistance to Biafra,[147] and Lisbon allowed South African planes to fly over Angolan territory *en route* to Libreville, then proceeding to Biafra.[148]

Pretoria's military support continued until P.W. Botha reviewed the situation following meetings with Bongo, Houphouët-Boigny and Debré in October 1969. According to a provisional itinerary, he and Loots were to fly to Libreville on 26 October, where van Tonder and General Rudolph Christian Hiemstra, the SADF Commandant – Chief of the SADF from 1973 – and Broederbond member,[149] would join them. After talks with Bongo, who had already invited P.W. Botha and Loots to visit him in August,[150] the company was to proceed to Abidjan in a Mystère 20, an eight-passenger plane provided by either Bongo or Houphouët-Boigny,[151] to hold discussions with Houphouët-Boigny. Subsequently, they were to fly to Paris to hold meetings with Debré. P.W. Botha, Loots and Hiemstra were to arrive back in Pretoria on 30 October.[152] That trip did take place, but a few days earlier than envisaged, as can be deduced from later correspondence.

After these meetings, P.W. Botha reconsidered the Nigerian Civil War involvement. Although not cited specifically, Biafra's dwindling chance of winning the war was one reason. In addition, van Tonder reported a "weak reception" from Debré;[153] according to Ambassador Burger's letter to Brand Fourie, Botha did not share with Debré the "spirit of understanding"[154] he had with Pierre Messmer, the French Defence Minister until June 1969. As a result, Botha wrote to van Tonder on 29 October: "Regarding further arms and weapons deliveries to Biafra, we shall make it available only if the French Minister of Defence informs me in writing that such armaments are still considered to be necessary".[155] Whether he made such a further request is unclear, but Mauricheau-Beaupré, on behalf of Houphouët-Boigny, requested additional supplies during October.[156] In any case, the relevant military archive box suggests Pretoria did not provide further armaments. Before turning to the results of the military activities, we need to discuss the role of French mercenary Bob Denard and his South African colleagues.

Denard participated in many conflicts and was probably the most notorious mercenary of the twentieth century. With the French navy from the mid-1940s, he became a policeman in Morocco in 1953. His move to the former Belgian Congo in 1960, working as a security officer for a mining company, marked the beginning of his mercenary career; in that decade, Denard fought for Tshombe's secessionists in Katanga and for President Mobutu.[157] Although Foccart claims to have "never had any relation with Bob Denard",[158] it is a reasonable assumption he acted with, at least, an "orange light" from Foccart's Africa agency; Denard thus became a "banal instrument of French Africa policy", as Foccart's interviewer suggests.[159] Denard himself described it as follows: "I never had direct contact with the French services. But it's their job to watch, to control, to manipulate".[160] In the Nigerian Civil War, Denard's mercenaries fought for Biafra.

Washington's Ambassador to Gabon, Francis McNamara (1981-84), suggests, they were stationed in Libreville, prior to nocturnal airlifts into Biafra, with Foccart proposing Mauricheau-Beaupré and Ambassador Delauney were in charge of them.[161] In any event, with the knowledge of an insider, Denard's memoirs describe Mauricheau-Beaupré as the "great architect of the rapprochement" between Pretoria and Paris, and their alliance with Houphouët-Boigny and Bongo. Denard also knew Loots was P.W. Botha's personal envoy to Houphouët-Boigny, claiming he was "sometimes" present during their meetings. Although we cannot verify this information, we have little doubt Paris and Pretoria were aware of Denard's role and some co-ordination took place among them. Given the sparse and contradictory information from the secondary literature, Denard's memoirs and interviews with van Tonder and Deon Fourie – a South African academic in strategic studies – no clear picture emerges as to how many South African mercenaries were involved and on whose side.[162]

With the end of the Nigerian Civil War, our interest turns to the question whether the military was successful in finding friends in the countries that surfaced in the context of that war.

Ghana

Interaction with Ghana was only incidental to the Nigerian Civil War. Paris held an interest in making this former British colony part of Francophone Africa. Apart from further strengthening interaction with Paris, it would have represented a considerable success for the military to have the backing of this African country; under Kwame Nkrumah, the country's leader until 1996, Ghana became the symbol for African liberation.

Wishing to install democratic rule, Ghana's military leadership had set presidential elections for August 1969, with Kofi Busia as one of the candidates. According to van Tonder's discussion with Muller within weeks of the elections, Houphouët-Boigny had "undoubted influence" on Busia, whose chances of winning were estimated at 85 per cent. Therefore, Muller was urged to discuss with Houphouët-Boigny "modalities of support to Ghana" and, offering Busia help "in such a way that he would accept it in the best spirit".[163] The military tried to convince the foreign service officials it was worthwhile to support Busia, presumably with economic lures, in the hope the president-to-be would remember the assistance and take a Pretoria-friendly stance. Foccart's and Mauricheau-Beaupré's mediation attempts were again of crucial importance. On 7 July, Mauricheau-Beaupré "discussed" Ghana with Muller,[164] and Loots wrote to P.W. Botha in May 1970: "they [Foccart and Mauricheau-

Beaupré] have gone out of their way to be helpful to make contact in Africa. So, for example, we have to thank them for our contact with Ghana".[165] We suggest Pretoria did provide Busia with some assistance, because, after his election to the presidency, he adopted Houphouët-Boigny's Dialogue approach towards Pretoria. In a speech before the National Assembly in December 1970, he argued "dialogue and armed pressure are not necessarily incompatible".[166] Yet, Accra's government was divided over the issue. While Victor Owosu, Foreign Minister until 1971, rejected Dialogue, his successor, William Ofori-Atta, favoured this approach, producing conflicting statements by Busia and his foreign minister during 1971.[167] In any event, Accra's pro-Dialogue stance ended in January 1972, when Busia was ousted in a military coup.

Gabon

Pretoria's Nigerian Civil War involvement resulted in a strong and long-lasting military bond with President Bongo. In April 1970, they provided three T6 planes, used for pilot training, low-intensity warfare and border surveillance,[168] which can be seen as a gesture of gratitude for Bongo's co-operation. Mirroring the Nigerian Civil War alliance, a Portuguese aircraft escorted the planes across Angola and a frigate in the area where they would fly across the sea. A French plane accompanied the squadron to its final destination.[169] In November 1970, through Loots' services, Bongo appealed to P.W. Botha's anticommunist stance to convince him of Gabon's need for an additional three T6 planes with spare parts and coastal patrol boats. In particular, Bongo argued Gabon was surrounded by the communist-inspired countries Cameroon, the Congolese Republic and Equatorial Guinea.[170] P.W. Botha replied on 2 December: "It gives me pleasure to inform you that I have approved of both requests and that the items in question will be delivered to you in accordance with ar-rangements to be made by Maj Genl Loots in consultation with our mu-tual friend Mr Beaupré [sic]. No charge will be levied on these items". Regarding the naval equipment, however, he proposed: "the French Government might be in a better position to assist you".[171] In supplying the three additional T6 planes, P.W. Botha referred to anti-communism as his guiding principle, as reflected in his letter to Bongo in February 1971: "With regard to the communist threat which is the cause of your serious concern, I wish to assure you that we are equally concerned".[172]

Ivory Coast

Contact with Abidjan as a result of the military's engagement in the Nige-rian Civil War was Pretoria's most significant success. In November 1969, opening a congress of the country's ruling Democratic Party, Houphouët-Boigny advocated Dialogue with Pretoria, reiterating his stance at a well-attended international press conference a year later[173] and again at a widely noted press conference in April 1971: "Apartheid is South Africa's domestic problem. It is not through the means of force that we will ensure its disappearance in the Republic of South Africa. (...) allow me to come back (...) to the necessity of dialogue with South Africa".[174] Once Houphouët-Boigny had made this bold step, more hesitant African leaders followed, for example Ghana's Busia.

The counting game of which African countries were pro- and anti-Dialogue was a tricky issue, with speculation abounding in the South African media and the contemporary literature. The Pretoria government, on occasion, deliberately fuelled these conjectures, while avoiding exposing an African state involved in Dialogue to political pressure from other African nations.[175] For instance, in May 1969, Minister Muller told Parliament Pretoria was in contact with more African states than he was able to mention.[176] This, however, was also due to the DFA not always being fully informed of the activities of other departments. Contradictory statements from a minister and the head of state, for example in the case of Ghana, gave further impetus to the controversy. Africa's political instability caused additional problems; previously pro-Dialogue countries, such as Ghana and Madagascar, could change sides overnight because of a coup d'état. Finally, Dialogue was not interpreted uniformly and unconditionally. Several African countries committed themselves unreservedly to the concept, while others, such as Uganda wanted it to encompass all aspects of Pretoria's apartheid policy, including domestic ones.[177]

Uganda

Within months of assuming power through a military coup, Idi Amin sought contact with Pretoria. While attending a conference in the US in April 1971, a Ugandan participant approached science Professor John Phillips from the University of Natal with the message Amin "would be prepared to meet Mr. Vorster if given the opportunity".[178] Phillips conveyed this to the Prime Minister, who invited Amin, in September 1971, to visit South Africa. In his reply, Amin proposed deploying a "10 man delegation (...) to study conditions prevailing in South Africa and to make a report to me which will also be submitted to the Organisation of African Unity".[179] It appears Vorster inquired from the DFA officials how to respond, as this would explain why he rejected Amin's proposal, arguing it could "only be construed in my country as an attempt to interfere in our internal affairs and would, therefore, be unacceptable".[180] Their subsequent interchange until October 1971,[181] partly exposed by the *Rand Daily Mail*,[182] did not lead to any rapprochement.

Mogadishu Declaration

Meetings of the OAU and regional African bodies during 1971 clarified the confusion regarding Dialogue. In January, a meeting of the Organisation commune africaine, malgache et mauricienne (OCAMM), alliance of Francophone African states, discussed the issue. The final communiqué merely took note of Houphouët-Boigny's argument that "there is no other solution than contact and dialogue",[183] without proposing further action. In June, the OAU Council of Ministers rejected Dialogue, requiring such an exchange first to take place between the Pretoria government and the country's majority, subsequently tabling the issue at the Summit of Heads of State and Government in Addis Ababa. Of the 39 countries present – the C.A.R. and Uganda were absent – only six voted pro-Dialogue, namely Gabon, the Ivory Coast, Lesotho, Madagascar, Malawi and Mauritius.[184] The Conference of East and Central African States (18-20 October) in Mogadishu put the final death knell to Dialogue:

> We (...) therefore do declare (...) that there is no way left to the liberation of Southern Africa except armed struggle to which we already give and will increasingly continue to give our fullest support; that the policy of dialogue advanced by a small group of African leaders which has already been rejected by the OAU is again rejected because it is a ploy to hoodwink the African people.[185]

In this context, we need to discuss the visit of the Progressive Party's Colin Eglin and Helen Suzman to Botswana, Gambia, Ghana, Kenya, Malawi, Senegal, Tanzania and Zambia, only days before the Mogadishu Declaration was adopted.[186] Given that none of the party's members had previously toured Africa, we corresponded with Eglin to establish their motives for doing so then. He explained it reflected his strategy as the party's leader from 1971 to reverse the Progressive's popularity, which had steadily declined since its establishment, and visiting African nations aimed at countering the apartheid ideology:

> It was important to show that white South Africans representing an anti apartheid party like the P[rogressive Party] were welcome in 'black' Africa. It was important to come back with a message to white South Africans that the black leaders we met were not anti white or anti South Africa, but that they were anti the policy of apartheid.[187]

Further, Eglin rejected the idea that the Progressives went to Africa to counter economic sanctions against South Africa "to do the bidding of Anglo American", the party's main financier: "While the PP representatives did not shy away from the fact that they did not believe comprehensive economic sanctions were the appropriate policy to apply, indeed hardly any of the countries were applying this policy in practice, the issue of sanctions was not the main thrust of our discussions".[188] Yet, whether intended or not, their Africa initiative favoured the business community, benefiting from any attempt to alleviate South Africa's isolation.

Returning to Pretoria's Dialogue policy, of the six African countries approving that policy at the 1971 OAU Summit, only Gabon and the Ivory Coast could really be considered as successes. Madagascar had been won over although it was not overly dependent on South Africa in economic terms, but its political standing in Africa was relatively low key In any case, Antananarivo no longer promoted Dialogue after Tsiranana was removed from power in 1972. Regarding Lesotho and Malawi, their economic dependence left them with little choice but to establish contact, although Banda's conservative political style favoured Lilongwe's move. We now discuss the reasons for Mauritius' pro-Dialogue attitude.

Mauritius

The island's stance can be partly explained with the role played by Gaëtan Duval, leader of the main opposition party. During 1969, attempting to quell this opposition, Prime Minister Seewoosagur Ramgoolam included Duval's party in a government of national unity and made him the Minister of External Affairs, Tourism and Emigration. In contrast to Ramgoolam, Duval advocated Dialogue, paying a visit to South Africa in May 1971,[189] within weeks of the OAU Summit. However, Mauritius' position must also be seen against its economic dependence on South Africa.

Trade and tourism were the main aspects of interaction between the two countries, illustrated by the presence of a South African Honorary Trade Commissioner on the island since 1957.[190] Mauritius was economically dependent for its tea export, second only to sugar, a dependency that gradually increased. Yet, Pretoria did not need to make specific use of that situation to demonstrate Dialogue was in Ramgoolam's best interest; Ramgoolam already followed the prescribed line, cognisant of Pretoria's ability to use tea and sugar export as leverage. Further, the DFA files record a number of reciprocal economic missions from the late 1960s,[191] with the Durban Chamber of Commerce's Trade Mission to Madagascar, Reunion and Mauritius in September/October 1971 deserving special mention. Mauritius was the primary motivation for the mission; similar to the Malawi missions mentioned previously, Kenneth Hobson, the Chamber's Manager, had personal connections with and knowledge of Mauritius. Given his marriage to a Mauritian, he was well acquainted with the Indian Ocean islands,[192] explaining the Chamber's missions to the Seychelles, Mauritius and Reunion in October 1973 and to Reunion, Mauritius and Malawi in April/May 1979.[193] Turning to tourism, South African Airways had an office on the island from 1969, flying to Port Louis four times weekly thereafter, two of them proceeding to Australia, the other two to Reunion.[194] In recognition of Mauritius being an important holiday destination, Southern Sun became interested in a hotel project. After the positive outcome of related feasibility studies, Southern Sun approached Jan Bouwer in May 1971 to assess Credit Guarantee's willingness to insure a credit. The estimated cost was $3.5 million, with $1.4 million being equity capital from Southern Sun and the rest a long-term CGIC loan. Bouwer informed the Department of Commerce of this development and Sol Kerzner mentioned the project to Counsellor Pretorius in April 1972.[195] The next section on Secret Diplomacy looks at the outcome of this project.

Let us now return to the implications of Dialogue for the future course of Pretoria's foreign policy towards Africa. In particular, we revealed this policy originated in the military's engagement in the Nigerian Civil War, causing jealousy among the foreign service officials and leading to interdepartmental rivalry.

Hawks versus Doves

The Nigerian Civil War illustrated the friction between the military, the hawks, and the Department of Foreign Affairs, the doves. On the French side, given their military and intelligence backgrounds, Foccart and Mauricheau-Beaupré, shared the military's realist view. In Mauricheau-Beaupré's letter of 19 November 1970 to P.W. Botha, these socio-ideological affinities are very pronounced. Their importance justifies a lengthy quotation:

> You, an old Afrikaner, should know, to what extent your black brothers are not considered as normal strangers. There is no "foreign affairs" possible with them (...). When I accepted, almost two years ago, on your formal demand, to introduce him [Muller] to HB [Houphouët-Boigny] in Geneva, I knew that I made a mistake and he himself gave me the proof: the only specific subject that he seriously dealt with HB, was his desire to have his name published in a communiqué after the meeting had taken place (...) it is really sad to come to such a position with regard to less important things such as the possible establishment of diplomatic relations that is but an unimportant factor of that which we must do. This will also happen, but at the right time.[196]

These differences had implications on Pretoria's relations with Gabon post-Nigerian Civil War.

P.W. Botha had initially given the foreign affairs ministry permission to utilise van Tonder's services for an agricultural project in Gabon,[197] our focus below. This facility-sharing deal, however, proved to be difficult and led to disputes over who had the right and permission to do what.[198] This developed into confrontation after the Nigerian Civil War, with the DFA trying to escape from its perceived position of weakness. It appears Brand Fourie now took the lead, sidelining Muller in the DFA's dealings with the Prime Minister. During a meeting with van Tonder on 27 May 1970, Fourie argued: "we ought to build our own communication with African states because tomorrow or the next day Foccart and Beaupré [sic] may not be there and then we will have no contact with these countries".[199] He wanted to use diplomatic channels of communication, urging a direct meeting, notably with Mauricheau-Beaupré's assistance, between Bongo, Houphouët-Boigny, Muller and another, unspecified, South African minister in Europe.[200] Mauricheau-Beaupré wanted to know the identity of the unspecified minister, but Fourie either was not prepared to, or could not divulge this, causing the Frenchman to say he "unfortunately" had concluded this was an attempt to "bypass him and the responsible French authorities". He therefore requested to discuss "the matter with the Prime Minister in detail",[201] which Fourie flatly rejected. According to van Tonder's notes on his meeting with Fourie, the latter accused Mauricheau-Beaupré of having dragged South Africa into the already lost Nigerian Civil War and "wanted to know who Mr. Beaupré [sic] thinks he is to dictate to us, and where he thinks he comes from to demand to see the Prime Minister".[202] Fourie's attitude caused the military great concern. On 29 May, Loots wrote to P.W. Botha: "This can only result in the collapse of everything that was built up with difficulty in the past years".[203] However, possibly by citing the military's failed involvement in the Nigerian Civil War, the DFA, and particularly Secretary Fourie, won the upper hand and convinced Vorster to henceforth use diplomatic channels of communication, as can be deduced from Bongo's subsequent letter of complaint to P.W. Botha: "I do not agree with the new dispositions that seem to have been adopted by your government with regard to the form that our future relations should take".[204] Mauricheau-Beaupré also disapproved, writing to P.W. Botha: "you had a system of relations with HB that worked very well. (...) Now you have nothing left".[205] Despite these warnings, later developments suggest Pretoria's inter-departmental clashes did not seriously affect the link with neither Gabon nor the Ivory Coast. Regarding the latter, Houphouët-Boigny retained his Dialogue stance, as the next section will show. In Gabon, the DFA came to play a more significant part. It had already established some contact unrelated to the Nigerian Civil War, but benefiting from the situation brought about by the military's endeavours, it now became involved in providing technical assistance and support for development/investment projects.

Gabon

The DFA's initial contact involved a visit of three Gabonese doctors to the Republic in August 1969, the result of a trip to Gabon earlier that year by medical authorities Chris Barnard and Jack Penn. They informed that department, through the South Africa Foundation, of which they were later to become Trustees, of their wish to invite the doctors.[206] We had neither access to the Foundation's archival material nor could we interview Barnard, who died in 2001, or Penn to ascertain their motivation for this approach. On 20 August, as a likely outcome of the above visit, Hilgard Muller informed President Bongo of Pretoria's willingness to deploy an "economic mission"; Bongo accepted the offer, requesting to include representatives from the mining, agricultural, industrial, fisheries, road-planning and pharmacy sectors.[207] The mission, however, was only deployed in April 1970, due to what Fourie called an "unfortunate delay" during a preparatory meeting in March.[208] In contrast, Deputy Secretary Montgomery had led a different mission to Gabon in September 1969, comprising his working colleague Shearar, van Tonder, three officials from the Departments of Agriculture and of Mining and Frans Swarts, South African Airways' Commercial Manager.[209] It appears the delay of the first mission occurred because of friction with the military over the Nigerian Civil War; the report on Montgomery's mission reveals Mauricheau-Beaupré had organised that visit, but not Fourie's mission. The purpose of the Montgomery mission, then, was to obtain information on Gabon's requirements, meeting with Bongo, and visiting several sites where assistance could possibly be provided. Montgomery concluded assistance was urgently needed to upgrade the transport infrastructure, while also mentioning agriculture and mining.[210]

However, for reasons we could not establish, this mission was not followed-up; Muller's original proposal of sending an economic mission now received preferential treatment. At the above-mentioned preparatory meeting, attended by Robert Montgomery and, *inter alia*, seven officials from five different government departments, Brand Fourie itemised agriculture, mining, trade, housing and pharmaceutical equipment as priorities.[211] The DFA-funded mission to Gabon in April 1970, led by the Secretary for Commerce, Gabriel Josef Johannes Fourie 'Joep' Steyn, included, among others, the military's man and the Agricultural Counsellor at the Paris Embassy, Neels van Tonder and Jan Boyazoglu respectively, and three members from the private business sector involved in mining and pharmaceuticals.[212] After their return, the government officials discussed the outcome. Fourie stated Gabon's needs were "unlimited", the crux of the matter being how to provide assistance in a "practical manner", without "burdening the Treasury too much". In June 1970, the Department of Foreign Affairs offered medical services, assistance in the development of stock-breeding, seed supply to improve agricultural production and assistance to preserve fauna.[213] After Bongo's acceptance, Pretoria deployed a "technical assistance mission" in September, composed of Under-Secretary Best, van Tonder, Boyazoglu and four medical doctors, to further clarify Gabon's needs, concluding medical and agricultural assistance should take immediate effect.[214] The medical doctors recommended supplying vaccines and drugs to combat "the major endemic diseases", to invite Gabonese medical officials for an exchange of experience, to despatch medical experts to Gabon to solve particular problems and to treat Gabonese patients with special needs in South Africa.[215] Vaccines, pharmaceutical products, blood plasma, transport vehicles and two mobile X-ray units were delivered in November 1970. Fourie supported all of the remaining proposals and concrete offers were made to Bongo.[216] Yet, in February 1973, DFA official Glenn Babb reported the X-ray units "proved to be white elephants", the visit of Gabonese medical teams had been abandoned, no further action had been taken regarding the visits by medical teams to Gabon and training Gabonese doctors in South Africa proved too difficult because of language problems.[217]

In contrast to the DFA's medical assistance, what became known as the agricultural project OGAPROV, standing for Gabonese Office for the Improvement and Production of Meat, found Bongo's keen interest. Jan Boyazoglu and Julian Thomas, Agricultural Attaché, later Counsellor, at the Paris Embassy, were Pretoria's men responsible for its agricultural/technical aspects. They had a strong academic and agricultural experience, both having worked with the Department of Agricultural Technical Services from the early 1960s. OGAPROV became a show piece for Pretoria's technical assistance. In conversation with us, Boyazoglu and Thomas emphasised its solidity as an agricultural technical pilot project, with the purpose of making livestock production and farming in Gabon sustainable; they aimed at overcoming the obstacles imposed by the tropical climate, inappropriate vegetation and animal diseases such as sleeping sickness.[218] Former DFA official Runge, based in Gabon in the mid-1980s, still recalled in 1999 it had demonstrated "South Africa's core competency in agricultural research; cattle breeding under very difficult circumstances".[219] It was also an ambitious project in terms of finance, with the credit for the first five years amounting to $1.1 million.[220] Located in Bongo's home province Haut-Ogooué in western Gabon, OGAPROV comprised a cattle ranch and two sheep and goat farms.[221] The project, "planned to be self-supporting after 5 years", was intended to reduce Gabon's dependency on meat import,[222] with the DFA attempting to make inroads to Bongo with this practical aspect of its technical assistance. Boyazoglu and Thomas convincingly vitiated our assumption that department had selected Bongo's home province as location to increase its appeal to the president. Rather, they explained maybe 95 per cent of Gabon's territory was not suitable for such a project from the point of view of agro-ecological conditions.[223] Albert Cognard, Chief Technical Adviser in the Gabonese Agriculture Ministry, suggested the Frenchman Jean Muxart as the project's local director, given his previous involvement in similar projects for the French development agency. Boyazoglu also argued: "It is believed that he is

Boyazoglu also argued: "It is believed that he is politically quite secure and can be considered as a friend of South Africa".[224] Having introduced the project's principal characteristics, we now turn to the developments leading to its establishment, highlighting the conflict between the foreign affairs ministry and Mauricheau-Beaupré.

The OGAPROV project resulted from the mission that visited Gabon in September 1970, recommending assistance to develop livestock production. Accepting this proposal, Bongo launched OGAPROV in April 1971, establishing a management Board on which Boyazoglu and Thomas represented South Africa.[225] Clashes between the DFA and the relevant Gabonese authorities versus Mauricheau-Beaupré's and his men overshadowed the project's early days. According to his report of August 1971, Boyazoglu initially took decisions "in agreement with, and in many cases on the proposals of" President Bongo's personal adviser and officials from Libreville's Agriculture Ministry. Mauricheau-Beaupré's indirect involvement changed with the deployment of seconded French staff. As Boyazoglu reported to Pretoria, they tried to give orders to Muxart who had accepted the South Africans "as his only direct bosses, and might not easily agree to orders from any other source", according to Boyazoglu. Mauricheau-Beaupré, upset his men were not given the expected respect, summoned the DMI's van Tonder and Boyazoglu. So as not to endanger the link with Bongo, Boyazoglu smoothed over the situation as one of "a simple misunderstanding", concluding: "Whatever the situation might be, it would be preferable not to risk the withdrawal of Jean's caution from the project".[226] To prevent a similar incident, he suggested to Mauricheau-Beaupré, who agreed, he could second two agriculturally trained men to Muxart, while writing to Pretoria: "I personally feel that it would be better if it is we South Africans that pay these people and not Jean's organisation".[227] However, the problems persisted. After his visit to Gabon in October 1971, Julian Thomas stated "personnel/human difficulties" were "handicapping the development of the project".[228] For the diplomats, the main problem lay in the clashes between Cognard and Muxart on the one hand, and Mauricheau-Beaupré's men seconded to the project on the other, as Ambassador Burger described to Under-Secretary Best: "Jean [Mauricheau-Beaupré] cannot or will not draw the line between matters of high policy and technical detail. We are playing matters as coolly as ever we can. But the position is quite as difficult and complicated as Jean is himself".[229] Towards the end of 1971, Mauricheau-Beaupré and his men withdrew, with Boyazoglu and Thomas suggesting to us he had "understood that it was essentially a technical/developmental operation and that it represented no interest/advantage/risk with regard to his functions and responsibilities".[230]

By April 1972, some 530 cattle were on the ranch, most of the equipment had arrived; Boyazoglu concluded the "project has reached take-off point".[231] By May 1973, some $86,600 remained unused and the project was well on track.[232] In the ensuing months, numerous South African missions, usually composed of officials from the Departments of ATS and Foreign Affairs, joined by Boyazoglu and Thomas from the Paris Embassy, visited the project to follow its progress. By late 1973, the $1.1 million was almost spent, some 500 hectares of pasture had been cleared and approximately 600 cattle were on the ranch. This development was also due to military assistance, with the South African Air Force (SAAF) flying cattle and equipment to Libreville numerous times.[233] Given OGAPROV's success, Boyazoglu and Thomas strongly motivated for an extension of Pretoria's commitment, arguing it had "become one of the show pieces in the country, thus gaining the confidence and support of certain influential people, including President Bongo".[234] Ambassador Burger concurred with their recommendation to continue, as did Brand Fourie.[235] During a meeting with Boyazoglu in May 1974, Bongo equally stated "he would welcome the continuation of the co-operation", provided the project remained confidential.[236] However, it was only in 1976, after Bongo had approved an additional $1.15 million to his annual contribution of $330,000 that Minister Muller agreed to allocate some $3.45 million for five years, beginning in 1979. This shows the DFA's growing scepticism vis-à-vis Bongo, who tried to drain Pretoria's finances without coming out in favour of Dialogue. Presumably for the same reason, it scaled down its financial commitment to $172,500 annually from 1976 to 1978.[237] Access to the DFA's Gabon files was restricted to 1979, but we know from Paul Runge, Project Liaison Officer in Gabon during 1985/6, that OGAPROV continued at least until the mid-1980s.[238] Yet, Pretoria significantly reduced its technical and financial involvement,[239] something we will equally note in the following chapter with other development/investment projects after 1978. On a personal level, given what he described to us as "global opposition to the South African authorities" by 1978, Boyazoglu ceased to represent Pretoria on the OGAPROV Board, while now representing Gabon in this organ.[240] Julian Thomas' involvement ended during 1983. After this presentation of the technical assistance, we will examine two development/investment projects in which the DFA became involved around the same time and which furthered its political ambition of winning Bongo's support.

Regarding the smaller of the two projects, the firm LTA informed the foreign affairs ministry in August 1971 of its contact with Libreville over a housing project. The cost of the envisaged 1,000 housing units was estimated at $8.5 million, for the financing of which LTA had previously approached the IDC, with Credit Guarantee acting as the insurer. In terms of repayment, the Gabonese government objected to the 20 per cent initial cash payment the IDC required. After discussions with Credit Guarantee and the Department of Commerce, the IDC reconsidered the issue and lowered it to 10 per cent; the remaining credit had to be repaid in ten annual instalments commencing one year after the project's completion. In addition to these soft terms, the loan was granted at the low interest rate of 6.5 per cent.[241] It is a reasonable assumption the DFA's interest in closer contact with Bongo was such that it was prepared to step in with financial assistance to enhance LTA's chances of getting the job. The LTA's Spencer Whiting informed us his company originally provided six sample houses.[242] According to a report from Under-Secretary Best, LTA was ready to commence constructing the housing units, when Bongo intervened in July 1972 "to cancel the arrangement for reasons which are not clear but he apparently felt the houses were too expensive and not suitable for Gabon". Consequently, LTA demanded payment, within three months, for the sample houses. Finding himself in an "embarrassing situation", according to Best's report, Bongo approached Mauricheau-Beaupré for help. He, in turn, approached van Tonder who discussed the matter with Norman Best. Van Tonder's information to Best was for the DFA to "intervene with L.T.A. to get them to agree to payment in six months, so as to avoid litigation and consequent harm to relations between Gabon and South Africa".[243] Best presented the matter to Secretary Fourie, who approached the Department of Commerce, while Deputy Secretary François Abraham Jacobus Viljoen discussed the matter with the LTA Chairman "in veiled terms" and was assured "L.T.A. would co-operate with the government to the fullest extent possible".[244] On its part, LTA contacted Credit Guarantee, and they resolved the matter by downplaying the problem and putting the blame on misunderstandings.[245] Even three decades later, Spencer Whiting commented: "The sum was minimal after all, which we could have easily written off, but one tried to avoid establishing precedents!"[246] In any case, in terms of its contract with the government, Pretoria reinsured Credit Guarantee's financial risk. Credit Guarantee could, thus, reassure LTA it would recover its money. The outstanding payment was made by November 1972, when Credit Guarantee's Jan Bouwer flew to Libreville to "convey apologies" to Bongo for the problems that had arisen.[247]

The second development/investment project was the construction of a railway line, in which Roberts Construction was interested. In August 1971, Cecil Jeffries 'Jeff' Miller and Derek Marriott from the company's International Division informed Pretoria's Ambassador in London, Robert Montgomery, of their London office's interest in the so-called Transgabonais railway project.[248] This cost some $200 million and was some 800 km long, running from the Atlantic Ocean to central Gabon (Section I), then splitting to the north-east (Section II) and Franceville in the south-east (Section III). Its main purpose was to transport iron and manganese for export and to access the vast timber potential, but the project would only be viable after completion of either Section II or III, ensuring the export of the mineral resources. By early 1972, Bongo had acquired the interest of several international donors, inter alia the European

pean Development Fund (EDF), Brussels' development assistance instrument, and the World Bank in financing the project. During discussions with Deputy Secretary Viljoen, Jeff Miller stated his firm was "very
interested", proposing Pretoria should also tender given the "implications
[that] go much further than that of just a normal construction project",
implying this would aid Pretoria's Dialogue with Gabon. In further promoting Roberts Construction's financial interest, Miller suggested Pretoria should undercut the loan conditions offered by others.[249] Viljoen
informed Fourie about the meeting, whom the Treasury advised not to
arrange a "soft loan" for a project that, referring to Section I, "looks like
a bottomless pit".[250] Roberts Construction was informed accordingly,
subsequently approaching Credit Guarantee. Yet, Jeff Miller later informed François Viljoen Credit Guarantee was not in a position to make
a commitment, while indicating "it was possible for us to offer a loan
facility" to the amount of $12.95 million, with repayment conditions
similar to the LTA's housing project and at a 6 per cent interest rate.[251]

By February 1973, however, the situation had changed; World Bank
President Robert McNamara informed Bongo he was not in a position to
provide the expected $30 million, causing Bongo to turn to South Africa
for help.[252] Two months later, Jan Bouwer informed Bongo Credit Guarantee was in a position to offer the necessary guarantees for Roberts
Construction to tender for the Transgabonais project with a contract
value of $21.7 million and for the IDC to negotiate with Libreville a loan
covering 85 per cent of that amount. Repayment would commence four
years after the project's completion; the interest rate was set at 6.5 per
cent.[253] Credit Guarantee's change of attitude may be explained by a
reading of *To the Point*, the Department of Information's secretly funded
magazine. Trying to belittle its rival's ambitions, it read that although
Bongo approached Pretoria as a last resort, "the South Africans", evidently meaning the foreign service officials, "would certainly welcome a
prestige coup of this kind".[254] In November 1973, an IDC official, Jan
Bouwer and an interpreter participated at a meeting with other donors
and the Gabonese government to discuss the project.[255] According to the
available evidence, in June 1974, the European Commission decided in
favour of the EDF's financing of the railway's Section I with some $20
million.[256] Initially, Roberts Construction was meant to participate,[257] but
by September 1974, Bongo awarded the contract to a French consortium,
financing the entire project from the country's reserves that had received
a substantial boost from the discovery of oil. Roberts Construction was
left with a small contract to build a bridge costing some $2-3 million, but
even this fell through in the end, Jeff Miller informed us.[258] This outcome
supports our argument that Bongo only approached the South Africans
when all other channels seemed closed, but dropping them when a different source became available.

In 1972, South Africa's daily *The Star* appropriately summarised the results Pretoria's Outward-Looking Policy: "The outward policy may not be quite dead, but these days it is looking very moribund".[259] This type of analysis formed the basis for what we term as Secret Diplomacy.

Secret Diplomacy

Friction between the foreign affairs ministry and the military over strategy dominated Pretoria's foreign policy making during the first half of Vorster's premiership. Inter-departmental struggles also characterised the remaining period of his rule, but the spectrum of actors was extended, with the Department of Information and the Bureau for State Security entering the scene. While working together, they pursued individual goals, conducting unconventional diplomacy and collecting intelligence respectively, resulting in Secret Diplomacy and Détente respectively. Given our access to the DFA files, we discuss several diplomatic activities during the Secret Diplomacy period. Détente ran parallel to some of these initiatives, but we consider it separately in the next section, as it was dominated by rivalries between BOSS and the military.

Deon Geldenhuys described the reasons for Secret Diplomacy with the Department of Information's "strong feeling of dissatisfaction and impatience (...) about the results achieved by Foreign Affairs' conventional diplomacy", and for them "there was a clear-cut case to supplement conventional diplomacy with unconventional or unorthodox means". The Department's methods to break South Africa's isolation can be succinctly summarised as buying, bribing or bluffing their way to the opinion and decision makers of the world, by launching clandestine propaganda operations.[260] Given both Secretary Rhoodie's and Deputy Secretary de Villiers' journalistic background, special attention was paid to the press and, in 1971, their department established the current affairs magazine *To the Point*, with Rhoodie as Deputy Editor until 1973. The secondary literature has ascribed Secret Diplomacy solely to the Department of Information. However, due to the lack of knowledge about the military's crucial role in bringing about Dialogue, the motivation for BOSS to become involved has been neglected. We argue the Bureau's activities during Secret Diplomacy and Détente resulted from van den Bergh's ambition to outmanoeuvre the military given the rivalry between the two state actors. Attempting to gain advantages over their respective rivals, BOSS and the Department of Information assisted each other in gaining a powerful position, an endeavour greatly enhanced by van den Bergh's and Rhoodie's personal relationship with Vorster.

We will first probe the Department of Information's undertakings, followed by the DFA's parallel activities, Pretoria's concern in obtaining overflying rights for South African Airways and its relations with the western Indian Ocean islands and finally the roles played by two non-state actors.

Ivory Coast and Senegal

The Department of Information shaped Pretoria's Africa policy by focusing on contact with the Ivory Coast and Senegal, judged to hold such political influence in African political matters that South Africa could find continental acceptance by securing their joint support.[261] Houphouët-Boigny's pro-Dialogue attitude had remained unchanged since 1969. As for Senegal's President Léopold Senghor, *To the Point* noted in January 1972 he had recently "called for an OAU summit to discuss the question of dialogue".[262] However, the Department of Information does not seem to have approached Senghor vigorously until early 1973; its budget only increased drastically in that year, and Senghor's pro-Dialogue position was uncertain. In April 1973, in an interview with *To the Point*, he stated: "In some respects I am a man for dialogue. (...) In the first place dialogue would have to take place, not between us and Mr Vorster, but between the Vorster government and the black majority in South Africa".[263] Furthermore, we will see later in this section Senghor preferred contact with the Progressive Party.

When the Department of Information tried to establish contact with Senghor during 1973, it utilised its favourite propaganda tactic, enlisting the services of Bernard Lejeune, a Johannesburg-based French journalist.[264] Rhoodie had established this contact while the Deputy Editor of *To the Point*.[265] Lejeune was specifically chosen because he spoke French, essential in contact with Francophone Africa, and because he "knows Africa like the back of his hand, especially French West Africa, and will help us to make good contacts out there, including people around President Houphouët-Boigny and President Senghor", Deputy Secretary Les de Villiers recalls in his autobiography.[266] Lejeune had passed away in 2000, but his wife Mauricette informed us they had moved from France to South Africa in 1955, her husband then teaching himself to become a freelance journalist. She also explained that he became acquainted with West Africa as a result of an exploratory mission there in 1971 to investigate the investment potential for South African firms.[267]

Bernard Lejeune first visited Dakar and Abidjan on behalf of the Department of Information in May 1973. According to his report to Minister Mulder, this trip had been "very successful" due to meetings with Bara Diouf and Laurent Dona-Fologo, the Editor-in-Chiefs of the Senegalese daily *Le Soleil*, and the Ivorian daily *Fraternité Matin* respectively. We further learn these two newspapermen were "scheduled to come to South Africa towards the end of this year", Diouf was "married to President Senghor's niece, and he enjoys the full confidence of the President", while Dona-Fologo was "very closely associated to the work of his President (...) and he is a member of the political bureau, with a recognised influence on the political trends of his country". Lejeune thus hoped to gain access to both Senghor and Houphouët-Boigny through them. In the case of Dona-Fologo, this strategy was very productive; Houphouët-Boigny gave Lejeune "a personal assurance that I can go back to him any time to discuss any problem with him whenever it may prove necessary to ease up the Dialogue issue". In Dakar, Lejeune could arrange a future meeting between Senghor and Mulder. Nonetheless, mirroring Senghor's ambivalence towards Dialogue, Lejeune argued: "the more we will be able to encourage an association between Ivory Coast and Senegal the greater advantage we will derive from it, bearing in mind that the real leadership for the Dialogue is unmistakably in Abidjan".[268] To compensate the lack of Department of Information sources, limiting us in reconstructing the follow-up initiatives, and the DFA files apart, we draw on Rhoodie's and de Villiers' autobiographies and our interviews with Bara Diouf and Mauricette Lejeune; Laurent Dona-Fologo declined to answer our questions. We thus established Bernard Lejeune returned to both the Ivory Coast and Senegal "several times",[269] certainly twice to Dakar,[270] meeting Diouf, Dona-Fologo, Senghor and Houphouët-Boigny. Information Secretary Rhoodie was most active, shuttling between Pretoria, Paris, Abidjan and Dakar as part of what was termed Operation Wooden Shoe.[271] Mulder came to see Houphouët-Boigny in the Ivory Coast, but Senghor never invited him.[272] Thus, while contact with Abidjan had a secure foundation, Senghor still had to be won, with relevant DFA papers indicating the problems experienced in wooing Senghor. Their examination reveals a genuine willingness of this African leader to conduct Dialogue, dependent on Pretoria making significant moves in changing the apartheid system.

In correspondence with Vorster from March to September 1974, the Senegalese President expressed his concern over an ongoing court case against Barend van Niekerk,[273] a white Law Professor at the University of Natal and "avid crusader for human rights and the need for a just legal system in South Africa".[274] This made him highly unpopular in government circles, and court cases were conducted against him in 1970, 1972 and 1975, the last of which triggered Senghor's interest; it concerned the newspaper publisher South African Associated Newspapers Ltd and van Niekerk v Estate Pelser, managed by Petrus Cornelius Pelser, the Minister of Prisons and Justice until 1974. Given his background as a poet and writer, Senghor was concerned about Pretoria's restrictions on the freedom of speech, and by intervening he more than probably wanted to assess the seriousness of Pretoria's Dialogue. His particular interest in this case, however, was due to van Niekerk having written a book about Senghor's literary work.[275] Senghor expressed "his satisfaction" with Vorster's attitude in a letter in June 1974.[276] In addition, in September 1974 and in May 1975, John Barratt, the Director of the South African

Institute of International Affairs, informed Deputy Secretary Killen that Senghor had expressed "it was a useful example of dialogue".[277] Barratt's information was based on a meeting with Senghor during a group visit to Senegal and the Ivory Coast in mid-August 1974, the background to which provides some insight into Secret Diplomacy. We argue the Department of Information attempted to convince the leaders of both countries, and especially Senghor, that a dialogue took place among all South Africans and that not all whites supported apartheid. Referring to the Policy Network concept (Chapter 1), Figure 2 illustrates a web of *verligte* individuals involved in fostering this strategy. In disentangling their links with the Department of Information, we need to discuss the apartheid idea of separate development.

The Verwoerd government aimed at establishing eight homelands, accommodating the Pretoria-defined black ethnic groups; they would develop into self-governing units and could, if so desired, attain full independence. The first homeland, Transkei, was formed in 1963, with Pretoria significantly promoting news homelands from the early 1970s, influenced by the International Court of Justice's Advisory Opinion in 1971 on S.W.A./Namibia. Reversing its 1966 ruling, the ICJ now concluded: "South Africa's continued presence is illegal", reasoning it refused "the Namibians the right to determine their own future".[278] In March 1971, Pretoria promulgated the Bantu Homelands Act (No 21), resulting in seven additional self-governing entities, among them KwaZulu, by the end of 1972.[279] While these activities can be seen as *verkrampte* attempts to accommodate the minority's needs and external pressure, the *verligte* used them to improve relations with Africa. In the forefront of the latter was Eschel Rhoodie, who appears to have convinced Minister Mulder of his views. Although known for his otherwise conservative leanings, Mulder recognised the potential of the homelands concept in breaking Pretoria's isolation: "He acknowledged that the policy was a stumbling block to South Africa's foreign relations, but saw this as being caused by the caricature made of the policy abroad. The way out of the dilemma was by correcting the distorted image through improved salesmanship".[280] Probably due to both Mulder's and Rhoodie's increasing influence on him from the early 1970s, Vorster intensified his interaction with the homeland leaders to justify Dialogue with African countries. In July 1971, one month after the OAU Summit had stipulated Dialogue must first take place among all South Africans, Vorster undertook a week-long journey through several homelands, at the end of which he rejected the accusation he only talked to the leaders in the rest of Africa.[281] Vorster interacted particularly with Transkei Chief Minister Kaizer Matanzima and KwaZulu Chief Executive Mangosuthu Gatsha Buthelezi,[282] due to their policies being moderate and compatible with those of Pretoria's.

Of relevance in Rhoodie's and Mulder's strategy of utilising the homelands concept to convince African leaders of Pretoria's willingness

Figure 2: Policy Network Supporting the Department of Information's Secret Diplomacy

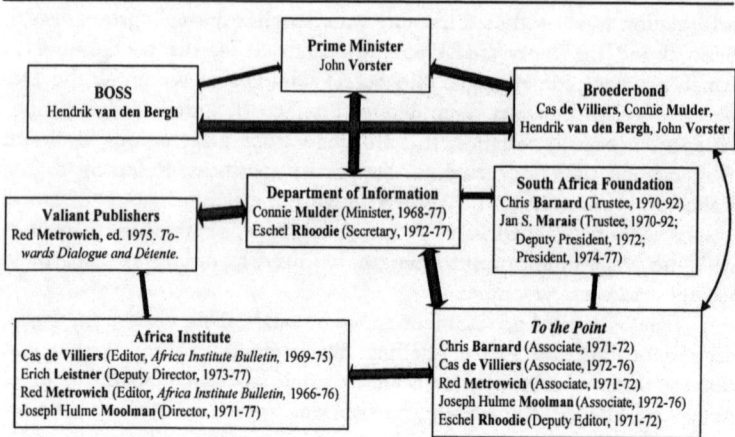

for reform and to talk with the majority were Caspar Francois 'Cas' de Villiers and Frederick Redvers 'Red' Metrowich. They both enjoyed a close relationship with Rhoodie dating from their days as Associates of *To the Point*,[283] publishing titles in co-operation with the Department of Information and Valiant Publishers,[284] covertly financed by the same department.[285] Subsequently, they headed two front organisations that department set up under the guise of think tanks. From 1975, de Villiers directed the Foreign Affairs Association, financed by five Afrikaner millionaires, among them Louis Luyt, whom we will introduce later; Metrowich was the Executive Officer of the Southern African Freedom Foundation (1976-79).[286] *To the Point* described de Villiers as a "strong believer in separate development", one who argued that "we must create a marketing value for separate development via Africa to the rest of the world".[287] During our interview, de Villiers confirmed he conveyed this message during numerous visits to African countries, having a "remote hope" for this to succeed in influencing African leaders to accept Pretoria's domestic policies. While not at the bidding of the Department of Information, these activities supported its Secret Diplomacy.[288]

The strategy also entailed demonstrating to African leaders not all South Africans supported apartheid, related to which was the above-mentioned visit of members from the South Africa Foundation and the Africa Institute to Senegal and the Ivory Coast in August 1974. Regarding the former's connections with the Department of Information, Deon Geldenhuys explains: "the former Department of Information no doubt saw the Foundation as a valuable ally in promoting South Africa's interests in a hostile world, particularly because of the Foundation's independence from government".[289] We argue Chris Barnard and Jan Marais personified this sort of link. In addition to being an Associate of *To the Point*, Barnard put his fame at that department's disposal to promote several of its projects.[290] The links of Marais, Foundation Deputy President during 1972/3 and then President until 1977, with this department were manifold, with *To the Point* praising him: "Marais (...) has not only built it [Trust Bank] up into an institution with assets exceeding $1 billion (...). He is also known outside South Africa for his enlightened views". He was an Associate of *To the Point*, giving him a platform for his views, notably in the article 'There is no alternative to dialogue' in 1972.[291] The abridged text of his address delivered in Germany was reprinted in Metrowich's *Towards Dialogue and Détente*.[292] Marais provided the Department of Information with offices in his bank to publish *To the Point*, as the magazine's editorial address indicates. Further, after his visit to the Ivory Coast and Senegal in 1973, Lejeune suggested regarding the newspaper editors Dona-Fologo and Diouf coming to South Africa: "Although I ignore what procedure you usually follow in regards to air tickets and other material arrangements, I heard that Dr. J. Marais will very much appreciate it if you would consider dealing with Trust Express".[293] Finally, in 1975, after a journey through the US, Marais reported to Connie Mulder, the section "South Africa – what to note and what to do", suggesting: "there is much confusion about the basics of the separate development programme. Once explained, one could say that the concept is saleable!" In his letter of acknowledgement, Mulder agreed to Marais' thoughts, promising to "give more attention to these matters".[294] We contacted Marais about his above interactions, but he did not answer our questions. The Africa Institute's links with the Information Department's policy network were also through personal contacts; Cas de Villiers and Red Metrowich worked at the Africa Institute, as Assistant Editor and Editor respectively, and Director Moolman served as an Associate with *To the Point*. Former Africa Institute researcher Richard Cornwell suggested the Department of Information used that institute's academic output as "intellectual gloss" for selling the separate development concept to African leaders.[295] Lejeune's report after his initial trip to the Ivory Coast and Senegal provides some evidence to this effect: "It has been unanimously agreed that the invitation [to Diouf and Dona-Fologo] should be issued under the auspices of the Africa Institute".[296]

Let us now examine the role of the above personalities and organisations in the Department of Information's Africa approach. In our interview, Erich Leistner recalled Africa Institute Director Moolman had arranged the visit of the South African group to Senegal and the Ivory Coast in August 1974 together with Lejeune, who "helped to somehow prepare the ground", with both Moolman and himself being aware of Lejeune's role as the Information Department's middleman.[297]. We could not contact Moolman, who has passed away, but a report on this visit in the DFA files reveals the group comprised Moolman, Leistner, South

African Institute of International Affairs Director Barratt, William Kgware, the black Vice-Chancellor of the University of the North, and the Indian financier Jayaaram Reddy, the last two being South Africa Foundation Trustees from 1970. They went to Dakar, holding talks with Senghor and Bara Diouf, and Abidjan, attending the Society for International Development's World Conference on 'Confrontation or Cooperation?' and meeting Dona-Fologo, now Ivorian Information Minister.[298] We argue the Department of Information engaged these academic and business circles to place its Secret Diplomacy on a broader foundation. Among the group, Barratt certainly was not connected to this department. In correspondence, Leistner explained: "We had a cordial working relationship with Barratt's Institute (...). You can be assured that he would not have come with us if there had been even the vaguest whiff of suspicion that State funds were involved!"[299] Barratt confirmed this to us, although adding with hindsight "I later came to suspect, correctly it seems, that Information had a hand in arrangements", and explaining his motivation to join: "in those days we had very few opportunities of visiting other parts of Africa".[300]

We do not want overemphasise the visit's significance, but we argue it was a contributory factor prompting Senghor to meet Vorster some five weeks later. Of greater importance, Houphouët-Boigny had "pushed" Senghor into this meeting, according to Bara Diouf.[301] In any event, reflecting the Department of Information's involvement, aboard the plane from Cape Town to Abidjan on 22 September 1974 were Vorster, his son, his personal physician and his private secretary, van den Bergh, Mike Geldenhuys, Rhoodie and Brand Fourie. BOSS agent Albie Geldenhuys and journalist Lejeune awaited the party in Abidjan, acting as interpreters and accompanying the party to Yamassoukro, where the meeting took place in Houphouët-Boigny's presidential palace.[302] The journey was cloaked in secrecy; the plane, parked far away from the terminal, left before dawn from Cape Town airport, which was less frequented than Johannesburg's Jan Smuts Airport. In December 1974, the *Rand Daily Mail* claimed Vorster had gone to the Ivory Coast, but the news was only officially released in May 1975,[303] while Senghor still denied his participation. Foccart, Mauricheau-Beaupré and South Africa's Ambassador to France, Burger, do not seem to have played a role in Vorster's visit; the DFA files contain no evidence, Rhoodie argues the Department of Information did not use their services,[304] Foccart's memoirs suggest he tried to decelerate Houphouët-Boigny's Dialogue initiative[305] and French political scientist Bach mentions France's Ambassador in Abidjan was only informed about the meeting two weeks after it had taken place.[306] It is most unlikely Foccart and Mauricheau-Beaupré offered their services to either the Department of Information or BOSS, the military's rival. We may even argue Vorster's excursion to the Ivory Coast could only become reality after Foccart had left office in May 1974.

Regarding Pretoria's contact with both Abidjan and Dakar until Vorster's premiership ended in 1978, Dona-Fologo and Balla Keita, the Minister of Scientific Research, came to South Africa in September 1975, invited by Information Minister Mulder and accompanied by both agent Geldenhuys and Lejeune.[307] Dona-Fologo, in Mulder's company, also visited the Africa Institute,[308] supporting our claim the think tank played an important role in the Secret Diplomacy. Furthermore, Africa Institute Deputy Director Leistner visited the Ivory Coast in January 1976. He could not recall the exact circumstances, but agreed that, "in all probability", this reciprocated Dona-Fologo's stay in South Africa, as Leistner met both this Ivorian Minister and Balla Keita while in Abidjan.[309] Coinciding with Leistner's visit, and as gleaned from internal Africa Institute documents, Louis Luyt had flown to Abidjan in his plane, accompanied by, *inter alia*, Lejeune and Cas de Villiers. Although not co-ordinated undertakings, Leistner's travel itinerary reveals he spent considerable time with the latter.[310] This constellation shows the importance of the above policy network. Luyt was an influential Afrikaner businessman, running Triomf Fertilisers Ltd, one of the world's largest producers of finished product at the time, while acting as a front man in two of the Department of Information's principal covert projects, the establishment of *The Citizen* newspaper and the Foreign Affairs Association.[311] Luyt informed us he had been in contact with Houphouët-Boigny since 1968, allowing him to land with his Lear Jet in Abidjan "en route to Brazil", his "biggest [fertiliser] customers". Concerning the 1976 visit, Luyt explained Dona-Fologo had invited him and: "I was contacted by (...) Cas de Villiers when news of the visit leaked out for a ride (...). I went there (...) as possible supplier of fertilisers to the country. The minister, together with the president, supplied us with contacts".[312] In March 1976, Connie Mulder led a party to Abidjan, composed of Eschel Rhoodie, DFA Deputy Secretary Killen, as well as Lejeune and Justus de Goede as their respective translators, holding talks with Houphouët-Boigny and Dona-Fologo.[313] The DFA's interest was to obtain landing rights for SAA, attempts for which began after Dona-Fologo's stay in South Africa.[314] After an exchange of correspondence and the visit of a SAA delegation to the Ivory Coast in February 1976, led by Chief Executive Salomon 'Pi' Pienaar (1975-77), the Ivorian authorities granted technical stopover facilities from May that year.[315] After Houphouët-Boigny's meetings with Brand Fourie and John Vorster in Geneva, in February and May 1977 respectively, SAA was furthermore "allowed to place a technical representative in Abidjan".[316] These developments underline the depth of Houphouët-Boigny's support to Pretoria in assisting it to overcome the negative consequences of its apartheid policy. However, the death of Steve Biko, the leader of the Black Consciousness Movement, in September 1977,[317] strained the relations. A DFA report noted: "several Ivory Coast spokesmen had expressed condemnation of the South African Government".[318] Abidjan now followed the African Group at the UN, which pushed the Security Council to adopt Resolution 418 in November 1977, imposing a mandatory arms embargo on South Africa.[319] The S.W.A./Namibia issue also weighed on the Abidjan-Pretoria relationship, with *The Star*, in December 1976, citing the Ivorian UN Ambassador, appealing to Pretoria to "see reason and to co-operate with the UN on the South West African issue".[320] A DFA report on the bilateral relations during 1978 read: "representatives of Liberia, the Ivory Coast and Senegal said in interviews that they had concluded that their peaceful approach to South Africa had produced no significant change".[321]

His more hesitant attitude towards Pretoria notwithstanding, a contributing factor for Senghor to meet Vorster in 1974 was their correspondence over a court case against Barend van Niekerk. Senghor was similarly pleased with Vorster's reply to his letter of concern regarding the fate of Breyten Breytenbach,[322] a white South African writer in French exile since the early 1960s, but jailed during a clandestine return home in August 1975.[323] In particular, Vorster assured Senghor in October 1975 Breytenbach's life was not threatened.[324] However, by 1976, Senghor became disillusioned with Pretoria. In January 1976, he hosted the international conference "Namibia and Human Rights", indicating his concern regarding the S.W.A./Namibia case. Christopher John Robert Dugard, simply referred to as John, Law Professor at Johannesburg's University of the Witwatersrand and author of many publications on that issue also attended this conference,[325] accompanied by his "friend and colleague", Barend van Niekerk, as Dugard informed us.[326] According to Counsellor Pretorius' brief, Dugard had "revealed" to André Jaquet from the Francophone Africa Desk "in a private conversation" Senghor "felt that his attempts at dialogue had been rebuffed by South Africa".[327] Senghor's view was based on his having sent two letters to Vorster in early 1975, expressing the intention to despatch a fact-finding mission with Senegalese jurists to South Africa and asking Vorster to free political prisoners as a gesture of goodwill, without receiving a reply. Subsequent evidence suggests Senghor's fact-finding mission idea led to controversy between the Departments of Information and Foreign Affairs. Rhoodie, who had had emphasised the importance of a positive reply necessary to sustain contact with Dakar, recounts Vorster had "refused to reply to Senghor's two letters".[328] In contrast, the foreign service officials, were against such a mission, representing an act of interference in the country's domestic affairs. Importantly, in the above-mentioned brief, destined for Fourie, Pretorius states their "records show no evidence" of Senghor's letters.[329] Confronted with this information, Jaquet suggested to us:

> Rae [Killen] was the consummate bureaucrat and a very cautious chap indeed. He always made his comments or instructions on documents in pencil in the margins and

regularly drew files to review how events had unfolded. If with hindsight he had made an unwise decision or had given a directive that later proved to be wrong, he would erase his initial comment and (...) write an insightful new remark in the margin.[330]

Indeed, Pretorius' brief went to Deputy Secretary Killen, and it is not certain whether it ever reached the Secretary. Counsellor Anton Loubser's hand-written note, dated 25 January 1978 at the end of this document reads: "This brief (prepared by Mr J. Pretorius on 4/2/76 and handed over to Mr Killen) was returned to me today by Mr Killen with the request to file it".[331] As we know, Senghor retreated from contact with Pretoria after Vorster's non-reply to his fact-finding mission proposal. Given that Killen had kept the document to himself suggests he and/or Fourie had been against Senghor's idea, obscuring a judgement which caused the demise of Pretoria's important link with Dakar. We could not obtain the comments of the late Killen, but we queried Loubser. Reflecting the importance of the situation at the time, he recalled even 26 years later "fairly well" what he referred to as "the issue of the 'phantom' correspondence": "References to the matter, in the media and by different sources, had caused considerable embarrassment" and the "Department [DFA] had been searching high and low for the missing correspondence. Alas, without any success!" Although admitting Killen "had a rather unique way of dealing with documentation", Loubser added: "It was totally unthinkable that we would have ignored his [Senghor's] approaches".[332] Whatever the matter, the Department of Information's initiative leading to Vorster's meeting with Houphouët-Boigny and Senghor in 1974 did not result in a stable relationship, due to Pretoria's intransigence over the S.W.A./Namibia issue and their becoming dissatisfied with South Africa's domestic situation.

Parallel to these developments, the Department of Foreign Affairs was active in two other relatively important African countries.

Liberia

Reflecting the DFA's jealousy towards its sister department's achievements in West Africa, Brand Fourie's autobiographical accounts do not make any reference to them.[333] Attempting to prove their ability, the foreign service officials also tried to produce a breakthrough in Africa. Liberia did not have a high political standing, but it was important for other reasons; together with Ethiopia, it had taken Pretoria to the International Court of Justice over the S.W.A./Namibia issue in 1966. Pretoria's first interaction with Monrovia is noted in April 1974, when Harold 'Tassie' Taswell, Ambassador at the Permanent Mission to the UN in Geneva, held informal talks with his Liberian counterpart, David Thomas. Thomas "remarked that he would very much like to visit South Africa", but he had "to act with caution" because "undue friendliness would not stand him in good stead with many of his African colleagues".[334] Subsequent activities took place at the UN in New York and Geneva, seemingly pursued more vigorously after Vorster's trip to the Ivory Coast. In October, UN Ambassador Pik Botha met Thomas in Geneva, following which Liberian President William Tolbert signalled preparedness to meet Pik Botha in November, on the fringes of the UN General Assembly.[335] In December 1974, probably encouraged by these developments, Vorster invited Tolbert to Pretoria, alternatively proposing he himself would go to Monrovia.[336] Then, attempting to henceforth organise a Tolbert-Vorster meeting, Pik Botha and BOSS's van den Bergh took Ambassador Thomas on a confidential mission through South Africa and Namibia from 17 to 23 December,, and from 31 December 1974 to 6 January 1975, KwaZulu leader Buthelezi visited Liberia, also meeting Tolbert. The aim was to convince Monrovia of Pretoria's respect for the freedom of the South African majority and of its intention to grant Namibia self-autonomy. The idea of generating goodwill through homeland leaders suggests an imitation of the Information Department's more aggressive style; the July 1972 *To the Point* editorial suggested: "South Africa would have to include in its delegation to any talks the leaders of its planned non-white states".[337] Buthelezi's trip met the DFA's goals; one week after Vorster's visit to Liberia in February 1975, Tolbert stated in a press communiqué: "As I had been informed by Chief Buthelezi that the South African Government had undertaken dialogue with the black people of that country, the criterion for dialogue with that Government had been met and the stage was now set for direct communication between us".[338] Further, after Thomas' journey, Pik Botha reported it was the Ambassador's "firm conviction that there is now a definite desire, conscious effort and determination" on Pretoria's part "to bring about a favourable change which will totally eliminate inequity and injustice. (...) in view of its efforts (...), [it] deserves a sympathetic listening ear instead of complete condemnation".[339] Resulting from this successful strategy, Vorster spent 11/12 February 1975 in Liberia.

The list of people accompanying Vorster reflected the influence of the players behind this meeting: Vorster's Private Secretary, his medical doctor, Minister Muller, Secretary Fourie, Pik Botha, van den Bergh and Mike Geldenhuys.[340] While the DFA publicised the meeting at once to demonstrate the effectiveness of its policy,[341] it was overtaken by the media coverage on Vorster's trip to the Ivory Coast three months later. Thus, during our interview, Pik Botha insisted angrily both BOSS and the Department of Information had "jumped on the bandwagon" and stolen the merits of the Liberia trip.[342] At the same time, intelligence support had been essential for the DFA; Fourie's unpublished memoirs reveal BOSS agent Gerhardus 'Gert' Rothmann was involved in the run-up to

Vorster's meeting with Tolbert.[343] However, Tolbert also became disillusioned and ceased all contact, due to Pretoria's uncompromising attitude towards Namibian independence and the treatment of South Africa's majority. During a discussion with Ambassador Thomas in June 1975, Tolbert pleaded with Pretoria: "if some dramatic statement were made (...), e.g. if within two years plans would be undertaken to prepare for granting the people of Namibia independence, the President would be able to present something tangible to his colleagues".[344] The Turnhalle Conference in 1975, mentioned in the next section, was only a half-hearted solution, however. Even less promising was Vorster's attitude towards Tolbert's written plea of December 1975, to allow Robert Sobukwe, a prominent PAC figure, to attend a political ceremony in Liberia.[345] Vorster rejected the idea, possibly influenced by foreign service officials, reasoning this constituted an interference in domestic matters. Notably, Fourie instructed Pik Botha in New York: "invitation is regarded as transparent move which if permitted would establish dangerous precedent".[346] After his two years deadline, Tolbert contacted Vorster in September 1977, raising the issues of Namibian independence, hospital treatment for Sobukwe and the oppression of the majority in South Africa. More than likely on diplomatic advice again, he declared the enquiries constituted "interference in domestic affairs".[347]

Apart from their Liberian venture to outshine the Department of Information's exploits, the foreign service officials applied their favourite policy-levers, namely technical assistance and development/investment projects, in the Central African Republic.

Central African Republic

The DFA's initial interest in this country was President Jean Bokassa's pro-Dialogue attitude, although questionable in content. His statements to this effect in June 1971[348] remained unconfirmed at the OAU Summit two weeks later, given the country's non-attendance. Furthermore, the country's Foreign Minister supported the Mogadishu Declaration in October, which terminated the Dialogue debate, and attacked South Africa at the UN. Substantial contact only took place from 1973, initiated by both BOSS and the military. In July, Jack Kagan of a Johannesburg-based import-export company implicated in a development programme for the C.A.R. met Joël Barkan, Bokassa's Technical Adviser, in Paris, subsequently informing BOSS he might be in a position to establish contact with Bokassa. A month later, Kagan also consulted with Military Intelligence Major George van Rhyn and reported the event to Defence Minister P.W. Botha, who subsequently informed Hilgard Muller and Brand Fourie. However, the DFA's "enthusiasm was (...) only weak"; Muller and Fourie received Kagan in January 1974.[349] The military retained an important position in the DFA's contact, although its interest in the C.A.R. was apparently not due to co-operation with France. Hein du Toit, then Chief of Staff: Intelligence and appearing in the present context, informed us the "C.A.R. was not a contact country for us such as e.g. Gabon or the Ivory Coast".[350] However, Barkan's background may have been of some relevance. According to DFA documentation, he was in the service of the Israeli Foreign Ministry before being seconded to Bokassa in the early 1970s, then possibly becoming the contact man for the Israeli intelligence, which had close links with Pretoria.[351] We queried du Toit, who claimed to have "no further recollection of my contacts with him".[352] In any event, DMI personnel met with both Kagan and Barkan and were present when DFA officials held meetings with them; Colonel Louw J. 'Oosie' Oosthuizen met Barkan in September 1973 in Paris, du Toit saw Barkan in South Africa in March and he was present when Kagan met Deputy Secretary Killen in June 1974.[353]

Barkan's visit in March 1974 led to the DFA's significant interaction with the C.A.R. During meetings with Barkan and Maurice Methot, Director of Services at the Presidency, Muller, Fourie and Killen raised the issue of overflying rights for SAA, so important in Pretoria's Africa policy, as we shall investigate later in this section. Talks were also held with the Department of Commerce Secretary, Joep Steyn, and representatives from the parastatal and private business community, namely Credit Guarantee, the Bantu Development Corporation (BDC), the IDC, LTA and Roberts Construction.[354] The BDC was established in 1959 to promote the economic and industrial development in the homelands.[355] Its presence in this instance can be seen as Pretoria's attempt to create political goodwill by demonstrating its work benefited the majority. Following Barkan's and Methot's feedback,[356] Bokassa met a South African delegation in Paris in September 1974, composed of, *inter alia*, Counsellor Pretorius, who acted as translator, and representatives of the enterprises who had attended the March meetings to discuss development/investment projects.[357] After Bokassa acknowledged to Vorster the "extremely positive" results of the Paris talks, emphasising the importance of the proposed projects for his country, Barkan met Vorster in October in Pretoria.[358] In November 1974, Ambassador Burger, joined by Rae Killen and Johan Pretorius, led a delegation with representatives from the Department of Commerce and the invited business sector to the C.A.R.[359] This resulted in what the DFA code-named 'Operation Bokassa', comprising assistance for a hotel complex of 500 bedrooms, a railway line, 500 prefabricated houses, mineral research and exploitation, an agricultural-industrial complex, tourist facilities, a second hospital in the capital, Bangui, educational projects and a paper pulp mill.[360]

Bokassa's motivation to seek contact with Pretoria was "a matter of economic expediency rather than part of an overall ideology", as one journalist wrote at the time.[361] The prime example was his wish of a hotel, named Hotel Intercontinental Bokassa, for the reasons indicated in a

DFA report: "[the hotel] must be completed before January, 1976, when 65 countries of the O.A.U. will confer in his country".[362] Muller being the cautious Minister he was, argued in October 1974 "the Republic cannot participate in prestige projects".[363] However, despite his reputation as a corrupt and eccentric politician and possibly overruled by Secretary Fourie, the DFA pursued the plans for the prestige-building exercise to win Bokassa's sympathies. For this purpose, it approached the companies Brian Colquhoun and its associate, Cereal and General Exports, representatives of which formed part of the group that visited the C.A.R. in November 1974. Several problems soon became apparent, however. The provision of credit finance was most critical, as Cereal and General Exports was responsible only for delivering the material, with no involvement in construction activity. Further, Bangui's credit repayment request exceeded the five years Credit Guarantee usually stipulated, the cost of $8.8 million was considered too high and the necessary cement was not readily available in South Africa. To complete the entire hotel by January 1976 therefore was no feasible proposition and the South Africans decided to build only sections.[364] In December 1974, Ambassador Burger communicated Pretoria's preparedness to provide a $2.2 million credit over ten years at 5 per cent interest, with a moratorium of two years before repayment, to be completed in 16 instalments with interest payments every six months. Two days later, Cereal and General Exports obtained CGIC insurance.[365] In a letter to Vorster in February 1975, Bokassa accepted the offer, deploying Barkan, the Minister of Housing and the Permanent Secretary of Housing to Pretoria the same month to sign the loan agreement; the IDC provided an export credit of $4.1 million and Pretoria added a $1.4 million loan.[366]

Second on the list of priorities in Operation Bokassa was a railway line to Cameroon's port of Douala, facilitating import to and export from the landlocked C.A.R. While in South Africa in March 1974, Barkan and Methot discussed this project with Fourie and Michael Catacuzene from Roberts Construction.[367] It again figured in Bokassa's discussions with the South African delegation in September[368] and Catacuzene was part of the delegation that visited the C.A.R. in November 1974. Yet, given the project's size, it could only be done by a consortium of companies, following which Catacuzene made it clear Roberts Construction would merely undertake sub-contractual work;[369] eventually, the firm did not take part. The third project in Operation Bokassa was the construction of 500 prefabricated houses in Bangui. The parties involved were LTA, the IDC and Credit Guarantee. Spencer Whiting from LTA and Jan Bouwer from Credit Guarantee were part of the group that went to the C.A.R. in November 1974. For the same reasons applicable to the hotel project, the provision of credit finance proved critical. However, judging this project to be "the only one [of Operation Bokassa] which appears capable of being dealt with on a normal commercial basis", the South Africans insisted on the normal five year repayment period.[370] On 14 March 1975, during their visit to South Africa, a C.A.R. delegation and the South African parties signed several financial agreements; the project's total cost to be undertaken by LTA was some $13.7 million, the IDC provided the credit, insured by Credit Guarantee. Repayment was to begin three years after the commencement of the contract, in six-monthly instalments over a period of ten years, with an interest rate of 7.25 per cent.[371] Sections of the agreement were thus not consistent with what the South Africans termed a "normal commercial basis". Bokassa's request for technical assistance in mineral research and exploitation of its reputedly rich mineral resources is the final aspect of Operation Bokassa we examine. During the talks in November 1974, the C.A.R. representatives asked for assistance from private South African mining companies, but the relevant DFA report mentions no names.[372] However, wanting to display the government's expertise, the South Africans proposed sending geologists from the National Metallurgical Institute. The geologist who visited the C.A.R. sometime between November 1974 and June 1975 recommended the concentration of operations on diamonds.[373] After this overview of the key projects within Operation Bokassa, we present their development until the end of Vorster's premiership.

By early 1976, the Hotel Intercontinental Bokassa encountered financial difficulties. Bokassa informed Muller, who led a delegation to Bangui in February, another $4.6 million was required,[374] and the OAU congress, raison d'être for the hotel, would no longer take place in Bangui. Although the South Africans "noted with surprise"[375] the additional money was needed, the IDC drafted contracts for a credit of $1.7 million.[376] It is likely the foreign service officers displayed such generosity to gain overflying rights for SAA and to find Bokassa's approval of Pretoria's homelands policy,[377] as the DFA included George Matanzima, Transkei's Justice Minister and Kaizer Matanzima's brother, in the delegation that went to Bangui in February 1976. While the foreign service officials' promise of additional financing for the hotel was not reciprocated with SAA overflying rights, they could report some success in their second aim; Bokassa indicated "he would accept the independence of Transkei" and "establish, without delay, diplomatic relations on an ambassadorial level".[378] The hotel project was again the main issue of discussion when Rae Killen and André Jaquet led ten businessmen, inter alia from CGIC, LTA, the IDC, Cereal and General Exports and Brian Colquhoun to Bangui in August 1977. The IDC provided further credit, while Cereal and General Exports continued their responsibility for the hotel's building material and LTA supervised the construction of the hotel, now scaled down to 270 rooms.[379] In contrast, regarding the 500 prefabricated houses, Johan Pretorius reported in March 1978 most "of the houses have been bought or let and the scheme is a great success".[380] Pretoria's technical assistance for mineral research resulted in the engagement of a geologist for exploration purposes by June 1975. Following his indication further assistance was worthwhile, the delegation going to Bangui in February 1976 conveyed Pretoria's offer: some $6.3 million until 1977, a visit by the C.A.R. Director of Mines to South Africa for talks with the Department of Mining and private mining companies, Safair's delivery of technical material to establish the extent of the diamond areas, the secondment of a South African geologist for a year and the training of three C.A.R. geologists by Pretoria's Geological Service.[381] However, a DFA report of March 1978 noted "a private company of Israeli and American interests has been formed to develop the diamond deposits",[382] putting an end to this aspect of co-operation.

On the whole, the DFA's contact with neither Liberia nor the Central African Republic was conducive to its ambition of establishing itself vis-à-vis the Department of Information. Pretoria's contact with Bangui proved to be a very difficult exercise and only one of the projects advanced well by 1978; their final outcome is examined in the next chapter. More importantly, the DFA's initiatives did not produce any tangible results; Bokassa did not recognise Transkei as a sovereign state when Pretoria declared its independence in October 1976 and South African Airways did not obtain overflying rights,[383] an aspect of Pretoria's foreign relations that constitutes our present focus.

Air Routes for SAA

Established in 1934, South African Airways ensured a connection to the developed world and to Western Europe in particular. Given South Africa's location, "far from principal trading partners, far from the major hubs of commerce, industry and innovation of the world, far from the Anglo-European cultural hearth to which many South Africans remain firmly bound",[384] this was of vital importance. The first non-stop flights to Europe took place from 1962,[385] but with independence sweeping across Africa in that decade, the direct routes became disrupted. Exploiting their geographical location, African countries began to withdraw both landing and overflying rights from SAA. This posed a severe problem for the Pretoria government. By having to fly around the western bulge of Africa, "distance to all European centres increased by at least 1 400 kms (...) and fuel usage soared"[386] (Figure 3). Yet, if SAA increased prices, they would lose passenger volume and income to competing airlines on these profitable routes. The result was great additional expenditure by Pretoria to sustain SAA flights. The DFA files apart, a particularly useful source to reconstruct the airline's and the government's initiatives to circumvent Africa's air sanctions were interviews and correspondence with the former SAA Chief Executives, Frans Swarts (1982-83) and Gerrit Dirk 'Gert' van der Veer (1983-93).

Figure 3: *Africa in South African Airways' International Network*

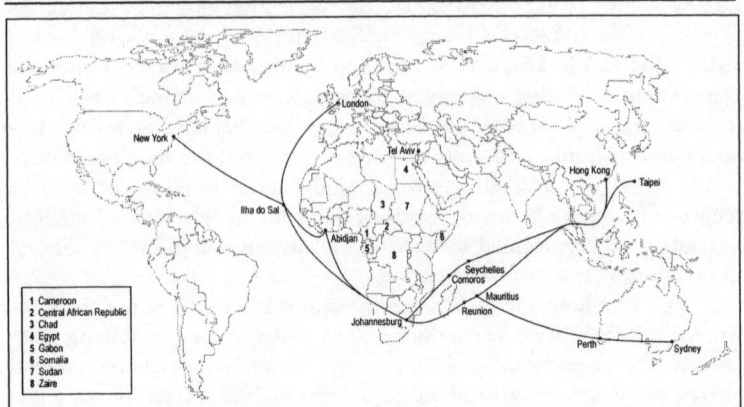

According to them, "numerous African countries were targeted on an on-going basis since August 1963 to reduce costs and also flying time in order to stay competitive on the European route".[387] The Spanish Canary Islands became an important stopover initially,[388] permitting planes to start with less fuel in Johannesburg, thus increasing their passenger capacity and making the flights more economical. During the early 1970s, SAA increasingly stopped over on Cape Verde, especially the New York flights that commenced in 1973; Las Palmas was still used for other flights until 1983.[389] In return for the landing rights on Ilha do Sal, Pretoria offered financial compensation and technical assistance to maintain airport standards,[390] $69,000 for the period 1977/9, for example. Additionally, in 1979, it provided the Cape Verde government with a loan of $15.75 million at an interest rate of 6 per cent to repair and improve the runway, apron and control tower.[391] At the same time, it saved the South African government a great deal of money in subsidising SAA flights. Former DFA official Paul Runge candidly stated in 1999: "there were projects that paid off nicely. In Cape Verde, for example, we only uplifted the runway, and in return we could put through three SAA flights a week. One flight paid for the project".[392] Cape Verde's dependence on that income was such it could not afford to cancel the landing rights, despite the condemnation of the apartheid system.[393]

SAA's efforts to circumvent the African air sanctions increased from 1974 for one important reason. Despite different measures, since the 1950s, to search and develop their own commercial gas and oil fields, South Africa depended on the oil-producing countries to obtain the precious raw material. The Arab states were an important source until the Yom Kippur War between Israel and Egypt in October 1973. To pressurise Israel into withdrawing her troops, the oil-producing Arab states embargoed its allies, among them South Africa.[394] The only Arab country to continue supplying oil to South Africa was Iran until the fall of Mohammed Reza Shah Pahlavi in 1979,[395] a relationship allegedly also involving co-operation in nuclear development and arms manufacturing.[396] The restricted access to the oil and the dramatic rise in the price of the available oil further increased the cost of the flights around the bulge of Africa. The stopover on Cape Verde apart, SAA considered two options to alleviate the problem: "i.e. over West Africa, cutting the bulge of Africa and over East Africa and the Red Sea".[397] Regarding the latter, Deon Geldenhuys indicates both BOSS's van den Bergh and Information Secretary Rhoodie supported the airline's endeavours, trying to secure overflying rights in Sudan and Egypt respectively during 1976.[398] Not having consulted the Egypt files, we cannot verify Rhoodie's advances, but we can document van den Bergh's enterprise in Sudan failed because he rejected Khartoum's demand of a $200 million loan and a $50 million grant in return.[399] Given that "Sudan proved to be the major stumbling block", Swarts and van der Veer informed us: "The possibility of overflying Somalia, Djibouti and up the Red Sea was seriously considered and theoretically possible, but never introduced due to the high risk of passing between Yemen and Ethiopia where a Russian no-go area (Submarine base) was proclaimed. Any adverse weather conditions would have forced us over either Yemen or Ethiopia, both of which would not have given us any rights. The risk of running a commercial service under such conditions was totally unacceptable".[400] Regarding the West African route, overflying rights were neither obtained for the C.A.R., as seen above, nor for Cameroon, as we established.[401] In any case, according to Swarts and van der Veer, overflying rights for these countries would have been of little use, as the same rights could not be obtained from Algeria and Libya, necessary for a complete air corridor.[402]

We have so far presented the strategies of the Departments of Foreign Affairs and Information to break South Africa's isolation. Geostrategic concerns shaped Pretoria's relations with those African countries beyond southern Africa that formed the western Indian Ocean area, namely the Comoros, Madagascar, Mauritius, Reunion and Seychelles. Both BOSS and the military, therefore, played important roles.

Western Indian Ocean

We first outline the strategic relevance of the western Indian Ocean during the Cold War to understand Pretoria's activities. Great Britain held the colonial administration over Mauritius and Seychelles until 1968 and 1976 respectively, and in 1966 signed an agreement allowing the US to use both islands for defence purposes. Yet, in 1968 London announced it was going to withdraw from east of the Suez Canal by 1971. Shortly thereafter, Moscow sent four warships to the area, regularly deploying naval units thereafter. The strategic importance of the western Indian

Ocean also relates to the closure of the Suez Canal (1967-75), forcing shippers to sail around South Africa's Cape of Good Hope to reach either Europe or North America. Consequently, and "by virtue of their potential for command of the Cape route", the Comoros, Madagascar and the Seychelles gained particular significance, more so than the further distant Mauritius and Reunion. When the Arab states cut off their oil supply to Israel and its allies after 1973, a military or intelligence presence there became even more important to monitor the movement of oil tankers around the Cape. This aspect remained highly significant even after the Suez Canal reopened in 1975; its closure had led to the construction of more voluminous tankers to make the long route around the Cape more economical and they were now too large to pass through the canal, therefore having to sail around the Cape.[403] A note on the French presence in the western Indian Ocean is also important. Its military forces on Madagascar were moved to the Comoros, to Reunion and Djibouti after Ratsiraka took power in 1972. The presence on Reunion remained unaffected due the island's status as an Overseas Department, administered by Michel Debré (1963-88), whom we encountered as Defence Minister in the context of the Nigerian Civil War. The Comoros declared their unilateral independence from France in 1975, a development Paris accepted by the end of that year, as it could retain its military presence on Mayotte, part of the Comoros.[404] We now investigate Pretoria's activities in the western Indian Ocean.

The only information in the DFA files related to Madagascar reveals BOSS held an interest in gathering intelligence. In January 1973, agent Albie Geldenhuys reported from Paris on the "existing possibility that the Bureau [BOSS] could again establish contact with the Malagasy Intelligence",[405] after Ratsiraka had terminated contact between the two countries in 1972.

We have seen Mauritian-South African relations were primarily based on trade and tourism. Together with the role played by Minister Gaëtan Duval, this resulted in the island's pro-Dialogue stance at the 1971 OAU Summit. However, in October 1973, Mauritius' UN Ambassador, simultaneously Chairman of the African Group, prevented Minister Muller from addressing the General Assembly, calling him a "criminal".[406] Pretoria now used the economic lever to exert political pressure; in September 1973, the two countries had reached an understanding whereby South Africa bought tea at a price 15 per cent above world price, thus increasing Mauritius' dependency.[407] In retaliation for the diplomat's behaviour, Pretoria stopped all tea import. Trying to alleviate the tension, Minister Duval wrote to Muller, explaining the ambassador "had not acted in accordance with Government instructions" and had been "recalled for consultation".[408] Duval's action and the visit of Mauritius' Minister for Trade and Industries to South Africa in October soothed Pretoria sufficiently to resume the import of tea in November.[409] Regarding the tourism sector, Sol Kerzner directed the Mauritius Southern Sun Hotels Ltd that opened a hotel, casino and golf club in 1975,[410] financed partly by a loan provided by the IDC and insured by Credit Guarantee.[411] Bureau for State Security activity was linked to Prime Minister Ramgoolam sacking Minister Duval in December 1973. Their political coalition was "shaky from the outset", according to Larry Bowman, because Duval "tended to run a pro-Western, pro-French, and pro-South African foreign policy that was often at variance with the more muted pro-British, pro-Indian, and somewhat more nonaligned stance" promoted by Ramgoolam.[412] In January 1974, BOSS agent Rothmann was planning on going to Mauritius, obviously entailing intelligence work in view of Mauritius' overtures towards the communist camp, reflected in Ramgoolam's visit to Moscow in August and the presence of a Soviet warship in Port Louis in December 1973.[413] The DFA was equally concerned. In January 1974, David Vrede Louw, Minister at the Washington Embassy, saw Herman 'Hank' Cohen, then Director for Central African Affairs in the State Department, who had just returned from Mauritius, to obtain his views on the current situation.[414] Prior to leaving for Mauritius, Rothmann asked Deputy Secretary Killen whether he could do anything for his ministry. Being interested in trying to ascertain the political climate, he took up the offer.[415] Rothmann spent 24/25 January on Mauritius, meeting the Prime Minister, his Security Adviser and the Commissioner of the Police's Special Branch; on his return, he reported to Secretary Fourie on Ramgoolam's affirmation that "contact must continue".[416] While these events reflect mutual acceptance by BOSS and the DFA for their respective roles, friction was an inherent risk. In particular, Rae Killen lamented to his superior, Rothmann "had entered diplomatic terrain" in having met Ramgoolam and this "had gone further than what we had asked".[417]

On Reunion, due to the island's status as a French colony and its importance for the French military, Paris was not prepared to let Pretoria benefit from its advantageous position. For example, SAA could only obtain landing rights because it was prepared to perform the weekly flight to Saint-Denis, and onwards to Mauritius, in co-operation with the French airline Union des Transports Aériennes (UTA). Furthermore, Holiday Inn's and Southern Sun's attempts in establishing casino hotels remained unsuccessful due to the strong position of the French hotel chain Novotel and Air France's share in a casino hotel nearing completion in 1976.[418] Consequently, the flow of South African tourists to Reunion remained low.[419] The establishment of an official mission is a final example of Pretoria's difficult standing on Reunion. The DFA contacted sister departments to determine their viewpoints on such a mission. The Department of Commerce, arguing "trading possibilities (...) have been neglected", favoured the "opening of a Consulate".[420] That position was quite likely influenced by the Durban Chamber of Commerce's assessment. In June 1973, Joep Steyn, the Department's Secretary, had contacted the Chamber to ascertain its views regarding the appointment of a trade representative; after returning from the Seychelles, Mauritius and Reunion in October, General Manager Kenneth Hobson replied in the affirmative.[421] The military also supported the idea of a permanent mission. In March 1974, the Naval Chief of Staff, Hugo Hendrik Biermann, wrote to Fourie it was "desirable to have a listening post in the area".[422] Only the French attitude was prohibitive, causing Counsellor Pretorius to suggest to Fourie in August 1974: "perhaps we should consider bringing pressure to bear via Mr Debré".[423] It is not recorded whether this avenue was pursued, but the Consulate was established in late 1974, with Johan von Gernet as the first Consul.[424] We do not know whether Military Intelligence posted a representative, such as indicated by Pretorius' report in January 1975: "D.M.I. are also likely to place one of their people there".[425]

Pretoria's contact with the Comoros began before its independence in 1975 and through the Eilande Sending, literally translated as Mission to the Islands. Its visit to the Comoros in early 1974 resulted in the island approaching Pretoria for technical assistance.[426] Following this up, Killen led government officials in charge of fisheries, trade, agriculture and a SAA representative on an "exploratory visit" to the Comoros in July 1974 to establish the requirements.[427] The DFA's interest in providing assistance was to obtain landing rights for SAA en route to Asia.[428] The military was interested for strategic reasons,[429] but the files contained no evidence of related activities. In September, based on the findings of the above visit, Muller offered Ahmed Abdallah, the President of the Comoros' Governing Council, chickens and assistance in cattle breeding, seven fishing boats, an ambulance and protein supplements to combat malnutrition.[430] On Abdallah's acceptance of the offer, Killen led another delegation with officials from the Departments of Fisheries and Agriculture to the Comoros in February 1975, taking along the promised items.[431] The relatively fruitful relations came to a standstill when mercenaries led by Bob Denard deposed Abdallah in August 1975. Nonetheless, the DFA's minimal technical assistance had been enough to secure SAA landing rights. The airline did not use them until 1983,[432] when tourism to the island increased.

Finally turning to the Seychelles, the DFA files record no diplomatic interaction prior to the island's independence in 1976. However, the Bureau for State Security showed an interest for intelligence reasons, leading to a joint BOSS-Department of Information venture. As part of the independence preparations, presidential elections were set for April 1975, with the pro-capitalist James Mancham competing against the leftist France René. According to Eschel Rhoodie's and Les de Villiers' autobiographies, the Department of Information supported Mancham financially in the run-up to the election so the island would be directed by a Western-oriented leader favouring contact with Pretoria.[433] Aware of

Mancham's lavish lifestyle,[434] they code-named their strategy Operation Playboy. Mancham won the election and became President upon the island's independence in June 1976, making René Prime Minister. The Department of Information's contact with Mancham continued post-independence. In January 1977, Rhoodie and de Villiers, accompanied by their families and friends, spent a luxury holiday on the Seychelles, also meeting Mancham.[435] Crucially, the holiday makers used Louis Luyt's Lear Jet.[436] According to Mancham's memoirs, Rhoodie, on behalf of Luyt, enquired if it was possible to register a plane for the purpose of promoting the latter's business in Africa.[437] In our correspondence, Luyt tried to distance himself from these developments: "My BAC 111 aircraft was chartered on different occasions, through a charter company, but I believe to carry government officials".[438] In any case, it again indicates this influential Afrikaner businessman was part of the network supporting the Department of Information's policies. In June 1977, René, with Tanzanian assistance, ousted Mancham. He initially pursued a pragmatic approach towards Pretoria, whose intelligence community retained an interest in the island. Notably, Luyt and BOSS agent Albie Geldenhuys together informed Brand Fourie in January 1978 of their separate meetings with President René in the previous December.[439] Luyt informed us he visited the island twice a year with his family, but never in Geldenhuys' company, while divulging: "Albie Geldenhuys started to work for me after I entered into an agreement with Gasocean, the French Shipping company in 1976, because he could speak French fluently".[440] However, René's pragmatism changed; in August 1978, "René announced his country would be severing trade and tourism ties with South Africa" and the Seychelles Tourist Office in Johannesburg was closed in December.[441] However, depending on the money spent by South African tourists, René did not completely break relations and did not terminate SAA's landing rights.[442] In return, Pretoria provided technical assistance to ensure the safety of the Mahé international airport.[443] However, the stopover used *en route* to Hong Kong since 1974 ceased in September 1980. This service, together with the one to Taipei from November 1980, was re-routed via Mauritius henceforth.[444]

Having analysed the endeavours by the Departments of Information and Foreign Affairs, as well as Pretoria's interests related to SAA and the western Indian Ocean, we will now discuss the Africa initiatives by the opposition Progressive Party and the South Africa Foundation.

Non-State Initiatives

Visits by Progressive Party members to the following African states are of interest to this period: Senegal, Gambia (Eglin, Suzman; 1972); Botswana, Zambia, Kenya, Nigeria (Eglin, Slabbert; 1974); Zaire (Eglin; 1975); Mauritius (Suzman; 1975); Tanzania (Eglin; 1975); Kenya, Senegal, Gambia

(Eglin; 1977); Zaire (Eglin; 1978); Nigeria, Senegal (Eglin; 1979).[445] While Suzman's trip to Mauritius "was simply a stopover visit to address students at the university there on my return from (...) Australia",[446] boosting the party's relevance was a key motivation for the other trips. Contact with Senegal, the only country to be visited three times, bore special significance; the Dialogue section noted both Eglin's and Suzman's first visit there in 1971. Elaborating on the close link with Senghor, Eglin proposed: "I found his views on the liberation of Africa, negritude, and on the form of democracy that he was trying to establish fascinating. These discussions, supplemented by discussions with Senegalese journalists and business entrepreneurs, gave me an insight into the Francophone perspective, one which was very difficult to get from SA".[447] Given the last reason, we queried Eglin why they had not gone to the Ivory Coast. Crucially, he responded both he and Suzman had tried to see Houphouët-Boigny, but they were prevented from entering the country: "Suzman and I had visas and an appointment but we were refused entry upon arrival at Abidjan airport. Years later in Paris I was told that the French government, at the request of the SA government, had put pressure on H-B not to meet with us".[448] While the special access to Abidjan seemingly allowed Pretoria to prevent the Progressives from intruding their important contact with Houphouët-Boigny, the party enjoyed privileged treatment by Senghor, leading to friction with the government. According to Eglin's interview prior to departing for Dakar in September 1977, Senghor had invited him "to discuss the South African situation", referring to Vorster's non-reply to Senghor's request in 1976 to send a fact-finding mission to South Africa. Upon returning, Pik Botha criticised Eglin had played ""a negative role" in South Africa's African policy" and if President Senghor "knew what Mr Eglin and the PFP stood for, he would have nothing whatsoever to do with Mr Eglin".[449] This reaction was related to the election amongst the white population, due in two months, criticising Eglin's goal of having sought party-political gains through his visit.[450] Eglin's and Slabbert's tour of four African countries in 1974 drew similar criticism. The Information Department's mouthpiece *To the Point* decried it as party politics: "Leaders from various political groupings are outbidding each other in their enterprise, the idea being to talk with as many African leaders as possible (...). The Progressive Party, with an eye to arming itself with plenty of ammunition for the coming parliamentary session, has been extraordinarily busy in this field within the past two weeks".[451] Defence Minister P.W. Botha even "assailed Eglin for sitting around the table with "terrorists" and falling over his feet in front of President Kaunda of Zambia".[452]

In contrast, Pretoria generally welcomed the South Africa Foundation's activities involving two countries. The first account relates to Uganda through the services of Edwin Stanton 'Ned' Munger, a Professor in Political Geography at the California Institute of Technology.[453] As a member of the American Universities Field Staff (1950-60), he had travelled extensively in Africa and got to know the politically powerful.

Munger had especially close ties with South Africa and Pretoria's political elite; he was a Research Fellow at the University of Stellenbosch during 1955/56, married to Ann Boyer, South Africa's Cultural Attaché in Washington during the 1970s, and a Trustee of the important US-South African Leadership Exchange Program (USSALEP),[454] which promoted communication between the two countries. He published widely on the US-South African relationship and South African political affairs, holding a favourable view towards the minority in this country.[455] Obviously aware of his position, the South Africa Foundation approached him during 1977, enquiring if he knew "anyone from East Africa" "to soften the SA image and maybe make a convert", as Munger informed us. Given his favourable stance toward South Africa, he was willing to assist and, in his words, "thought that my old friend Martin would be effective",[456] meaning Martin Aliker from Uganda. Their friendship had begun during concurrent studies at Uganda's Makerere College in the 1940s and continued thereafter, especially as Aliker studied dentistry at Northwestern University in Evanston.[457] Aliker then became politically influential, was Uganda's Ambassador Plenipotentiary in the early 1960s, a successful businessman and married to an American. In 1971, when Amin came to power, Munger went into Kenyan exile.[458] The DFA files' sparse documentation on subsequent developments and our interview with Aliker allowed us to clarify the contents of interaction, although contradictions regarding certain dates remained. Aliker's first visit to South Africa – in 1977 according to Aliker, in 1978 according to the files – took place on the invitation of the South Africa Foundation and in the company of mediator Munger. Aliker explained his motivation was to see for himself and "satisfy (...) [his] curiosity" what apartheid signified, and he was "willing to talk", recalling having met Foundation Secretary General Sorour and the Trustees Basil Hersov, Jan Marais and Harry Oppenheimer. Regarding the contents of their discussions, Aliker did not divulge much, except they revolved around exploring "the possibility of business activities". Exemplifying its co-operative relationship with the government, the Foundation arranged for Aliker to meet with politicians and civil servants. In particular, the Ugandan told us rather proudly Prime Minister Vorster was prepared to meet him on the very day he had asked for such an encounter. Aliker also lunched with almost the entire Cabinet and saw BOSS's van den Bergh, who was "interested in the situation in Uganda", as Aliker indicated meaninglessly.[459] Considering his stay in South Africa "very successful", Aliker maintained contact with Pretoria. He returned in July 1978 and August 1979 according to the DFA documents, but Aliker claims he returned only once, one year after the initial visit.[460] In any case, both sources agree the Pretoria government had invited Aliker on this occasion, without Munger. This time, Aliker was motivated by "selfish reasons" and, during his discussions with Vorster and Minister Pik Botha, "specifically requested armaments" for Ugandan rebel groups to topple Amin.[461] Pretoria's willingness to assist did not substantiate, as the South Africans were only prepared to supply through a third party. In return, Aliker offered to ensure South Africa's participation in the 1980 Olympic Games and landings rights for SAA in Mombasa, Kenya.[462] However, neither became reality[463] and Aliker's contact with Pretoria ceased.

The second South Africa Foundation activity, the only recorded example of friction with Pretoria, relates to Kenya, involving heart specialist and Trustee Chris Barnard. Diplomatic contact with Nairobi became possible when Daniel arap Moi came to power in 1978; his political leanings were towards the West, with Deputy Secretary Killen judging him to be "a business-orientated man". The same year, the DFA files record Under-Secretary Hendrick 'Hennie' Geldenhuys met one Mr. Marende, a Kenyan businessman, member of the Board of Commerce and Trade and "well acquainted" with arap Moi and Charles Njonjo, Kenya's Attorney-General.[464] Probably linked to this meeting, the DFA now actively courted Njonjo, who was highly influential in Kenyan politics and close to arap Moi at the time.[465] According to a report from Deputy Secretary von Hirschberg, it made "many attempts" to bring him to South Africa.[466] Queried about these developments, von Hirschberg wrote to us Killen had been the "primary intermediary", adding: "I am not sure how Rae established contact with Njonjo (...) but it developed over time and resulted in Rae occasionally visiting Njonjo in Nairobi"; Njonjo confirmed this in our correspondence.[467] Von Hirschberg further recalled: "Njonjo was pro-dialogue, an attitude which we earnestly tried to promote amongst African leaders. (...) We had no direct contact with arap Moi. We relied on Njonjo to influence Government policy on South Africa".[468] Njonjo's pro-Dialogue stand, expressed in a Kenyan TV interview in August 1978, was related to Chris Barnard's heart transplantation on a Kenyan girl, the second of its kind within months, in Cape Town in July.[469] Njonjo remembered: "I was interested in Barnard's work as a transplant pioneer. His operation on the Kenyan girl took place after his visit to Kenya".[470] However, Barnard's interaction with Njonjo caused friction with the DFA. In mid-August 1978, the Kenyan Foreign Affairs Minister had attacked Njonjo as "interfering in the country's foreign policy and contradicting Government policy".[471] Pik Botha feared this undermined their intended contact with arap Moi, as von Hirschberg confirmed: "Njonjo was already in the firing line and the publicity impacted further on his political standing in Kenya. Pik Botha was concerned it would further undermine Njonjo's influence in Kenya and negate his usefulness to us".[472] Pik Botha complained to the Foundation's President and Secretary General, Hersov and Sorour respectively, who saw the Minister regarding their visit to Kenya in 1979: "the professor just did not understand the political situation in Kenya. Instead of keeping quiet about his plans he had publicised it. The Minister felt that we should be more sophisticated about the way we set about inviting people of the stature of Njonjo".[473] The DFA subsequently withdrew from contact with Njonjo, justifiably so, as friction between Njonjo and arap Moi resulted in their fall-out in 1983.[474]

This concludes the Secret Diplomacy period. While this section mentioned some BOSS and military activity, we now separately examine the Détente phase, during which these two state actors were the principals.

Détente

African independence during the 1960s notwithstanding, Angola and Mozambique remained Portuguese colonies, white minority rule continued in Rhodesia and Pretoria still occupied Namibia. Thus, South Africa was surrounded by what became known as a *cordon sanitaire*, on which its "security and relative isolation had relied for so long to keep the black insurgent movements at a distance from its own frontiers".[475] Yet, in April 1974, a military coup in Lisbon ignited Portugal's retreat from Africa, eliminating the *cordon sanitaire*. Pretoria consequently needed to find an arrangement to safeguard the position of the white minority. Its reaction became an intense struggle between the Bureau for State Security and the military, propagating Détente and war respectively, in the Cold War context and of great significance given the implications on Pretoria's foreign relations with the countries further north.

Superpower and South African Détente

Détente relates to the Cold War between the superpowers, with Henry Kissinger, Assistant for National Security Affairs (1969-76) and US Secretary of State (1973-77), as the driving force.[476] His principal motivation was to extricate the US from Vietnam, where they had become embroiled in a conflict they could not win. Co-operation was sought, first with Moscow, then with Beijing, to terminate Washington's traumatic experience. Kissinger's approach resulted in respectable successes during 1972/73.[477] Regarding Washington's Détente with China, Kissinger and President Richard Nixon visited Beijing in 1971 and 1972 respectively, restoring Sino-American relations.[478] Relations with Moscow became strained due to differing interpretations over how Détente related to the superpowers' behaviour in the Third World; Washington linked it to a Soviet restraint, while for Moscow, Détente "never meant renunciation of their support for national liberation and other 'progressive' struggles".[479]

Evidence of the term Détente entering Pretoria's political vocabulary as a strategy with which to come to terms with the situation in southern Africa dates from late 1974. A *To the Point* editorial outlined its purpose, arguing Pretoria's strained relations with Africa could only improve if it settled the situation in Rhodesia and S.W.A./Namibia.[480] Based on evidence presented later, we argue BOSS, given its privileged access to Vorster and co-operation with Washington's CIA, instigated Détente. In addition, Détente had backing from significant parts of the Afrikaner community, especially the Broederbond, and the policy network supportive of Secret Diplomacy. With these considerations, Vorster began appraising both the Rhodesian and S.W.A./Namibia problems. With the choice of continued support for Ian Smith, resulting in Pretoria's further isolation, or withdrawing from Rhodesia and improving relations with Africa, he chose the latter. The activities of BOSS and the DFA to resolve the impasse contributed to the holding of the Victoria Falls Conference in August 1975, attended by the protagonists of the Rhodesian conflict.[481] Shortly before the meeting, Vorster withdrew the remaining police units from Rhodesia to indicate Pretoria's negotiation commitment. While he was quite prepared to sacrifice Rhodesia in pursuit of Détente, Pretoria considered what it called South West Africa as South Africa's fifth province;[482] abandoning this territory, therefore, was a highly sensitive issue. At the same time, this was a matter of prime concern to African leaders and internationally, as we have shown. As was characteristic of his premiership, Vorster bumbled his way through the conflict, launching less than half-hearted initiatives, such as the Turnhalle Conference to discuss Namibia's political future, while adamantly remaining against granting the country independence.[483]

Parallel to these developments, BOSS, the DFA and the Department of Information tried drawing Zaire into the Détente strategy.

Zaire

Mobutu did not seek contact with Pretoria after his coming to power in 1965; still in August 1974, Rae Killen noted: "Our present day relations with Zaïre are limited to our mutual trade".[484] This changed towards the end of 1974, linked to the Angolan war, with Mobutu supporting the pro-western National Front for the Liberation of Angola (FNLA), which, together with the National Union for the Total Independence of Angola (UNITA), opposed the communist-oriented Popular Movement for the Liberation of Angola (MPLA). During 1975, having unsuccessfully tried to solicit US support for the pro-western liberation movements, Mobutu turned to South Africa's intelligence and military community,[485] discussed later. Our present interest lies with the civilian aspect in diplomatic contact with Pretoria.

In early 1975, the DFA interacted with Etienne Kallos, owner of a Cape Town-based firm, which exported foodstuff to Zaire through the Zairian Société Africaine des Produits Alimentaires (SAPA), directed by Justin Bomboko, Zaire's former Foreign Minister (1960-63, 1965-69); through him, the DFA gained access to Mobutu, who invited a South

African business delegation in April. Reflecting his wider interest in gaining Pretoria's support for Angola's FNLA, he courted a representative each from the Commerce Department and the IDC, Jan Bouwer from Credit Guarantee and Counsellor Pretorius as translator. They discussed providing a $4.1 million credit to SAPA and a similar firm, while Bomboko mentioned three development/investment projects for possible assistance.[486] In May 1975, Department of Commerce and IDC representatives, in Pretorius' company, made a follow-up visit, offering the Zairian authorities an additional $6.8 million credit for the import of South African goods.[487] Given the DFA's interest in promoting Détente, the IDC concluded four agreements with Bomboko's SAPA until February 1976, providing a total credit of some $18 million for the purchase of South African foodstuff, pharmaceutical and medical goods.[488]

After successfully promoting South African export to Zaire, the DFA launched development/investment projects. In July 1975, Commerce Secretary Joep Steyn, with the DFA's de Goede as translator, led seven business representatives to Zaire. Those destined to play an important role were Paul Hoogendyk (Bessemer Steel), Douglas J. Hamilton (Brian Colquhoun), Michael Thomas 'Mike' Ridley (LTA) and Derek Marriott (Roberts Construction). Following their report, identifying an "enormous potential" and recommending "an energetic follow-up",[489] the Departments of Foreign Affairs and Commerce selected ten projects considered suitable for participation.[490] For closer investigation, Bomboko arranged the visit of 14 business representatives to Zaire in October.[491] Those from the engineering firms were interested in the construction of the 150 km railway line to a seaport to facilitate Kinshasa's import and export. The project would cost an estimated $41 million, 85 per cent of which the IDC was prepared to finance with Credit Guarantee as the insurer. Yet, the proposed railway line covered only part of the route from the coast to Kinshasa; the construction of the remaining 200 km posed geographical problems and the seaport did not have the necessary facilities. Therefore, Jan Bouwer expressed caution regarding participation.[492] The LTA's Ridley confirmed our impression no South African activity ever took place: "The idea of a railway line was absurd, in relation to the fact that the use of the Congo River was way below capacity – even then 75% of the barges were out of action and in a state of disrepair".[493] As a second project, the Bessemer Steel was interested in providing "silos to contain grain" for import and export and of "storage facilities for food supplies". The estimated cost was $5.4 million, to be made available by the IDC and insured by Credit Guarantee. Hoogendyk and his two colleagues remained behind to inspect the silo sites.[494] However, a DFA report, dated end of 1976, states "not much progress"[495] had taken place since, suggesting this project was not implemented either. Finally, in October 1975, Justin Bomboko wrote to Secretary Fourie concerning the establishment of an agro-industrial complex in Gbadolite, Mobutu's birth-place, which he tried to develop during the 1970s.[496] The project was to include "a palm-plantation of more than one thousand hectares, an oil-pressing factory, tabacco [sic] plantations, cattle breeding, the breeding of more than 20,000 pigs and other agricultural undertakings". Hoping to gain Mobutu's support for Détente by providing assistance to a project close to him, it Fourie replied "in principle we are absolutely ready (...) to provide our assistance (...) such as desired". In December, Bomboko àsked Fourie whether South African agricultural experts could visit Gbadolite in January 1976.[497] Thereafter, however, the Department of Information took over this initiative for reasons not recorded. According to Rhoodie's autobiography, van den Bergh, himself and BOSS agent Albie Geldenhuys as translator flew to Zaire in early 1976 in Louis Luyt's private jet to meet Mobutu,[498] confirming the significance of the above policy network. According to a later DFA document, two representatives of Luyt's Triomf Fertiliser company went to Zaire in May 1976 in connection with that project.[499] This was the only additional information on the issue in the files; Luyt claimed in our correspondence he had no knowledge of any such activity.[500] The following case study details a special kind of interaction between Pretoria and Kinshasa, one that became a Cold War issue.

Its diamond mining activities aside (Chapter 3), Anglo American held an interest in the fields of copper and cobalt in Tenke Fungurume, province of Katanga. The state-owned Générale des carrières et des mines (Gécamines), established in 1967 to explore the deposits there, was not in a position to function effectively given Zaire's worsening financial situation. Thus, in 1970, Kinshasa concluded an agreement with foreign enterprises to form the Société Minière de Tenke Fungurume (SMTF), with Charter Consolidated, the London-based Anglo American subsidiary, and the US Standard Oil Company of Indiana, as the largest shareholders, with 28 per cent participation each.[501] By 1973, several SMTF feasibility studies established the resources were sufficient to make mining viable. During 1974, Washington's export credit agency, the Export-Import Bank, provided an export credit of $232 million, a Chase Manhattan-led bank consortium made available bank loans of $195 million and shareholder's funds accounted for $234 million to implement the project. Yet, originally estimated at $500 million,[502] the cost estimate rose to $812 million, causing the Chase Manhattan bank consortium to withdraw in January 1976; Anglo American and Standard Oil decided not to further invest for three years. At this point, the US administration became involved, interested in keeping Mobutu in power as a guarantor of political stability in Central Africa and as an ally against the communist MPLA in Angola.[503] Yet, Kissinger's State Department was aware the country's economic crisis threatened "the Mobutu government at a time when its help over Angola was needed most",[504] fearing the SMTF project's postponement would further undermine Mobutu's standing. Therefore, in

January 1976, the State Department invited Harry Oppenheimer and a Standard Oil representative to discuss possibilities of keeping the project alive; whether Kissinger was present is not known. Furthermore, Robert McNamara, former US Secretary of Defence and now World Bank President, was contacted to obtain the $150 million estimated sufficient to get the project off the ground. This powerful link was not helpful, however, as Oppenheimer informed Hilgard Muller in April 1976.[505] Washington also approached Pretoria. In February 1976, Deputy Assistant Secretary of State for Africa, Edward Mulcahy, held discussions with Minister Plenipotentiary Shearar at the South African Embassy and Robert Anderson went to Pretoria to raise the required $150 million.[506] Anderson, former Secretary of the Navy and the Treasury, had carried out diplomatic missions on behalf of President Johnson until 1968, was State Department Press Secretary in 1974, time during which he became close to Kissinger, and later became "an investment adviser for wealthy individuals and corporations in New York".[507] Furthermore, Anderson was engaged in Standard Oil, maintaining close ties with David Rockefeller, the business magnate who presided over Chase Manhattan.[508] We thus argue Anderson's mission was related to his link with Kissinger, representing Standard Oil's and Chase Manhattan's financial interests. This web was enlarged with Iran entering the picture.

Trying to resuscitate their investment of $35 million,[509] Harry Oppenheimer and Anglo American Executive Director Julian Ogilvie Thompson went to Tehran in February 1976. Benefiting from Pretoria's alleged politico-military contacts with Iran, they used the services of Colonel Charles Alan 'Pop' Fraser, Consul-General in Tehran; he set up a meeting on 11 February, when Oppenheimer, Ogilvie Thompson and himself held talks with Iran's Prime Minister and two ministers. Three days later, the Shah gave Oppenheimer and Fraser an audience. According to Fraser's report, and although Oppenheimer had emphasised the need for co-operation in Zaire's SMTF project, nothing specific resulted in this regard.[510] In January 1976, supplementing these initiatives, US mediator Anderson introduced a proposal whereby Pretoria would purchase extra oil from Iran to the amount of $150 million, to be repaid by putting the money into the SMTF project, making the Shah a shareholder. Pretoria replied in the negative, stating it had no funds available. Anderson then devised a proposal whereby two US oil companies would buy the extra oil and sell it at a price somewhat lower than prescribed by the Organisation of the Petroleum Exporting Countries (OPEC), with Pretoria making good the shortfall. This would have made it a shareholder with $10 million, with Iran's share still amounting to $150 million. Pretoria again declined, citing a lack of clarity.[511] However, its negative attitude on both occasions can be seen as a consequence of the deteriorating US-South African engagement in the Angolan war, examined later.

As all attempts to obtain the necessary financing had failed, Anglo American and Washington engaged Maurice Tempelsman, an apt choice. He had close ties to all US Presidents from the 1960s and to the CIA, "enjoyed excellent access to the State Department",[512] was a successful businessman and senior partner in his father's firm, Leon Tempelsman & Son, engaged in mining and mineral trading, for example holding a 3 per cent share in the SMTF project.[513] These connections led Richard Mahoney to state Tempelsman "had a liking for mixing conspiracy with commerce in his African trade". Such interaction was particularly fruitful with Mobutu, who made Tempelsman Zaire's Honorary Consul in New York during the 1970s.[514] This took place in co-operation with Anglo American, a contact dating back to the 1950s, when Tempelsman became uniquely important as the middleman supplying diamonds from the Central Selling Organisation (CSO) to the US. The CSO was De Beers' monopolistic diamond marketing subsidiary, barred by Washington from trading in the US in retaliation for under-supplying tool diamonds during the Second World War.[515] Furthermore, Tempelsman exploited diamonds in western Kasai, an area not controlled by the government-owned Société Minière de Bakwanga (MIBA); the British Zaire Diamond Distributors (Britmond), De Beers' Zairian subsidiary, sold both MIBA's and Tempelsman's production through the CSO.[516] Thus, Anglo American Executive Director Spicer referred to Tempelsman as Oppenheimer's "personal friend".[517]

In April 1976, after his first mission to safeguard the SMTF project, Tempelsman informed Oppenheimer he and Anderson had met Iran's Finance Minister to discuss the oil-for-copper deal. The Minister informed them Kissinger had encouraged the Shah "to consider participation",[518] mirroring "his geo-political view that southern Africa was now a focal point in the East/West global struggle and a threat to superpower *détente*".[519] Oppenheimer lobbied with equal vigour, submitting, in April 1976, two memoranda to Charles Robinson, Under-Secretary of State for Economic Affairs, who was to accompany Kissinger to Zaire shortly thereafter. In South Africa, he provided Minister Muller and Secretary Fourie with the same documentation given to Robinson and including the above-mentioned letter from Tempelsman. On 30 March, Oppenheimer met with Muller, indicating Anglo American "would, naturally, welcome any assistance the South African Government might be in a position to offer". On 22 April, Oppenheimer despatched a letter with similar contents to Fourie.[520] However, Muller only replied on 4 May and very curt: "It was certainly very useful to have had an exchange of views on the subject. I also appreciate your kind offer to keep my Department informed of any new developments".[521] Pretoria's diminished interest in assisting Anglo American and the Americans in the SMTF project, can again be attributed to failed US-South African intervention in the Angolan war. A similar fate befell another example of co-operation between Pretoria, Washington and Anglo American in keeping Mobutu in power. Given Zaire's oil shortage during 1975, Justin Bomboko approached the DFA for help, sending Larry Devlin as an intermediary to Pretoria in October, the ideal man to help solve the problem.[522] The department knew Devlin was a "former official" of the US government with "long experience" in Zaire who now worked for Leon Tempelsman & Son as their representative there and who was "well known to (…) H. Oppenheimer and General van den Bergh".[523] It is uncertain, however, whether they knew Devlin was the CIA's key person for Zaire. The secondary literature informs us he was formerly CIA Station Chief in Kinshasa (1960-63, 1965-67); it was in this role that he had reported South African mercenary activity in the Congo (Chapter 3). After his departure from Kinshasa, Devlin remained in close contact with Mobutu as Head of the CIA's Africa Division (1971-74). Thereafter, and until 1987, he put his connections at the disposal of Leon Tempelsman & Son, consolidating a connection from Devlin's days in the Congo.[524] Devlin's stay in South Africa served to convey Zaire's needs. He again visited the Republic in November, meeting with Brand Fourie and private business representatives. A scheme was devised whereby US Mobil Oil International would supply Kinshasa with oil and oil products worth $50 million to bridge the gap until the expected assistance from the International Monetary Fund (IMF) arrived. However, given Zaire's dire economic situation, Mobil Oil insisted on bank guarantees, and this is where Mobutu hoped to obtain South African assistance. Among the businessmen Devlin consulted was Harry Oppenheimer, who either knew him related to De Beers' diamond mining in Zaire and/or through Tempelsman. In any event, Oppenheimer could not assist Devlin, possibly because Union Acceptances Ltd, Anglo American's own private merchant bank, experienced financial problems,[525] but he referred him to Frank Dolling, the Managing Director of South Africa's Barclays Bank, advice probably related to that bank's involvement with UAL.[526] With Oppenheimer's recommendation, Dolling unsurprisingly provided the bank guarantee; Oppenheimer offered to cover any shortfalls in Kinshasa's repayments to Mobil Oil International through Britmond, De Beers' diamond agency in Zaire, by using the income from MIBA's diamond sales. Oppenheimer had previously obtained Mobutu's permission for such sales and had contacted Secretary Fourie to ascertain the DFA's preparedness to reinsure the deal.[527] The State Security Council, the principal decision-making body during P.W. Botha's era, discussed the proposal in November 1975,[528] making this one of the few times the SSC met during the Vorster era. The DFA files do not contain its final decision, but again referring to the failed US-South African military intervention in Angolan, it is unlikely Pretoria co-operated.

We have now discussed Pretoria's Détente activities. Yet, the destruction of Pretoria's *cordon sanitaire* caused the military to pursue another approach towards southern Africa. In this context, the following section details its relations with Gabon, which served as a stopover for armament transports to South Africa. These supplies are important in understanding its involvement in the Angolan war, representing the apogee in the conflicting approaches by the military and BOSS.

Gabon

President Bongo had become a reliable partner to Pretoria's military from the Nigerian Civil War. Although this gave the DFA access to Gabon, supporting development/investment projects and launching the OGAPROV agricultural project, Bongo favoured dealing with the military. Patrick Monier-Vinard and Jean-Pierre Daniël served as Bongo's advisers in political, military and intelligence matters until 1975 and 1979 respectively. Daniël was an agent of the French intelligence agency SDECE,[529] and we assume the same of Monier-Vinard. We had contact with Monier-Vinard, but he flatly refused to verify this and other information. Reflecting their importance to both Pretoria's military and the DFA in providing a conduit to Bongo, they were awarded the Order of Good Hope in 1975 (Monier-Vinard) and 1979 (Daniël).[530]

In May 1975, probably following interventions of Monier-Vinard and Pretoria's military, Bongo granted Safair the right to use Libreville airport as a refuelling stop-over on its routes to and from Europe.[531] The airline made frequent use of the facility until late 1976, with at least one north- and southbound weekly flight.[532] Thereafter, for reasons not recorded, the number of landings was drastically reduced.[533] The Safair flights occasionally transported material for the technical assistance and development/investment projects in the C.A.R. and Gabon,[534] but their main purpose was to deliver parts for armament production in South Africa by the Armaments Development and Manufacturing Corporation (Armscor). Established in 1968 to counter the 1963 UN voluntary arms embargo, it became the SADF's main armaments supplier.[535] The destinations for which Safair frequently required clearance from Libreville were Milan's Malpensa Airport, Glasgow Prestwick International Airport and Bordeaux.[536] The French armament supplies after 1963 explain the Bordeaux destination, while Malpensa possibly served as a trade centre for the alleged US and Italian deliveries.[537] A clearance request sheds some light on Glasgow: "Freight from Prestwick consists of Jet engine starter cartridges and detonators from Nobel's Enterprises to Naschem (Pty) Limited".[538] The Armscor subsidiary Naschem was described as "one of the largest ammunition producers in the southern hemisphere".[539] Regarding the provider, Nobel's Enterprises, Alfred Nobel had established the British Dynamite Company south of Glasgow. Renamed Nobel's

Explosives in 1877, it later merged with other chemical companies to form Imperial Chemical Industries.[540] While satisfied with the Safair landing arrangement, Bongo expressed concern over the visibility of the Safair stopovers.[541] The Safair deal was only one element of what Rae Killen described as the "package",[542] supplemented by Bongo's interest in the Gabonese but Rhodesia-registered air cargo carrier Affretair[543] and SAA's desire to obtain landing rights in Gabon. Jack Malloch, a South African-born pilot and Rhodesian resident, had established Air Trans Africa, the operator of Affretair, in 1970, and had co-operated with President Bongo by flying Rhodesian support, via Gabon, to Biafra.[544] Concerning the other elements of the 'package', Gabon was almost entirely dependent on imported meat, with Rhodesia as one of the principal suppliers, contravening the 1966 mandatory UN sanctions against Salisbury. Affretair, in which Bongo was averred to hold "a financial interest", according to a DFA document,[545] transported this commodity to Gabon before proceeding to European destinations. On their return trip to Rhodesia via Libreville, the Affretair planes were usually empty and this lack of economic viability was not in Bongo's financial interest.[546] Furthermore, given the economic sanctions against Rhodesia, the Libreville stop-over posed a political problem. To resolve this situation, Bongo approached Pretoria. In May 1975, Malloch met SAA Planning Manager Frans Swarts in South Africa, proposing a weekly Affretair cargo flight from Europe to Johannesburg, "wet-leased"[547] by SAA, and then onwards to Salisbury.[548] Monier-Vinard had previously discussed the controversial aspect of cargo traffic rights on the Johannesburg-Salisbury route with Brand Fourie, agreeing that Affretair would be apportioned a weekly flight.[549] Probably in return for this concession, Bongo offered SAA to use Franceville airport as a technical stopover. These elements were consolidated in an agreement Air Trans Africa and SAA officials signed in June 1975.[550] Bongo used the services of Monier-Vinard, and later Daniël, to resolve any problem in this deal. When Affretair encountered difficulties landing in Johannesburg, Monier-Vinard contacted Julian Thomas at the Paris Embassy, who informed Secretary Fourie, who, in turn, intervened through Pi Pienaar.[551] The matter was quickly resolved and Affretair made its first landing in Johannesburg on 17 July.[552]

As South African Airways had fulfilled its obligations, its use of Franceville airport was next on the agenda. However, this airport could neither handle large aircraft nor always guarantee the availability of jet fuel.[553] Therefore, based on its interest in extending SAA's landing and overflying network in Africa, Pretoria offered Gabon a loan of $4.1 million "for a basic improvement" of Franceville airport to ensure adequate landing facilities for the large SAA aircraft used on the European routes. An additional $13.7-16.4 million loan for the "development" of Franceville airport and the construction of "a small project" at Libreville airport was promised.[554] In late July 1975, Daniël informed Brand Fourie and SAA Chief Executive Pienaar a SAA Boeing 747 would be able to land at Franceville airport in early August, but "discreetly, on a Sunday, and during dusk".[555] However, SAA soon lost interest in co-operating with Affretair and the Franceville option. In particular, Affretair, had concealed a similar arrangement with the French airline and SAA pool partner, UTA, while other pool partners complained about it undercutting cargo tariffs on the Europe-South Africa route.[556] SAA's attitude endangered Pretoria's package deal with Bongo, especially the important armament deliveries. As a result, the military put pressure on both the DFA and SAA to sustain the Safair landings, approaching Bongo's adviser, Daniël, who now intervened. On 17 August, he phoned Boyazoglu at the Paris Embassy and "appeared to be disillusioned" about SAA's waning interest in Franceville, according to the Agricultural Attaché. Feeling the situation could cause a complete breakdown in bilateral relations, Boyazoglu informed Secretary Fourie and Deputy Secretary Killen.[557] Not to further damage the Gabon-South African relationship, they retained the $4.1 million loan offer, the possibility of an additional $12.3 million loan, the weekly Affretair flight to Johannesburg and the Safair deal, while proposing the "principle of SAA eventually landing at Franceville, and with deviation rights at Libreville", the latter being the airline's main interest.[558] Satisfied with this, Bongo authorised his Economics and Finance Minister to sign the $4.1 million loan agreement for the improvement of Franceville airport with Pretoria in September 1975.[559] Its soft conditions comprised a 4 per cent interest rate and repayment in 40 half-yearly instalments from January 1977; Pik Botha later approved Bongo's request for a two-year moratorium.[560] The involvement of Roberts Construction in the planned construction of "aeroplane parking facilities and fuel storage tanks" at Franceville airport is doubtful, as the available DFA files up to 1979 contain no further related documentation. Julian Thomas confirmed the airport was not upgraded until he departed from OGAPROV in 1986.[561] Frans Swarts equally informed us SAA never used Franceville, while being granted emergency landing rights in Libreville.[562]

In assessing Pretoria's package deal, Bongo "had become master in the art of driving a wedge between each clan and to then profit from the conflict",[563] as Péan described it, linking Safair's landing rights which served the military to the DFA's interest in obtaining SAA landing rights and his own in Affretair and meat transport. Bongo kept his agreement with the military, while the offer of Franceville airport to SAA was only a token, the airline becoming something of a pawn. The Safair deliveries for Armscor's armament production contributed to the military's confidence in becoming involved in the Angolan war. Investigating this war is necessary as we have mentioned it regarding Pretoria's refusal to participate in two schemes related to the SMTF project in Zaire. Furthermore, it highlights the rivalries between BOSS and the military, with implications for Pretoria's subsequent foreign relations with Africa.

Angolan War

After Portugal's retreat from both Angola and Mozambique, the possibility of communist forces coming to power at South Africa's borders was imminent. In Mozambique, the Portuguese government recognised the Mozambique Liberation Front (FRELIMO) as the only liberation movement and its leader, Samora Machel, led the country to independence in June 1975. In contrast, three liberation movements were opposed over who was to govern an independent Angola, the western-oriented FNLA and UNITA fighting the communist-Marxist MPLA. South Africa's national intelligence and military exploited this, hoping to bring a Pretoria-friendly movement to power, BOSS siding with the FNLA, the military favouring UNITA. Having established contact with their respective leaders, Holden Roberto and Jonas Savimbi, in February 1975, General Constand Viljoen, Director General of Operations and Principal Staff Officer to the Chief of the SADF, and Hendrik van den Bergh, after Vorster's approval, delivered their covert assistance to them in June. In this context, Gleijeses suggests BOSS had co-ordinated its activities with the CIA.[564] Indeed, the CIA was predisposed to support both movements, but Congress "had no stomach for another intervention so soon" after Vietnam and banned all military assistance.[565] However, Kissinger circumvented this embargo by including Mobutu in his plans; the CIA arranged "for Zaire to supply armaments to the FNLA and then simply replenished Mobutu's stocks".[566] In August, the situation changed with Cuba sending military advisers to the MPLA.[567] In response, Vorster decided to deploy troops into Angola, bringing to a head the conflict between the military and BOSS, aided by the DFA, over Pretoria's southern African policy. Minister Muller had opposed sending troops, but given his weak profile, was "largely excluded from the decision". Van den Bergh also opposed troop deployment and, following upon the CIA's desires, favoured arms supplies to the FNLA through Zaire. However, the arguments of powerful Defence Minister Botha to deploy troops evidently convinced Vorster.[568]

The subsequent developments produced a shift in the power balance among the three state actors. In December 1975, when it became clear South Africa could not win the war, BOSS and foreign service officials – after three meetings with Vorster – managed to push through a decision for the phased troop withdrawal from January 1976;[569] the FNLA offensive had virtually collapsed, South African and UNITA troops were still fighting MPLA soldiers with heavy Cuban and Soviet support south of Luanda. The capital's capture was critical as the MPLA had declared Angola's independence in November 1975, installing itself as the government, but Washington undermined Pretoria's plans. In December, Congress banned further covert US military assistance, and the Ford Administration appealed to Pretoria not to attack Luanda[570] due to geo-political considerations. In particular, Washington and Beijing had undertaken successful steps towards Détente; following Kissinger's trips in October and November there, President Gerald Ford and Kissinger met with China's leader, Deng Xiaoping, in Beijing in December 1975.[571] The Angolan war was part of the talks.[572] China also channelled support to the FNLA through Zaire,[573] but Deng realised the apartheid regime's concurrent support for the FNLA jeopardised Beijing's idea of bolstering its global position by supporting African liberation movements. Gleijeses, using declassified documents from the US National Archives, reveals that Washington was prepared to withdraw from Angola, leaving South Africa behind, in order not to endanger the fruitful contact with Beijing.[574]

Pretoria's last troops withdrew in March 1976, with the bitter feeling of betrayal by the US administration. P.W. Botha expressed this very pointedly before Parliament in April 1978: "I know of only one occasion in recent years when we crossed a border and that was in the case of Angola when we did so with the approval and knowledge of the Americans. But they left us in the lurch".[575] While the military complained of unfair treatment, it was itself accused of destroying Pretoria's Détente. Strong criticism came from the DFA. For example, career foreign service officer Sole argued the military had "ruined" its ambitions in Africa.[576] However, our discussion of Pretoria's relations with the Ivory Coast, Liberia and Senegal revealed they suffered no setbacks due to involvement in the Angolan war. Rather, we suggest the military invasion conveniently served to cover up the DFA's failed attempt at instigating Dialogue and allowed the DFA to apportion blame onto the military for Pretoria's isolation. In any case, the military suffered the biggest losses within Vorster's Outward-Looking Policy. It established a fruitful cooperation with Bongo, but suffered a setback in the Nigerian Civil War, the result of which, Pretoria's Dialogue, was not even counted to its credit. Its humiliating withdrawal from Angola impinged on South Africa's domestic political arrangements. The Information Scandal served to camouflage the struggle between the Information Department and BOSS, represented by Mulder, and the military, led by P.W. Botha, over Vorster's succession. While a fight for the political control of South Africa, it was also about Pretoria's foreign relations with Africa. Thus, when the National Party caucus voted for P.W. Botha as the next Prime Minister, it chose a hard-line politician.

5

The Military in Command:
P.W. Botha, 1978-89

Securocrats

The military dominated P.W. Botha's foreign policy towards Africa beyond southern Africa throughout the 1980s, representing a *volte-face* in the rivalry between government departments during Vorster's premiership. In a continuation of the performance during his long incumbency as the Minister of Defence, and as evidenced by the Nigerian Civil War and the Angolan war involvement, P.W. Botha pursued a realist approach, considering power effective to achieve political ends. The military's primary concern was South Africa's security after its *cordon sanitaire* had ceased to exist. In interpreting these events, set against the Cold War background, it reasoned the Soviet Union would next conquer mineral-rich and strategically important South Africa in its quest for global communist domination. They would then provide assistance to the Angolan and Mozambican governments, which, in turn, supported the ANC, PAC and the South West Africa People's Organisation (SWAPO).[1] This appraisal went by the label 'Total Onslaught', as formulated by Defence Minister Malan.[2] The corresponding reaction became termed 'Total Strategy',[3] forcing the neighbours to succumb to Pretoria's hegemony. A central aspect was support for Angola's UNITA and the Mozambican National Resistance (RENAMO) to undermine their communist governments, an approach that became known as Destabilisation.[4] Southern Africa now effectively constituted the region with South Africa as the regional power.

The military acted in a geo-political framework, characterised by heightened Cold War tension, seeing and presenting "its role within the international system as the Southern African bulwark against communist aggression and on the side of the West in a 'war of proxy', between the United States and the former USSR [Union of Soviet Socialist Republics".[5] The stance against communism became important to appeal to Western governments for political support. This was especially successful with Republican US President Ronald Reagan (1981-88) and Conservative British Prime Minister Margaret Thatcher (1979-90), who both pursued a Pretoria-friendly policy. The one principal Western power taking an increasingly critical position was France, due mainly to the stance of Socialist President François Mitterrand (1981-95).[6] This constellation paralysed the Contact Group's work, established in 1977 to advance Namibia's independence and composed of France, Great Britain, the US, Canada and Germany.[7] Crucially, in 1981, US Assistant Secretary of State for African Affairs, Chester Crocker, introduced the Cuban Linkage, stipulating South Africa would only have to leave Namibia once the Cuban troops had withdrawn from Angola.[8] In a sense, an international protective shield had replaced South Africa's *cordon sanitaire*. The international backing for Pretoria began to crumble from the mid-1980s, when the Reagan and Thatcher policies attracted both domestic and external criticism.[9] While these international developments impacted on South Africa's policy in the region, we argue they equally influenced Pretoria's foreign relations with the countries beyond, as the military's undertakings there took place predominantly in the first half of the 1980s, feeling confident enough under the protective shield. In contrast, France tried to undermine Pretoria's activities. In 1985, Director Glenn Babb suggested: "France's actions (...) aimed at frustrating South Africa's attempts in expanding our relations with French-speaking African countries". Three years later, Paul Runge communicated to Babb from Cameroon: "France (...) has watered down our influence in certain neighbouring countries".[10]

Neither intending to establish diplomatic relations nor break the country's isolation, the military's core initiatives in the African countries of interest can be summarised into three categories: gaining access to the western Indian Ocean islands, armament sales and co-operation with Gabon's President Bongo. Given the military's powerful position, we first outline the relevance of other actors.

Assistants, Bystanders and Outsiders

The military significantly curtailed the DFA's influence, causing political scientist Jaster to describe its designated primary responsibility in this domain as "more formal than real".[11] Although the DFA files after 1979 were only partly accessible, they suggest its activities in Africa beyond the neighbourhood became subordinate to the military's regional security considerations, as seen in a report, dated May 1983, from Deputy Director-General Killen to Pik Botha: "It is clear that the RSA does not have the necessary financial means at its disposal to provide development assistance to the rest of Africa to approximately or to the same amount as the assistance provided to the neighbouring countries."[12] Crucially, there is no evidence of any major development/investment project. The DFA's only lever still to be applied was technical assistance, but only to supplement operations in countries of interest to the military. An important reason for this was quite likely the pitiful lack of success experienced through development/investment projects. Possibly with the exception of the Lilongwe Capital Project, none of the others had achieved a measurable political benefit for Pretoria. This also applied to Operation Bokassa in the C.A.R., introduced in Chapter 4 and whose outcome we now outline. Operation Bokassa entailed two main components, the construction of Hotel Intercontinental Bokassa and 500 prefabricated houses, both of which made little progress. While the multiplying costs[13] made the hotel project difficult, Bokassa's fall in September 1979 put an end to it. In December, Under-Secretary Loubser, Credit Guarantee's Bouwer, David Lewis from Cereal and General Exports and LTA's Spencer Whiting and Brian Melhuish travelled to Bangui to ascertain the situation. The Minister of Public Works and Housing informed them: "although his Government felt that the hotel was very necessary for Bangui (...), it was regarded as a prestige object and had to take lower rating in the urgent development needs of the country". Nonetheless, he asked Pretoria "to consider putting in money to complete the hotel". Yet, Bouwer noted "there was a general feeling in South Africa that we had reached the limit of the financial resources we could allocate".[14] Pretoria consequently withdrew and the Hotel Intercontinental Bokassa is a five-storey ruin that still forms part of the Bangui landscape.[15] Concerning the prefabricated houses, a C.A.R. mission had visited South Africa in January 1979, requesting another $1.5 million and a two and a half year moratorium to repay the previous IDC loans. Spencer Whiting explained the reasons for this unexpected situation to us: "The original contract (...) was the delivery of 500 prefabricated houses (...) to Pointe Noire. [The] C.A.R. would take delivery there and were responsible for transporting them to Bangui and for the erection at their cost. It turned out eventually that they were unable to fund this part".[16] In fact, some 300 houses had already been erected in Bangui, and this concerned the remaining 200. Credit Guarantee considered the additional loan to be "very high", requiring "consideration by the South African Ministers of Economic Affairs and Finance".[17] Eventually, the additional loan was granted to the Société Nationale d'Habitat (SNH), responsible for implementing the housing project, resulting in the construction of the remaining 200 houses, not in Bangui, but in Pointe Noire, "as CAR had again run out of funds".[18] Furthermore, the South African delegation visiting Bangui in December 1979 was informed Maurice Methot, instrumental in establishing contact with Pretoria in 1974 and now Director of the SNH, would soon leave this organisation, with Jan Bouwer reporting on the project's state of affairs: "the 200 houses which the Government had taken are being left unoccupied and are deteriorating, looters are stripping the houses and also stealing from the supplies for the 200 houses to be erected".[19]

In sum, Operation Bokassa was a failure, another venture for Pretoria resulting in considerable financial wastage without gaining any political advantage, as highlighted by the *Rand Daily Mail* after Bokassa's fall.[20] While Pik Botha promptly denied this report,[21] the foreign service corps probably had more difficulty to defend Operation Bokassa vis-à-vis the military. Therefore, this was proof positive such ventures should be curtailed, the military merely allowing the DFA to offer technical assistance within its own operations. Asked about resulting tensions with the military, Paul Runge and Neil van Heerden, both with the DFA in the 1980s, downplayed. Runge argued: "If it hadn't been for military support, we couldn't have run the aid programmes we had in Africa. Because we used their aircraft, we used their engineering services". Van Heerden added: "Were there any agreements, disagreements or conflicts? Not really. (…) Disagreement was mostly confined to not being informed. (...) P.W. [Botha], egged on by his colonels and his generals, was fundamentally opposed to the idea of having to tell any other minister what he does. So that tension was there, but I don't think it is a major conflict in terms of objectives.[22] However, in a brief to Pik Botha of May 1983, Deputy Director-General Killen clearly expresses ill-feelings about being sidelined by the military and the National Intelligence Service:

> It is an evidently unhealthy situation that the named departments concentrate on the furtherance of the tasks entrusted to the relevant department, i.e. information gathering, while paying little attention to the political aspects of government-to-government contacts which (...) is the responsibility of the Department of Foreign Affairs and Information. The result is a one-sided and half-hearted foreign policy towards the rest of Africa.[23]

Considering the other state actors formerly involved in Pretoria's foreign policy making, the Department of Information, reintegrated into the DFA in 1980, ceased to exist three years later. The Bureau for State Security became the Department of National Security in 1978 and the National Intelligence Service in 1980. To avoid confrontation with the military as in the past, P.W. Botha held this ministerial portfolio and made Niël Barnard NIS Director-General. In the interim period, the available sources reveal only one independent national intelligence activity, namely oil shipments from Nigeria to South Africa, the only hard evidence Pretoria attempted to obtain the precious resource from Africa's largest producer. In March 1979, the S.S. Jumbo Pioneer was prevented from loading oil in Nigeria and transporting it to its presumed destination of Cape Town. A month later, the Safmarine tanker S.T. Kulu[24] was seized by the Lagos authorities after it had been loaded with crude oil.[25] The Nigerian government presented the two cases as Pretoria's "meticulously planned high powered propaganda campaign" to sabotage its resolute anti-apartheid position.[26] While this may have been the result, the Department of National Security's main interest was to obtain oil. According to an intelligence document, verifying its involvement in the second case, the tanker Kulu had called at a Nigerian port on ten previous occasions.[27] The only other notable endeavour by national intelligence prior to 1980 relates to the attempted coup in the Seychelles in 1981, as we will discuss.

Now turning to the role of the non-state actors, the South Africa Foundation makes one significant appearance. Prior to leaving for Kenya in May 1979, President Hersov and Director General Sorour informed Pik Botha and Deputy Secretary von Hirschberg of their visit, further reflecting the rather co-operative interaction between the Foundation and the DFA. Apart from Pik Botha's complaint about Chris Barnard's contact with Njonjo (Chapter 4), he and von Hirschberg showed interest in obtaining their assistance in one particular area: "if the opportunity arose", they "might enquire" whether Pretoria would be allowed to be accredited to the UN Centre for Human Settlements (Habitat), "a convenient way of arranging a South African presence in Nairobi".[28] Regarding their own motivation to visit Kenya, Sorour wrote to us: "We listened to a debate in Parliament and called on a few friends and correspondents to renew contact and hear something about current affairs in that part of the world. (...) if I recall correctly, Mr Hersov was going there on business anyway in his own aircraft and we made use of the opportunity". Apart from that, they also "called on" Charles Njonjo, whom they "knew".[29] On their return, Hersov and Sorour briefed the Minister and von Hirschberg that Habitat "saw no reason why South Africa should not have a mission accredited", while the Kenyan Minister of Foreign Affairs had "refused to see them".[30] Regarding the Progressive Federal Party, Geldenhuys notes P.W. Botha strongly disliked its foreign affairs ambitions, certainly since Colin Eglin had called the military's invasion in Angola before Parliament in January 1976 "an error of political judgement".[31] In response, P.W. Botha bluntly told Eglin in Parliament in February 1979: "Don't you show your face in my office again".[32] When Frederik van Zyl Slabbert became the PFP leader in 1979, the situation improved for a short while, Geldenhuys further notes.[33] While the available DFA files contain no information on PFP undertakings in Africa, we know from our correspondence that Eglin's close link with Senegal continued even after Senghor's departure from the presidency in 1980.[34]

Having examined the minor roles of other state and non-state actors, we now analyse three aspects central to the military's considerations, following the order indicated above.

Western Indian Ocean

Chapter 4 explored the western Indian Ocean's geo-strategic importance during the 1970s. Control of the entire Indian Ocean gained in importance after the Soviet invasion of Afghanistan in 1979, raising Western fears over continued access to the oil reserves in the Persian Gulf, with the US increasing its military presence in the area.[35] Pretoria's military also showed an interest in the western Indian Ocean for strategic reasons. While it undertook endeavours on the Comoros, on Madagascar and on the Seychelles, Mauritius and Reunion are notable absentees, them being comparatively less important in strategic terms.

Comoros

The DFA had provided some technical assistance to the Comoros in the early 1970s and we suggested the military may have held an interest due to the island's strategic location. Pretoria's subsequent activities were determined by French mercenary Denard, who overthrew Ahmed Abdallah's government in 1975, terminating the DFA's technical assistance. Denard, alias Saïd Moustapha M'hadjou, intervened again in 1978 to reinstate Abdallah, although, Denard's Presidential Guard effectively ruled the island. Given the presumed contact with Denard during the Nigerian Civil War, the military grabbed the opportunity to establish a presence on the island with his help. The secondary literature suggests the Comoros served as a listening post to monitor shipping movements through the Mozambique Channel and to track ANC activities in Mozambique and Tanzania, as a springboard from which to support RENAMO in Mozambique and "as a transshipment centre for South African arms, bartered for Iraqi crude".[36] Given the unavailability of military sources and access to the DFA files to November 1980, we can only partly substantiate these proposals.

In April 1979, Deputy Secretary von Hirschberg noted "numerous" advantages of renewed contact, the island, for example, becoming "an important stopover for SAA and a tourist haven for South Africans".[37] According to his report after a mission there in December 1979, the military was greatly interested in the archipelago for "surveillance operations".[38] Consequently, both actors aimed at establishing themselves, with the military taking the lead. Those to have the first recorded meeting with Denard on the Comoros in October 1979 were three DMI officials, *inter alia* Colonel Martin Knoetze, and von Hirschberg.[39] Denard's memoirs indicate Knoetze acted as the DMI contact,[40] for example being present at Rae Killen's meeting with Denard on the island in September 1980, the latter proposing a petroleum products-against-crude oil exchange between the Comoros and South Africa.[41] Glenn Babb reported back to Killen: "The Department of Mineral and Energy Affairs says it has no objection to the arrangement and will grant permits to oil companies exporting the petroleum products to the Comoros. It is up to the Comoros and Mr Denard to arrange for the exchange via a registered South African oil company".[42] The Comoros therefore may have been used as a trans-shipment centre for oil, but the files contain no indication of weapons deals. However, the military had entered a mutually beneficial agreement with Denard; he allowed it to establish a "presence on the main island", while it partly financed the Presidential Guard.[43] Denard, reveals Pretoria's financial assistance for 1985 and 1987 was $2 and $2.9 million respectively.[44] The significance of this and other military involvement is reflected in Abdallah's visit to Pretoria in April 1983, meeting with Pik Botha, with whom he signed a secret Memorandum of Understanding.[45] Upon our enquiry, the DFA was not prepared to comment on its contents or even acknowledge its existence.[46] In addition, Magnus Malan went to the Comoros in December 1986.[47] The military appears satisfied with its activities, judging by the available evidence presented. The opposite is true for the foreign service officials.

As mentioned, their interest was a SAA stopover *en route* to the Far East and tourism. During von Hirschberg's discussion with Denard in October 1979, querying what they could offer in return, Denard replied "cattle breeding, agriculture, fishing and tourism".[48] To assess the situation, von Hirschberg went to the Comoros in December 1979, joined by, *inter alia*, Julian Thomas from the Department of Agricultural Technical Services and Southern Sun Director Peter Venison.[49] Finding the island's socio-economic situation deplorable, and due to Pretoria's focus on southern Africa, von Hirschberg concluded the cost for technical assistance with any meaningful result was beyond its capacity. Further, he stated the "absence of suitable beaches" ruled the Comoros "out as a tourist attraction". All that remained was von Hirschberg's proposal of a "small Ogaprov project", with costs for the first three years estimated at $450, 290 and 95 thousand. This seemed a worthwhile investment for Pretoria, because Abdallah was "keen to develop the cattle industry to reduce their dependency on imported meat if not entirely to eliminate imports".[50] Abdallah had probably learnt about OGAPROV through Denard; according to Péan, Gabon's President had "lent" the French mercenary in order for Abdallah to come to power.[51] Lacking additional primary sources, Denard's memoirs reveal the Sangani "pilot farm", administered by the Presidential Guard and comprising 600 hectares, was launched in 1983, costing Pretoria $140, 180 and 295 thousand in 1984, 1985 and 1987 respectively.[52]

Equally in the mid-1980s, the hotel firm World Leisure Group Ltd nevertheless undertook the development and management of two resort and casino properties; Kerzner had established this company on the British Virgin Islands in the Caribbean, a tax haven, and subsequently chaired it.[53] The hotels cost some $22.5 million, with the IDC providing and Credit Guarantee insuring the credit.[54] Kerzner's expansion strategy due to limited possibilities in South and southern Africa finds reflection in the parallel developments on Mauritius. Incorporated in 1983, and with Kerzner as its Director, Sun Resorts Ltd expanded on that island, taking over the management of an existing casino resort and a tourist hotel.[55] Although having obtained landing rights in 1975, and linked to this development, SAA flew South African tourists to the Comoros from 1983, an extension of the service to Blantyre.[56] In the following years, Sun Resorts increased the number of managed holiday resorts to five.[57]

Returning to the Comoros, the foreign affairs ministry became increasingly sceptical towards Abdallah; in 1982, it granted the island the right to open a Trade Mission with diplomatic status, without being accorded a reciprocal privilege and in 1985, on the occasion of the OAU's 40th Anniversary Meeting, Abdallah attacked Pretoria. Consequently, apparently also due to deteriorating relations with Denard, the DFA withdrew from the Sangani farm by July 1989. According to Denard, Glenn Babb argued "the time has passed of giving and aiding and to only receive slaps in return".[58]

Madagascar

In June 1979, the Chief of Staff: Intelligence and Broederbond member,[59] Pieter van der Westhuizen, summarised Pretoria's interest in this island: Madagascar did not currently pose a security threat to South Africa, but this could change, considering "the increasing activity of the USSR, Cuba and other East European countries on the island"; a final attempt should be made "to win the goodwill of the Ratsiraka Government by rendering economic assistance"; if this failed, Pretoria should support resistance movements, which would have to prepare a detailed plan of how they intend to overthrow the Government (...) as well as their requirements as far as the RSA is concerned".[60] There is no indication the military undertook any such activities, however, possibly because Madagascar was the only western Indian Ocean island maintaining "armed forces of any size".[61] It is possible such considerations influenced the military's involvement in an attempted coup on the Seychelles.

Seychelles

Albert René had ousted Mancham in 1977 with both Tanzania's and China's help. The files reveal subsequent attempts by exiled Seychelles groups to obtain support in overthrowing René, none of which seems to have found Pretoria's support.[62] Nonetheless, in November 1979, President René accused South African and French mercenaries of fomenting protests to overthrow him.[63] His concern may have been founded by knowledge about contact of DMI Brigadier Hamman and Colonel Knoetze with Denard around that time.[64] The subsequent developments and the activities of these two military intelligence officials relate to their interest in the western Indian Ocean, and their particular involvement in the attempted Seychelles coup in 1981. We can state three reasons why this was not executed by the French mercenary Denard, but by Mike Hoare, although he had seemingly remained inactive after his Congo engagement and had reached the age of 62 by 1981.[65] First, Hamman explained to us: "I was not in favour of Mike being involved and I asked Bob Denard on one of his visits to the RSA whether he would be interested in leading a group to the Seychelles. He was prepared to do it but the Seychelles group could not afford his services and he was never again involved as far as I know."[66] Second, having interviewed Denard in the early 1990s, Samantha Weinberg suggests one of Hoare's motives may have been competition: "One of the aspects that must have rankled most bitterly, was that his despised rival, Colonel Bob Denard, was still sitting happy and wealthy on the nearby, larger, more populous Comoros".[67] Third, the Durban area had become home to many former Rhodesians who had fought alongside Hoare in the Congo; nine of them accompanied him to the Seychelles.[68] Contact between the Seychelles exile movement and Hoare is therefore possible, prompting him to action. We now outline the events surrounding Hoare's attempted coup.

On 25 November 1981, Hoare and 42 of his men boarded an aircraft in Swaziland. On their arrival at Mahé airport, a customs officer discovered their weapons, leading to a brief gun-battle. Seeing the coup had failed, Hoare and most of his men hijacked a plane that had landed during a scheduled stopover. René, who had meanwhile been advised, gave permission for the plane to take off for South Africa.[69] Hoare's own account and the TRC report suggest Martin Dolinchek, a Durban-based Department of National Security agent, had approached Hoare in 1979, further indicating military intelligence then took over the coup plans after some infighting between the two units over respective areas of responsibility.[70] Daan Hamman indirectly substantiated our argument: "as I have it, NIS was going to do the operation and wanted the military to supply the arms and equipment; the plan was already in place. It was at this stage that it was decided, I do not know by whom, that MI was to facilitate Mike Hoare to execute the plan".[71] Thereafter, Dolincheck remained NIS liaison officer, while Hamman and Knoetze were charged with the DMI operation, providing the necessary armaments to Hoare.[72] While the extent, to which Pretoria's political leadership gave the instructions is unclear,[73] it tried to minimise the damage; the Progressive Federal Party proposal of establishing a commission of enquiry was blocked, P.W. Botha prevented any further investigation by invoking national security legislation, Hoare was only reluctantly put on trial after international pressure and Defence Minister Malan invoked a security law, barring Hoare and his men from giving evidence.[74]

Hoare was sentenced to ten years imprisonment for hijacking, defined as the unlawful interference in the smooth operation of civil aviation in terms of the Civil Aviation Offences Act (No 10 of 1972),[75] indicating Hoare either did not have the South African nationality and/or was not a member of the SADF or its Reserve, because only then did the 1957 Defence Act apply. However, Hoare was already released in 1985, as part of an amnesty declared by President Botha.[76] Of the more than 40 other men put to trial, only nine were convicted and given a minimum sentence of five years, but they were all released after six months. The six men who had remained behind after the coup plot were sentenced, four of them to death, but Pretoria paid a ransom of $3 million and all six prisoners could return to South Africa in July 1983.[77] This suggests Pretoria did not need to worry about international reaction, sufficing for it to only show initial severity toward the perpetrators to ease the situation. In particular, it quite likely had Cold War backing from Washington, which considered the Seychelles of strategic importance, having a satellite tracking station there since 1963.[78] In fact, the *New York Times* suggested Hoare had informed a CIA official of coup plans beforehand.[79]

The military's engagement in the western Indian Ocean aside, a central theme in its undertakings in Africa beyond the region was to sell surplus arms.

Armament Sales

Armscor had been created to counter the impact of the 1963 UN voluntary arms embargo. Given Pretoria's growing regional military involvement and the 1977 UN mandatory arms embargo, the need to develop ever more advanced weapons made it "one of the world's largest producers of armaments".[80] During the early 1980s, faced with "economic problems due to rising production costs, excess capacities, and a drop in domestic demand",[81] Armscor initiated arms exports, such as to Somalia and Sudan.

Somalia

During the mid-1970s, Somalia became a Cold War zone when President Siad Barre began to side with the Soviet Union, invading the Ogaden region in 1977. However, as Moscow subsequently switched its support to Ethiopia, Barre lost the war that crippled the country's economy, a situation exacerbated by the drought. In his search for assistance, Barre found US support from 1980/81[82] and approached South Africa. Mogadishu considered Pretoria a potential partner because of its own war against communist forces; during the stay of a South African delegation in Somalia in May 1984, the Somali Defence Minister declared the "RSA and Somalia have the same aggressors".[83] An important person in establishing contact between the two countries was Hassan Wehelie, a Somali citizen and director of two Johannesburg-based trade and finance companies.[84] Military intelligence was involved from the beginning, with Colonel Knoetze bringing Rae Killen together with Wehelie. During that meeting in Knoetze's presence in February 1980, Wehelie declared Mogadishu was particularly interested in obtaining arms.[85] However, Killen was cautious, arguing "the sale of arms (...) could jeopardise our relations with Kenya because of the troubled border situation".[86] Possibly due to this concern, in 1981, the State Security Council decided "Somalia was not a priority", while "the possibility for contact should be explored at a later point".[87] Wehelie again sought contact in 1982, when Somalia's border conflict with Kenya was resolved, meeting Babb in August.[88]

According to our correspondence with Babb, their meeting triggered "several visits, meetings with Barre and the Vice-President",[89] leading to Barre's invitation, in January 1984, to both Pik and P.W. Botha to visit Somalia. Pik Botha replied he could not come "at this stage" due to "pressing obligations at home and long-standing arrangements abroad",[90] but proposed sending a delegation, which took place in February. Reflecting Pretoria's interests, its members were Glenn Babb, Brigadier Hamman, Mike Kühn from NIS and Jacobus Gustavus 'Gus' Schoeman, SAA Chief Director for Flight Operations (1979-86). Talks were held with, *inter alia*, President Barre, First Vice-President and Defence Minister Mohamed Ali Samatar, the head of the Somali intelligence agency and the Deputy Minister of Water and Mineral Resources. The military's armament sale constituted the key theme in the discussions, linked to which became the SAA's ambition to obtain overflying and/or landing rights, as we will see. On their fringes, Kühn and his Somali counterpart "agreed to a meeting between a South African representative and their man in Rome to establish a permanent liaison system", while the Somali Deputy Minister expressed interest in joint economic ventures focusing on mineral resources.[91] Back in Pretoria, and probably to strengthen the DFA's bargaining position regarding overflying rights, Babb and Wehelie met separately with representatives from the mining companies Gold Fields (South Africa) and Anglo American in April to establish their position. The former explained its London branch was responsible for that part of Africa. The discussion with Anglo American's Deputy Technical Director (Mining), Theodore Pretorius, and its Metal Studies Consultant, Stefan Landsberg, was no cause for hope either. Pretorius elaborated "some members of the Board, because of experiences in Zaire and Zambia, were fundamentally opposed to ventures in Africa";[92] Anglo American abandoned the SMTF project in 1984 due to huge losses[93] and the Konkola Copper Mine in Zambia posed geological problems, according to information we obtained from Landsberg.[94] As a result, Anglo American never became involved in Somalia.[95]

Returning to Pretoria's main interest in contact with Mogadishu, Babb noted after his visit to Somalia: "Military collaboration is the most important facet of our future relations".[96] In December 1983, the State Security Council had approved $225,000 for humanitarian aid and $270,000 for supplying light weapons and ammunition, more than likely hoping to win Mogadishu as an armaments buyer. Armscor was the driving force due to its economic difficulties, interested in Somalia as a stepping stone to reach markets in the Middle East.[97] The military subsequently included the DFA officers to obtain a package deal, holding first discussions with a Somali delegation in South Africa in May 1984, comprising First Vice-President and Defence Minister Samatar, the Deputy Minister of Minerals and Water Resources, Somalia's Ambassador to Mozambique and the heads of its armed forces and national intelligence. They met with Defence Minister Malan, the Chief of Staff: Intelligence, Pieter van der Westhuizen, Brigadier Hamman, DFA Deputy Minister Louis Nel, Babb, SAA Chief Executive van der Veer, the NIS agents van der Merwe and Kemp and go-between Wehelie. Nel's presence is astonishing, as the DFA Deputy Minister, a post established in 1982, generally did not play a role in negotiations, but "concerned himself largely with liaison between Government and the media".[98] Queried about Nel's present and subsequent role, Babb explained to us: "the Africa policy was almost entirely driven by officials with politicians being the stalking horses for the objectives of expanding relations and having a figure to place in the meetings and carry things to Cabinet. Nel's tenure as Deputy Minister was always on a knife-edge and his political decisions were more dictated by his own precarious position than by a genuine interest in the Africa venture".[99]

Officials from Nimrod, the Armscor division promoting arms exports,[100] showed the Somali military representatives a range of weapons.[101] Thereafter, Samatar held talks with Magnus Malan and Louis Nel to find common ground on the package deal. Malan offered a $7 million loan to purchase weapons at the following conditions: $1.7 million, repayable over ten years, to finance a required 23 per cent deposit, plus $5.3 million at an interest rate of 10.5 per cent, to be repaid over five years. SAA promised an additional $7 million if it was granted overflying rights. However, as such rights for Somalia alone were worthless without similar agreement from both Sudan and Egypt, Samatar was requested to use his influence to secure them. In return, Samatar offered a base to station a DMI agent, extending the offer to the DFA and the NIS. Samatar also promised President Barre would use his friendship with his Egyptian counterpart to secure SAA overflying rights.[102] Yet, Mogadishu was not satisfied, requesting softer loan conditions. Pretoria's military subsequently juggled the figures, strongly supported by Deputy Minister Nel. The South Africans made a number of further visits to resolve the dilemma. In June 1984, Nel presented a new offer with a loan of $2.1 million for the deposit, at 5 per cent interest and repayable over ten years, a $350,000 grant from the SADF and the remaining of $4.55 million at 6 per cent interest, to be repaid over 12 years.[103] In July, Glenn Babb, Daan Hamman, a SAA representative and Wehelie visited Mogadishu. Their offer stood firm regarding the SADF grant, the loan at 5 per cent interest was now only repayable over 15 years, while the $4.55 million loan had to be repaid over eight years and at an interest rate of 10.25 per cent. SAA offered its $7 million at 6 per cent interest. However, Samatar expressed disappointment both at the amount and the repayment facilities.[104]

A few days later, go-between Wehelie again approached Babb, highlighting the SAA overflying rights and promising to make an attempt to obtain the same from both Egypt and Sudan, and claiming Barre would use his influence to promote the South African case in Africa and the Arab world.[105] On 23 August, Deputy Minister Nel met Killen and Babb, arguing the DFA should offer the $2.1 million loan at no interest as it would save SAA some $28 million for jet fuel per annum. However, Killen replied SAA's savings would only amount to $7 million, as overflying rights for Sudan were estimated at $21 million.[106] However, the package deal never materialised, the Somalis trying to reap all rewards whilst Pretoria would have had to settle for modest returns. Van der Veer revealed to us SAA never gained overflying rights[107] and Armscor did not deliver any arms. With hindsight, Glenn Babb argued: "[Barre] turned out to be more rapacious than we had imagined. Somalia would never have been in a position to be a client of ARMSCOR – it was almost a bankrupt state. (...) Repayment (...) might have come out of the overflight rights had we ever got to that point".[108]

Sudan

Much the same kind of relationship existed with Sudan, with maverick Francis Nzeribe establishing and maintaining the Pretoria-Khartoum liaison from 1984. Nigerian of origin, he had been Biafra's ambassador during the Nigerian Civil War and a member of Nigeria's Senate (1979-83), subsequently making his "wealth from oil, arms trade, banking, and insurance business".[109] Jimmy Kruger, the former Minister of Justice, Police and Prisons (1974-79), introduced Nzeribe to the DFA,[110] with Glenn Babb explaining to us: "Nzeribe (...) got in contact with Jimmy Kruger himself, latching on to the latter's unforgivable "Biko's death leaves me cold", imagining (...) that despite his political career's limbo he would still have influence with the boys in the Cabinet – and so it turned out to be: Kruger approached [Pik] Botha, only too pleased to be in the loop again, and convinced Botha that we should receive him".[111] However, the foreign service officers did not presently show an interest, maybe feeling his assistance was not required in achieving SAA overflying rights for Sudan. The middleman with Somalia, Wehelie had indicated President Barre would try to obtain these rights in both Sudan and Egypt, and in July 1984, the SAA's van der Veer wrote directly to the Director General of Sudan's Civil Aviation Department regarding landing rights,[112] supported by the DFA's simultaneous relief aid offer to Khartoum.[113] Yet, these activities did not bear any fruit and only gained in momentum in late 1984 when the military became involved. Nzeribe came to South Africa in November, holding talks with Pik Botha, Mineral and Energy

Affairs Minister Daniël 'Danie' Steyn and Defence Minister Malan. He asked Pik Botha for financial assistance to run a publishing house in Nigeria to produce magazines advocating a pro-Pretoria stance, offered Steyn oil supply from his refinery in Saudi Arabia and proposed Malan to act as a salesman for South African weapons.[114]

Pretoria now displayed serious interest in Nzeribe's propositions. Regarding the publishing house, and according to our correspondence with Babb, Pik Botha was "impressed" by Nzeribe's "swashbuckling style". However, the go-between "ran away with the funds" made available at a later stage,[115] and the project was abandoned.[116] SAA's ambitions enjoyed top priority according to Babb's February 1985 report: "The SSC has decided that all possibilities must be investigated to establish a way for SAA through Africa and the Government was even prepared to offer Somalia a considerable amount to convince Sudan to accord SAA overflying rights".[117] Equally important were the armament sales. When Nzeribe again held separate talks with Ministers Malan, Steyn and Pik Botha, the latter in Babb's presence, in Pretoria in February 1985, Malan declared "ARMSCOR (..) is looking to get rid of redundant stock". Nzeribe claimed to have a list of ten African countries interested in purchasing South African arms, adding he would "only sell to countries miles from RSA borders";[118] Armscor provided Nzeribe with a list of arms ready for sale.[119] In discussing the oil issue, Minister Steyn displayed little interest due to previously negative experiences with middlemen. In contrast, the talks with Minister Botha on SAA overflying rights and relief aid were productive;[120] in February 1985, the DFA provided $245,000 to combat the drought and promote the airline's cause.[121] However, after having met Nimeiri in March, Nzeribe reported to Rusty Evans at the London Embassy his president was "not overly impressed" by the amount of drought aid, suggesting "that as a further indication of serious intent on our part, one aircraft of equipment be donated in the near future".[122] Babb was then in contact with DMI Colonel Johan Pretorius, "who indicated that there is a strong possibility that the SADF could manage to provide a load of outdated stock", as he reported to Killen and Magnus Malan.[123] However, Pretoria's efforts in obtaining SAA overflying rights through armament deliveries and relief aid came to naught when Nimeiri was toppled in April.

In the following and final account of military engagement in the African countries of interest, it co-operated with Gabon's President, its long-standing friend from the Nigerian Civil War.

Co-operation with Gabon

Given Bongo's importance to both the military and the DFA, the latter holding a keen interest in SAA overflying rights, they assisted him on several occasions during the 1980s.

Chad

Chad experienced political instability through the 1970s. In 1975, Felix Malloum assassinated President Tombalbaye in a military coup. The new government was paralysed by a split between the Frolinat rebels Goukouni Oueddei and Hissène Habré, who co-operated with and opposed Libya respectively. Attempting to strengthen the government, President Malloum appointed Habré as Prime Minister. However, a power struggle erupted between them; in March 1979, Habré-loyal forces overthrew Malloum. Around the same time, Wadal Kamougué formed his own government in southern Chad. African mediation brought about a government of national unity, presided over by Oueddei, and with Habré and Kamougué as members, but fighting between the two arch-enemies resumed, with Oueddei, supported by Libya, forcing Habré out of N'Djamena in April 1980. In this situation, Bongo approached Pretoria for assistance.

According to the secondary literature, he supported Kamougoué's move in southern Chad to flex his muscle against Paris, due to disagreement over Mitterrand's policy towards Gabon.[124] Based on Rae Killen's report, Bongo's adviser, a certain Colonel Jules from the French intelligence agency SDECE,[125] came to South Africa in October to discuss Pretoria's assistance to Kamougoué,[126] meeting Pik Botha and DMI people. In November 1980, Brigadier Hamman and Agricultural Counsellor Jan Boyazoglu met Brand Fourie and Killen, briefly discussing "the matter of military aid to Col Kamougué"; the OGAPROV project in Gabon was the main issue.[127] Pik Botha had assured Colonel Jules they would provide "goods worth about R200 000 [$257,000]", comprising "medical equipment", as Boyazoglu recommended, and military supplies, as Killen wrote: "It would therefore seem that we should obtain a special allocation for R200 000 which would then enable us to include the weapons and ammunition". In addition, Pik Botha had obtained the support of Magnus Malan for this offer.[128] Yet, during the November meeting it became clear military intelligence, according to Hamman, "had no funds", causing Glenn Babb to note: "It therefore seems that we are to foot the bill".[129] In piecing these fragments of information together, the DFA apparently tried to impress Bongo by supplying Kamougué with medical supplies, believing the military would be interested in sending arms and covering the delivery costs. The primary sources do not record what was delivered and who paid and Daan Hamman's correspondence with us was rather vague: "As far as I recall medical supplies were delivered".[130] It is certain, however, that the material was supplied at Bongo's request, as Babb noted in June 1981: "The original decision to help Col Kamougué was taken in order to satisfy Pres. Bongo".[131] Yet, towards mid-1981, Pretoria became sceptical towards Kamougué, who was now striving towards the fully-fledged secession of southern Chad. Babb recommended the cessation of support, arguing that to "become further emeshed in an intractable situation beyond the requirements of our relations with Gabon, would not bring any real benefit to us".[132] We could not establish the subsequent developments; the relevant files contain no further documents and Babb did not comment when queried.

In 1982, the military took a definite stance and, following Bongo's request, provided assistance to Chad. By then, the situation was different. In June 1982, Habré had forced Libyan-supported Oueddei to withdraw to the north, while Kamougué had fled the country. To avert a further deterioration of the situation, the OAU deployed a peacekeeping operation. In this context, and with the DFA's knowledge, French mercenary Denard, alias Rémy Destrieux, provided seven officers to facilitate Habré's accession to power.[133] Furthermore, Chad became a Cold War hot spot; under President Reagan, the CIA had supported Habré since 1981 to overthrow Oueddei and to curb Libya's influence.[134] Concern over the communist influence was an important reason for Pretoria to support Habré, illustrated by Pik Botha's letter to him in October 1982: "South Africa and Chad themselves are facing common enemies and have mutual interests therefore to defend".[135] A report from Africa Director Jan Francois 'Frans' Wentzel and Deputy Director-General Killen to Babb lists additional factors: the "good relations" between Habré and Bongo; "the possibility of exchanging intelligence with Chad interests the SADF in view of its proximity to Libya"; discovery of oil in the north of Chad; and Habré's "friendship with Sudan", where Pretoria attempted to obtain SAA overflying rights. Given these considerations, they recommended consultation "with the SADF on the possibility of sending a message to Chad to form a channel of communication and to find grounds for mutual understanding".[136] Having assisted Habré in assuming power, having been Bongo's adviser since 1971 and given his co-operation with Pretoria on the Comoros from 1979, Bob Denard, alias Gilbert Bourgeaud,[137] "offered to take to Mr Habré a letter from us (...) in which we (...) express interest in future contact", as Wentzel and Killen noted in June 1982. Subsequently, military intelligence took the initiative, because of their organisational means and reflecting Armscor's interest of selling surplus weaponry, indicated in the same brief.[138] It appears Denard took the communication to Habré, who requested arms supplies in December.[139] Brigadier Hamman and Colonel Jurie Bosch, together with the requisite ammunition, flew to N'Djamena in February 1983, discussing the mission with Bongo's security advisers during a stopover in Libreville.[140] Hamman substantiated our assumption that Bongo was a crucial factor in the military's decision to support Habré[141] with some 15 tons of ammunition, according to Denard.[142] DMI had invited Babb to join them, as the plane also contained equipment for the OGAPROV project, but: "After consultation with Mr Killen, Col Bosch was informed that I would not be accompanying the flight".[143] The military went into areas the DFA officers could not, because of their diplomatic rules. While Killen applied them strictly, Babb wanted to go, otherwise he would not have bothered discussing the matter with his superior.

Equatorial Guinea

Bongo sought renewed co-operation with the military over Equatorial Guinea, cementing their close contact. Pretoria's military, for its part, appears to have been interested in establishing a listening post there. The first trace of a military interest is recorded in a discussion between Glenn Babb and Colonel Bosch in June 1982. Babb reported Bosch's "extreme interest. He had had the intention of going there himself, since from a logistical point of view and also because of the SADF's relations with Gabon, the SADF would like to establish a working relationship with that country".[144] This ambition received impetus when Colonel Philippe Cauvin, Bongo's Security Adviser, visited South Africa in November 1983. In a report on his meeting with Cauvin, Rae Killen stated: "President Bongo has given special instructions to Col. Cauvin to approach the Hon. Minister of Foreign Affairs and Information concerning Equatorial Guinea". Bongo was "particularly anxious that we involve ourselves in EG", because of his friendship with President Obiang and the country's Fang population, with whom he was "attempting to form an alliance in view of the large Fang population in Gabon", and because of their common concern over the Soviet role in the area.[145] Bongo's appeal was again successful; in December 1983, a South African delegation visited Equatorial Guinea, the last record of contact we could obtain from the files. Babb led this mission, which consisted of a NIS agent, an official each from the Agriculture and the Fisheries department and a representative from the state-owned petroleum company, Soekor.[146] While their meeting with Teodoro Obiang is recorded, the content of their discussions is not. However, secondary sources reveal South Africa became involved in a cattle-breeding project from 1986, the foundation for which was probably laid in those days.

The project was situated on Bioko island, site of the capital Malabo. It began with some 200 cattle and 40 sheep and still existed in 1990, albeit without South African participation.[147] Interviewed in 1999, Neil van Heerden, then Deputy Director-General, commented: "It was really a project that you could be excited about beyond description".[148] Yet, given the island's short distance of some 200 km to Nigeria, and especially the oil-rich Bight of Biafra, Nigerian authors and the ANC claimed Pretoria pursued military-strategic objectives.[149] The Lagos government concluded a non-aggression pact with President Obiang in 1987 and Foreign Affairs Minister Ike Nwachukwu described the South African presence as a "threat" to Nigeria's security.[150] Queried about these allegations, van Heerden countered the "prime motivation" for the project had been "a political one",[151] a claim backed by DFA reports of March and September

1987 from the Nigeria files, providing no indication of military activity.[152] Yet, given Pretoria's military and intelligence activities in other African countries beyond the region and the above-mentioned interest displayed by both the NIS and the SADF, it would not surprise if the project was used for intelligence gathering purposes. Thus, in 1987 Pretoria concluded a contract with Malabo "for the construction of a satellite tracking station", according to a reliable secondary source.[153] While we cannot conclusively state Pretoria's true intentions, Nigerian pressure on Obiang resulted in South Africa's withdrawal from Equatorial Guinea by mid-1988.[154]

These case studies suggest Bongo, probably apart from Malawi's Banda, was Pretoria's most constant partner in Africa. While the military was seemingly satisfied with its contact, the DFA did not achieve a single aim. Glenn Babb described the situation in retrospect: "Bongo, being what he was, was only interested in using us as an instrument to help his pals in the region".[155] In addition, SAA never obtained overflying rights from Chad, thus preventing it from establishing an air corridor across Africa.[156] In any case, Pretoria's illegal occupation of Namibia and the domestic apartheid policy still prevented it from joining the international community as a respected member. However, in the context of the rapprochement between Washington and Moscow after 1986, the two superpowers aimed at resolving the S.W.A./Namibia issue.

End of Cold War

The waning of the Cold War crucially impacted on South Africa[157] and its foreign relations with Africa. Reagan and his Soviet counterpart, Mikhail Gorbachev, acknowledged superpower involvement in regional conflicts inhibited the improvement of their bilateral relations. Crucially, the resolution of the conflicts in southern Africa was among the topics discussed by the two leaders at the Washington Summit in 1987.[158] An important stumbling block was Pretoria's illegal occupation of Namibia, tied to the Cuban troop withdrawal from Angola through the Cuban Linkage, introduced by Chester Crocker in 1981. Reflecting the new superpower relationship, the deadlocked situation began to improve; the Assistant Secretary of State for African Affairs now mediated between Angola, Cuba and South Africa.[159] With the demise of the Cold War, the military's predominance in Pretoria's foreign policy making declined, while the DFA took the lead in the negotiations; Namibia's eventual independence was primarily its achievement.[160] These talks resulted in the Namibia Accords, signed by the three parties at the UN Headquarters in New York on 22 December 1988. While Havana agreed to withdraw its troops from Angola, Pretoria committed itself to applying Security Council Resolution 435 of 1978, allowing the UN to organise and monitor the country's independence. After the elections in November 1989, the independence celebrations took place in March 1990.[161] This significantly improved Pretoria's foreign relations with African countries beyond the region. Geldenhuys aptly argues South Africa had taken "a giant step towards removing a major source of conflict with the international community, black African states in particular",[162] for example the Congolese Republic. While access to the Congolese file was restricted to 1979, Crocker's autobiography reveals President Sassou Nguesso arranged meetings between himself and the leaders of Gabon, the Ivory Coast and Zaire, all of whom supported the pro-Western UNITA in Angola.[163] Significantly, on 13 December, the relevant parties concluded the Brazzaville Protocol in the Congolese capital that led to the signing of the Namibia Accords.[164] Linked to these developments, P.W. Botha had officially met with Mobutu in Zaire on 1 October and with Houphouët-Boigny in the Ivory Coast two weeks later.[165] In addition, Pretoria's Ambassador Albert Warnich was stationed in the Ivorian capital from September 1988,[166] and Ambassador Hermann Hanekom headed the under-cover Liaison Office in Kinshasa from September 1989,[167] concurrently being accredited to the Congolese Republic.

Parallel to these international and continental developments, South Africa's domestic situation had changed considerably. Most notably, the banned African National Congress had risen to such a prominent position that Pretoria could no longer ignore it; during 1987, the ANC entered into an alliance with the country's largest trade union, the Congress of South African Trade Unions (COSATU), and the United Democratic Front (UDF), a powerful coalition of civil society groups.[168] Building on this, the ANC gained regional, continental and eventually international acceptance as South Africa's leading liberation movement.[169] Acknowledging this situation, a number of rapprochement meetings took place from 1985 to 1990 between ANC representatives, South African big business and the Afrikaner intelligentsia.[170] Two highly significant events took place in Zambia (September 1985) and Senegal (July 1987). Regarding the former, three top Anglo American leaders, Chairman Gavin Relly and Directors Tony Bloom and Zacharias 'Zach' de Beer, joined by South Africa Foundation Director General Peter Sorour, met ANC President Oliver Tambo and other leading figures from the ANC and its other partner, the South African Communist Party (SACP). Frederik van Zyl Slabbert was the initiator of the other meeting, at which 17 ANC representatives, among them Thabo Mbeki, held discussions with 61 Afrikaner intellectuals. Slabbert had resigned as the Progressive Federal Party's leader and as the party's Member of Parliament in 1986. He subsequently co-founded and directed the Institute for a Democratic Alternative for South Africa through which he organised the Dakar meeting.[171] Senegal was chosen not because of the links Colin Eglin had established during his party leadership.[172] The above encounters were a diplomatic coup for the ANC, as we have concluded elsewhere: "they reflected the status the ANC had achieved among important segments of South Africa's white society. There can be little doubt that this contributed to Pretoria's realisation that this liberation movement could no longer be ignored and wished away".[173]

The domestic, regional and international changes now outlined required policies other than the use of military force to resolve South Africa's problems. Consequently, and his deteriorating health aside, P.W. Botha was no longer considered fit to rule the country. In September 1989, he was succeeded by F.W. de Klerk, with considerable consequences for both South Africa's domestic situation and external relations.

6

New Diplomacy:
F.W. de Klerk, 1989-94

Preliminaries

F.W. de Klerk brought a very different political style to Pretoria, breaking fundamentally with the apartheid ideology of his National Party. In the domestic arena, he presented himself as the reformer, symbolised by his announcement, in February 1990, of the release of Nelson Mandela after 27 years of imprisonment. The subsequent negotiations between the government and the ANC form the background to this chapter, but our main concern is to show how they related to Pretoria's foreign relations with the African states beyond the region. In doing so, we argue the negotiations were a tactical power play, each group trying to manage the balance of power to its advantage to achieve a particular outcome.[1] In this context, African diplomatic support became vital, especially following the Boipatong massacre in June 1992. With this premise, we first explore the goals of both sets of actors at the outset of the talks, followed by an investigation into the key negotiation issues, the relevance of the African continental dimension therein and developments post-Boipatong.

New Diplomacy

De Klerk's unexpected reforms notwithstanding, it was never his intention to simply hand over political power to the country's majority. As late as August 1991, he vehemently rejected "one man, one vote" elections.[2] While it was not de Klerk's ambition to retain apartheid, his negotiation strategy was best characterised as follows: "It is to maintain the initiative so that Pretoria can force previously banned organisations to compromise on a whole range of issues that, in turn, will enable the government to realise its goal of entrenching a constitution that will guarantee the protection of minority or group rights".[3] To strengthen the government's bargaining position, de Klerk's foreign policy aimed at ending South Africa's international isolation, him making overseas visits to explain the reform initiatives so that sanctions would be lifted. De Klerk's autobiography suggests he considered the amelioration of relations with Africa as crucial: "We also had to break out of our international isolation, and in particular improve our relations with our immediate neighbours in southern Africa and in the continent as a whole. (...) It was for this reason that my first visits as state president were to countries in Africa".[4] In these endeavours, de Klerk benefited from P.W. Botha's contacts; as Acting State President (15 August-20 September), he with met Mobutu in Zaire on 25 August,[5] while his first presidential visit abroad took him to the Ivory Coast in December 1989, meeting with Houphouët-Boigny.[6]

In his foreign policy making, de Klerk took the advice of the foreign service officials, which steadily re-emerged from their subordinate position under P.W. Botha, illustrated by the co-operation with the French mercenary Denard on the Comoros. While the DFA had halted its involvement in the Sangani farm project by July 1989, financial and military support for Denard's Presidential Guard continued. Then, on 26 November, President Abdallah was assassinated under unresolved circumstances, although Denard was a suspect, bringing to a head the rivalry between the DFA and the military over whether or not to maintain a presence on the Comoros. The former's view prevailed and, on 4 December, Pretoria announced all assistance would cease. Once Paris and Pretoria had pressured Denard to withdraw from the island, and mirroring his close links with Pretoria's military, a Safair aircraft flew Denard and 25 members of his Presidential Guard to South Africa, where he was granted temporary residence rights until he left for France in 1993.[7]

Minister Pik Botha and his confidant, Director-General van Heerden, played important roles. In 1989, van Heerden formulated the principles of foreign relations with Africa that became known as 'New Diplomacy', reflecting South Africa's aspiration to be both part of Africa and a regional power with substantial development capacity, while also attaching great importance to trade and commerce.[8] Its application was facilitated by the end of the Cold War, which had resulted in Africa's economic and political marginalisation.[9] This required closer economic co-operation, making South Africa as the most economically sound African country an attractive partner. A letter sent to 30 African heads of state and government on 23 May 1991, within days of the OAU Summit in Abuja, Nigeria, verifies de Klerk specifically referred to these developments to appeal to African leaders:

> Abuja 91, Mr President, will take place against a backdrop of dramatic changes in the international environment, of shifts in economic patterns and in power balances which provide both challenges and opportunities for our Continent. The emergence of a unified European market in 1992, coupled with changes in Eastern and Central Europe

and in the USSR, represent potential threats to continued economic investment and involvement in Africa by the industrialised countries. There is a school of thought that Africa runs the risk of being marginalised. We in Africa should urgently consider steps to counter this tendency. (...) We believe that it has become imperative that cooperation in all fields of development be established to safeguard and advance our common interests.[10]

Technical expertise aside, South Africa's manufactured goods were low in price compared to international products and suitable for African conditions.[11] As a result, trade figures in Appendixes B and C show significantly increased economic interaction. South African export experienced a strong upswing and we will see the prospering trade relations became a lever to establish political contact.

Compared to Pretoria's position at the outset of the negotiations, the ANC conducted a diplomacy of liberation during the exile period,[12] but clearly did not have the political experience of a government. Furthermore, the ANC was relatively unprepared for de Klerk's announcements in 1990 and the subsequent negotiations. Its guiding document was the Discussion Paper on the Issue of Negotiations from June 1989.[13] It stipulated five conditions – unconditional release of all political prisoners and detainees; lifting of bans and restrictions on all proscribed and restricted organisations and persons; troop removal from the townships; end the state of emergency, political trials and political executions – that had to be met before substantial negotiations could begin. The ANC had Africa's diplomatic support, a crucial advantage over the government. In August 1989, the OAU ad hoc Committee on Southern Africa had endorsed its position paper in Zimbabwe, the document therefore becoming known as Harare Declaration, with the UN's African Group ensuring the General Assembly endorsed it in December.[14]

Negotiations

The negotiations after 1990 can be divided into three phases, the 'Talks about Talks' until October 1991, the Convention for a Democratic South Africa (CODESA) until May 1992 and the Multiparty Negotiation Process until December 1993. Following our earlier argument, the period until the Boipatong massacre constitutes the focus, because Pretoria's foreign relations with the African countries beyond the region were of crucial significance only until then. The complex negotiations are analysed elsewhere,[15] with a relatively brief survey sufficing for our purposes.

In the first phase, de Klerk outmanoeuvred the ANC, pressuring the movement into making substantial compromises, particularly the suspension of the symbolically important armed struggle. At the same time, Pretoria's negotiators had only fully implemented one of the Harare Declaration demands, namely the lifting of bans and restrictions on all proscribed and restricted organisations and persons. Six months after Mandela's release and unbanning the ANC, de Klerk could show the white electorate he had not surrendered any political power, while the ANC could not present its followers with any significant achievements. At its National Consultative Conference in December 1990, the grass-roots level expressed frustration over the lack of progress and the allied COSATU and SACP argued mass action had been neglected. Parallel to these developments, the international dimension was part of the power play. De Klerk travelled to 30 countries to end South Africa's international isolation, while Mandela paid visits to 49 countries to maintain anti-apartheid sanctions (Tables 3-4). We examine their journeys to African countries later. For the moment it suffices to note de Klerk's campaign was successful initially. His reforms were welcomed during his visits to European capitals and Washington during 1990. In anticipation of later developments, the European Community lifted its sanctions in April 1991, the US Congress abolished the 1986 sanctions in July and Japan removed its anti-apartheid measures by October 1991.[16]

The question of culpability for the domestic violence, with thousands of black South Africans being killed, was a major factor impacting on the negotiations. Initially, de Klerk retained the status as the "man of integrity", as Mandela described him on the day of his release from prison.[17] During the second half of 1990, however, the ANC started accusing him of pursuing a double agenda, negotiating while simultaneously fomenting the violence to weaken the ANC and co-operating with Inkatha leader and ANC rival Buthelezi in this. In April 1991, the ANC leadership addressed an open letter to de Klerk, demanding specific action against the violence and stating: "The government's inaction calls into serious question its true intentions and sincerity regarding the entire peace process and the democratization of South Africa".[18] In May, the ANC-COSATU-SACP alliance concluded "de Klerk has not demonstrated any willingness to end the violence",[19] feeling justified to break off the negotiations. In effect, the ANC had seized the initiative for the first time since 1990. At its National Conference in July, it also managed to close its internal ranks and to smooth over differences within the alliance. Finally, on 19 July, 'Inkathagate' made international headlines. According to documents published simultaneously in *The Weekly Mail* and its British partner, *The Guardian*, Pretoria had supported Inkatha both financially and with weapons after February 1990, causing de Klerk's international prestige to plummet. As a result, the National Peace Accord, concluded between the government and the ANC in September 1991, dealt with the role of the security forces, thus forcing Pretoria to acknowledge partial responsibility for the violence. On the whole, a more equal bargaining power existed when the negotiations resumed.[20]

Table 3: De Klerk's Journeys Abroad (1990 – June 1992)[21]

	May	France, Greece, Portugal, Italy, Belgium, Great Britain, Germany, Switzerland, Spain
1990	August	Madagascar
	September	United States
	October	Portugal, Great Britain / Luxembourg, Netherlands, Senegal
	April	Denmark, Great Britain
1991	June	Kenya
	November	Israel, Taiwan
	February	France, Hungary, Czechoslovakia, Poland
1992	April	Nigeria
	June	Russia, Japan, Singapore / Spain

Table 4: Mandela's Journeys Abroad (1990 – June 1992)[21]

	March	Tanzania
	May	Algeria, Angola, Egypt, Nigeria, Zimbabwe
	June-July	Geneva (UN), Germany, Luxembourg, Italy, Vatican, Netherlands, Canada, United States, Ireland, Great Britain,
1990		Uganda, Ethiopia, Kenya, Mozambique
	September	Uganda
	October	Kenya
	October-	India, Indonesia, Australia, Japan, Malaysia, Brunei,
	November	Great Britain, France
	February	Gabon
	May	Nigeria (OAU Conference of Ministers)
1991	June	Belgium
	July-August	Spain, Jamaica, Cuba, Mexico, Venezuela, Brazil
	November	Ghana, Ivory Coast
	December	United States
	January	Tunisia, Libya, Morocco
1992	February	France, Denmark
	May	Norway
	June	Malawi

The Convention for a Democratic South Africa I ushered in substantial negotiations on South Africa's political future, the bargaining taking place in five Working Groups. The success of the entire process depended on the progress made in Working Group 2, which defined the new constitution and therefore determined post-apartheid political arrangements. Current polls indicated the ANC would achieve majority rule in "one man, one vote" elections, allowing it to shape South Africa's future to its liking. To ensure some sort of say for the whites, de Klerk's negotiators attempted to restrict the ANC's post-apartheid influence, pushing for the fragmentation of power at the legislative and executive levels.[22] In May 1992, when CODESA II convened, all but Working Group 2 had successfully concluded their discussions. The government "still wanted a slow transition to power sharing", whereas the ANC "still wanted a quick majority rule".[23] At this moment, de Klerk again held a strong bargaining position; on 17 March, the white electorate had endorsed his reform process in a referendum he had announced in February. The magazine *SouthScan* commented, by "manufacturing a contest against the advocates of continued white domination, de Klerk's image-makers (...) were able to pose de Klerk as the champion of the other side".[24] De Klerk was applauded internationally for his commitment,[25] while the ANC was on the losing end again; major apartheid laws had been abolished, but for the ANC, the "book of apartheid" was not yet closed, no matter how successfully Pretoria reassured the international community to the contrary.[26]

In this politically tense situation, 40 people lost their lives in the Boipatong township on the night of 17/18 June. The massacre made international front-page news, unanimously presenting Pretoria as the main culprit. On 21 June, in an address to the Boipatong residents, Mandela announced he would request a special UN Security Council meeting;[27] two days later, the ANC leadership broke off the negotiations with Pretoria. The ANC's decision to call upon the UN was an ideal opportunity to regain international support; political commentator Stanley Uys aptly argued: "If evidence is produced to substantiate the ANC's repeated allegations of government "complicity" in the violence, international opinion will turn against President de Klerk".[28] The Boipatong massacre provided the ANC with such 'evidence', terming it solid proof of its allegation Pretoria deliberately fuelled the violence to weaken the movement.[29]

Prior to discussing the ensuing developments, we examine the African continental dimension, a pivotal factor at this particular moment.

Outreach into Africa

De Klerk's and Mandela's visits abroad reveal that both considered African diplomatic support a high priority. We presently focus on Pretoria's endeavours; the next section examines the ANC's efforts. The government pursued a two-pronged and sometimes overlapping Africa strategy; securing the support of the Organisation of African Unity, our focus later, and broadening the contact network via economic interaction, our present subject. Given Africa's increasing marginalisation from the late 1980s, Pretoria sought to engage with the continent through trade and other economic exchange, hoping this would result in political contact. We first summarise such interaction with those countries where we had to rely on secondary sources.

Economic Co-operation

In June 1990, Malawi government officials came to Pretoria to sign a trade agreement, replacing the one dating from 1967.[30] In August, "accompanied by a retinue of businessmen", de Klerk flew to Madagascar to conclude an air transport agreement and probably hold economic talks. Another agreement followed in April 1991, laying the foundation for the establishment of a South African Trade Mission in Antananarivo.[31] In December 1990, Dawid Jacobus 'Dawie' de Villiers, Minister of Mineral and Energy Affairs and Public Enterprises, led a delegation to the Ivory Coast, discussing political reforms and bilateral relations with Houphouët-Boigny.[32] In January 1991, seven businessmen went to the Congolese Republic,[33] with Hermann Hanekom, Ambassador in Kinshasa and accredited to neighbouring Brazzaville, acting as a facilitator, according to our correspondence.[34] The Shipping Research Bureau, established in 1980 to monitor the oil sanctions against South Africa, suggests technical assistance for oil exploration was discussed. The same source proposes the supply of oil featured in the talks Minister de Villiers while in Gabon in February 1991.[35] In November 1990, the DFA confirmed it had established a "representation of interests" in Togo.[36] Possibly as a result, three Togolese Ministers came to South Africa in March 1991, meeting Dawie de Villiers, evidently to discuss economic matters, and inviting interested parties, singling out the South African Foreign Trade Organisation, to come to Togo. In April 1991, Chief Director Christoffel 'Christo' Prins led a government delegation to Sao Tome e Principe, discussing SAA landing rights, tourism and agriculture.[37] A particularly important country within Pretoria's plan to approach African countries through economic interaction was Kenya, which Minister Pik Botha visited in November 1990. Undoubtedly as a result of his meeting with arap Moi, SAA was granted a weekly flight to Nairobi from December.[38] In June 1991, de Klerk visited Kenya, presenting arap Moi his vision of four African economic regions formed around Egypt, Nigeria, Kenya and South Africa to stimulate African economic growth.[39] Pretoria's contact with this heavyweight in African affairs intensified, climaxing with arap Moi's official one-day visit to Pretoria in June 1992.[40]

The above information was derived from secondary sources, with little indication regarding political implications of economic interaction. In contrast, the following case studies are based on DFA documents, revealing a connection between economic and political exchange.

Sudan and Cameroon

A meeting between Deputy Director-General Evans and President Omar Bashir during Namibia's independence celebration prompted Pretoria's present contact with Khartoum. In January 1991, Evans visited Khartoum, with subsequent contact focussing on military assistance, SAA overflying rights and economic interaction.[41] In February, probably linked to Evans' stay, SAA Chief Executive van der Veer requested landing rights,[42] necessary to close the Zaire-Sudan-Egypt air corridor, after

Egypt and Zaire had granted these rights by 1990.[43] In his letter of August to Bashir, de Klerk welcomed Khartoum's decision to grant the overflying rights;[44] which cost Pretoria $188,400 per month.[45] An important person in this context, and indicating the military dimension of the contact, was Elfatih Erwa, Minister of State in the Presidency, who met Pik Botha and van der Veer in April 1991.[46]

Three almost parallel reciprocal visits of South African and Sudanese delegations followed. From 18 to 22 September, the Minister of Energy Affairs and Natural Resources, Bashir's Economic Adviser and Sudan Airways' Deputy General Manager held meetings with representatives from the parastatal oil companies Sasol and Soekor, SAA, the mining firm Genmin and the petroleum company Engen.[47] Following de Klerk's announcement to Bashir to this effect,[48] a mission went to Sudan on 16/17 September, led by Rusty Evans and composed of officials from SAA and Engen. Only a few days later, representatives from arms producer Armscor's subsidiary Atlas Aircraft,[49] the National Intelligence Service, SAA, the South African Air Force and Spoornet, the former South African Railways, visited Sudan.[50] Soekor and Engen showed "a great deal of interest" in exploring the potentially rich southern oil fields, according to Deputy Director-General Auret's correspondence with Minister Erwa. Later briefs, however, suggest no investment was forthcoming.[51] Spoornet's intention to "upgrade the existing railway network in Sudan" was discussed with Bashir's Economic Adviser in South Africa in February 1992, but this idea did not materialise due to a lack of finances. Solely Atlas Aircraft's involvement produced a concrete result, providing expertise to restore ten helicopters and to upgrade the airforce base in Khartoum, cross-financed from SAA's overflying rights fees.[52] In contrast to this situation, Pretoria's economic interaction with Cameroon became linked to a diplomatic goal.

Pretoria was approached for assistance in a hydroelectric project, aimed at providing electricity for the city of Douala and to run an aluminium-from-bauxite smelter. The German company Siemens was in charge of the engineering, while a Bavarian bank provided the financing.[53] On 18 January 1991, the Director-General of Siemens' South Africa representation wrote to de Klerk: "It would be appreciated if a participation of your government, together with the banks of your country, your industrialists and your advanced technology, could assist in the carrying out of this project".[54] Cameroon's President Paul Biya had addressed a parallel request to the same effect to de Klerk, who welcomed the proposal "for I firmly believe that there is a growing need for closer cooperation between African countries as regards their economic development".[55] The relatively thin DFA files document two meetings between representatives of the Departments of Trade and Industry, Foreign Affairs and Finance, the electricity parastatal Eskom, Credit Guarantee, Siemens and the Bavarian bank in mid-1991 to assess the project's feasibility.[56] However, the South

Africans preferred not to get involved considering the high financial risk. According to a letter from the Eskom Engineering Proposal Manager to the Bavarian bank in August, the CGIC was not "prepared to guarantee the financing and would not support a recommendation for underwriting to the Government".[57] This stance remained unchanged, although Cameroon's Industrial and Trade Development Minister, during his visit in August, emphasised the project's importance to Pretoria's new Mineral and Energy Affairs Minister, George Bartlett, and conveyed Yaoundé's decision to grant SAA landing rights.[58] Pretoria's non-participation in the project notwithstanding, contact continued.

Derek Auret included Cameroon on his tour through West Africa in October 1991.[59] Its main purpose was to enlist African diplomatic backing for Pretoria's readmission to the FAO during the UN agency's upcoming annual meeting in Rome, raising the issue with the prime ministers of the Congolese Republic and Cape Verde, as well as with the foreign affairs ministers of the Ivory Coast, Cameroon and Senegal. However, he only obtained one clear indication of support; Yaoundé's Foreign Minister said "Cameroon will support and encourage the application both amongst African countries as well as in international fora". It is reasonable to argue this pro-active stance was motivated by the economic interest in contact with Pretoria over the hydroelectric project, as the issue figured in Auret's talks with the foreign minister.[60] During the FAO meeting in November, Cameroon kept its promise. According to Glenn Babb's feedback, then Ambassador to Italy and Permanent Representative to the FAO, to Deputy Director-General Jeremy Shearar, there was dissension among African countries over Pretoria's readmission. Cameroon's Ambassador, simultaneously the leader of the African Group within the FAO, "asked in a spirit of co-operation that South Africa withdraw its application". After consultations with Pretoria, Babb followed this advice, but Shearar concluded: "We thus experienced a surprisingly large measure of goodwill, much of it from unexpected quarters. But above all, valuable experience was gained on the manner in which countries should be lobbied to support our aspirations".[61]

Apart from the use of economic leverage, Pretoria's strategy of winning African support entailed a second aspect, namely to target the OAU. Contact with Ethiopia, its host, was apparently not sought. However, Pretoria tried to secure the backing of Uganda and Nigeria, the consecutive OAU Chairs from July 1990 to June 1992.

Uganda and Nigeria

The first recorded contact between Pretoria and Kampala post-1990 is NIS Director-General Niël Barnard's visit there on 3/4 July 1990, meeting President Yoweri Museveni.[62] Intelligence's interest stemmed, in all likelihood, from the training camps Kampala harboured for the armed wing of both the ANC, Umkhonto we Sizwe (MK), and the PAC, Azania People's Liberation Army (APLA), since late 1986;[63] this contradicts secondary literature suggestions whereby the camps been established after the 1988 Namibia Accords.[64] His report to President de Klerk and Director-General van Heerden indicates South African domestic matters were discussed, suggesting Barnard was in all probability promoting the reforms,[65] with de Klerk being eager to meet Museveni in his capacity as the OAU Chairman. The idea for this meeting came from John Kazzora, Museveni's Personal Adviser. According to a report of September 1990, Kazzora felt a meeting de Klerk-Museveni, "somewhere in Europe", would be "appropriate at this time".[66] De Klerk's plan to meet Museveni in London, at the end of his visit to Great Britain in October, did not materialise "due to private circumstances on the part of Museveni".[67] Thereafter, Pretoria did not undertake further moves towards Museveni, probably because he maintained a pro-sanctions stance until further steps towards the dismantling of apartheid were made.[68] This sharply contrasts Pretoria's efforts to gain access to Nigeria, a contact which bore great importance; as one of Africa's most powerful states, it generously supported liberation movements, especially those in southern Africa in their struggle against Pretoria, hosted ANC and PAC missions from 1975 and Nigerian foreign ministers chaired the UN Special Committee against Apartheid for 21 of the 31 years of its existence.[69] Pretoria fairly successfully applied two strategies to convince Lagos bilateral contact was to its advantage. First, emphasising the prospects economic interaction held for both countries,[70] also referring to de Klerk's concept of four economic regions, seeing Nigeria as West Africa's powerhouse Second, capitalising on Nigeria's aspirations for continental leadership, particularly during the OAU Chairmanship, commending President Ibrahim Babangida in correspondence and meetings on his statesmanship and underlining the country's seminal role in African and international politics.

The National Intelligence Service was instrumental in establishing significant interaction between Pretoria and Lagos; the DFA files contain communication to and from Lagos intercepted by NIS, suggesting they were stationed there from at least April 1984.[71] The text of a NIS document, dated 16 November 1984, might serve as an indication how this came about: "During December 1984, Nigeria will receive two C-130 aircraft from the RSA".[72] This suggests secret deals between South Africa's and Nigeria's intelligence community, with the former possibly providing the Hercules cargo planes to buy their way into Nigeria. The files contain no further material on this matter and we could not obtain Niël Barnard's view. In any case, given its long-standing presence, NIS had knowledge of the channels through which to establish contact. Thus, on 1/2 July 1990, Barnard went to Lagos, holding talks with Babangida on South Africa's domestic political situation.[73] Barnard's messenger duties were supplemented by similar activities by General Aliyu Mohammed Gusau,[74] Lagos' man in charge of intelligence. The DFA officers were not content with national intelligence's responsibility for all contact between Pretoria and Lagos.

Through their own lines of communication, they arranged a visit of former Nigerian President Olusegun Obasanjo (1975-79) to South Africa in July 1990, meeting, in this order, Pik Botha, van Heerden and de Klerk. Considering his friendship with Pik Botha, established while Co-chairman of the Commonwealth Eminent Persons Group that visited South Africa in 1986,[75] the DFA had successfully reactivated its contact without any apparent NIS involvement. Obasanjo told Pik Botha Lagos was eager to be "associated with the things happening in the RSA", encouraging Pretoria "to sustain the good being done". Crucially, van Heerden suggested "the OAU might now invite a South African delegation (not ANC or PAC or any of that sort) to go to the OAU as observers". De Klerk expressed the hope for "a real dialogue with a country so important as Nigeria", promoting the concept of Nigeria and South Africa boosting the continent's economic development. As Obasanjo concluded he "had come on his own and on behalf of the Nigerian Government and President Babangida",[76] de Klerk subsequently wrote to Babangida, stressing the need for economic co-operation between the two "major economic powers in Africa".[77] Obasanjo remained in contact with Pretoria through correspondence[78] and personally, acting almost as the DFA's mediator. In September 1991, his New York-based Africa Leadership Forum organised a conference on "The challenges of post-Apartheid South Africa" in Windhoek,[79] following which Obasanjo and 16 prominent Nigerians went to South Africa, calling for an end to its isolation.[80] Another avenue the DFA pursued in establishing contact with Nigeria without NIS involvement was diplomatic exchange at the UN in New York. In our interview, Jeremy Shearar, Pretoria's UN Ambassador at the time, indicated this began after the 1988 Namibia Accords through several meetings with his Nigerian counterpart Joseph Garba, Chairman of the Special Committee against Apartheid from 1984 and President of the General Assembly during 1989. This diplomatic link remained with Garba's successor from 1990, Ibrahim Gambari. In fact, Shearar mentioned to us contact intensified after de Klerk's February 1990 speech.[81] Discussions on South Africa's position at the UN and the country's domestic situation aside, Shearar's correspondence to Gambari reveals he tried to appeal to Nigeria emphasising "the need to combine our efforts to confront the compelling development needs of Africa".[82]

Pretoria's intelligence and diplomatic contact with Nigeria promised to open doors to the OAU, chaired by Babangida from July 1991 to June 1992, and the Commonwealth, whose current Secretary-General was Eleazar Chukwuemeka 'Emeka' Anyaoku, a distinguished Nigerian diplomat. According to a press communiqué by the Nigerian Permanent Mission to the UN in New York, reproducing Babangida's statement of

12 April 1991, Nigeria "would be fully prepared to promote and under-take initiatives at the forthcoming OAU Summit to lift sanctions on South Africa if the remaining apartheid laws are abrogated by May, 1991".[83] Thereafter, Pretoria seemingly felt the Nigerian government's pulse so as to make changes with the most appeal to Lagos. A telex from the Belgian Embassy in Lagos to Brussels on 14 May, intercepted by the NIS, contains the Belgian perception of the Nigerian attitude: "Nigeria stands for the following position: Sanctions should be maintained until the Pretoria Government abrogates three laws, the Population [Registra-tion] Act, the Group Areas Act, and the [Native] Land Act".[84] Being a pragmatist, de Klerk usually timed his actions to have the greatest politi-cal impact. In the above-cited letter to 30 African heads of state and government within days of the OAU Summit in Nigeria, he stressed "the political process leading to a new constitutional order in South Africa remains on track".[85] To substantiate his claim, possibly with knowledge of the telex intercepted by NIS, de Klerk undertook to repeal these three central apartheid acts. While he had announced their abrogation in Feb-ruary 1991, it was only on 5 June that de Klerk repealed both the Group Areas and the Native Land Act. While this delay was possibly due to dissension in Cabinet on the speed of these reforms, circumstantial evi-dence suggests the timing was also related to the OAU Summit from 2 to 5 June. Whether or not Nigeria lobbied for Pretoria's cause, the OAU did not propose the international community to lift sanctions, judging de Klerk's reforms as insufficient.[86]

The OAU's standpoint notwithstanding, de Klerk's exchange with Babangida continued, through national intelligence. On 17 June, the same day the Population Registration Act was repealed, Babangida reassured de Klerk in a message Niël Barnard conveyed: "he will do anything he can to assist Pres de Klerk in achieving his goals".[87] On 17 September, three days after the National Peace Accord was concluded, Babangida com-mended de Klerk for this initiative.[88] With this backing and given An-yaoku's position as the Commonwealth Secretary-General, de Klerk replied to Babangida on 26 September, lobbying for Nigeria's support in the forthcoming (16-22 October) Commonwealth Summit in Harare: "I would like to propose that the first such meeting [between Babangida and de Klerk] take place in Abuja before the forthcoming Commonwealth Conference. Accordingly I suggest that I arrive on October 13, 1991, accompanied by my Minister of Foreign Affairs".[89] Babangida did not act on de Klerk's proposal, possibly due to disagreement within his govern-ment over its attitude towards Pretoria; in August 1991, Foreign Affairs Minister Ike Nwachukwu had asked the US, the European Community and Japan to maintain economic sanctions.[90] Whether Lagos lobbied for Pretoria's cause in Harare is uncertain, but the DFA officials felt devel-opments during 1991 had "come to naught", such as UN Ambassador Vernon 'Jim' Steward's complained to his Nigerian counterpart, Gambari, in February 1992.[91] Furthermore, de Klerk's next correspondence to Babangida in the DFA files is only dated 11 February 1992, containing a summary of the political developments since CODESA I.[92] To bring new life to the Pretoria-Lagos contact, Steward proposed sending "an official, if not a Minister (...) to Nigeria for discussions", a suggestion to which Gambari "fully agreed".[93] Steward's statement reflected the DFA's discontent that all communication had to be channelled through the NIS, leading to interdepartmental friction over who took the lead in promoting contact. However, not only had the NIS been stationed in Nigeria for a long time, but the Nigerian government, and even its diplomatic corps, was divided regarding contact with Pretoria, both of which did not augur well for diplomatic relations. Nonetheless, the foreign affairs ministry managed to establish itself vis-à-vis national intelligence.

In a letter of 3 March to Babangida, de Klerk accepted his invitation to come to Abuja, stating this offer had been transmitted to Pretoria by Nigeria's High Commissioner in Botswana, Alaba Ogunsanwo.[94] While a report from Deputy Director-General Auret indicates this served as the DFA's principal channel of communication,[95] he revealed to us the NIS had originally established it.[96] In any case, Auret took de Klerk's letter to Abuja, as suggested by Pik Botha,[97] indicating national intelligence had been replaced as the transmission centre. Auret visited Nigeria from 7 to 11 March, informing Babangida in a "very relaxed and friendly atmosphere" of the white referendum on de Klerk's reforms, refuting allegations regarding Pretoria's involvement in the violence and asking him to play an important role in the reform process.[98] Regarding de Klerk's visit to Nigeria, this was contingent on the referendum's outcome;[99] as this was favourable to de Klerk, the Nigerian Foreign Affairs Ministry issued a press statement the following day, stating the ""Yes Vote" (...) has now removed a major obstacle to the efforts to transform South Africa from a racially segregated country to a non-racial, united and democratic society".[100] Consequently, on 23 March, Ogunsanwo confirmed de Klerk's visit could take place on 9/10 April.[101] Before discussing this breakthrough for Pretoria's diplomatic endeavours, we will consider the important role South Africa's business community played in the run-up to this event.

The delegation accompanying de Klerk to Abuja comprised key business representatives, namely Afrikaanse Handelsinstituut President Adriaan Sarel 'Attie' du Plessis, SAFTO Chief Executive Holtes and Jan Hendrik 'Hennie' Viljoen, President of the South African Chamber of Business (SACOB).[102] SAFTO was the most significant participant in this instance and within the framework of Pretoria's foreign relations with Africa more generally, as du Plessis and Viljoen confirmed to us.[103] The Togolese delegation that had visited South Africa in March 1991 specifically asked for a SAFTO mission to visit Togo. The trade organisation was also invited to a manufactured goods fair in Ghana in 1993[104] and it played a highly significant role in facilitating de Klerk's Nigeria visit. The establishment of the African Business Development Group (ABDG), in 1980, marked SAFTO's growing Africa interest.[105] Holtes, who stated in our interview to have had "a great interest in Africa",[106] and Paul Runge, who ran the ABDG (1989-91) and then the Africa and Europe section (1992-97), were SAFTO's driving forces in Africa. Runge, previously a foreign service official with postings related to West Africa, now maintained the personal link between the traders and the DFA. He was rather close to Neil van Heerden, whom he followed to the South Africa Foundation in 1997, and we argue SAFTO became something of an implementer of van Heerden's New Diplomacy, towards Nigeria in particular. In fact, the SAFTO Annual Report 1991/2 suggests the "the psychological effect of establishing business relationships with this leader on the African continent [Nigeria] cannot be underestimated".[107] Derek Auret confirmed our view that the activities of SAFTO's Africa Business Development Group in Nigeria supplemented Pretoria's ambition of winning over this important West African country.[108] Runge paid a "pilot visit" in March 1992 to "examine first-hand an important new market", to "set up logistics for a confidential South African trade delegation to visit Lagos from 3 to 10 May " and to "canvass for Nigerian participation in the SAFTO Africa conference scheduled for 28 and 29 April".[109] Significantly, Olusegun Obasanjo, the DFA's contact, attended this conference as seen in a photograph with Runge.[110] Thereafter, a 'Special SAFTO Group' visited Nigeria in May, a week later than planned and only after the DFA had "obtained official approval for the visit" from the Nigerian authorities.[111] Although these developments took place after de Klerk's visit, they illustrate DFA and SAFTO facilitated each other's tasks.

Regarding de Klerk's Abuja coup on 9/10 April, the DFA files contain relatively little documentation, indicating the NIS still managed to somewhat relegate the foreign service corps to the background. Still in August 1992, Director Justus de Goede's wrote to Derek Auret: "We are using a channel which is not a Foreign Ministry one. We have little choice in the matter, but it seems clear to us that the Nigerian Foreign Ministry is happy to keep this distance".[112] Nonetheless, one document lists the "Specific Points" to be raised by de Klerk in the talks with Babangida, verifying our above arguments: "Normalisation of trade and other relations", "Overflight rights for SAA", "Facilitation of SAFTO-delegation visit – 3 to 10 May 1992" and "Channel of Communication".[113] It is not known whether all of these points were discussed, as the only other relevant document, summarising de Klerk's 90-minute talk with Babangida, merely notes South Africa's domestic political developments as an issue.[114] According to secondary sources, oil surfaced, speculating Nigeria was going to be a future supplier.[115] The Joint Communiqué at the end of the visit focused on South Africa's internal situation, especially the violence, the last paragraph mentioning "close regional cooperation was essential for economic growth and progress".[116] In any event, de Klerk's venture was a tremendous breakthrough for Pretoria's Africa policy.[117]

The information we have now provided shows the economic lever was very important in Pretoria's endeavour to promote contact with African states beyond the region. This was relevant in the wider context of strengthening the bargaining position in the domestic negotiations, particular attention being paid to the OAU Chairs Uganda and Nigeria. In March 1992, Pik Botha argued: "It is important for us to gain membership of the organisation (...), I would like to see South Africa taking its rightful place in the OAU this year still".[118] By way of diplomatic backing from the OAU, Pretoria apparently hoped to achieve its central foreign policy objective of returning to the international community. De Klerk's visits to Paris, London and Washington aside, contact was also established with Moscow, the former archenemy and another permanent UN Security Council member; full diplomatic relations existed from February 1992 and de Klerk met Boris Yeltsin in Moscow on 1/2 June 1992, also discussing Pretoria's readmission to the UN General Assembly.[119] In 1999, Neil van Heerden admitted it was Pretoria's goal to secure the support of the permanent Security Council members in re-entering the UN as a fully fledged member: "Yes, of course, that was always in the back of one's mind".[120] Regarding the People's Republic of China, the fifth permanent member, South African newspapers revealed Pik Botha had paid a secret visit to Beijing in October 1991 to discuss the establishment of diplomatic relations. In February 1992, China's Foreign Minister came to South Africa.[121] Finally, during the visit to Moscow, Tokyo and Singapore in early June, de Klerk hoped to make a stopover in Beijing, but this did not materialise despite strong lobbying from Pretoria, the well-informed magazine *SouthScan* suggests.[122] Nonetheless, de Klerk stated on his return on 8 June: "South Africa is back in the international community. This time I am more convinced of it than ever before".[123]

We now resume our analysis of the developments after the Boipatong massacre, which had caused the ANC to break off the negotiations. At this particular juncture, the international and domestic dimension came together so critically.

Post-Boipatong Developments

The weeks following the Boipatong massacre saw a flurry of diplomatic moves. The ANC's goal was the re-imposition of international pressure on Pretoria, while the government aimed at refuting the accusation it was not committed to negotiating the demise of apartheid, fomenting the violence against the ANC.

The massacre occurred days before the OAU Conference of Ministers (22-27 June), followed by the Heads of State and Government meeting in Dakar (29 June-1 July). Capitalising on these, the ANC requested the OAU to draft a resolution condemning Pretoria for submission to the UN Security Council. Although the OAU had recognised the ANC as South Africa's principal liberation movement and endorsed its negotiation paper in the Harare Declaration, Mandela's organisation could not rely on this backing, given that Pretoria had made significant inroads into Africa. Reflecting the high priority the ANC attributed to continental diplomatic support, 20 of the 49 countries Mandela visited until mid-1992 were in Africa, pursuing three goals: lobby for OAU support was important, with Mandela going to Uganda in 1990 and Nigeria in 1991; second, win politically important Kenya, by going there twice; third, broaden the diplomatic network by going to Nigeria (1990), Gabon, the Ivory Coast and Ghana (1991), countries critical towards recognising the ANC as the main liberation movement or that had not allowed it to establish a presence during the exile period.[124] Despite these activities, the *Africa Research Bulletin* pointedly commented after de Klerk's Abuja breakthrough: "For the ANC this marks a major and almost total defeat in an area which, six months before – when the movement won widespread agreement to delay further normalisation until an interim government – seemed to have been uncontested ANC turf".[125] Reflecting the great significance attached to rally Africa's support at the OAU Summit in Dakar, Mandela himself went there, accompanied by nine ANC representatives, most notably Thabo Mbeki, urging Africa's leaders to think again before "hastily re-establishing relations with Pretoria".[126]

Parallel to these developments, Pretoria tried to rally diplomatic support through Nigeria's assistance. In furtherance of his African leadership ambition, Babangida convened UN Secretary-General Boutros Boutros-Ghali and South African government representatives in Abuja on 27 June. Two separate rounds of talks were held between Boutros-Ghali, Pik Botha and Roelof 'Roelf' Meyer, Pretoria's chief negotiator, and between Babangida, Foreign Minister Nwachukwu, Pik Botha and Meyer. Also present were Deputy Director-Generals Auret and Shearar, UN Ambassador Steward and Deputy Director Anton van Dalsen, the son of former Director-General Hans van Dalsen. The violence issue dominated. One day prior to the Abuja meetings, de Klerk and Pik Botha wrote to their Nigerian counterparts: "The charges of Government complicity in the tragedy in Boipatong or in any other instance of killing, are without any substance whatsoever". While questioning the legal justification for action by the UN Security Council, Pretoria left room for compromise: "If the Security Council feels that it needs to be reliably informed on events in South Africa, the Government would certainly be prepared to assist by participating in any meeting in this respect".[127] Pretoria's officials adopted the same stance during the talks in Abuja. Pik Botha argued the ANC used Boipatong as an "opportunity to cancel Codesa and proceed with mass action".[128] The arguments were repeated during the meeting with the UN Secretary-General, with Pik Botha and Meyer emphasising

Meyer emphasising Pretoria's steps to curb the violence and its commitment to negotiations. Boutros-Ghali replied "he was willing to assist in trying to find a solution to the problems", while indicating he had lost some of his faith in Pretoria: "how it is possible that with all its infrastructure and means, the SA Government is still unable to cope with such acts of violence after two years. This leads to possible international perceptions that there is something fishy going on".[129] In contrast, Babangida confirmed his support for de Klerk: "The position of President de Klerk is appreciated and there is faith in his sincerity".[130]

The OAU's Dakar meeting revealed the success of the ANC's and Pretoria's endeavours in securing African diplomatic support. The ANC's networking had evidently found acceptance by the majority of states, as the heads of state and government adopted the draft resolution prepared by the Conference of Ministers,[131] and on 2 July, on behalf of the African Group, Madagascar requested a special Security Council meeting to discuss that resolution.[132] In contrast, Pretoria's link with Abuja bore some fruit during the Security Council debates on 15/16 July; in comparing the OAU draft resolution and what became Security Council Resolution 765, the sections in which Pretoria was held responsible for the violence and the Boipatong massacre were either strongly toned down or deleted entirely.[133] Crucially, according to well-informed *Africa Confidential* and *SouthScan*, these alterations were also due to Nigerian lobbying.[134] The Security Council meetings of 15/16 July impacted on South Africa's subsequent political development. Resolution 765 requested the Secretary General to send an envoy. Boutros-Ghali chose former US Secretary of State Cyrus Vance,[135] who went to South Africa from 22 to 31 July, consulting with parties and groups involved in the political transition process. Based on his findings, the Security Council adopted Resolution 772 on 17 August, stipulating the creation of a UN Observer Mission in South Africa (UNOMSA); 50 observers were deployed in early September.[136]

Thus, following the Boipatong massacre, the ANC had successfully raised the necessary African diplomatic support to re-establish international pressure on Pretoria. With UNOMSA, it had some assurance the government could no longer sabotage the negotiation process, as Mandela had accused de Klerk of doing. Between 1990 and 1992, Pretoria had accepted fact finding missions from Amnesty International, the International Commission of Jurists and even the OAU,[137] but it had always resisted the deployment of a permanent international observer mission. On 23 April 1992, de Klerk had stated: "South Africa is a sovereign state (...). Demands for international involvement (...) are (...) rejected".[138] Therefore, the international community's engagement in South Africa represented a major victory for the ANC; de Klerk could no longer procrastinate on rapid political change while attempting to secure a maximum number of concessions for the minority. Yet, despite the public hostility, Pretoria's and the ANC's chief negotiator, Roelf Meyer and

Cyril Ramaphosa respectively, met behind the scenes to work out a deal acceptable to both parties, resulting in the signing of the Record of Understanding on 26 September 1992.[139]

We do not need to examine the subsequent developments until South Africa's first democratic elections in April 1994, as the African continental dimension no longer played a significant role. The days of soliciting the support of African states were over. In particular, the DFA files for those 12 countries where access was granted until September 1993, or beyond, do not record any relevant interaction post-Boipatong. In spite of all the undertakings from de Klerk to gain recognition for his reforms, Pretoria could never find acceptance as a fellow African state until the country's majority had the vote. This fundamental reality was the cause for Africa's renewed diplomatic activity post-Boipatong. New Diplomacy had achieved some concrete results, particularly overflying and landing rights for South African Airways, the establishment of missions in Madagascar and Togo, diplomatic support from Cameroon in the forum of the FAO and important meetings with the presidents of Kenya and Nigeria. However, these were not substantial enough and more than 30 African states would not relinquish their anti-apartheid stance. On 10 May 1994, Nelson Mandela was sworn in as President, terminating the last outpost of white minority rule in Africa and subsequently putting South Africa's foreign relations with the continent on a sound basis.

Conclusion

This study examined South Africa's foreign relations with the African states beyond southern Africa within the framework chartered by Pretoria's apartheid policy and Africa's fundamental opposition to this ideology. While a Diplomatic History, having the advantage of access to different South African archives, we underlined the relevance of concepts provided by the disciplines of Political Science and International Relations. In acknowledging their importance for an understanding of the evolution of South Africa's foreign relations of interest, we proposed Pretoria's Africa policy resulted from an interplay of domestic, regional, continental and international environments. Our focus was the first, looking at the role of both state and non-state actors. Regarding the state actors, we argued throughout that competition and rivalry, but also a degree of co-operation, prevailed between the Departments of Foreign Affairs and Information, the military and national intelligence in trying to influence Pretoria's foreign policy direction. We now evaluate how the different agencies fared over time.

Gradually, the DFA, the supposedly predominant foreign policy actor, was relegated to the background. Its attempt to maintain its position by launching an Interdepartmental Committee on African Affairs failed, as other departments were not prepared to relinquish their independent axis to decision-making. Consequently, the early 1960s appears as the only period during which the DFA was unrivalled in conducting foreign policy. Certainly, officials from this ministry were not exposed to discernible bureaucratic competition in their later contact with the Central African Republic, Liberia, Malawi and Madagascar. However, they were never the sole players in the African countries of interest to us. Above all, the DFA's central approach of providing technical assistance and support for development/investment projects did not help to break Pretoria's international isolation through acceptance by African states. This weakened its position in the decision-making process and made it vulnerable to interference from sister departments. The DFA's attempt to secure the support of Gabon's President illustrates the unsuitability of a strategy based on technical assistance. The OGAPROV agricultural project attracted some of Bongo's attention, but on the 101 anti-apartheid sanctions resolutions adopted by the UN General Assembly between 1962 and 1989, Gabon abstained only six times, approving in all other instances.[1] A similar situation prevailed on the Comoros during the 1980s, where the Sangani farm project did not result in diplomatic recognition or other forms of diplomatic support. The department's only engagement we could judge as worthwhile was the upgrading and maintenance of the airport on Cape Verde, in return for which South African Airways obtained landing rights.

An equally sobering conclusion must be drawn from the development/investment projects, namely the Transgabonais railway and the Hotel Intercontinental Bokassa. While eager to secure South Africa's participation, several African leaders exploited the DFA's almost desperate attempt to gain a foothold in Africa. Malawi was the only country to exchange ambassadors and its voting behaviour at the UN General Assembly was at least more supportive of Pretoria than that of Gabon; on the above-mentioned 101 anti-apartheid sanctions, it cast a no-vote three times, abstained 70 times, while approving in 28 instances. When we asked Neil van Heerden about this dearth of results, he downplayed: "We certainly didn't get a regular return for the money, but this was as one would say in the Bible: it is bread on the water. You are putting the bread on the water and you are hoping that it will (...) [be] an investment for the future. And you know full well that you would not get a one-to-one return".[2] Pretoria's focus on southern Africa and South Africa's declining economic performance in the 1980s aside, the ineffectiveness of the DFA's Africa approach caused the P.W. Botha government to freeze technical assistance and development/investment projects. The end of the Cold War contributed to Africa's economic marginalisation. Consequently, trade became an important feature during de Klerk's tenure, making South Africa an attractive partner for African states. In return, SAA obtained landing and overflying rights in several countries and Pretoria established wider political contacts. The DFA's Africa policy thus only took a promising form towards the end of de Klerk's term.

The military was, after P.W. Botha became the assertive Defence Minister in 1966, the first actor to invade the DFA's domain, initially acting on the 1949 Africa Charter, proposing South Africa's co-operation with the colonial powers to maintain Western control over Africa and defend the continent against communism. Its ambition of this nature was detected in the Congo crisis, providing assistance to western-oriented Katangese Prime Minister Tshombe alongside Washington and giving at least tacit approval to related mercenary activity. The French arms supplies from 1963 strengthened the military's foreign policy making position. Resulting from a working relationship with France's intelligence and military community, and joined by two key Francophone African leaders, Presidents Bongo and Houphouët-Boigny, it provided arms to Biafra in the Nigerian Civil War. South Africa sought to create a military network with the politically stable and anticommunist African states, with Prime Minister Vorster, in September 1970, offering to conclude non-aggression pacts with the independent African countries.[3] Yet, the impending independence of Angola and Mozambique after 1974 removed Pretoria's *cordon sanitaire*, compelling the military to concentrate on safeguarding South Africa's national security in the immediate neighbourhood. Furthermore, the Department of Information, assisted by the Bureau for State Security, had became the primary foreign policy actors.

The Department of Information's privileging was based upon the strong ties between Secretary Rhoodie and BOSS head van den Bergh, Prime Minister Vorster's long-time friend. The resulting access to large budgets allowed it to launch what we called Secret Diplomacy, best characterised as a "middle way" between the DFA's conventional diplomacy and the military's realist approach. Its officials conducted a "marketing foreign policy", a concept introduced by South African IR scholar Janis van der Westhuizen.[4] A cornerstone of Secret Diplomacy was to sell the separate development concept as Pretoria's intention of reforming apartheid. Although benefiting from the military's co-operation with Abidjan over the Nigerian Civil War, the Department of Information managed to convince both the Ivorian and Senegalese President of Pretoria's reform intention, resulting in Vorster's breakthrough visit to the Ivory Coast in September 1974. This caused the DFA to imitate Secret Diplomacy, sending homeland leader Buthelezi to Liberia in December 1975, undoubtedly facilitating Vorster's meeting with President Tolbert in Monrovia in February 1975. Furthermore, Transkei leader Matanzima was included in the delegation to the UN General Assembly in 1974, something Geldenhuys called "multiracial diplomacy".[5]

Co-operation with the Bureau for State Security greatly facilitated the Information Department's work. Its intelligence gathering to safeguard South Africa's national security included: monitoring the western Indian Ocean area; securing access to oil, for example from Nigeria; obtaining SAA overflying rights; and arranging high-level visits, such as those of Vorster to West Africa. However, after South Africa's *cordon sanitaire* collapsed, its regional Détente goals clashed with those of the military. The central point of division was how best to ensure white South Africa's security following the establishment of Marxist governments in neighbouring Angola and Mozambique. In October 1975, the military succeeded in convincing Vorster of the necessity to deploy troops to Angola, thus winning an important battle against BOSS. While the invasion ended with a defeat, the struggle for policy ascendancy was not over. The final showdown came after Vorster's resignation, with Defence Minister Botha winning the executive position against Information Minister Mulder.

Following the demise of BOSS, the national intelligence agency eventually became the National Intelligence Service, headed by Niël Barnard, who shared P.W. Botha's politico-ideological views. His appointment resulted in close co-operation between the NIS and the military. Given the military's focus on southern Africa, ventures beyond concentrated on co-operation with Gabon's President and French mercenary Bob Denard, armament sales and the western Indian Ocean. The military's principal success was the fruitful partnership with Bongo. With the end of the Cold War, however, its dominance in foreign policy making waned, because its realist policies of power were no longer suited to resolving South Africa's problems. However, as a remainder of the military's dominance, the NIS retained an influence in contact with Uganda and Nigeria, while the DFA gradually rose in prominence, facilitated by de Klerk, who relied on the advice of the foreign service corps.

In turning to a discussion of the roles played by the different non-state actors, it is appropriate to form four clusters: Progressive Party and *Rand Daily Mail*, think tanks, Broederbond and the business sector.

The opposition party and the relatively liberal daily shared a critical stance towards Pretoria's policies. The Progressive Party's leader, Colin Eglin, went to several African countries during the 1970s to offset the impression all white South Africans supported apartheid, while also intending to strengthen the party's political profile. Pretoria's politicians criticised Eglin's excursions on various occasions, and the government, through its network with France, ensured Eglin and Suzman could not intrude upon its relations with Houphouët-Boigny. No comparable developments appear to have occurred during Frederik van Zyl Slabbert's leadership until February 1986. However, as the Director of the Institute for a Democratic Alternative for South Africa, he organised the Dakar meeting between members of the ANC and the Afrikaner intelligentsia in 1987, a seminally important event in the abolition of apartheid. Regarding the *Rand Daily Mail*, it was the first newspaper to suggest Vorster had gone to the Ivory Coast in 1974 and its reports led to the Information Scandal, causing his resignation. It also exposed the financial wastage in development/investment projects in the C.A.R. Later on, *The Weekly Mail* and *The Guardian* were responsible for uncovering Inkathagate, which weakened de Klerk's negotiating position. Thus, both the Information Scandal and Inkathagate significantly changed the course of South African political developments.

Researchers from the two think tanks Africa Institute and South African Institute of International Affairs analysed Pretoria's foreign relations with African states. However, we traced one instance in which the Africa Institute was crossing the border of being a think tank, independent of government, referring to the visit of Director Joseph Moolman and Deputy Director Erich Leistner, joined by South African Institute of International Affairs Director John Barratt, to Senegal and the Ivory Coast in 1974. In this instance, due to concurring politico-ideological views regarding Pretoria's separate development policy, the Africa Institute members, and especially Moolman, were drawn into the policy network supportive of the Information Department's Secret Diplomacy; Barratt's Institute retained its non-partisan character. The Foreign Affairs Association and the Southern African Freedom Foundation were not think tanks due to their being funded by that same department.

Regarding the Broederbond's relevance, personal contact and informal networking ensured an influence on political decisions. Importantly, almost all Cabinet Ministers in the period under review were Broederbonders. Important among the values the brotherhood promoted was the idea of white supremacy, which, we suggest, underpinned Pretoria's Africa policy. The clearest evidence of such indirect influence can be detected during Vorster's premiership, when it was part of the policy network supportive of the Pretoria's policies of the day. However, after P.W. Botha's rise to Prime Minister, the Broederbond's standing decreased,[6] only to increase under de Klerk who suggests its views supported his move to undertake the reforms.[7]

In examining the business sector's significance, we will discuss two issues raised in Chapter 2, namely its relationship with apartheid politics and the division between Afrikaner and English-speaking business. Regarding the latter, we showed English-speaking business dominated, while the Afrikaner counterpart played a negligible role. Among the organised business, the Afrikaanse Handelsinstituut's sole independent venture was Malawi, while the Durban Chamber of Commerce dispatched five business missions. The South African Foreign Trade Organisation and the South Africa Foundation, although not purely English-speaking institutions, were equally active, mostly in a mutually beneficial exchange with government. Talking about SAFTO's relationship with the DFA from the late 1980s, Paul Runge explained in 1999 it "was a particularly good one. There was a lot of interaction. (...) It was a quite natural thing to move from the Department of Foreign Affairs into SAFTO. It was all very well received".[8] Asked about the inherent dilemma that by promoting South Africa's export industry, SAFTO inevitably supported the policy goals of the apartheid government, Holtes admitted in 1999: "We did a lot of things which perhaps should not be done by a trade organisation, but our attitude was always in the broad support of trade (...). [business] is supportive of anything that ensures stability".[9] We also revealed South Africa Foundation executives and Trustees interacted rather closely with the government. Former Director General Sorour elaborated: "The Foundation never ostracised the Government, but we made contact the exception rather than the rule".[10] While appreciating his distancing from the apartheid regime, we showed the Foundation's and Pretoria's interests coincided more often than not, rendering the line of separation between them somewhat blurred.

The Afrikaner's limited business involvement aside, the DFA officials seemed more at ease with English-speaking business. Such firms were involved or showed interest in several development/investment projects during the 1970s: Roberts Construction with railway projects in Malawi, Gabon, the C.A.R. and Zaire; LTA with housing and hotel projects in Gabon and the C.A.R. and the Zairian railway project. Sol Kerzner's hotel firms and the Anglo American Corporation were cases apart. Southern Sun became part of the DFA's development/investment projects approach with a hotel on Madagascar and Mauritius. However, Kerzner's other activities in the 1980s on Mauritius and the Comoros reflecting an expansionist strategy, unrelated to government policies. Anglo American played in a different league altogether, with its status resembling that of a foreign policy actor. The multinational company did not need Pretoria's assistance to achieve its business goals, although their interests did at times overlap. We did not reveal any clashes of interest with Pretoria, and Anglo American had minor exchanges with the DFA over the Congo (early 1960s), Madagascar (late 1960s) and Somalia (1984). A rather close relationship evolved over the SMTF copper project in Zaire during 1975, when Pretoria's Détente coincided initially with Anglo American's mining interests. Often, however, Anglo American seemingly went its own way; the secondary literature mentions mining operations in the C.A.R. and the Ivory Coast, in Gabon, Liberia, Mauritania, Sierra Leone and Tanzania,[11] but the DFA files do not contain any documents on related contact. For example in Tanzania, De Beers was an equal joint partner with the country's government in the mining firm Williamson Diamond Ltd.[12] As Anglo American Executive Director Spicer explained in 1999: "The Tanzanians (...) had a very strict policy towards South Africa. And yet, De Beers officials went backwards and forwards (...) with British passports. (...) [Tanzania's President] Nyerere and [Harry] Oppenheimer: close personal friends".[13]

In assessing the business sector's relationship with apartheid politics, we concentrate on the English-speaking firms, given their leading role. By examining hitherto unavailable statistics on South Africa's trade with sub-Saharan Africa, we challenged Tim Shaw and Roger Southall's thesis, explaining Pretoria's Outward-Looking Policy in Africa as an expression of South Africa's political economy. Empirically, we demonstrated that the reverse applied; the DFA needed the business sector in its ambition to establish contact with African countries. So much so that the state-controlled Industrial Development Corporation often offered loans on soft conditions, insured by the Credit Guarantee Insurance Corporation with the government's backing. Soft loan examples were the Lilongwe Capital Project, the hotel on Madagascar and the housing projects in the C.A.R. and in Gabon; Credit Guarantee insured the loan to finance Malawi's railway link with Mozambique, although this only involved 60 per cent local content, and not 70 per cent as its statutes stipulated. The Truth and Reconciliation Commission examined the role of business during the apartheid period. However, given that only 40 of the close on

2,800 pages total report relate to this subject, one cannot escape the impression it shied away from probing this delicate issue too deeply.[14] Nonetheless, it introduced a helpful classification of business culpability:

> *First order involvement*: "Direct involvement with the state in the formulation of oppressive policies or practices that resulted in low labour costs (or otherwise boosted profits)";
> *Second order involvement*: "businesses that made their money by engaging directly in activities that promoted state repression (...). Businesses that provided armoured vehicles to the police during the mid-1980s would fall into the former category";
> *Third order involvement*: "business activities that benefited indirectly by virtue of operating within the racially structured context of an apartheid society".[15]

Although business activities in Africa did not directly contribute to the oppression of the deprived in South Africa, this categorisation is of some use, because private firms participated in development/investment projects that aimed at finding African diplomatic acceptance, therefore potentially prolonging the apartheid system. The relevant companies benefited financially from these projects, while practically no risk was involved, as payment was usually forthcoming from the IDC, insured by Credit Guarantee and reinsured by the Treasury. This suggests all the companies examined in this study displayed an involvement of the third order. Taking into account the size of the projects in which they participated, we propose LTA's and Robert Construction's engagement was of the second order. This judgement can also be made on the CGIC and Safmarine with its aviation subsidiary, Safair. Without the former's financial backing, the DFA could not have pursued its Africa approach. Importantly, the firm's executives were aware of the political connotations of their role; Credit Guarantee General Manager Klaus Oppenheimer commented in our correspondence on the firm's involvement as outlined in this study: "There is no doubt that (especially in later years) the export credit financing facility also played the political role that you have described".[16] Safmarine's sanction-busting represents an equally strong case of economic-cum-political association with Pretoria: its airline subsidiary, Luxavia, circumvented the African air sanctions; Safmarine tankers shipped Nigerian oil to South Africa; and Safair flew arms from Europe to South Africa. Anglo American's interaction over Zaire, finally, bore significant political importance, and can therefore also be rated as second order involvement. Having discussed, based on the Political Science concept, the relevance of the state and non-state actors in Pretoria's Africa policy, we now briefly, and in conclusion, explore the International

Relations premise whereby the structural inequality among states shaped Pretoria's relationship with African states.

We proposed interaction between unequal states could take the form of either dominance, hegemony or primacy/leadership, reflecting a decrease in the use of power and force by the preponderant state, proposing South Africa was a preponderant force on the African continent. Pretoria's approach towards the region from the mid-1970s was one of dominance, while its approach fluctuated beyond southern Africa. Capitalising on the country's preponderance, the DFA could offer technical assistance and support for development/investment projects, while the military was in a position to become involved in a war as far away as Biafra, to provide armaments to Chad and Gabon and to establish a presence in the western Indian Ocean. The Department of Information's marketing strategy equally relied on South Africa's preponderance. Yet, as we emphasised, for a preponderant state to assume the role of a leader requires it to provide not only material, but also normative/moral resources. While offering all kinds of assistance and support, Pretoria's apartheid ideology fundamentally clashed with the idea of pan-Africanism. As Denis Venter suggested, the white governments had no comprehension of the basic premise that "treating other people differently on the basis of race and treating them as inferior on the basis of race would not be acceptable" by African states.[17] This, more than anything else, separated South Africa from Africa. Crucially, the end of apartheid altered entirely South Africa's position on the African continent, with several authors stipulating Pretoria was now in a position to attain middle power[18] leadership in both African and international politics.[19] South Africa's preponderance on the African continent and its role as a middle power now permits it to play a respected and recognised role in world politics and, of particular interest to this study, in Africa.[20] While acceptance by African states now proves to be essential in realising its ambition of attaining middle power status, diplomatic recognition was the vital key necessary for South Africa to break its international isolation during the apartheid era, underlining the central argument of this study.

Notes

Chapter 1: Introduction

1. Geldenhuys. 1984. *The Diplomacy of Isolation*, p.187; Olivier. 1982. 'South Africa's relations with Africa', p.269; Venter, T.D. 1980. *South Africa and Black Africa*, p.3.

2. Pretoria referred to it as South West Africa (S.W.A.) until its independence in 1990. In 1966, the UN General Assembly named it Namibia. We use S.W.A./Namibia when referring to the legal case, Namibia in all other cases.

3. For example Albright. 1991. 'South Africa in Southern Africa'; Butts & Thomas. 1986. *The Geopolitics of Southern Africa*; Chan. 1990. *Exporting Apartheid*; Falk. 1986. *The Geopolitics of Southern Africa*; Makinda. 1992. 'South Africa as a regional great power'; Olivier. 1988. 'South Africa as a regional power'; Price. 1984. 'Pretoria's Southern African strategy'.

4. DoD, HS/11/1/2/6, Vol. 30.

5. *Foreign Affairs List*.

6. Venter, T.D. 1980. 'Black Africa and the Apartheid issue', p.82-5.

7. Geldenhuys. 1984. *The Diplomacy of Isolation*, p.1.

8. Burchill. 1996. 'Introduction', p.23; Craig. 1983. 'The historian and the study of International Relations', p.1-11; Elman & Elman, eds., 2001. *Bridges and Boundaries*; Gaddis. 1990. 'New conceptual approaches to the study of American foreign relations', p.403-25; Holsti. 1991. 'International Relations models', p.57-88.

9. Elman & Elman. 1997. 'Diplomatic History and International Relations theory', p.5.

10. Evans & Newnham. 1998. *The Penguin Dictionary of International Relations*, p.274-5; McMahon. 1991. 'The study of American foreign relations', p.20-1.

11. Holbo. 1977. 'Editor's Note', p.vi. Emphasis in the original

12. Elman & Elman. 1997. 'Diplomatic History and International Relations theory', p.7-11.

13. Holsti. 1991. 'International Relations models', p.88.

14. Craig. 1983. 'The historian and the study of International Relations', p.9.

15. Rosenau. 2001. 'International Relations', p.424.

16. Gill. 2001. 'Hegemony', p.354.

17. Bull. 1977. *The Anarchical Society*, p.214-5.

18. Mathews. 1989. 'The Organisation of African Unity in World Politics', p.36-7; Shaw. 1979. 'The actors in African international politics', p.370; Zartman. 1967. 'Africa as a subordinate state system in international relations'.

19. Muller, M.E. 1996. 'South Africa's changing external relations', p.126.

20. Ruggie. 1996. *Winning the Peace*, p.48.

21. Hill. 2001. 'Foreign policy', p.290.

22. Rosenau. 1987. 'New directions and recurrent questions in the comparative study of foreign policy', p.3; Neack, Hey & Haney. 1995. *Foreign Policy Analysis*, p.9.

23.   Barber & Barratt. 1990. *South Africa's Foreign Policy*, p.1; de St. Jorre. 1977. 'South Africa', p.53; Jaster. 1988. *The Defence of White Power*, p.xiii; Legum. 1980. 'South Africa in the contemporary world', p.281-96; Pottinger. 1988. *The Imperial Presidency*, p.200; Schrire & Silke. 1997. 'Foreign policy', p.3; Spence. 1965. *Republic Under Pressure*, p.3-4, 15-23; van Wyk, K. 1991. 'Foreign policy orientations of the P.W. Botha regime', p.45-65; Venter, T.D. 1980. 'Black Africa and the Apartheid issue', p.98.

24.   Neack, Hey & Haney. 1995. *Foreign Policy Analysis*, p.203-4; Clapham. 1977. 'Sub-Saharan Africa', p.98; Shaw. 1987. 'Foreword', p.viii; Aluko. 1977. 'The determinants of the foreign policies of African states', p.1-2.

25.   Clapham. 1988. *Third World Politics*, p.124-5; Schraeder. 1996. 'African International Relations', p.131; Tordoff. 1984. *Government and Politics in Africa*, p.5-6.

26.   Gilpin. 1987. *The Political Economy of International Relations*, p.9.

27.   Gourevitch. 1993. 'Political Economy', p.716.

28.   Gilpin. 1987. *The Political Economy of International Relations*, p.38.

29.   Fine & Rustomjee. 1996. *The Political Economy of South Africa*, p.193-8; Holden. 1989. 'Trade policy debate', p.31-6; Holden. 1990. 'The growth of exports and manufacturing in South Africa from 1947 to 1987', p.363-6; Houghton. 1976. *The South African Economy*, p.212-3, 218-9, 233; Jones & Müller. 1992. *The South African Economy, 1910-90*, p.341-2; Moll. 1990. 'From booster to brake?', p.78-9.

30.   'Report of the Private Sector Export Advisory Committee for the period 1972-1974', 10 July 1975, p.1 (DFA, 34/2, Vol. 5); Vols. 2-5, AJ 1974.

31.   Shaw. 1977. 'Kenya and South Africa', p.375-94; Southall. 1984. 'South Africa', p.221; Southall. 1999. *South Africa in Africa*.

32.   Southall. 1984. 'South Africa', p.233.

33.   Decter. 1976. *South Africa and Black Africa*, p.3; Guelke. 1974. 'Africa as a market for South African goods', p.72-3; Holtes. 1983. *The Future of Trade between the Republic of South Africa and Black Africa*, p.2.

34.   Telephone interview with Trevor van Heerden (Commissioner, South African Revenue Service), 8 March 1999.

35.   Interview with Wim Holtes, 31 March 1999; *ARB: Economic, Financial and Technical Series* 16, 3, 1979: 5048; Legum. 1980. 'South Africa in the contemporary world', p.286; *SAFTO & the State of SA Trade*. 1984. p.21; *Finance Week* 20-26 June 1991: 24.

36.   This has previously been suggested by Chettle. 1984. 'Economic relations between South Africa and Black Africa', p.121-33; Esterhuysen, Fair & Leistner. 1994. *South Africa in Sub-Equatorial Africa*, p.65; Kerdellonton. 1989. 'Afrique', p.48; Thomas. 1979. 'South Africa and Black Africa', p.103, 114.

37.   Southall. 1999. *South Africa*, p.12; Southall. 1984. 'South Africa', p.235.

38.   Guelke. 1974. 'Africa as a market for South African goods', p.87-8.

39.   <http://www.uovs.ac.za/support/library/E_library_arca.php>

40.   <http://www.ufc.ac.za/collections/anc.htm>

41.   Pfister. 2003. 'Gateway to international victory'.

42.   Carstens. 2001. *In the Company of Diamonds*.

43.   <http://www.national.archives.gov.za>

44.   Harris. 2002. 'The archival sliver', p.138-9.

45.   Mandated to analyse and describe the causes, nature and extent of gross violations of human rights that occurred from 1 March 1960 to 10 May 1994.

46.   *TRC Report. Vol. 1*. 1999. p.233.

47.   Correspondence with André Jaquet, December 2002.

48.   Brits. 1995. 'The historian and the archives', p.70.

49. Cape Verde, Central African Republic, Congolese Republic, Djibouti, Gabon, Guinea, Ivory Coast, Kenya, Madagascar, Malawi, Mauritius, Reunion, Sao Tome and Principe, Senegal, Togo, Zaire (all until December 1979); Seychelles (April 1980), Comoros (November 1980), Equatorial Guinea (February 1984), Somalia (August 1984), Tanzania (May 1985), Burkina Faso (July 1987), Mali (September 1987), Gambia (November 1988), Guinea Bissau (May 1991), Cameroon (July 1992), Ethiopia (February 1993), Sudan (September 1993), Burundi (October 1993), Rwanda (November 1993), Nigeria (January 1994), Benin, Chad, Ghana, Liberia, Mauritania, Niger, Sierra Leone, Uganda (all until April 1994).

50. *TRC Report. Vol. 1.* 1999. p.201, 219, 229; Harris. 2000. "They should have destroyed more", p.30, 38-41, 55 (note 2).

51. *TRC Report. Vol. 1.* 1999. p.223.

Chapter 2: South Africa's Foreign Policy System

1. Vale & Mphaisha. 1999. 'Analysing and evaluating foreign policy', p.89-90; McGowan & Nel. 1999. 'The study of International Relations', p.10-1.

2. Neack, Hey & Haney. 1995. *Foreign Policy Analysis*, p.123-4.

3. Bealey. 1999. *The Blackwell Dictionary of Political Science*, p.222-3.

4. Said, Lerche Jr. & Lerche III. 1995. *Concepts of International Politics in Global Perspective*, p.39.

5. Carlsnaes. 2002. 'Foreign policy', p.337-9.

6. Art. 1993. 'Bureaucratic Politics', p.99.

7. Vale & Mphaisha. 1999. 'Analysing and evaluating foreign policy', p.97.

8. Interview with Richard Cornwell, 19 February 1999.

9. Interview with Maxi Schoeman, 1 March 1999.

10. Interview with Greg Mills, 3 March 1999.

11. Plano & Olton. 1988. *The International Relations Dictionary*, p.13.

12. Cited in Sole. 1994. 'South African foreign policy assumptions and objectives from Hertzog to de Klerk', p.109.

13. Barratt. 1972. 'South Africa's Outward Policy', p.546; Breitenbach. 1974. *South Africa in the Modern World (1910-1970)*, p.511; Geldenhuys. 1994. 'The head of government and South Africa's foreign relations', p.263; Nolutshungu. 1975. *South Africa in Africa*, p.83; Olivier. 1975. 'South African foreign policy', p.293.

14. Jaster. 1988. *The Defence of White Power*, p.26; Geldenhuys. 1984. *The Diplomacy of Isolation*, p.74-5.

15. Geldenhuys. 1984. *The Diplomacy of Isolation*, p.74.

16. Rees & Day. 1980. *Muldergate*.

17. Jaster. 1988. *The Defence of White Power*, p.34; Pottinger. 1988. *The Imperial Presidency*, p.7; O'Meara. 1996. *Forty Lost Years*, p.210-9.

18. Barber & Barratt. 1990. *South Africa's Foreign Policy*, p.247-8; Prinsloo. 1997. *Stem uit die Wilderness*.

19. Geldenhuys. 1984. *The Diplomacy of Isolation*, p.89-90.

20. Plano & Olton. 1988. *The International Relations Dictionary*, p.7.

21. Jaster. 1988. *The Defence of White Power*, p.28-9.

22. Pottinger. 1988. *The Imperial Presidency*, p.35.

23. O'Meara. 1996. *Forty Lost Years*, p.281. The SSC generally comprised the Prime Minister (Chairman), the Ministers of Defence, Foreign Affairs, Finance, Justice, Law and Order. Barber & Barratt. 1990. *South Africa's Foreign Policy*, p.252-

4; Geldenhuys. 1984. *The Diplomacy of Isolation*, p.95; Pottinger. 1988. *The Imperial Presidency*, p.334-5; van Nieuwkerk & van Wyk. 1989. 'The operational code of PW Botha', p.74-5.

24.   Barber & Barratt. 1990. *South Africa's Foreign Policy*, p.247-51; de Beer, J.H. 1998. 'Integration of the Departments of Foreign Affairs and Information in 1980 and adjustments up to 1993', p.116-7; Davies. 1986. 'The military and foreign policy in South Africa', p.310; Jaster. 1988. *The Defence of White Power*, p.29, 137; Muller. 1989. 'The Department of Foreign Affairs', p.245; Pottinger. 1988. *The Imperial Presidency*, p.35-43; Seegers. 1996. *The Military in the Making of Modern South Africa*, p.162; van Wyk, K. 1991. 'Foreign policy orientations of the P.W. Botha regime', p.45.

25.   Gastrow. 1992. *Who's Who in South African Politics*, p.50-4; de Klerk, F.W. 1998. *The Last Trek*; De Klerk, W.J. 1991. *F. W. de Klerk*.

26.   Arnold. 1992. *South Africa*.

27.   Geldenhuys & Kotzé. 1991. 'FW de Klerk', p.39, 32.

28.   Muller, C.F.J. 1998. 'The creation of the Department of External Affairs in 1927'; Muller, M.E. 1989. 'The Department of Foreign Affairs', p.243.

29.   Evans & Newnham. 1998. *The Penguin Dictionary of International Relations*, p.304-6; Plano & Olton. 1988. *The International Relations Dictionary*, p.7.

30.   Interview with Pik Botha, 20 April 1999.

31.   *Foreign Affairs List.*

32.   Letter from Douglas David Forsyth (Secretary for External Affairs) to all heads of department, 14 October 1954 (DoD, Group 5, KG/AOC/4/7, Vol. 22).

33.   Given that DFA, 1/99/13 contains no material.

34.   Geldenhuys. 1984. *The Diplomacy of Isolation*, p.15, 20; van Wyk, A.J. 1998. 'Eric Louw'.

35.   Barratt. 1975. 'The Department of Foreign Affairs', p.334; Muller, M.E. 1976. *Suid-Afrika se buitelandes verteenwoordiging (1910-1972)*, p.84; Muller, M.E. 1989. 'The Department of Foreign Affairs', p.246.

36.   Sole. 1994. 'South African foreign policy assumptions and objectives from Hertzog to de Klerk', p.108; Stevens. 1970. 'South Africa and independent Black Africa', p.27.

37.   Barber & Barratt. 1990. *South Africa's Foreign Policy*, p.65; Geldenhuys. 1984. *The Diplomacy of Isolation*, p.22-3; Nolutshungu. 1975. *South Africa in Africa*, p.79.

38.   Jooste. 1977. *Diensherinneringe*, p.185-205.

39.   Geldenhuys. 1984. *The Diplomacy of Isolation*, p.15, 27; Jooste. 1977. *Diensherinneringe*, p.187.

40.   Barber & Barratt. 1990. *South Africa's Foreign Policy*, p.65; Geldenhuys. 1984. *The Diplomacy of Isolation*, p.23; Munger. 1965. *Notes on the Formation of South African Foreign Policy*, p.31-2; de Beer, K.J. 1981. 'Die diplomatieke strategie van dr. Hilgard Muller teen die totale aanslag op die Republiek van Suid-Afrika'; Meiring. c1985. *Die lewe van Hilgard Muller*.

41.   Sole. 1989. 'This Above All', p.261. He was, *inter alia*, Minister Plenipotentiary, Permanent Mission to the UN, New York (1955-57) and Mission, Vienna (1957-61), Ambassador to Germany (1969-77) and the United States (1977-82). Barber & Barratt. 1990. *South Africa's Foreign Policy*, p.113, 182; Geldenhuys. 1984. *The Diplomacy of Isolation*, p.17, 123.

42.   Bach. 1990. 'Les initiatives franco-sud africains de «dialogue» avec l'Afrique francophone', p.206 (translated from French).

43.   Barber & Barratt. 1990. *South Africa's Foreign Policy*, p.213-4; Geldenhuys. 1984. *The Diplomacy of Isolation*, p.98; Harber & Ludmann. 1994. *A-Z of South African Politics*, p.9-10; Pottinger. 1988. *The Imperial Presidency*, p.210.

44.   Interview with Neil van Heerden and Paul Runge, 7 April 1999.

45.   Sole. 1984. 'Review of "The Diplomacy of Isolation"'.

46.   Interview with Paul Runge, 18 January 2003.

47.   Second to Ambassador, this post was a diplomatic appointment, as opposed to the politically appointed Ambassador.

48.   Barber & Barratt. 1990. *South Africa's Foreign Policy*, p.214; Geldenhuys. 1984. *The Diplomacy of Isolation*, p.131; Murray. 1989. 'The quiet South African', p.7-10.

49.   Interview with Neil van Heerden and Paul Runge, 7 April 1999.

50.   List provided by Ethel-Louise Mostert, Department of Defence Information Centre, Pretoria, 5 April 2002.

51.   *Paratus: Official Magazine of the South African Defence Force* 24, 5, May 1973: 50.

52.   Wilkins & Strydom. 1980. *The Super-Afrikaners*, p.A143.

53.   *Foreign Affairs List.* 1971.

54.   Interview with Neil van Heerden, 7 April 1999.

55.   Crocker. 1993. *High Noon in Southern Africa*, p.406; Hamann. 2001. *Days of the Generals*, p.82; TRC Report. *Vol. 2.* 1999. p.321-2.

56.   Ellis. 1998. 'The historical significance of South Africa's third force', p.269; Geldenhuys. 1984. *The Diplomacy of Isolation*, p.99-100.

57.   Wilkins & Strydom. 1980. *The Super-Afrikaners*, p.A99.

58.   Geldenhuys. 1984. *The Diplomacy of Isolation*, p.99-100.

59.   Sole. 1989. *'This Above All'*, p.262.

60.   De Villiers, L.E.S. 1980. *Secret Information*, p.17; Rhoodie. 1983. *The Real Information Scandal*, p.23, 38, 58, 65.

61.   De Villiers. 1980. *Secret Information*, p.119; Gastrow. 1985. *Who's Who in South African Politics.* Johannesburg: Ravan Press, 208-10; Starcke. 1978. *Survival*, p.132-47; Wilkins & Strydom. 1980. *The Super-Afrikaners*, p.196, A54, A163.

62.   Geldenhuys. 1984. *The Diplomacy of Isolation*, p.16-7; Muller, M.E. 1989. 'The Department of Foreign Affairs', p.250.

63.   Geldenhuys. 1984. *The Diplomacy of Isolation*, p.85, 108.

64.   Rhoodie. 1983. *The Real Information Scandal*, p.98.

65.   Geldenhuys. 1984. *The Diplomacy of Isolation*, p.147.

66.   Terblanche. 1983. *John Vorster*; Marx, C. 1994. 'The Ossewabrandwag as a mass movement'.

67.   D'Oliveira. 1978. *Vorster*, p.84-7, 243-4; Geldenhuys. 1984. *The Diplomacy of Isolation*, p.147; Seegers. 1996. *The Military in the Making of Modern South Africa*, p.127, 130-1, 153-4; Wilkins & Strydom. 1980. *The Super-Afrikaners*, p.5-6, 107, A239; Winter. 1981. *Inside BOSS*, p.19, 34, 36, 38-9, 42.

68.   'Instructions of the Prime Minister in Regard to the Intelligence Set-up for the Republic of South Africa', April 1969, p.2, 4. Document obtained from the National Intelligence Agency, Pretoria.

69.   De Villiers. 1980. *Secret Information*, p.62, 148-9; Rhoodie. 1983. *The Real Information Scandal*, p.74.

70.   Geldenhuys. 1984. *The Diplomacy of Isolation*, p.87, 148.

71.   Rhoodie. 1983. *The Real Information Scandal*, p.84, 99-100; Geldenhuys. 1984. *The Diplomacy of Isolation*, p.148.

72.   De Villiers. 1980. *Secret Information*, p.149.

73.   Barber & Barratt. 1990. *South Africa's Foreign Policy*, p.249-51; Ellis. 1998. 'The historical significance of South Africa's third force', p.266, 269; Geldenhuys. 1984. *The Diplomacy of Isolation*, p.120, 147; Jaster. 1988. *The Defence of White Power*, p.33-4; Pottinger. 1988. *The Imperial Presidency*, p.45.

74.   De Villiers. 1980. *Secret Information*, p.94-5; D'Oliveira. 1978. *Vorster*, p.194 (note 10); Rhoodie. 1983. *The Real Information Scandal*, p.71; Winter. 1981. *Inside BOSS*, p.45, 416.

75.   *Parliamentary Register.* 1991. p.5. On the Department of National Security, see Ellis. 1998. 'The historical significance of South Africa's third force', p.270; Geldenhuys. 1984. *The Diplomacy of Isolation*, p.36, 149; Pottinger. 1988. *The Imperial Presidency*, p.12, 14, 21; Winter. 1981. *Inside BOSS*, p.225.

76.   Gastrow. 1992. *Who's Who in South African Politics*, p.37-9; 'Wily lawyer who won Madiba's trust: Former champion of apartheid dies with integrity intact', *Sunday Times* 30 July 2000.

77.   Geldenhuys. 1984. *The Diplomacy of Isolation*, p.149; Gastrow. 1992. *Who's Who in South African Politics*, p.7.

78.   On Barnard, see Gastrow. 1987. *Who's Who in South African Politics*, p.16-7; Kotzé & Greyling. 1994. *Political Organisations in South Africa*, p.288; Seegers. 1996. *The Military in the Making of Modern South Africa*, p.248.

79.   *The Daily News* 21 November 1979, p.9; <http://www.anc.org.za/anc/newsbrief/1994/news0520>

80.   For example Barnard, L.D. 1977. 'Angola in die internasionale magskonstellasie'.

81.   *o the Point* 13 June 1980, p.19.

82.   Hackland. 1984. 'The Progressive Party of South Africa, 1959-1981'; Williams & Hackland. 1988. *The Dictionary of Contemporary Politics of Southern Africa*, p.210-2.

83.   Gastrow. 1987. *Who's Who in South African Politics*, p.85-9, 302-5.

84.   Slabbert. 1987. *The Last White Parliament*, p.5, 53; Gastrow. 1987. *Who's Who in South African Politics*, p.292-5.

85.   Slabbert. 1987. *The Last White Parliament*, p.177.

86.   <http://www.idasa.org.za>

87.   Williams. 2001. 'Intellectuals and the end of Apartheid', p.86, 96.

88.   Pelzer. 1970. *Die Afrikaner-Broederbond*; Serfontein. 1979. *Brotherhood of Power*, Wilkins & Strydom. 1980. *The Super-Afrikaners*.

89.   Geldenhuys. 1984. *The Diplomacy of Isolation*, p.31.

90.   Serfontein. 1979. *Brotherhood of Power*, p.145; Williams. 2001. 'Intellectuals and the end of Apartheid', p.94.

91.   Stone. 2001. 'Think Tanks', p.15668-9.

92.   Munger. 1965. *Notes on the Formation of South African Foreign Policy*, p.53; Geldenhuys. 1984. *The Diplomacy of Isolation*, p.17, 30, 170; Nolutshungu. 1975. *South Africa in Africa*, p.72.

93.   Geldenhuys. 1984. *The Diplomacy of Isolation*, p.170; Munger. 1965. *Notes on the Formation of South African Foreign Policy*, p.52.

94.   Williams. 2001. 'Intellectuals and the end of Apartheid', p.180, 190, 203.

95.   Cadet (1954-57); Third Secretary, Permanent Mission to the UN, New York (1958-66). 'Profile: John Barratt'; Starcke. 1978. *Survival*, p.47-55.

96.   Williams. 2001. 'Intellectuals and the end of Apartheid', p.184, 191-2; Geldenhuys. 1984. *The Diplomacy of Isolation*, p.30, 170.

97.   *The South African Institute of International Affairs.* 1984. p.5.

98.   Williams. 2001. 'Intellectuals and the end of Apartheid', p.226-7.

99.   Walker. 1982. *Powers of the Press*, p.314, 321-3.

100. Pogrund. 2000. *War of Words*.
101. Walker. 1982. *Powers of the Press*, p.313-35.
102. Frederikse. 1987. 'South Africa's media', p.642; Merrett & Saunders. 2000. 'The Weekly Mail'.
103. Manoim. 1996. *"You Have Been Warned"*.
104. Rutherford. 1992. *Dictionary of Economics*, p.342.
105. Nattrass. 1991. 'Controversies about capitalism and Apartheid in South Africa'.
106. Barber & Barratt. 1990. *South Africa's Foreign Policy*, p.257, 287; Geldenhuys. 1984. *The Diplomacy of Isolation*, p.161-5; Pottinger. 1988. *The Imperial Presidency*, p.117.
107. Geldenhuys. 1984. *The Diplomacy of Isolation*, p.161.
108. Fine & Rustomjee. 1996. *The Political Economy of South Africa*, p.63; Dollery. 1989. 'Capital, labour and state'.
109. Jones & Müller. 1992. *The South African Economy, 1910-90*, p.179.
110. Esterhuyse. 1986. *Anton Rupert*.
111. Sampson. 1987. *Black and Gold*, p.82.
112. Sampson. 1987. *Black and Gold*, p.129-31.
113. Fine & Rustomjee. 1996. *The Political Economy of South Africa*, p.149-174; Terreblanche & Nattrass. 1990. 'A periodization of the Political Economy from 1910', p.14-7.
114. ARCA, PV.203, File PS 5/1/1 contains the list of representatives.
115. Kotzé & Greyling. 1994. *Political Organisations in South Africa*, p.114.
116. DFA, 34/2, Vols. 2-3.
117. Kotzé & Greyling. 1994. *Political Organisations in South Africa*, p.117; O'Meara. 1983. *Volkskapitalisme*, p.143-8; Pretorius. 1994. 'The head of government and organised business', p.214-5, 243.
118. DFA, 34/3/4.
119. Wilkins & Strydom. 1980. *The Super-Afrikaners*, p.A221.
120. *Who's Who of Southern Africa, 1985*, p.492.
121. *SAFTO & the State of SA Trade*. 1984. p.17.
122. AHI: *Kongresagenda, Jaarverslag*, IDC: *Annual report and accounts, Directors' report and accounts, Annual report; Annual Report of the South Africa Foundation; Xhosa Development Corporation: annual report, 1973*, p.2; *Who's Who of Southern Africa, 1989-90*, p.266.
123. Wilkins & Strydom. 1980. *The Super-Afrikaners*, p.13, A106.
124. *Xhosa Development Corporation: annual report*, 1973-77.
125. Budlender. 1976. *Transkei Independence*, p.37.
126. AHI: *Kongresagenda, Jaarverslag*, IDC: *Annual report and accounts, Directors' report and accounts, Annual report; Who's Who of Southern Africa, 1989-90*, p.339-40.
127. Correspondence with Geoffrey Tyler, 26 February 2002. On Tyler: *Who's Who of Southern Africa, 1988-89*, p.507.
128. The mission's reports were provided by courtesy of Sheila de Villiers from the Chamber's head office in Durban.
129. Meiring. 1973. *Inside Information*, p.141.
130. NAT.ARC. MNL, IN10/1, 2; MNL, INL22, 74/7; MNL, INL26/1, 76; INL, 16/1/2/A, Vols. 1/2/26, 1/2/27/2, 1/2/27/3; Geldenhuys. 1984. *The Diplomacy of Isolation*, p.30, 175-6; Munger. 1965. *Notes on the Formation of South African Foreign Policy*, p.56-7; Sampson. 1987. *Black and Gold*, p.119.
131. Geldenhuys. 1984. *The Diplomacy of Isolation*, p.176.

132. *Annual Report of the South Africa Foundation.*

133. Correspondence with Peter Sorour, 31 January 2004; *Annual Report of the South Africa Foundation: 1959-89, 30 years,* p.16.

134. *Annual Report of the South Africa Foundation.*

135. Hudson. 1999. 'Christian Neethling Barnard'.

136. Penn. 1974. *The Right to Look Human.*

137. Trustee (1970-73), Member of the Council (1973-76), Deputy President (1976-77), President (1977-79), and Honorary President (1979-96). Information provided by courtesy of Rose Fitzpatrick from the South Africa Foundation.

138. *Who's Who of Southern Africa, 1990-91,* p.260, 262; Sampson. 1987. *Black and Gold,* p.91, 115; <http://www.mbendi.co.za/vpsabeh.htm>

139. Membership Campaign Manager (1962-65); Deputy Director (1966-67); Financial Director (1968-72); Director General (1973-87). Information provided by courtesy of Rose Fitzpatrick, South Africa Foundation, January 2002.

140. Executive Trustee (1967-70), Trustee (1970-92), Deputy President (1972-73), President (1974-77), Honorary President (1983-92). Information provided by courtesy of Rose Fitzpatrick, South Africa Foundation, January 2002.

141. Verhoef. 1992. 'Afrikaner nationalism in South African banking', p.115-53.

142. *SAFTO: annual report, 1994/5,* p.3.

143. '30 years of exports: Wim Holtes reflects', *SAFTO Exporter* 29, 4, April 1992: 1.

144. *SAFTO & the State of SA Trade.* 1984. p.9.

145. *SAFTO & the State of SA Trade.* 1984. p.11; *SAFTO: annual report, 1987/8,* p.2.

146. *SAFTO & the State of SA Trade.* 1984. p.9; interview with Wim Holtes, 31 March 1999.

147. DFA, 34/2, Vols. 2-3.

148. Geldenhuys. 1984. *The Diplomacy of Isolation,* p.163-4; *SAFTO & the State of SA Trade.* 1984. p.16-7.

149. 'Policy and initial operations plan', 1963, p.1-2. (ARCA, PV.799, File S33/14/13/2(1)); *SAFTO Annual Report, 1967/8,* p.5; *1968/9,* p.4; *1970/1,* p.4; *1976/7,* p.6; *1977/8,* p.6; *1984/5,* p.5; *1986/7,* p.5; *1987/8,* p.6-7.

150. Adresses contained in ARCA, PV.118, File 3/2/6 and File 3/2/9.

151. Interview with Wim Holtes, 31 March 1999.

152. 'Angola floating exhibition' (10-27 May 1969) on a ship that sailed from Durban to Luanda (ARCA, PV.799, File S33/14/3/C(2); *SAFTO Newsletter* 5, 1, January 1969; 'Angola: explosion on our doorstep. An export seminar', 3 December 1969, Johannesburg (ARCA, PV.799, File S33/14/13/2(2)); 'Angola: rich, natural market on South Africa's doorstep', *SAFTO Exporter* 5, 9, September 1968: 1, 3-5; 'Afrika subkomitee', Annexure 3(C), from the Department of Commerce, 16 May 1969, p.4 (DFA, 34/2, Vol. 4).

153. *SAFTO: annual report, 1974/5,* p.3; *1976/7,* p.5; *1977/8,* p.5; *1978/9,* p.10; *1979/80,* p.2; *1980/1,* p.11.

154. *IDC: annual report, 1980,* p.2; Clark. 1994. *Manufacturing Apartheid,* p.108, 130-2, 160, 208 (note 80); IDC of South Africa Ltd. 1992. 'The Industrial Development Corporation of South Africa Ltd', p.150.

155. Clark. 1994. *Manufacturing Apartheid,* p.166.

156. IDC of South Africa Ltd. 1992. 'The Industrial Development Corporation of South Africa Ltd', p.151-2.

157. IDC: *Annual report and accounts, directors' report and accounts.*

158. Interview with Wim Holtes, 31 March 1999.

159. Meinardus. 1980. *Die Afrikapolitik der Republik Südafrika*, p.351-3.
160. Innes. 1984. *Anglo American and the Rise of Modern South Africa*, p.13.
161. Kanfer. 1993. *The Last Empire*; Roberts. 2003. *Glitter and Greed.*
162. Vincent. 1999. 'Non-state actors in International Relations', p.128.
163. De Villiers, F. 2003. 'Julian Ogilvie Thompson'; *The Giants.* 1991. p.6, 12, 41; Fine & Rustomjee. 1996. *The Political Economy of South Africa*, p.10, 143; Innes. 1984. *Anglo American and the Rise of Modern South Africa*, p.204, 221, 229, 231-2, 234, 274; Sampson. 1987. *Black and Gold*, p.30, 251.
164. Waldmeir. 1997. *Anatomy of a Miracle*, p.29.
165. Interview with Michael Spicer, 7 April 1999.
166. Munger. 1965. *Notes on the Formation of South African Foreign Policy*, p.62.
167. *Argus* 15 May, *The Star* 15 May 1975.
168. *The Star* 22 November 1979, cited in Shelton. 1986. 'Theoretical perspectives on South African foreign policy making', p.11.
169. <http://www.bessemer.co.za>
170. *SAFTO Exporter* 24, 7, July 1987: 1.
171. 'Profile of the Firm of BCHOD ', dated September 2001. Document provided by courtesy of Tim Ashford from the company's Johannesburg office.
172. *SAFTO & the State of Trade.* 1984. p.43.
173. *Export Project Insurance.* c1998. p.2-3, 5-6, 9, 11, 13-4; *Credit Guarantee.* 1991. p.3-4, 7, 27, 45.
174. Interview with Wim Holtes, 31 March 1999; Meinardus. 1980. *Die Afrikapolitik der Republik Südafrika*, p.351-5.
175. *Credit Guarantee.* 1991. p.3. All amounts in this study were calculated from South African Rand according to *International Financial Statistics.* Washington, DC: IMF.
176. Correspondence with Christoph Leisewitz, 27 May 1999; *Credit Guarantee.* 1991. p.7
177. DFA, 34/2, Vols. 2-3.
178. *Who's Who of Southern Africa, 1979*, p.133; Oppenheimer & Mynhardt. 1996. *Make the World Your Market*, p.45-7; *SAFTO: annual report*; Bouwer. 1988. 'Trade credit and trade credit insurance'.
179. Interview with Wim Holtes, 31 March 1999.
180. Oppenheimer & Mynhardt. 1996. *Make the World Your Market*, p.46-7.
181. Correspondence with Christoph Leisewitz, 27 May 1999; *Who's Who of Southern Africa, 1999*, p.273; *SAFTO: annual report.*
182. Innes. 1984. *Anglo American and the Rise of Modern South Africa*, p.204; Pallister, Stewart & Lepper. 1987. *South Africa Inc.*, p.10; *Anglo American Corporation: annual report*; *LTA Limited: centenary review, 1889-1989.* 1989. p.1, 19-20, 25; *LTA Limited: annual report.*
183. *Business Day* 11 July 2000; <http://www.lta.co.za>
184. Innes. 1984. *Anglo American and the Rise of Modern South Africa*, p.204; *LTA Limited.* 1989. p.20-5.
185. Correspondence with Spencer Whiting, 21 April 2004.
186. *Murray & Roberts.* 1976. p.19-23; *Financial Mail* 27 July 1984; *Murray & Roberts: annual report.*
187. *Murray & Roberts.* 1976. p.48.
188. Cited in Ryan. 1991. 'Trade roots'; *Business Day* 7 October 1992.
189. Interview with Neil van Heerden and Paul Runge, 7 April 1999.
190. Telephone interview with Aliki Boyazoglu, Johannesburg, niece of Steve Boyazoglu, 21 April 1999.

191. *Who's Who of Southern Africa, 1979*, p.133; his interview in *Murray & Roberts*. 1976. p.70; *Murray & Roberts: annual report*, 1968-79.
192. Wilkins & Strydom. 1980. *The Super-Afrikaners*, p.A24.
193. Correspondence with Donald Sole, 2 February 2004; Sole. 1989. *'This Above All'*, p.314.
194. Correspondence with Jan Boyazoglu, 6 March 2004.
195. *ARB: Economic, Financial and Technical Series* 16, 3, 1979: 5048.
196. Clark. 1994. *Manufacturing Apartheid*, p.149; *Safmarine*. 1976. p.18-21; Stuttaford. 1986. *Safmarine*.
197. Meredith. 1995. *Sky Trek*.
198. Uys, F. 1993. 'Airlines of Africa', p.23.
199. His interview in *Safren*. 1991. p.34; Dodgen. 1991. 'The sky is open', p.12; Ingpen & le Roux. 1996. *Safmarine 50*, p.106-7, 157; 'Safair'. 1993; *Financial Mail* 13 May 1988, p.84; Stuttaford. 1986. *Safmarine*, p.55-6.
200. Interview with Pieter van Aswegen, 2 November 2001.
201. *The Giants*. 1991. p.28; Innes. 1984. *Anglo American and the Rise of Modern South Africa*, p.221; Pallister, Stewart & Lepper. 1987. *South Africa Inc.*, p.7.
202. Hall. 1995. 'The legend of the Lost City', p.196.
203. Rogerson. 1990. 'Sun International', p.346.
204. *Sun International*. 1985. p.11.
205. *Who's Who of Southern Africa, 1985*, p.299; *Annual Report of the South Africa Foundation*; Silber. 1999. 'Solomon Kerzner'.
206. 'Allegations of collusion with Sol Kerzner', ANC Department of Information and Publicity, Johannesburg, 1 August <http://www.anc.org.za/ancdocs/pr/1996/pr0801a.html>; 'Mandela confirms Kerzner did contribute funds to ANC kitty', 10 August <http://www.doj.gov.za/trc/media/1996/9608/s960810a.htm>; *Mail & Guardian* 13 September 1996.
207. *Daily Dispatch* 3 February 1999. According to apartheid legislation, casinos were only allowed in the homelands.
208. 'Sale and distribution of book about Sol Kerzner remains suspended', 29 October 1997 <http://fxi.org.za/alerts/1997/upkerz.htm>

Chapter 3: Wind of Change

1. Barratt. 1985. 'South African diplomacy at the UN', p.192; Boutros-Ghali. 1994. 'Introduction', p.8, 18; Mathews. 1988. 'The African Group at the UN as an instrument of African diplomacy'.
2. Andemicael. 1976. *The OAU and the UN*, p.134; Boutros-Ghali. 1994. 'Introduction', p.40-1; Kay. 1970. *The New Nations in the United Nations*, p.25-6, 66.
3. Term borrowed from Olivier. 1973. 'Die grondslae van Suid-Afrika se buitelandse beleid', p.239.
4. Breitenbach. 1974. *South Africa in the Modern World (1910-1970)*, p.512.
5. Nolutshungu. 1975. *South Africa in Africa*, p.102.
6. Louw, E.H. 1959. *The Union and the Emergent States of Africa*, p.3, 7; Louw, E.H. 1957. *Union's Africa Policy*.
7. Biermann. 1963. *The Case for South Africa, as Put Forth in the Public Statements of Eric H. Louw, Foreign Minister of South Africa*, p.86; Jooste. 1977. *Diensherinneringe*, p.210-5; Sole. 1994. 'South African foreign policy assumptions and objectives from Hertzog to de Klerk', p.108.
8. Spence. 1965. *Republic Under Pressure*, p.73.

9. Barratt. 1972. 'South Africa's Outward Policy', p.546-7; Muller, M.E. 1976. *Suid-Afrika se buitelandes verteenwoordiging (1910-1972)*, p.137, 143-4; Nöthling. 1998. 'South Africa and Africa'.

10. *Foreign Affairs List*. 1964.

11. Barber & Barratt. 1990. *South Africa's Foreign Policy*, p.77.

12. Cockram. 1970. *Vorster's Foreign Policy*, p.134; Geldenhuys. 1984. *The Diplomacy of Isolation*, p.14.

13. Cockram. 1970. *Vorster's Foreign Policy*, p.133; Olivier. 1973. 'Die grondslae van Suid-Afrika se buitelandse beleid', p.224.

14. DFA, 22/12, Vols. 2-3.

15. *The Star* 12 December 1967.

16. Barratt. 1972. 'South Africa's Outward Policy', p.544; Barber & Barratt. 1990. *South Africa's Foreign Policy*, p.76; Cockram. 1970. *Vorster's Foreign Policy*, p.140; Geldenhuys. 1984. *The Diplomacy of Isolation*, p.13, 50.

17. Abi-Saab. 1978. *The United Nations Operation in the Congo.*

18. De Witte. 2002. *The Assassination of Lumumba.*

19. For basic historic facts about African states: Esterhuysen. 1998. *Africa A-Z.*

20. Barratt. 1975. 'The Department of Foreign Affairs'; Berridge. 1992. *South Africa, the Colonial Powers and "African Defence"*; Nöthling. 1998. 'South Africa and Africa', p.29-33; Nolutshungu. 1975. *South Africa in Africa*, p.39-59; Olivier. 1973. 'Die grondslae van Suid-Afrika se buitelandse beleid', p.213-9; Olivier. 1977. *Suid-Afrika se buitelandse beleid*, p.126-33; Olivier. 1982. 'South Africa's relations with Africa', p.269-85.

21. DoD, Group 5, KG/GPW/2/5/1, Vol. 341; KG/GPW/2/5/2, Vols. 1-4, Vol. 342, KG/GPW/2/5/3, Vol. 342; Barber & Barratt. 1990. *South Africa's Foreign Policy*, p.57-8.

22. *New York Times* 13 March 1954.

23. Barber & Barratt. 1990. *South Africa's Foreign Policy*, p.100-1.

24. Verwoerd. 1964. *I. Crisis in World Conscience; II. The Road to Freedom for Basutoland, Bechuanaland, Swaziland*, p.4; his first interview after having taken office: *Rand Daily Mail* 15 December 1958.

25. NAT.ARC., BTS 22/1/112/1+PL, Vol. 1; Guelke. 1972. 'South African foreign policy in Africa', p.218-9; Meinardus. 1980. *Die Afrikapolitik der Republik Südafrika*, p.421-2; Nolutshungu. 1975. *South Africa in Africa*, p.86-7.

26. DoD, Group 5, DKG/EXT/6/6, Vol. 175.

27. *The New Encyclopaedia Britannica, Vol. 8*. 1986. p.27.

28. Botha, C.B. 1993. 'Soldiers of Fortune or Whores of War?', p.84.

29. Hoare, M. 1967. *Congo Mercenary*; Hoare, M. 1989. *The Road to Kalamata*; Lunel. 1991. *Bob Denard*; Denard. 1998. *Corsaire de la république*; McNamara. 1989. *France in Black Africa*, p.176-8; Rogers. 2000. *Someone Else's War*, p.16-31; Weinberg. 1994. *Last of the Pirates*, p.64-5.

30. Hoare, M. 1989. *The Road to Kalamata*; Hoare, C. 1986. 'Mad Mike's own story'.

31. *The Star* 25 August 1964.

32. Letter from Brand Fourie to Gerhardt Jooste, New York, 31 March 1961 (NAT.ARC., BTS 1/112/5/1, Vol. 1).

33. Hocking. 1973. *Oppenheimer and Son*, p.95, 119, 204; Jessup. 1979. *Ernest Oppenheimer*, p.9, 132, 138-9, 162, 177-8, 191, 227; Newbury. 1989. *The Diamond Ring*, p.240, 248, 250, 358.

34. Letter from Harry Oppenheimer to Hendrik Verwoerd, 13 September 1960 (ARCA, PV.93, File 1/53/2/4).

35.   Letter from Hendrik Verwoerd to Harry Oppenheimer, 13 September 1960 (ARCA, PV.93, File 1/53/2/4).

36.   *The Star* 19 October 1964.

37.   'Huursoldate in die Kongo', from Tassie Taswell (Under-Secretary, Africa Division), 13 October 1964; 'The Congolese Army and the white volunteers', from Albie Burger to Gerhardt Jooste, 5 April 1965 (DFA, 1/112/5/1, Vol. 3).

38.   Hoare, M. 1967. *Congo Mercenary*; *The Star* 25 August 1964; Lunel. 1991. *Bob Denard*, p.272, 275, 279; Rogers. 2000. *Someone Else's War*, p.31-6.

39.   'Die Republiek se verhoudings met Afrika in die algemeen en met die Demokratiese Republiek van die Kongo in die besonder', 3 September 1964; *Rand Daily Mail* 27 August 1964.

40.   'Press statement by the Hon. the Prime Minister of the Republic of South Africa', Department of Information, 1 September 1964 (DFA, 1/112/3, Vol. 4).

41.   Gleijeses. 2001. *Conflicting Missions*, p.126.

42.   Gleijeses. 2001. *Conflicting Missions*, p.126-7.

43.   Barratt. 1971. *Dialogue in Africa*, p.101; Breytenbach, W.J. 1977. *South Africa Looks to Africa*, p.1; Johns. 1971. 'South Africa's diplomatic opening to the north', p.784-5; Molteno. 1971. 'South Africa's forward policy in Africa', p.342; Woldring. 1975. 'South Africa's Africa policy reconsidered', p.84-5.

44.   'Attitude of Zaïre towards the Republic', from Johan Pretorius, 16 January 1973, p.1 (DFA, 1/112/3, Vol. 5).

45.   Geldenhuys. 1984. *The Diplomacy of Isolation*, p.31, 172-3, 187; Serfontein. 1979. *Brotherhood of Power*, p.149; Wilkins & Strydom. 1980. *The Super-Afrikaners*, p.401, A33, A294; Williams. 2001. *Intellectuals and the End of Apartheid*, p.95-6; Steyn. 2002. *Penvegter*.

46.   Cillié. 1968. 'Outwards', p.8.

47.   Geldenhuys. 1984. *The Diplomacy of Isolation*, p.26.

48.   Geldenhuys. 1984. *The Diplomacy of Isolation*, p.19, 256 (note 176).

Chapter 4: What Relations with Africa?

1.   Geldenhuys. 1984. *The Diplomacy of Isolation*, p.192.

2.   *News/Check* 4, 6, 24 September 1965: 32-3, 35, 37.

3.   Vorster. 1970. *South Africa's Outward Policy*.

4.   Barber & Barratt. 1990. *South Africa's Foreign Policy*, p.143-50; Geldenhuys. 1984. *The Diplomacy of Isolation*, p.34-8; Geldenhuys. 1994. 'The head of government and South Africa's foreign relations', p.268-70; Guelke. 1972. 'South African foreign policy in Africa', p.228-9; Meinardus. 1980. *Die Afrikapolitik der Republik Südafrika*, p.60-8.

5.   Barratt. 1970. 'South Africa's Outward Movement', p.129-31; Barratt. 1972. 'South Africa's Outward Policy', p.549-51; Breitenbach. 1974. *South Africa in the modern world (1910-1970)*, p.511-2; D'Oliveira. 1978. *Vorster*, p.218-9; Geldenhuys. 1984. *The Diplomacy of Isolation*, p.34; Guelke. 1972. 'South African foreign policy in Africa', p.270; Meinardus. 1980. *Die Afrikapolitik der Republik Südafrika*, p.55-6; Nolutshungu. 1975. *South Africa in Africa*, p.114; Swanepoel. 1982. 'Die diplomasie van adv. B.J. Vorster', p.252.

6.   Geldenhuys. 1984. *The Diplomacy of Isolation*, p.19; Guelke. 1972. 'South African foreign policy in Africa', p.252.

7.   Geldenhuys. 1984. *The Diplomacy of Isolation*, p.130.

8. 'Visit to the Comoros Islands, 4-7 December 1979', from Carl von Hirschberg to Brand Fourie, 1 May 1980, p.4 (DFA, 1/203/3, Vol. 4).

9. Christiansen & Kydd. 1983. 'The return of Malawian labour from South Africa and Zimbabwe'; Hughes. 1973. 'Malawi and South Africa's co-prosperity sphere'.

10. 'Initial contact between South Africa/Malawi', 22 September 1976, p.6-7 (DFA, 1/158/3, Vol. 14); letter from Hastings Banda to Albie Burger, 15 June; letter from Hastings Kamuzu to Albie Burger, 4 July 1966 (DFA, 1/158/3, Vol. 8).

11. Guelke. 1972. 'South African foreign policy in Africa', p.266.

12. DFA, 1/158/3, 2PL.

13. 'Malawi', p.4-11, 14 (DFA, 1/158/3, AJ 1979).

14. *Rand Daily Mail* 8 March 1967; Sindima. 2002. *Malawi's First Republic*, p.176.

15. *Foreign Affairs List*.

16. ARCA, PV.118, File 3/2/8; DFA, 1/158/3, Vol. 4; Barratt. 1970. 'South Africa's Outward Movement', p.133-4; Barratt. 1973. *Southern Africa*, p.12; D'Oliveira. 1978. *Vorster*, p.218; Guelke. 1972. 'South African foreign policy in Africa', p.263; Kalley. 2001. *South Africa's Treaties in Theory and Practice*, p.527, 545, 557; Swanepoel. 1982. 'Die diplomasie van adv. B.J. Vorster', p.176-82.

17. Letter from Lang Piet Rautenbach to Hastings Banda, May 1969 (DFA, 1/158/3, Vol. 5); letter from Hastings Banda to Lang Piet Rautenbach, 3 June 1969 (DFA, 1/158/3, Vol. 8; ARCA, PV.132, File 2/6/1/19).

18. Provided by courtesy of Hester van der Berg, SA Media, University of the Free State.

19. M.Comm and D.Comm, University of Pretoria (1953, 1957); Department of National Resources (1957-60); Director for Planning, Department of Trade and Industry (1960-64); Chairman, Resources and Planning Advisory Council (1964-70). *Suid-Afrikaanse Oorsig* 1 February 1980, p.12-3; correspondence with Renée Conradie, 29 February 2004; *Who's Who of Southern Africa, 1970*, p.790.

20. Africa Institute annual reports; correspondence with Erich Leistner, 13 January 2004; Rhoodie. 1983. *The Real Information Scandal*, p.80.

21. Correspondence with Renée Conradie, 29 February 2004.

22. Planning Adviser to the Prime Minister (1969-75); Chairman, Planning Advisory Council (1976-82) and Public Service Commission (1976-82); Ambassador Extraordinary and Plenipotentiary on Special Assignment (1982-84). Correspondence with Renée Rautenbach, 29 February 2004; *Who's Who of Southern Africa, 1985*, p.429; *Suid-Afrikaanse Oorsig* 1 February 1980, p.12; *Rand Daily Mail* 7 May 1982.

23. Correspondence with Renée Conradie, 29 February 2004; Wilkins & Strydom. 1980. *The Super-Afrikaners*, p.10, 402, A193; *Die Afrikaner* 21 April 1982, p.4.

24. Literally translated "(coloured) maidservant, servant-girl", a term generally used in a somewhat derogatory sense when referring to black or mixed-blood females.

25. Correspondence with Erich Leistner, 13 January 2004 (emphasis in the original).

26. Correspondence with Renée Conradie, 29 February 2004.

27. Potts. 1985. 'Capital relocation in Africa', p.188.

28. Letter from Hastings Banda to Hilgard Muller, 4 September 1967, p.2 (DFA, 1/158/3, Vol. 2PL).

29. 'Malawi', p.15 (DFA, 1/158/3, AJ 1979).

30. *Malawi Hansard* 29 January 1968, p.238 (ARCA, PV.377, File 1/A1, Vol. 1).

31. *The Star* 22 November 1966 and 31 May 1967; *Rand Daily Mail* 7 October 1966.

32. Innes. 1984. *Anglo American and the Rise of Modern South Africa*, p.166.

33. Biddlecombe. 1966. 'IMEX'; *Financial Mail* 19 January 1968, p.153.

34. Correspondence with Klaus Oppenheimer, 26 March 2002.

35.   *The Star* 4 May 1968; Cockram. 1970. *Vorster's Foreign Policy*, p.142; Guelke. 1972. 'South African foreign policy in Africa', p.265; Sindima. 2002. *Malawi's First Republic*, p.177.

36.   Cockram. 1970. *Vorster's Foreign Policy*, p.143.

37.   *Rand Daily Mail* 8 May 1968; Cockram. 1970. *Vorster's Foreign Policy*, p.143.

38.   Potts. 1985. 'Capital relocation in Africa', p.183.

39.   Letter from Hastings Banda to Hilgard Muller, 4 September 1967, p.3 (DFA, 1/158/3, Vol. 2PL).

40.   *Rand Daily Mail* 8 May 1968; Cockram. 1970. *Vorster's Foreign Policy*, p.141-3; Guelke. 1972. 'South African foreign policy in Africa', p.265; *SAFTO Exporter* 5, 6, June 1968: 4-5.

41.   *Report of the 1968 Business & Goodwill Mission to Malawi.* 1968; Sindima. 2002. *Malawi's First Republic*, p.177.

42.   ARCA, PV.132, File 2/6/1/23. Mentioned by Cockram. 1970. *Vorster's Foreign Policy*, p.144.

43.   *Report of the 1968 Business & Goodwill Mission to Malawi.* 1968. p.14 (ARCA, PV.799, File S33/14/3/D(1)).

44.   *Report of the 1973 Trade Mission to Malawi.* 1973. p.5, 12.

45.   *Reunion, Mauritius, Malawi . . . report of 1979 trade mission.* 1979. p.17.

46.   Correspondence with Geoffrey Tyler, 27 February 2002; *Who's Who of Southern Africa, 1981*, p.323.

47.   ARCA, PV.799, File S33/14/3/D(1) (translated from Afrikaans).

48.   ARCA, PV.799, File S33/14/3/D(1), p.16.

49.   Reuvid. 1995. 'The petroleum industry', p.232-5.

50.   O'Meara. 1983. *Volkskapitalisme.*

51.   DFA, 1/115/3, Vols. 1A, 2PL.

52.   DFA, 1/115/3, Vols. 1, 5; 1/115/4, Vol. 3.

53.   Letter from Albie Burger, 8 April 1968 (DFA, 1/115/3, Vol. 3).

54.   Innes. 1984. *Anglo American and the Rise of Modern South Africa*, p.234; Meinardus. 1980. *Die Afrikapolitik der Republik Südafrika*, p.360.

55.   Interview with Michael Spicer, 7 April 1999.

56.   O'Meara. 1983. *Volkskapitalisme.*

57.   Report of that mission, p.1, 9 (DFA, 1/115/3, Vol. 3).

58.   'Compte-rendu d'une visite à Madagascar', from Lang Piet Rautenbach, 19 March 1969, p.3, 6-7 (DFA, 1/115/4, Vol. 1); DFA, 1/115/3, Vols. 3-4.

59.   DFA, 1/115/3, Vol. 5; 1/115/4, Vol. 3; 1/115/4/1, Vol. 1.

60.   Letter from Albie Burger, 8 April 1968 (DFA, 1/115/3, Vol. 3).

61.   Interview with Michael Spicer, 7 April 1999.

62.   'Hotel project – Nossi Be', 8 December 1969, p.1-3 (DFA, 1/115/4/1, Vol. 1); *The Star* 20 January 1970.

63.   'Working paper: Nossi Bé', 22 June 1970, p.1-4 (DFA, 1/115/4/1, Vol. 2).

64.   DFA, 1/115/4/1, Vol. 1.

65.   DFA, 1/115/3, Vol. 6.

66.   'Loan agreement entered into by and between the Government of the Republic of South Africa and the Government of the Malagasy Republic', 20 November 1970 (DFA, 1/115/4/1, Vol. 3).

67.   'Memorandum of agreement entered into by and between the Government of the Malagasy Republic and la Société Anonyme Malgache des Hotels "Southern Sun" and Southern Sun Hotel Corporation (Proprietary) Limited and the Export Finance Company of South Africa (Proprietary) Limited', p.3-4 (DFA,

1/115/4/1, AJ 1970); 'Press release: South Africa/Madagascar loan agreement, p.1-2 (DFA, 1/115/4/1, Vol. 3); *Rand Daily Mail* 14 November 1970; Guelke. 1972. 'South African foreign policy in Africa', p.268.

68.　Banda's speech on 9 April 1969 in DFA, 1/115/3, Vol. 4.

69.　DFA, 1/115/3, Vols. 3-4; *Who's Who of Southern Africa, 1972*, p.988.

70.　DFA, 1/115/4/2, AJ 1970; 1/115/4/2, Vol. 2.

71.　'Summary of discussions in Cape Town on 1 March 1971 between the Minister of Foreign Affairs, the Secretary for Foreign Affairs and Mr P.J. Ullmann, Inter-Afrique Advisory Services', 3 March, p.6, 8; 'The Narinda Bay project', April 1971, p.5 (DFA, 1/115/4/2, Vols. 1-2).

72.　DFA, 1/115/3, Vol. 6, AJ 1971; 1/115/4/2.

73.　'Relations with Madagascar: discussions with Mr P.J. Ullmann, Pretoria, 23 June 1971', June 1971, p.2 (DFA, 1/115/4/2, Vol. 1).

74.　Correspondence with Basil Hersov, 9 February 2004.

75.　'Relations with Madagascar: discussions with Mr P.J. Ullmann, Pretoria, 23 June 1971', June 1971, p.5, 2 (DFA, 1/115/4/2, Vol. 1).

76.　*Matin* (Antananarivo) 24 June 1972.

77.　*Sunday Express* 25 June 1972.

78.　DFA, 1/115/4/1, Vols. 4-5; 1/115/4/1/1, Vol. 3; Rogerson. 1990. 'Sun International', p.346-7.

79.　*Matin* (Antananarivo) 24 June 1972.

80.　*Pretoria News* 25 August 1972.

81.　Reprinted in *Africa Contemporary Record, 1969-70*: C41-5.

82.　Burundi, Central African Republic, Chad, Congolese Republic, Democratic Republic of Congo, Ethiopia, Kenya, Rwanda, Somalia, Sudan, Tanzania, Uganda, Zambia.

83.　Barber & Barratt. 1990. *South Africa's Foreign Policy*, p.146-7; Barratt. 1973. *Southern Africa*, p.14-5; Guelke. 1972. 'South African foreign policy in Africa', p.270-1.

84.　Serfontein. 1970. *Die verkrampte aanslag*, p.110-6; Schoeman, B.M. 1974. *Vorster se 100 dae*.

85.　Muller. 1967. 'South Africa in today's Africa', p.305.

86.　De St. Jorre. 1977. 'South Africa', p.78-80.

87.　Muller, H. 1967. 'South Africa in today's Africa', p.305.

88.　Panter-Brick. 1988. 'Independence, French style'.

89.　Chafer. 2001. 'French African policy in historical perspective', p.177; Chipman. 1989. *French Power in Africa*, p.8, 115-20, 149, 227, 232, 241, 256; McNamara. 1989. *France in Black Africa*, p.149, 210; Nwokedi. 1989. 'France's Africa', p.192-3.

90.　Andereggen. 1994. *France's Relationship with Subsaharan Africa*, p.77; Chipman. 1989. *French Power in Africa*, p.233.

91.　McNamara. 1989. *France in Black Africa*, p.187.

92.　Faligot & Krop. 1985. *La piscine*, p.11-5, 223-5; McNamara. 1989. *France in Black Africa*, p.190; Shennan. 1993. *De Gaulle*, p.78; van Meter. 1980. 'The French role in Africa', p.30-2; *Who's Who in France, 1989-1990*, p.678; Yao. 1996. 'Jacques Foccart', p.60-76.

93.　McNamara. 1989. *France in Black Africa*, p.187; Andereggen. 1994. *France's Relationship with Subsaharan Africa*, p.76-7.

94.　Samuel. 1999. *Michel Debré*, p.198.

95.　Minister of Justice (1958-59); Prime Minister (1959-62); Minister of Economy and Finances (1966-68); Minister of Foreign Affairs (1968-69). *Who's Who in France, 1989-1990*, p.522.

96.   Renamed General Directorate for External Security (DGSE) in 1982
<http://www.dgse.org/informations/histoire.php>
97.   Chipman. 1989. *French Power in Africa*, p.233; Faligot & Krop. 1985. *La piscine*, p.228-31; McNamara. 1989. *France in Black Africa*, p.192-3; Péan, Pierre. 1983. *Affaires africaines*, p.8; <http://www.africaintelligence.com/ps/FR/Arch/LC-/LC-_314.asp>
98.   Faligot & Krop. 1985. *La piscine*, p.253-4 (translated from French).
99.   Foccart. 1997. *Foccart parle. Vol. II*, p.110 (translated from French).
100.   Faligot & Krop. 1985. *La piscine*, p.253; Foccart. 1995. *Foccart parle. Vol. I*, p.213; Lunel. 1991. *Bob Denard*, p.396-7, 404; Samuel. 1999. *Michel Debré*, p.105-6; Weinberg. 1994. *Last of the Pirates*, p.246.
101.   Interview with Neels van Tonder, 19 March 2002; Grundy. 1973. *Confrontation and Accommodation in Southern Africa*, p.143.
102.   Stockholm International Peace Research Institute. 1976. *Southern Africa*, p.208-9; Cuddumbey. 1996. 'France and South Africa', p.70-1.
103.   Interview with Pik Botha, 20 April 1999.
104.   DFA, 22/3/26, Vol. 2; Bach. 1990. 'Un système autonome de relations', p.184.
105.   Harshe. 1983. 'France, Francophone African states and South Africa', p.56-7; Bach. 1990. 'Un système autonome de relations', p.175-80.
106.   Darbon. 1990. 'Les rapports franco-sud africains depuis 1977', p.233.
107.   Alden. 1996. 'From policy autonomy to policy integration', p.18-9; Bach. 1990. 'Un système autonome de relations', p.174.
108.   Alden & Daloz. 1996. 'Introduction', p.2; Alden. 1996. 'From policy autonomy to policy integration', p.14; Bach. 1990. 'Un système autonome de relations', p.184-7; Harshe. 1983. 'France, Francophone African states and South Africa', p.55.
109.   'Voorgenome ontmoeting: Dr Muller en 'n ander minister – Presidente Houphouet-Boigny en Bongo', from Fritz Loots to P.W. Botha, 29 May 1970, p.3 (DoD, MV/56/16, Vol. 26) (translated from Afrikaans).
110.   DFA, 1/184/4, Vol. 1.
111.   DFA, 1/184/3, AJ 1971 and 1/184/4, AJ 1966.
112.   Letter from John Vorster to François Tombalbaye, 1 March 1967 (DFA, 1/184/3, Vol. 1PL).
113.   Letter from François Tombalbaye to John Vorster, 31 March 1967 (DFA, 1/184/3, Vol. 1PL).
114.   Letter from Hilgard Muller to François Tombalbaye, 14 May 1967; letter from François Tombalbaye to Hilgard Muller, 14 February 1970 (DFA, 1/184/3, Vol. 1).
115.   'Tsjaad (24-26 April 1967)', from Neels van Tonder, p.1 (DFA, 1/184/3, Vol. 1); DFA, 1/184/3, Vols. 1, 1PL; 1/184/4, Vols. 2PL, 3PL.
116.   Letter from Hilgard Muller to François Tombalbaye, 14 May 1967, p.2 (DFA, 1/184/3, Vol. 1).
117.   Letter from Neels van Tonder to Fritz Loots, 11 July 1969, p.4 (DoD, MV/56/16, Vol. 26) (translated from Afrikaans).
118.   Letter from François Tombalbaye to John Vorster, 31 March 1967 (DFA, 1/184/3, Vol. 1PL).
119.   'Tsjaad (24-26 April 1967)', from Neels van Tonder, p.2 (DFA, 1/184/3, Vol. 1).
120.   Letter from François Tombalbaye to John Vorster, 10 May 1967 (DFA, 1/184/3, Vol. 1).
121.   Letter from Hilgard Muller to François Tombalbaye, 14 May 1967, p.2 (DFA, 1/184/3, Vol. 1).

122. Letter from Neels van Tonder to Fritz Loots, 11 July 1969, p.4 (DoD, MV/56/16, Vol. 26) (translated from Afrikaans).

123. DFA, 1/184/4, Vol. 3PL.

124. Letter from François Tombalbaye to Hilgard Muller, 14 February 1970, p.2 (DFA, 1/184/3, Vol. 1).

125. Letter from Hilgard Muller to François Tombalbaye, 17 April 1970 (DFA, 1/184/3, Vol. 1).

126. Cronjé. 1972. *The World and Nigeria*, de St. Jorre. 1972. *The Nigerian Civil War*, Stremlau. 1977. *The International Politics of the Nigerian Civil War, 1967-1970*.

127. Nweke. 1976. *External Intervention in African Conflicts*, p.38, 41-3.

128. Daddieh. 1984. 'Ivory Coast', p.135; Foccart. 1995. *Foccart parle. Vol. I*, p.345; McNamara. 1989. *France in Black Africa*, p.180; Nweke. 1976. *External Intervention in African Conflicts*, p.37, 54; Péan. 1983. *Affaires africaines*, p.12, 285. Delauney's memoirs: 1982. *De la casquette à la jaquette*, p.176-82; 1986. *'Kala-kala'*, p.193-217.

129. Péan. 1983. *Affaires africaines*, p.72 (translated from French); Faligot & Krop. 1985. *La piscine*, p.264.

130. Akinyemi. 1994. 'Origins, articulations and continuities in foreign policy and foreign policy formulation', p.62; Bach. 1980. 'Le Général de Gaulle et la guerre civile au Nigeria', p.262, 271; McNamara. 1989. *France in Black Africa*, p.180; Samuel. 1999. *Michel Debré*, p.235-6.

131. Foccart. 1995. *Foccart parle. Vol. I*, p.342; Foccart. 1997. *Foccart parle. Vol. II*, p.269 (translated from French); Akinyemi. 1994. 'Origins, articulations and continuities in foreign policy and foreign policy formulation', p.62; Bach. 1980. 'Le Général de Gaulle et la guerre civile au Nigeria', p.260, 263-4, 271; Chipman. 1989. *French Power in Africa*, p.126-7; McNamara. 1989. *France in Black Africa*, p.180; Nweke. 1976. *External Intervention in African Conflicts*, p.6, 19-20.

132. 'Jean Maurichaux Beaupré [sic]', from Johan Pretorius, 9 November 1972, p.2 (DFA, 1/99/19, Vol. 1) (translated from Afrikaans).

133. .Gifford & Louis. 1971. *France and Britain in Africa*, Shennan. 1993. *De Gaulle*, p.16-36; Gallo. 1998. *De Gaulle. Vol. II*, p.55-128.

134. Letter from Jean Mauricheau-Beaupré to P.W. Botha, 19 November 1970, p.2-3 (DoD, MV/56/16, Vol. 26) (translated from French).

135. Foccart. 1995. *Foccart parle. Vol. I*, p.342; 'Biafra – Shell-BP', from Neels van Tonder to Albie Burger, 6 November 1969 (DFA, 1/129/3, Vol. 1).

136. Vallée. 2000. 'Une Afrique sous influence', p.24.

137. Foccart. 1995. *Foccart parle. Vol. I*, p.343.

138. 'Gesprek met Mnr Beaupre op 7/7/69', from Neels van Tonder to Fritz Loots, July 1969, p.3 (DoD, MV/56/16, Vol. 26).

139. 'Onderhoud tussen sy Edele Mnr P.W. Botha en Pres F. Houphouët-Boigny in Parys op 19 Maart 1969' (DoD, MV/56/16, Vol. 26).

140. Daddieh. 1997. 'South Africa and Francophone African relations', p.186; Nolutshungu. 1975. *South Africa in Africa*, p.295.

141. Letter dated 21 April 1969 (DoD, MV/56/16, Vol. 26) (translated from French).

142. 'Onderhoud met Dr. Muller op 9/7/69', from Neels van Tonder to Fritz Loots, July, p.2, 6; letter from Neels van Tonder to Fritz Loots on a meeting between Houphouët-Boigny and Muller, 11 July 1969, p.3-4 (DoD, MV/56/16, Vol. 26).

143. Foccart. 1997. *Foccart parle. Vol. II*, p.110.

144. 'Onderhoud met Dr. Muller op 9/7/69', from Neels van Tonder to Fritz Loots, July 1969, p.5 (DoD, MV/56/16, Vol. 26) (translated from Afrikaans).

145.   Letter from Neels van Tonder to Fritz Loots, 11 July 1969, p.3 (DoD, MV/56/16, Vol. 26) (translated from Afrikaans).

146.   Letter from Neels van Tonder to Fritz Loots on a meeting between Houphouët-Boigny and Muller, 11 July 1969, p.2-3 (DoD, MV/56/16, Vol. 26). In comparison, Faligot & Krop. 1985. *La piscine*, p.264 (note 1), note that Biafra received 350 tons of armament per week from the second half of 1968.

147.   'Notes on the talks between Dr. Hilgard Muller, Minister of Foreign Affairs of the Republic of South Africa, and Dr. Franca Nogueira, Minister of Foreign Affairs of Portugal, on Monday, 16th June, 1969', p.2 (DFA, 22/3/29, Vol. 3).

148.   Cronjé. 1972. *The World and Nigeria*, p.185, 237, 323-4; Stremlau. 1977. *The International Politics of the Nigerian Civil War, 1967-1970*, p.233-5.

149.   Wilkins & Strydom. 1980. *The Super-Afrikaners*, p.A105.

150.   Letter of invitation from Albert Bongo to P.W. Botha, 1 August; letter of receipt from P.W. Botha to Albert Bongo, 27 August 1969 (DoD, MV/56/16, Vol. 26).

151.   They both owned one: *Jeune Afrique* 767, 19 September 1975: 37; Péan. 1983. *Affaires africaines*, p.196.

152.   'Voorgestelde reisplan vir die voorgenome besoek van die Minister en KG, SAW', September 1969 (DoD, MV/56/16, Vol. 26).

153.   Document undated (DoD, MV/56/16, Vol. 26) (translated from Afrikaans).

154.   Letter from Albie Burger to Brand Fourie, 13 November 1969, p.2 (DFA, 1/99/19, Vol. 1) (translated from Afrikaans).

155.   DoD, MV/56/16, Vol. 26 (translated from Afrikaans).

156.   'Opsomming van 'n gesprek: Mnr Fourie – Maj van Tonder: 27 Mei 70', from Neels van Tonder, May 1970, p.4 (DoD, MV/56/16, Vol. 26).

157.   Foccart. 1997. *Foccart parle. Vol. II*, p.259 (note 1); McNamara. 1989. *France in Black Africa*, p.181; Weinberg. 1994. *Last of the Pirates*, p.58-60.

158.   Foccart. 1997. *Foccart parle. Vol. II*, p.122; Weinberg. 1994. *Last of the Pirates*, p.246.

159.   Foccart. 1997. *Foccart parle. Vol. II*, p.259-60, 263.

160.   Interviewed in Weinberg. 1994. *Last of the Pirates*, p.198.

161.   McNamara. 1989. *France in Black Africa*, p.180; Foccart. 1995/1997. *Foccart parle. Vol. I*, p.345; *Vol. II*, p.259 (note 1).

162.   Cronje. 1972. *The World and Nigeria*, p.187-8; Lunel. 1991. *Bob Denard*, p.410-1; interview with Deon Fourie, 22 April 1999; interview with Neels van Tonder, 19 March 2002.

163.   'Onderhoud met Dr. Muller op 9/7/69', from Neels van Tonder to Fritz Loots, July 1969, p.3 (DoD, MV/56/16, Vol. 26) (translated from Afrikaans).

164.   'Gesprek met Mnr Beaupre op 7/7/69', from Neels van Tonder to Fritz Loots, July 1969, p.3 (DoD, MV/56/16, Vol. 26) (translated from Afrikaans).

165.   'Voorgenome ontmoeting: Dr Muller en 'n ander Minister – Presidente Houphouet-Boigny en Bongo', from Fritz Loots to P.W. Botha, 29 May 1970, p.3 (DoD, MV/56/16, Vol. 26) (translated from Afrikaans).

166.   DFA, 1/106/3, AJ 1970.

167.   DFA, 1/106/3, Vol. 5.

168.   Potgieter & Steenkamp. 1981. *Aircraft of the South African Air Force*, p.138-43.

169.   Letter from Albert Bongo to P.W. Botha, 30 April 1970; letter from P.W. Botha to Albert Bongo, May 1970; 'Aflewering van drie Harvard-vliegtuie', April 1970 (DoD, MV/56/16, Vol. 26).

170.   Letter from Albert Bongo to P.W. Botha, 9 November 1970, p.1-2 (DoD, MV/56/16, Vol. 26).

171. Letter from P.W. Botha to Albert Bongo, 2 December 1970, p.1 (DoD, MV/56/16, Vol. 26).

172. Letter from P.W. Botha to Bongo, 17 February 1971, p.1 (DoD, MV/56/16, Vol. 26) (translated from French).

173. *Africa Contemporary Record, 1970-71*: C29-30; *Jeune Afrique* 515, 17 November 1970.

174. 'La conférence de presse du Président Felix Houphouët-Boigny', 28 April 1971, p.10-1 (DFA, 1/179/3, AJ 1971), reprinted in *Africa Contemporary Record, 1971-72*: C72-4.

175. *The Star* 31 March 1970; *The Argus* 29 March 1971.

176. Barratt. 1970. 'South Africa's Outward Movement', p.134.

177. Barratt. 1971. *Dialogue in Africa*, p.10-2; Barratt. 1972. 'South Africa's Outward Policy', p.555-7; Legum. 1972. 'Dialogue', p.A66-82; von der Ropp. 1971. 'Chancen eines Dialoges zwischen der Republik Südafrika und dem schwarzen Afrika', p.731-2; *Africa Contemporary Record, 1970-71*: C32-4. Newspaper clippings: ARCA, PV.59, File KN 59/A2/5/3; PV.451, File 1/11/35/1.

178. Letter from John Phillips to John Vorster, 4 May 1971 (DFA, 1/120/3, Vol. 1).

179. Telegram from Idi Amin to John Vorster, 28 September 1971 (DFA, 1/120/3, Vol. 1; ARCA PV.614, Plaakboek Nr. 53, Bylae A).

180. Telegram from John Vorster to Idi Amin, 1 October 1971, p.1-2 (DFA, 1/120/3, Vol. 1).

181. Telegram from Idi Amin to John Vorster, 3 October 1971; letter from John Vorster to Idi Amin, 5 October 1971 (DFA, 1/120/3, Vol. 1).

182. *Rand Daily Mail* 4 October 1971.

183. 'Peace in Africa through neutrality and in neutrality'. Declaration by President Houphouët-Boigny to the Conference of O.C.A.M. Heads of State, January 1971. 'Ivory Coast News', Embassy of the Ivory Coast, London (DFA, 1/179/3, Vol. 2).

184. Barratt. 1971. *Dialogue in Africa*, p.6-7; Klotz. 1995. *Norms in International Relations*, p.77-8; Olivier. 1982. 'South Africa's relations with Africa', p.281-2.

185. *Africa Contemporary Record, 1971-72*: C18-9; *Southern Africa Record* 2, 1975.

186. Newspaper coverage: ARCA, PV.59, Files KN 59/A2/5/3 and KN 59/D4/1/1; Suzman. 1983. *In No Uncertain Terms*, p.126-9; Nolutshungu. 1975. *South Africa in Africa*, p.293-4; von der Rop. 1971. 'Chancen eines Dialoges zwischen der Republik Südafrika und dem schwarzen Afrika', p.734; Strangwayes-Booth. 1976. *A Cricket in the Thorn Tree*, p.241-3.

187. Correspondence with Colin Eglin, 13 January 2003; Eglin. 1971. *Africa*.

188. Correspondence with Colin Eglin, 13 January 2003.

189. DFA, 1/62/3, Vol. 4; *The Star* 21 March 1972.

190. *Foreign Affairs List*.

191. DFA, 1/62/3, Vols. 1-2, 4, 7-8; 'Visitors from Mauritius to South Africa from beginning 1972', July 1974 (DFA, 1/62/3, Vol. 9).

192. Correspondence with Geoffrey Tyler, 27 February 2002.

193. *Report of the 1973 Trade Mission to Malawi*. 1973; *Reunion, Mauritius, Malawi . . . report of 1979 trade mission*. 1979.

194. Correspondence with Frans Swarts and Gert van der Veer, 11 February 2003.

195. Letter from the Director of Southern Sun to Jan Bouwer, 10 May; letter from Jan Bouwer to Joep Steyn, 12 May 1971 (DFA, 1/62/3, Vol. 1); DFA, 1/62/3, Vol. 4.

196. Letter from Jean Mauricheau-Beaupré to P.W. Botha, 19 November 1970, p.2-3, 5, 8 (DoD, MV/56/16, Vol. 26) (emphasis in the original; translated from French).

197. 'Voorgenome ontmoeting: Dr Muller en 'n ander Minister – Presidente Houphouet-Boigny en Bongo', from Fritz Loots to P.W. Botha, 29 May 1970, p.4; 'Gesprek met Mnr Beaupre op 7/7/69', from Neels van Tonder to Fritz Loots, July 1969, p.3 (DoD, MV/56/16, Vol. 26).

198. 'Gesprek met Mnr Beaupre op 7/7/69', from Neels van Tonder to Fritz Loots, July, p.2; letter from Neels van Tonder to Fritz Loots, 11 July 1969, p.2-5; 'Onderhoud met Dr. Muller op 9/7/69', from Neels van Tonder to Fritz Loots, p.2 (DoD, MV/56/16, Vol. 26).

199. 'Opsomming van 'n gesprek: Mnr Fourie – Maj van Tonder: 27 Mei 70', from Neels van Tonder, May 1970, p.2 (DoD, MV/56/16, Vol. 26) (translated from Afrikaans).

200. 'Verslag insake reëlings vir die voorgenome ontmoeting met Houphouet-Boigny en Bongo', from Brand Fourie, 25 May 1970, p.1 (DoD, MV/56/16, Vol. 26) (translated from Afrikaans).

201. 'Verslag insake reëlings vir die voorgenome ontmoeting met Houphouet-Boigny en Bongo', from Brand Fourie, 25 May 1970, p.3 (DoD, MV/56/16, Vol. 26) (translated from Afrikaans).

202. 'Opsomming van 'n gesprek: Mnr Fourie – Maj van Tonder: 27 Mei 70', from Neels van Tonder, May 1970, p.2, 4 (DoD, MV/56/16, Vol. 26) (translated from Afrikaans).

203. 'Voorgenome ontmoeting: Dr Muller en 'n ander Minister – Presidente Houphouet-Boigny en Bongo', from Fritz Loots to P.W. Botha, 29 May 1970, p.2-4 (DoD, MV/56/16, Vol. 26) (translated from Afrikaans).

204. Letter from Albert Bongo to P.W. Botha, 9 November 1970, p.1 (DoD, MV/56/16, Vol. 26) (translated from French).

205. Letter from Jean Mauricheau-Beaupré to P.W. Botha, 19 November 1970, p.6 (DoD, MV/56/16, Vol. 26) (emphasis in the original; translated from French).

206. 'Technical aid to Gabon to 31 December 1972', from Glenn Babb, p.1 (DFA, 1/178/3, Vol. 3).

207. Letter from Hilgard Muller to Albert Bongo, 20 August (translated from French). Letter from Albert Bongo to Hilgard Muller, 18 September 1969 (DFA, 1/178/3, Vol. 1).

208. 'Opsomming van besprekings by inderdepartementale vergadering oor voorgenome besoek van 'n ekonomiese sending aan Gaboen', 7 April 1970, p.1 (DFA, 1/178/4, Vol. 1).

209. DFA, 1/178/3, Vol. 1.

210. 'Besoek aan Gaboen: 21-27.9.1969', from Robert Montgomery to Brand Fourie, 6 October 1969, p.7-10; 'State mission to the Republic of Gabon, 21st – 27th September, 1969', from the Inspector of Mining Leases, 9 October 1969 (DFA, 1/178/3, Vol. 1).

211. 'Opsomming van besprekings by inderdepartementale vergadering oor voorgenome besoek van 'n ekonomiese sending aan Gaboen', 7 April 1970, p.1 (DFA, 1/178/4, Vol. 1).

212. DFA, 1/178/3, Vol. 2.

213. 'Notules van inter-departementele vergadering gehou te Uniegebou op Vrydag, 24 April 1970', from Jeremy Shearar, April (translated from Afrikaans); 'Aide-memoire', June 1970 (DFA, 1/178/4, Vol. 1).

214. Letter from Albert Bongo to Hilgard Muller, 16 July; letter from Hilgard Muller to Albert Bongo, 3 September; 'Technical assistance mission to Gabon', from Brand Fourie to Albie Burger, 14 September; 'South African mission to Gabon: 27 September-3 October 1970', from Norman Best to Brand Fourie, 13 October 1970 (DFA, 1/178/4, Vol. 1).

215. 'Report of the medical mission to Gabon, September 1970', October 1970 (DFA, 1/178/4, Vol. 2).

216. 'South African mission to Gabon: 27 September-3 October 1970', from Norman Best to Brand Fourie, 13 October, p.9-11; 'Technical aid to Gabon', from Brand Fourie, 19 October, p.1; 'Technical aid to Gabon: visit to R.S.A.: Gabonese officials', from J. Gilliand to Norman Best, 14 December 1970; letter from Brand Fourie to John Terblanche and J. Gilliand, 5 March 1971, p.1-3 (DFA, 1/178/4, Vols. 1-2).

217. 'Medical aid to Gabon', from Glenn Babb to Norman Best, 15 February 1973 (DFA, 1/178/4, Vol. 6).

218. Interview with Jan Boyazoglu and Julian Thomas, 1 April 2004.

219. Interview with Neil van Heerden and Paul Runge, 7 April 1999.

220. 'Report on the agricultural aid to Gabon following the visit from 27th September to 4th October 1970', from Jan Boyazoglu, 7 October 1970, p.3-4 (DFA, 1/178/4, Vol. 1).

221. Correspondence with Jan Boyazoglu, 12 April 2004.

222. 'Technical aid to Gabon', from Brand Fourie, 19 October 1970, p.1 (DFA, 1/178/4, Vol. 1).

223. Interview with Jan Boyazoglu and Julian Thomas, 1 April 2004.

224. 'Report on the agricultural aid to Gabon following the visit from 27th September to 4th October 1970', from Jan Boyazoglu, 7 October 1970, p.8 (DFA, 1/178/4, Vol. 1).

225. Letter from Albert Bongo to Hilgard Muller, 7 April; letter from Hilgard Muller to Albert Bongo, 23 April 1971 (DFA, 1/178/4, Vol. 2).

226. 'Re: visit to Libreville from 28 July to 1 August 1971', from Jan Boyazoglu to Albie Burger, 2 August 1971, p.4-6 (DFA, 1/178/4, Vol. 3) (emphasis in the original).

227. 'Re: visit to Libreville from 28 July to 1 August 1971', from Jan Boyazoglu to Albie Burger, 2 August 1971, p.6 (DFA, 1/178/4, Vol. 3).

228. 'Report on visit to the Gabon: 2 to 17 October 1971', from Julian Thomas to Jan Boyazoglu, 1 November 1971 (DFA, 1/178/4, Vol. 4).

229. Letter from Albie Burger to Norman Best, 29 October 1971 (DFA, 1/178/4, Vol. 4).

230. Correspondence with Jan Boyazoglu and Julian Thomas, 24 April 2004.

231. 'The O.G.A.P.R.O.V. project during 1971/72 and prospects for the future', from Jan Boyazoglu, April 1972, p.20-1 (DFA, 1/178/4, Vol. 5); 'Re: report on informal O.G.A.P.R.O.V. meeting held at Embassy on 25/26 January 1972', from Jan Boyazoglu to Albie Burger, 16 February 1972 (DFA, 1/178/4, Vol. 4).

232. 'OGAPROV: 1973/74 budget', from Norman Best to Brand Fourie, 16 May 1973, p.2 plus attachment 'O.G.A.P.R.O.V.' (DFA, 1/178/4, Vol. 7).

233. 'Technical aid to Gabon', from Brand Fourie, 19 October 1970, p.2; 'OGAPROV', from Norman Best to François Viljoen, 7 September 1972, p.1;

'File note', from Glenn Babb, 1 February, p.2; 'O.G.A.P.R.O.V. – report on visit to the Gabon, 19 to 26 February 1973 by Messrs. Hawkins and Thomas', from Julian Thomas, 29 March, p.1-2; 'OGAPROV: 1973/74 budget', from Norman Best to Brand Fourie, 16 May, p.1; 'Besoek aan Gaboen: Mnr. J.F. Pretorius', from Johan Pretorius, September, p.1; 'O.G.A.P.R.O.V. – report on visit to the Gabon: 3 to 25 September 1973', from Julian Thomas, 5 November 1973, p.2-3 (DFA, 1/178/4, Vols. 1, 5-8).

234.   'Memorandum on future financing of the O.G.A.P.R.O.V. project', from Julian Thomas, 14 November, p.1, 3, 5; 'Re: memorandum on future financing of the O.G.A.P.R.O.V. project', from Jan Boyazoglu to Albie Burger, 15 November 1973 (DFA, 1/178/4, Vol. 9).

235.   'The future financing of the O.G.A.P.R.O.V. project', from Albie Burger to Brand Fourie, 19 November 1973 (DFA, 1/178/4, Vol. 9); interview with Jan Boyazoglu and Julian Thomas, 1 April 2004

236.   'Re: recent visit to the Gabon', from Jan Boyazoglu to Albie Burger, 10 May 1974, p.1 (DFA, 1/178/4, Vol. 10).

237.   'Re: O.G.A.P.R.O.V. – final estimate of expenditure 1975/76', from Julian Thomas to Albie Burger, 15 May 1975, p.1-2; 'Re: Gabon – O.G.A.P.R.O.V. estimate of expenditure 1976/1977', from Julian Thomas to Albie Burger, 30 January, p.1; 'Re: Gabon – O.G.A.P.R.O.V. estimate of expenditure 1977/78', from Julian Thomas to Albie Burger, 10 December 1976, p.2; 'Background of OGAPROV', May 1978, p.4-5 (DFA, 1/178/4, Vols. 12-14, 16).

238.   Interview with Paul Runge, 18 January 2003.

239.   Interview with Jan Boyazoglu and Julian Thomas, 1 April 2004.

240.   Correspondence with Jan Boyazoglu, 6 March 2004 (emphasis in the original).

241.   'Housing project', from J. van der Walt (Secretary, IDC) to Mbouy Boutzit (Minister of Economic Affairs, Gabon), 6 August 1971, p.1-2 (DFA, 1/178/3, Vol. 2).

242.   Correspondence with Spencer Whiting, 21 April 2004.

243.   'Relations with Gabon: L.T.A. Ltd housing project', from Norman Best to François Viljoen, 20 July 1972 (DFA, 1/178/3, Vol. 2).

244.   'Relations with Gabon: L.T.A. Ltd. housing project', from François Viljoen to Paul Kruger (Department of Commerce), 2 August 1972 (DFA, 1/178/3, Vol. 2).

245.   Letter from Machiel de Klerk (Managing Director, Credit Guarantee) to J.P. Chassang (Union Gabonaise de Banque), 7 August 1972 (DFA, 1/178/3, Vol. 2).

246.   Correspondence with Spencer Whiting, 21 April 2004.

247.   Letter from Machiel de Klerk to J.P. Chassang, 27 November, p.2; 'Gabon – L.T.A.-kontrak', from Jan Bouwer to Norman Best, 29 November 1972 (DFA, 1/178/3, Vol. 2).

248.   'Roberts Construction: development projects in Ivory Coast and Gabon', from François Viljoen, 16 August 1971 (DFA, 1/178/3, Vol. 2).

249.   'Re: Transgabon railway project', from Jeff Miller to François Viljoen, 6 March 1972, p.3 (DFA, 1/178/3, Vol. 2).

250.   'Trans-Gaboen spoorwegprojek', from François Viljoen to Brand Fourie, 28 March; 'Trans-Gabon railway project', from the Secretary for Finance at the Treasury to Brand Fourie, 3 July 1972 (DFA, 1/178/3, Vol. 2).

251.   'Re: Transgabon railway project', from Jeff Miller to François Viljoen, 28 July 1972 (DFA, 1/178/3, Vol. 2).

252.   Péan. 1983. *Affaires africaines*, p.119, 121.

253. Letter from Jan Bouwer to Albert Bongo, 13 April 1973 (DFA, 1/178/3, Vol. 3).

254. *To the Point* 30 June 1973: 27-8 and 25 August 1973: 39.

255. 'Export finance – Gabon', November 1973 (DFA, 1/178/3, Vol. 3).

256. Letter from David de Villiers du Buisson (Ambassador, Brussels) to Brand Fourie, 5 June 1974, p.1 (DFA, 1/178/3, Vol. 4).

257. *The Star* 25 June 1974; Legum. 1976. *Vorster's Gamble for Africa*, p.16.

258. 'Gaboen' from Johan Pretorius, 21 November 1974, p.5 (DFA, 1/178/3, Vol. 4); Péan. 1983. *Affaires africaines*, p.123; interview with Jeff Miller, 17 April 2004.

259. *The Star* 6 October, *Sunday Times* 25 June 1972.

260. Geldenhuys. 1984. *The Diplomacy of Isolation*, p.84-6, 109-10, 114-9, 183-5.

261. Rhoodie. 1983. *The Real Information Scandal*, p.98, 123.

262. *To the Point* 29 January 1972: 42.

263. *To the Point* 21 April 1973: 20.

264. Geldenhuys. 1984. *The Diplomacy of Isolation*, p.117.

265. Rhoodie. 1983. *The Real Information Scandal*, p.123.

266. De Villiers. 1980. *Secret Information*, p.49.

267. Telephone interview with Mauricette Lejeune, 3 November 2003.

268. 'Report of my trip to Dakar and Abidjan', from Bernard Lejeune, May 1973, p.1-3 (NAT.ARC., MNL, INL22/6, Vol. 73).

269. Telephone interview with Mauricette Lejeune, 3 November 2003 (translated from French).

270. Interview with Bara Diouf, 8 October 2003.

271. De Villiers. 1980. *Secret Information*, p.49, 78-9; Rhoodie. 1983. *The Real Information Scandal*, p.122-32; Geldenhuys. 1984. *The Diplomacy of Isolation*, p.73, 117-8.

272. Interview with Bara Diouf, 8 October; telephone interview with Mauricette Lejeune, 3 November 2003.

273. 'Senegal: President Senghor and Détente', from Johan Pretorius to Brand Fourie, 4 February 1976, p.2 (DFA, 1/186/3, Vol. 2).

274. <http://www.nu.ac.za/law/fachistory.html>; Louw, R.H. 2000. 'The legacy of Barend van Niekerk'.

275. Van Niekerk. 1970. *The African Image (Negritude) in the Work of Leopold Sedar Senghor*.

276. 'Senegal: President Senghor and Détente', from Johan Pretorius to Brand Fourie, 4 February 1976, p.2 (DFA, 1/186/3, Vol. 2).

277. 'Prime Minister's correspondence with President Senghor', to Brand Fourie, 16 May 1975, p.1; 'Senegal: President Senghor and Détente', from Johan Pretorius to Brand Fourie, 4 February 1976, p.2 (DFA, 1/186/3, AJ 1978 and Vol. 2).

278. Dugard. 1972. 'Namibia (South West Africa)', p.14; Gross. 1973. 'The United Nations, self-determination and the Namibia opinions', p.534.

279. Horrell. 1973. *The African Homelands of South Africa.*

280. Geldenhuys. 1984. *The Diplomacy of Isolation*, p.110.

281. *Keesing's Archiv der Gegenwart* 1971: 16489-90.

282. *To the Point* 4 November 1972: 39.

283. Interview with Cas de Villiers, 18 January 2003; NAT.ARC., MNL, CP78, Vol. 42; Geldenhuys. 1984. *The Diplomacy of Isolation*, p.108-9; Rhoodie. 1983. *The Real Information Scandal*, p.61.

284. For example Metrowich & de Villiers. 1975. *The Communist Strategy*; Metrowich. 1975. *Towards Dialogue and Détente*.

285. Geldenhuys. 1984. *The Diplomacy of Isolation*, p.119.

286. Geldenhuys. 1984. *The Diplomacy of Isolation*, p.65, 119, 169; *Sunday Times* 9 March 1975.

287. *To the Point* 12 September 1975: 7.

288. Interview with Cas de Villiers, 18 January 2003.

289. De Villiers. 1980. *Secret Information*, p.177-8; Rhoodie. 1983. *The Real Information Scandal*, p.143, 150, 152, 309, 479, 572-3, 668, 673; Geldenhuys. 1984. *The Diplomacy of Isolation*, p.116.

290. Geldenhuys. 1984. *The Diplomacy of Isolation*, p.176.

291. *To the Point* 26 August 1972: 37-9.

292. Marais. 1975. 'South Africa'.

293. 'Report of my trip to Dakar and Abidjan', from Bernard Lejeune, May 1973, p.2 (NAT.ARC., MNL, INL22/6, Vol. 73).

294. 'South Africa and the United States of America: brief notes on a visit to the U.S.A. by Dr. Jan S. Marais', from Jan Marais to Connie Mulder, October (emphasis in the original); letter from Connie Mulder to Jan Marais, 20 November 1975 (translated from Afrikaans) (NAT.ARC., MNL, INL8, Vol. 52/5).

295. Interview with Richard Cornwell, 19 February 1999.

296. 'Report of my trip to Dakar and Abidjan', from Bernard Lejeune, May 1973, p.1 (NAT.ARC., MNL, INL22/6, Vol. 73).

297. Correspondence with Erich Leistner, December 2002 and interview, 26 February 2003; Moolman. 1974. 'South Africans visit West Africa'.

298. 'Africa Institute of S.A.: notes on visit to West Africa', August 1974 (DFA, 1/179/3, Vol. 4).

299. Correspondence with Erich Leistner, 20 January 2003.

300. Correspondence with John Barratt, 15 January 2003; Barratt. 1974. 'Report on a visit to Senegal and the Ivory Coast'.

301. Interview with Bara Diouf, 8 October 2003 (translated from French).

302. Barber & Barratt. 1990. *South Africa's Foreign Policy*, p.148-9; De Villiers. 1980. *Secret Information*, p.49, 78-9; Geldenhuys. 1984. *The Diplomacy of Isolation*, p.73, 117-8; Rhoodie. 1983. *The Real Information Scandal*, p.122-32; ARCA, PV.132, Bylae A, No. 12.

303. *Rand Daily Mail* 3 December 1974, 15 and 16 May, *Die Transvaler* 15 May 1975.

304. Rhoodie. 1983. *The Real Information Scandal*, p.104.

305. Foccart. 1997. *Foccart parle. Vol. II*, p.112, 281.

306. Bach. 1982. 'L'insertion ivoirienne dans les rapports internationaux', p.111.

307. 'Proposed programme for the official visit to the Republic of South Africa by the Hon. Laurent Dona-Fologo, Minister of Information of the Republic of the Ivory Coast', August 1975; *Fraternité Matin* (Abidjan) 22 September 1975 (DFA, 1/179/3, Vol. 5); *To the Point* 19 September 1975: 7-9; telephone interview with Mauricette Lejeune, 3 November 2003; Bach. 1982. 'L'insertion ivoirienne dans les rapports internationaux', p.111; Daddieh. 1997. 'South Africa and Francophone African relations', p.187-8; Rhoodie. 1983. *The Real Information Scandal*, p.133-5.

308. *Africa Institute: annual report, 1976*; Swanepoel. 1982. 'Die diplomasie van adv. B.J. Vorster', p.221.

309. Correspondence with Erich Leistner, 21 December 2002; Leistner. 1976. '"Dialogue and tolerance"'.

310. 'Verslag – Abidjan, G M E Leistner, 1976' and 'Enkele indrukke van n reis na Wes-Afrika, Wes-Europa en Israel 24 Januarie tot 4 April 1976, G M E Leistner, 1976', provided by courtesy of Amanda Wortman and Justa Kruger (Africa Institute), January 2003.

311. De Villiers. 1980. *Secret Information*, p.118-32; du Preez. 2001. *Louis Luyt*, p.19-25.

312. Correspondence with Louis Luyt, 23 and 25 February 2003.

313. 'Visit to Ivory Coast: Minister C.P. Mulder and party: 21-24 March 1976', from Rae Killen; 'Discussion between President Houphouët-Boigny and Minister C.P. Mulder: Abidjan, 22 March 1976'; 'Le dialogue continue', Ivorian Service Press, Information, Documentation, 25 March 1976 (DFA, 1/179/3, Vol. 6).

314. Telex from Brand Fourie to Laurent Dona-Fologo, 4 December 1975 (DFA, 1/179/3, Vol. 6).

315. Telex from Laurent Dona-Fologo to Brand Fourie, 16 January 1976; letter from Brand Fourie to Laurent Dona-Fologo, 17 March 1976 (DFA, 1/179/3, Vol. 6); *To the Point* 14 May 1976: 50.

316. 'Ivory Coast', 13 March 1978, p.1 (DFA, 1/179/3, Vol. 9); Yao. 1992. 'Le dialogue Yamassoukro – Prétoria', p.7; Yao. 1991. 'Côte d'Ivoire – Afrique du Sud', p.146.

317. Pityana. 1991. *Bounds of Possibility*.

318. '1978: annual review of relations with Ivory Coast', December 1978, p.1 (DFA, 1/179/3, Vol. 9).

319. Pfister. 1992. 'United Nations sanctions against Apartheid'.

320. *The Star* 6 December 1976.

321. '1978: annual review of relations with Ivory Coast', December, p.1; *Pretoria News* 2 June 1978; Bach. 1982. 'L'insertion ivoirienne dans les rapports internationaux', p.111.

322. Letter from Léopold Senghor to John Vorster, 29 September; letter from John Vorster to Léopold Senghor, 16 October 1975; 'Senegal: President Senghor and Détente', from Johan Pretorius to Brand Fourie, 4 February 1976, p.2 (DFA, 1/186/3, Vol. 2).

323. Breytenbach, B. 1986. *End Papers*.

324. 'Senegal: President Senghor and Détente', from Johan Pretorius to Brand Fourie, 4 February 1976, p.2 (DFA, 1/186/3, Vol. 2).

325. For example: 1973. *The South West Africa/Namibia Dispute*.

326. Correspondence with John Dugard, 4 December 2002.

327. 'Senegal: President Senghor and Détente', from Johan Pretorius to Brand Fourie, 4 February 1976, p.2 (DFA, 1/186/3, Vol. 2). In correspondence of 4 December 2002, John Dugard states there "was a steel wall" between him and the DFA, while confirming meeting Jaquet unofficially.

328. Rhoodie. 1983. *The Real Information Scandal*, p.132.

329. 'Senegal: President Senghor and Détente', from Johan Pretorius to Brand Fourie, 4 February 1976, p.1 (DFA, 1/186/3, Vol. 2).

330. Correspondence with André Jaquet, 2 December 2002.

331. 'Senegal: President Senghor and Détente', from Johan Pretorius to Brand Fourie, 4 February 1976, p.1 (DFA, 1/186/3, Vol. 2) (translated from Afrikaans).

332. Correspondence with Anton Loubser, 6 February 2004.

333. Fourie. c1986. *Buitelandse woelinge om Suid-Afrika*; Fourie. 1991. *Brandpunte*.

334. Report from Tassie Taswell (Ambassador, Embassy, Washington), 23 April 1974 (DFA, 1/13/3, Vol. 2).

335. 'Memorandum', from Pik Botha to Brand Fourie, 4 November; letter from Pik Botha to William Tolbert, 7 November; telegram from Pik Botha, 8 November 1974 (DFA, 1/13/3, Vols. 1A, 2).

336. Letter from John Vorster to William Tolbert, 8 December 1974 (DFA, 1/13/3, Vol. 1A).

337. *To the Point* 1 July 1972: 21.

338.   Official statement by Liberian President William Tolbert on 18 February, issued by the Embassy of Liberia, Rome, 11 March 1975, p.4 (DFA, 1/13/3, Vol. 1A).

339.   Report from Pik Botha to John Vorster, 6 January 1975, p.11-2 (DFA, 1/13/3, Vol. 1A).

340.   DFA, 1/13/3, Vol. 1A.

341.   Frank. 1975. 'Is Pretoria on the point of break-through to Africa?'; Swanepoel. 1982. 'Die diplomasie van adv. B.J. Vorster', p.228.

342.   Interview with Pik Botha, 20 April 1999.

343.   Fourie. c1986. *Buitelandse woelinge om Suid-Afrika*, p.132.

344.   'Memorandum', 23 June 1975 (DFA, 1/13/3, Vol. 3).

345.   Letter from William Tolbert to John Vorster, 3 December 1975 (DFA, 1/13/3, Vol. 3).

346.   Telegram from Brand Fourie to Pik Botha, 17 December 1975 (DFA, 1/13/3, Vol. 3).

347.   Letter from William Tolbert to John Vorster, 14 September; letter from John Vorster to William Tolbert, November 1977 (DFA, 1/13/3, Vol. 3).

348.   *Keesing's Archiv der Gegenwart, 1971*, p.16527.

349.   'Rol van Mnr. Jack Kagan in ons kontak met Pres. Bokassa', p.2-4 (DFA, 1/183/3, Vol. 5) (translated from Afrikaans); 'Interview with Mr J. Kagan of Union Fabrics, 20 June 1974', 20 June 1974, p.1; 'Draft letter to J. Kagan from SOCODEAF and FMDC' (DFA, 1/183/3, Vol. 2).

350.   Correspondence with Hein du Toit, 30 April 2004.

351.   Adams. 1984. *The Unnatural Alliance*.

352.   Correspondence with Hein du Toit, 30 April 2004.

353.   'Central African Republic: visit of Mr Joël Barkan, Technical Adviser to the President and Mr Maurice Methot, Director of Services in the Office of Life President Bokassa', 10 April, p.1; 'Note:', June 1974 (DFA, 1/183/3, Vol. 2); 'Oorsig van verhoudings en kontakte tussen die R.S.A. en Sentraal Afrikaanse Republiek', from Johan Pretorius, 30 January 1976, p.4 (DFA, 1/183/3, AJ 1976).

354.   'Central African Republic: visit of Mr Joël Barkan, Technical Adviser to the President and Mr Maurice Methot, Director of Services in the Office of Life President Bokassa', 10 April 1974, p.1-3, 12 (DFA, 1/183/3, Vol. 2).

355.   Swart, Adendorff & Louw. 1966. *The Economic and Administrative Development in Bantu Territories.*

356.   Letter from Jean Bokassa to Hilgard Muller, 6 September 1974 (DFA, 1/183/3, Vol. 2).

357.   DFA, 1/183/3, Vol. 2.

358.   Letter from Jean Bokassa to John Vorster, 3 October (translated from French); 'S.E. die Eerste Minister se onderhoud met Mnr. J. Barkan, gesant van Pres. Bokassa van die Sentraal Afrikaanse Republiek', from Johan Pretorius, 8 October 1974 (DFA, 1/183/3, Vol. 3).

359.   Letter from John Vorster to Jean Bokassa, 1 November; letter of invitation from Rae Killen to the various companies, 25 October 1974 (DFA, 1/183/3, Vol. 3).

360.   'Communiqué conjoint', 9 November 1974 (DFA, 1/183/3, Vol. 4); Decter. 1976. *South Africa and Black Africa*, p.5.

361.   *West Africa* 3624, 31 March 1975: 359.

362.   'Meeting with the President: France, 24/9/1974 at 8 P.M.', p.3 (DFA, 1/183/3, Vol. 2).

363. 'Principes directeurs indiqués pendant le vol à Londres par son Excellence le Ministre des Affaires Etrangères', October 1974, p.1 (DFA, 1/183/3, Vol. 3) (translated from French).

364. 'Report on working group I', p.1-4, 8-9 (DFA, 1/183/3, Vol. 4).

365. Letter from Albie Burger to Jean Bokassa, 17 December 1974 (DFA, 1/183/3, Vol. 5).

366. Letter from Jean Bokassa to John Vorster, 5 February; 'Dr Koornhof: visit to Bangui', from Johan Pretorius to Rae Killen, 17 November 1975, p.1 (DFA, 1/183/3, Vols. 5, 7).

367. 'Central African Republic: visit of Mr Joël Barkan, Technical Adviser to the President and Mr Maurice Methot, Director of Services in the Office of Life President Bokassa', 10 April, p.10-3 (DFA, 1/183/3, Vol. 2); letter from Hilgard Muller to Jean Bokassa, 29 March 1974, p.2 (DFA, 1/183/3, Vol. 1).

368. 'Meeting with the President: France, 24/9/1974 at 8 P.M.', p.1-2 (DFA, 1/183/3, Vol. 2).

369. 'Report on working group I', p.10, 4-5 (DFA, 1/183/3, Vol. 4).

370. 'Report on working group I', p.10, 6-7 (DFA, 1/183/3, Vol. 4).

371. 'Memorandum of Agreement entered into by and between the Central African Republic ("the Borrower") and Industrial Development Corporation of South Africa Limited ("the IDC")' (DFA, 1/183/3, Vol. 6).

372. 'Report on working group II', p.1-3 (DFA, 1/183/3, Vol. 4).

373. 'Barkan – 25.6.75' (DFA, 1/183/3, Vol. 7).

374. 'Official visit of our Foreign Minister to the Central African Republic: 21 to 24 February 1976', 3 March 1976 (DFA, 1/183/3, Vol. 8).

375. 'Procès-verbal de la séance de travail entre la délégation centrafricaine et certains membres de la délégation sud-africaine', 24 February 1976, p.2 (DFA, 1/183/3, Vol. 8) (translated from French).

376. 'Central African Republic', from Rae Killen to Hilgard Muller, 2 June 1976, p.1 (DFA, 1/183/3, Vol. 8).

377. 'Onderhoud met President Bokassa by die Presidensiele Paleis of 23 Februarie', from Johan Pretorius, 26 February, p.4; 'Procès-verbal de la séance de travail entre la délégation centrafricaine et certains membres de la délégation sud-africaine', from André Jaquet, 24 February 1976, p.1 (DFA, 1/183/3, Vols. 7-8).

378. 'Onderhoud met President Bokassa by die Presidensiele Paleis of 23 Februarie', from Johan Pretorius, 26 February 1976, p.2-3 (DFA, 1/183/3, Vol. 7) (translated from Afrikaans).

379. 'Visit to Bangui, Central African Empire: 10-17 August 1977', from Rae Killen, p.4-5, Annex A (DFA, 1/183/3, Vol. 8).

380. 'Main points of discussion with Minister Toleque and Mr Barkan of Central African Empire', from Johan Pretorius, 7 March 1978, p.2 (DFA, 1/183/3, Vol. 9).

381. 'Procès-verbal de la séance de travail entre la délégation centrafricaine et certains membres de la délégation sud-africaine', 24 February, p.4-5; 'Official visit of our Foreign Minister to the Central African Republic', 3 March 1976 (DFA, 1/183/3, Vol. 8).

382. 'Main points of discussion with Minister Toleque and Mr Barkan of Central African Empire', 7 March 1978, p.1 (DFA, 1/183/3, Vol. 9).

383. Interview with Frans Swarts, 7 December 2002.

384. Pirie. 1990. 'Aviation, Apartheid and sanctions', p.231.

385. *South African Airways*. 1964; <http://www.saamuseum.co.za/history.htm>; <http://www.saa.co.za>

386. Pirie. 1990. 'Aviation, Apartheid and sanctions', p.233.

387. Correspondence with Frans Swarts and Gert van der Veer, 11 February 2003.

388. Potgieter. 1986. *Aviation in South Africa*, p.11.

389. Griffiths. 1989. 'Airways sanctions against South Africa', p.255-6; correspondence with Frans Swarts and Gert van der Veer, 11 February 2003.

390. 'Summary of discussions between representatives of the Government of Cabo Verde and SA Airways: Ilha do Sal: 8 August 1975', p.1 (DFA, 1/224/3, Vol. 1).

391. DFA, 1/224/3, Vol. 1.

392. Interview with Neil van Heerden and Paul Runge, 7 April 1999.

393. Whann. 1998. 'The Political Economy of Cape Verde's foreign policy', p.46.

394. Adams. 1984. *The Unnatural Alliance.*

395. Whitehill. 1986. 'The sanctions that never were'.

396. Seidman & Makgetla. 1979. 'Transnational corporate involvement in South Africa's military build-up'.

397. Correspondence with Frans Swarts and Gert van der Veer, 11 February 2003.

398. Geldenhuys. 1984. *The Diplomacy of Isolation*, p.117.

399. 'Contact with Sudan: meeting with Dr van Riebenberg: SAR & H Headquarters', from Carl von Hirschberg, 13 August, p.4; 'Contact with Sudan: meeting between Minister and Dr van Riebenberg', from Carl von Hirschberg, 15 August 1979, p.1 (DFA, 1/163/3, Vol. 1PL).

400. Correspondence with Frans Swarts and Gert van der Veer, 11 February 2003.

401. Interview with Frans Swarts, 7 December 2002.

402. Correspondence with Frans Swarts and Gert van der Veer, 11 February 2003.

403. Bowman. 1982. 'African conflict and superpower involvement in the Western Indian Ocean'; Cooke. 1983. 'Strategic considerations', p.253-4, 256, 263; Sparks. 2001. 'Indian Ocean region', p.390.

404. Chipman. 1985. *French Military Policy and African Security*, p. 11-2.

405. 'Madagaskar/RSA: geheime onderhandelinge in Parys', from Albie Geldenhuys, 15 January 1973, p.3 (DFA, 1/115/3, Vol. 3PL) (translated from Afrikaans).

406. *Rand Daily Mail* 5 October 1972.

407. 'Mauritian tea question', from Johan Pretorius to Pik Botha, 15 January 1979 (DFA, 1/62/3, Vol. 12; Vol. 5 contains the agreement).

408. Letter from Gaëtan Duval to Hilgard Muller, 2 November 1973 (DFA, 1/62/3, Vol. 7).

409. DFA, 1/62/3, Vol. 7.

410. <http://www.semdex.com/company_profile/sun.htm>; *To the Point* 20 December 1974: 26.

411. *The Citizen* 24 December 1976.

412. Bowman. 1991. *Mauritius*, p.71, 73-4; Wickman. 1982. 'Mauritius', p.160.

413. *Pretoria News* 20 December 1973.

414. Letter from David Louw to Brand Fourie, 23 January 1974, p.2 (DFA, 1/62/3, Vol. 8).

415. 'Verhoudings met Mauritius', from Rae Killen to Brand Fourie, 7 February 1974, p.1 (DFA, 1/62/3, Vol. 8).

416. 'Mauritius – voortsetting van kontak met R.S.A.', from the Secretary, BOSS, to Brand Fourie, 30 January 1974, p.1 (DFA, 1/62/3, Vol. 8) (translated from Afrikaans).

417. 'Verhoudings met Mauritius', from Rae Killen to Brand Fourie, 7 February 1974, p.3 (DFA, 1/62/3, Vol. 8) (translated from Afrikaans).

418. DFA, 1/138/3, Vol. 1; letter from W.A.E. 'Ted' Hirst (Director of Development and Corporate Planning, Holiday Inn) to Rae Killen, 16 February; letter from Rae Killen to Ted Hirst, 3 March; letter from Ted Hirst to Rae Killen, 9 June; 'Holiday Inn hotel project', from Johan von Gernet to Brand Fourie, 10 November 1976, p.2 (DFA, 1/138/4, Vols. 1-2).
419. 'Reunion: end of stay report', from Johan von Gernet to Brand Fourie, 17 February 1978, p.2 (DFA, 1/138/3, Vol. 3).
420. 'Representation on Reunion', from Johan Pretorius to Brand Fourie, 7 August 1974, p.1 (DFA, 1/138/3, Vol. 1).
421. Letter from Kenneth Hobson to Joep Steyn, 26 October 1973, p.1-2 (DFA, 1/138/3, Vol. 1).
422. 'Réunion: possible South African representation', from Hugo Biermann to Brand Fourie, 4 March 1974 (DFA, 1/138/3, Vol. 1).
423. 'Representation on Reunion', from Johan Pretorius to Brand Fourie, 7 August 1974, p.1 (DFA, 1/138/3, Vol. 1).
424. DFA, 1/138/3, Vol. 1; *Foreign Affairs List*.
425. 'Establishment: St. Denis, Reunion', from Johan Pretorius, 31 January 1975 (DFA, 1/138/3, Vol. 2).
426. 'Proposed invitation to Comoros Head of State to visit South Africa', from Carl von Hirschberg to Brand Fourie, 29 April 1979, p.1 (DFA, 1/203/3, Vol. 3).
427. 'Summaries of discussions with Comorian ministers, 19-22 July 1974', from Rae Killen, 1 August 1974, p.2 (DFA, 1/203,3, Vol. 1).
428. 'Besoek aan die Comora-Eilandgroep op versoek van die Departement van Buitelandse Sake via die Sekretaris van Nywerheid', p.1; 'Visit of technical mission to Comoros: 18-23 July 1974', p.2; 'Summaries of discussions with Comorian ministers, 19-22 July 1974', p.3-4, all from Rae Killen, 1 August 1974 (DFA, 1/203/3, Vol. 1).
429. 'Visit of technical mission to Comoros: 18-23 July 1974', from Rae Killen, 1 August 1974, p.2 (DFA, 1/203/3, Vol. 1).
430. Letter from Hilgard Muller to Ahmed Abdallah, 3 September 1974 (DFA, 1/203/3, Vol. 2).
431. Letter from Ahmed Abdallah to Hilgard Muller, 11 September 1974; 'Visit to Comores [sic]: 14-21 February 1975', from Rae Killen, 25 February 1975, p.2-3, 6-7; 'Comoros: current position of Technical Assistance', from André Jaquet, 6 May 1977, p.1 (DFA, 1/203/3, Vols. 2-3).
432. Correspondence with Frans Swarts and Gert van der Veer, 11 February 2003.
433. De Villiers. 1980. *Secret Information*, p.142; Rhoodie. 1983. *The Real Information Scandal*, p.140; Geldenhuys. 1984. *The Diplomacy of Isolation*, p.118-9.
434. Franda. 1982. *The Seychelles*, p.49.
435. Letter from Eschel Rhoodie to Brand Fourie, 17 January 1977 (DFA, 1/194/3, Vol. 2).
436. De Villiers. 1980. *Secret Information*, p.142-3; Ellis. 1996. 'Africa and international corruption', p.171.
437. Mancham. 1983. *Paradise Raped*, p.176.
438. Correspondence with Louis Luyt, 23 February 2003.
439. 'Verhoudings met die Seychelle', 11 January 1978 (DFA, 1/194/3, Vol. 2).
440. Correspondence with Louis Luyt, 23 February 2003.
441. 'Relations between Seychelles and South Africa', from Rae Killen to Donald Sole, September 1978 (DFA, 1/194/3, Vol. 3); 'Seychelles: technical

assistance', from Carl von Hirschberg to Brand Fourie, July 1979, p.1; 'Seychelles', from Rae Killen, February 1980, p.1-2 (DFA, 1/194/4, Vol. 1).

442. 'Seychelles', from Rae Killen, February 1980, p.1 (DFA, 1/194/4, Vol. 1).

443. 'Seychelles: technical assistance', from Carl von Hirschberg to Brand Fourie, July 1979; 'Seychelles', from Rae Killen, February 1980, p.1-2 (DFA, 1/194/4, Vol. 1).

444. Correspondence with Frans Swarts and Gert van der Veer, 11 February 2003.

445. DFA, 1/62/3, Vol. 10; 1/129/3, Vol. 3, AJ 1974; 1/149/3, Vol. 1; 1/186/3, Vol. 2; 1/199/3, Vol. 5; correspondence with Colin Eglin, 13 and 15 January 2003; Slabbert. 1987. *The Last White Parliament*, p.31-3.

446. Correspondence with Helen Suzman, 18 November 2002.

447. Correspondence with Colin Eglin, 13 January 2003.

448. Correspondence with Colin Eglin, 15 and 19 January 2003.

449. *Rand Daily Mail* 13 and 23 September 1977.

450. Geldenhuys. 1984. *The Diplomacy of Isolation*, p.52.

451. *To the Point* 2 August 1974: 19.

452. Geldenhuys. 1984. *The Diplomacy of Isolation*, p.51; *The Star* 30 July 1974.

453. *Who's Who in America, 2002*, p.3776.

454. Geldenhuys. 1984. *The Diplomacy of Isolation*, p.176-7.

455. For example: 1968. *South Africa's Prime Minister*, 1979. *The Afrikaners.*

456. Correspondence with Ned Munger, 7 February 2002.

457. Munger. 1983. *Touched by Africa*, p.284-312.

458. Munger. 1983. *Touched by Africa*, p.355-6, 377.

459. Interview with Martin Aliker, 24 February 2004; Munger. 1983. *Touched by Africa*, p.360-73; DFA, 1/120/3, Vol. 2.

460. Telegram from the South African Embassy to Brand Fourie, London, 19 July 1978 (DFA, 1/120/3, Vols. 1PL, 3); DFA, 1/120/3, Vol. 2; interview with Martin Aliker, 24 February 2004.

461. Interview with Martin Aliker, 24 February 2004.

462. DFA, 1/120/3, Vol. 2.

463. Correspondence with Gert van der Veer, 5 January 2003.

464. 'Conversation with Mr Marende from Kenya', from Hennie Geldenhuys to Rae Killen, 25 October 1978, p.1 (DFA, 1/135/3, Vol. 7).

465. 'Médard. 1997. 'Njonjo'.

466. 'Meeting between the Minister and Messrs Hersov and Sorour of the South Africa Foundation', from Carl von Hirschberg, June 1979, p.1 (DFA, 1/135/3, Vol. 8).

467. Correspondence with Carl von Hirschberg, 12 January 2004, and Charles Njonjo, 23 December 2003

468. Correspondence with Carl von Hirschberg, 12 January 2004.

469. *Rand Daily Mail* 19 July, *The Citizen* 9 August 1978.

470. Correspondence with Charles Njonjo, 23 December 2003.

471. *Pretoria News* 15 and 21 August 1978.

472. Correspondence with Carl von Hirschberg, 12 January 2004.

473. 'Meeting between the Minister and Messrs Hersov and Sorour of the South Africa Foundation', from Carl von Hirschberg, June 1979, p.1 (DFA, 1/135/3, Vol. 8).

474. Médard. 1997. 'Njonjo'.

475. Legum. 1976. 'Southern Africa', p.20.

476. Bowker. 1983. *Superpower Détente*, Crockatt. 1995. *The Fifty Years War*, p.207-34.

477. Kissinger. 1994. *Diplomacy*, p.674-702.

478. Kissinger. 1994. *Diplomacy*, p.726; Kissinger. 1999. *Years of Renewal*, p.146, 876.
479. Bowker. 1983. *Superpower Détente*, p.97-113.
480. *To the Point* 6 December 1974: 17.
481. Venter, A.J. 1977. *Vorster's Africa.*
482. Philipps. 1969. 'South West Africa, South Africa's fifth province', p.181-98.
483. Barber & Barratt. 1990. *South Africa's Foreign Policy*, p.198-9.
484. 'Zaïre: technical assistance in the atomic energy field', from Rae Killen, 15 August 1974, p.1 (DFA, 1/112/3, Vol. 6).
485. Gleijeses. 2001. *Conflicting Missions*, p.287-9.
486. 'Besoek aan Zaïre deur 'n amptelike missie om die toestaan van 'n wentelkrediet aan twee staatsbeheerde invoerders van lewensmiddele te ondersoek, 1-4 April 1975', from Johan Pretorius, 7 April 1975 (DFA, 1/112/3, Vol. 6).
487. 'Tweede besoek aan Zaïre deur 'n amptelike missie om die toestaan van 'n wentelkrediet van R3 miljoen aan twee staatsbeheerde invoerders van lewensmiddele te beklink', from Johan Pretorius, 19 May 1975 (DFA, 1/112/3, Vol. 6).
488. 'Unpaid exports made from South Africa to Zaire', May 1977 (DFA, 1/112/3, Vol. 9).
489. 'Visit of delegation from private sector to Zaire, led by Secretary for Commerce: 5-10 July, 1975', July 1975, p.7 (DFA, 1/112/3, Vol. 6).
490. 'Notes for the discussions to be held with Mr. Steyn on Thursday July 17, 1975', 15 July 1975 (DFA, 1/112/3, Vol. 6).
491. Telex to Justin Bomboko, 9 October 1975 (DFA, 1/112/3, Vol. 7).
492. 'Memorandum: visit of group of contractors to Zaire', 23 October 1975, p.4-10 (DFA, 1/112/3, Vol. 7).
493. Correspondence with Mike Ridley, 9 May 2004.
494. 'Memorandum: visit of group of contractors to Zaire', 23 October 1975, p.10-2, 18 (DFA, 1/112/3, Vol. 7).
495. 'Suid-Afrikaanse hulp aan Zaire', November 1976, p.1 (DFA, 1/112/4, Vol. 1).
496. *Mail & Guardian* 12 July 1999.
497. Letter from Justin Bomboko to Brand Fourie, 17 October; letter from Brand Fourie to Justin Bomboko, 24 October (translated from French); telex from Justin Bomboko to Brand Fourie, 22 December 1975 (DFA, 1/112/3, Vol. 7).
498. Rhoodie. 1983. *The Real Information Scandal*, p.136.
499. 'Suid-Afrikaanse hulp aan Zaire', November 1976, p.2 (DFA, 1/112/4, Vol. 1) (translated from Afrikaans).
500. Correspondence with Louis Luyt, 23 and 25 February 2003.
501. Hocking. 1973. *Oppenheimer and Son*, p.417-8; Pallister, Stewart & Lepper. 1987. *South Africa Inc.*, p.254; Whyte. 1997. 'Taking a chance on Zaire'; <http://www.tenke.com/tenke/history.html>
502. 'Zaire', from Jeremy Shearar to Brand Fourie, 12 February 1976, p.3 (DFA, 1/112/3, Vol. 7).
503. Kissinger. 1999. *Years of Renewal*, p.945; Kelly. 1993. *America's Tyrant.*
504. Gleijeses. 2001. *Conflicting Missions*, p.258-9; Litwak. 1984. *Détente and the Nixon Doctrine*, p.181.
505. 'SMTF-Zaire copper project: memorandum number one', attached to Harry Oppenheimer's letter to Hilgard Muller, 14 April, p.5 (DFA, 1/112/4, Vol. 1); 'Confidential note on the activities of the Anglo American group in Zaïre', from Chris Stals (General Manager, South African Reserve Bank), 7 January 1976 (DFA, 1/112/3, Vol. 7). The Exchange Control required the Reserve Bank to approve Anglo American's investment in the SMTF project.

506. 'Zaire', from Jeremy Shearar to Rae Killen, 12 February 1976, p.1 (DFA, 1/112/3, Vol. 7).

507. Domhoff. 1967. *Who Rules America?*, p.105, 99; Kissinger. 1982. *Years of Upheaval*, p.1049; Kwitny. 1986. *Endless Enemies*, p.178; *The Complete Marquis Who's Who; Who's Who in America, 1984-1985*, p.76.

508. Gibbs. 1991. *The Political Economy of Third World Intervention*, p.112-4, 181 (note 114), 189-90.

509. 'Confidential note on the activities of the Anglo American group in Zaïre', from Chris Stals, 7 January 1976 (DFA, 1/112/3, Vol. 7).

510. 'Co-operation in development of Iranian mines', from Pop Fraser to Brand Fourie, 18 February 1976, p.1-2 (DFA, 1/112/4, Vol. 1); 'Iran', from Harry Oppenheimer (DFA, 1/112/3, Vol. 8).

511. 'Suid-Afrikaanse hulp aan Zaire', October 1976, p.3-4 (DFA, 1/112/4, Vol. 1).

512. Gibbs. 1991. *The Political Economy of Third World Intervention*, p.182.

513. 'SMTF-Zaire copper project: memorandum number one', from Harry Oppenheimer to Hilgard Muller, 14 April 1976, p.1 (DFA, 1/112/4, Vol. 1).

514. Mahoney. 1983. *JFK*, p.173; Gibbs. 1991. *The Political Economy of Third World Intervention*, p.108, 110-1, 180-3; Kwitny. 1986. *Endless Enemies*, p.9, 52-9; Roberts. 2003. *Glitter and Greed*, p.169-77, 198, 203-4.

515. Callaghy. 1985. 'Zaire and Southern Africa', p.69; Roberts. 2003. *Glitter and Greed*, p.115-30, 169-74.

516. Gibbs. 1991. *The Political Economy of Third World Intervention*, p.183 (note 166), 189; Kwitny. 1986. *Endless Enemies*, p.46-8, 87-8.

517. Interview with Michael Spicer, 7 April 1999.

518. Letter from Maurice Tempelsman to Harry Oppenheimer, 6 April 1976 (DFA, 1/112/4, Vol. 1).

519. Barber & Barratt. 1990. *South Africa's Foreign Policy*, p.201-2.

520. Letter from Harry Oppenheimer to Hilgard Muller, 14 April; letter from Harry Oppenheimer to Brand Fourie, 22 April 1976 (DFA, 1/112/4, Vol. 1).

521. Letter from Hilgard Muller to Harry Oppenheimer, 4 May 1976 (DFA, 1/112/4, Vol. 1).

522. Telex from Justin Bomboko to Justus de Goede, 30 September 1975 (DFA, 1/112/3, Vol. 7).

523. Telex from Justin Bomboko to Justus de Goede, 30 September; 'Zaire: versoek aan Suid-Afrikaanse regering om te borg te staan vir olievoorrade', 26 November, p.1; 'Zaire: versoek aan die Suid-Afrikaanse regering om betaling van brandstofaankope te borg', 28 November 1975, p.1, both from Johan Pretorius (DFA, 1/112/3, Vol. 7).

524. Kelly. 1993. *America's Tyrant*, p.33, 41, 57-9, 71; Kwitny. 1986. *Endless Enemies*, p.58-71; Prados. 1988. *Presidents' Secret Wars*, p.234-5, 283, 293, 340; Roberts. 2003. *Glitter and Greed*, p.177-81, 197-8; Stockwell. 1978. *In Search of Enemies*, p.71, 136-7; Weissman. 1980. 'The CIA and U.S. policy in Zaire and Angola', p.158-66.

525. Jones. 1992. 'Union Acceptances'.

526. *Finance Week* 25 June 1993.

527. 'Zaire: supply of $50 million oil by Mobil International', 22 November; 'Zaire: versoek aan Suid-Afrikaanse regering om te borg te staan vir olievoorrade', 26 November; 'Zaire: versoek aan die Suid-Afrikaanse regering om betaling van brandstofaankope te borg', 28 November, all from Johan Pretorius; telex from Justin Bomboko to Rae Killen, 4 December 1975 (DFA, 1/112/3, Vol. 7).

528. 'Dr. Smit', 26 November 1975 (DFA, 1/112/3, Vol. 8). 'Dr. Smit' refers to Robert van Schalkwijk Smit, Department of Finance Secretary (1964-67), IMF Alternative Executive Director (1971-74) and Finance Director in the Treasury (1975-76) (*Who's Who of Southern Africa, 1977-78*, p.817). In 1977, he was murdered under unresolved circumstances (*Sunday Times* 5 May 2002).

529. Péan. 1983. *Affaires africaines*, p.141, 236, 261.

530. 'Re: Gabon – award of the "Order of Good Hope" to Messrs. P. Monier-Vinard and J.M. Muxart', from Jan Boyazoglu to Brand Fourie, 23 November 1975, p.1-2; "Award of the "Order of Good Hope" to', from Anton Loubser, 2 July; Gaboen: eerbewys aan Mnr. J.P. Daniël', from Carl von Hirschberg to Brand Fourie, 9 July 1979, p.2 (DFA, 1/178/3, Vols. 7, 9).

531. 'Gabon: relations with South Africa and technical aid', from Anton Loubser, 2 October 1978, p.1 (DFA, 1/178/4, Vol. 16).

532. 'Klaring van Safair-vlugte', to Brand Fourie, 4 June; 'Re: supply of jet fuel to Franceville', from Pi Pienaar to Jean-Pierre Daniël, 30 June, p.2; 'Note', from Johan Pretorius, 20 June; 'Route clearances', from J.J. le Roux (Safair) to Johan Pretorius, 18 August; 'Re: Gabon – SAFAIR', from Julian Thomas to Albie Burger, 20 November 1975 (DFA, 1/178/3, Vols. 5-7).

533. 'Gabon: relations with South Africa and technical aid', from Anton Loubser, 2 October 1978, p.1 (DFA, 1/178/4, Vol. 16).

534. Documents in endnote 532 and 'Central African Republic', from Rae Killen to Hilgard Muller, 2 June 1976, p.2 (DFA, 1/183/3, Vol. 8).

535. Landgren. 1989. *Embargo Disimplemented*, McWilliams. 1989. *Armscor.*

536. DFA, 1/178/3, Vols. 4-6.

537. Klare. 1977. *U.S. Arms Deliveries to South Africa*, Landgren. 1989. *Embargo Disimplemented*, p.201-7, 215-6.

538. 'Route clearances', from J.J. le Roux (Safair) to Johan Pretorius, 18 August 1975 (DFA, 1/178/3, Vol. 6).

539. Landgren. 1989. *Embargo Disimplemented*, p. 125; 63-78, 95, 128-9, 215.

540. <http://www.nobel.se/nobel/alfred-nobel/industrial/dolan>

541. 'I/s Gaboen besoek', from Jan Boyazoglu to Brand Fourie, 26 July 1975, p.2; 'Re: visit to the Gabon: 19 to 23 November 1976', from Jan Boyazoglu to Brand Fourie, 3 December 1976, p.3 (DFA, 1/178/3, Vols. 5, 9).

542. 'Note', from Rae Killen, 19 July 1976 (DFA, 1/178/3, Vol. 8).

543. *African Business* 171, November 1992: 52.

544. Péan. 1983. *Affaires africaines*, p.80-1, 83.

545. 'Notes on a meeting at 10.30 hours Friday, 8th August in S.A. Airways Boardroom, Air Terminal, Johannesburg', August 1975, p.1 (DFA, 1/178/3, Vol. 6).

546. Péan. 1983. *Affaires africaines*, p.84.

547. The lease of plane and the entire crew. Interview with Pieter van Aswegen, 2 November 2001.

548. 'Resume of discussions between Capt. Jack M. Malloch of Air Trans Africa and Mr. F. Swarts of SA Airways', p.1 (DFA, 1/178/3, Vol. 5).

549. Letter from Patrick Monier-Vinard to Brand Fourie, 17 May 1975, p.1-2 (DFA, 1/178/3, Vol. 5).

550. 'Agreement between the South African Airways and AFFRETAIR companies', 13 June; 'Resume of understanding reached between South African Airways and Air Trans Africa – Salisbury, 13th June, 1975', 13 June 1975, p.1-2 (DFA, 1/178/3, Vols. 5-6).

551. Letter from Julian Thomas to Brand Fourie, 26 June, p.2; letter from Brand Fourie to Pi Pienaar, 2 July 1975, p.1-2 (DFA, 1/178/3, Vol. 5).

552. 'I.s. Gabon aangeleenthede', from Jan Boyazoglu to Brand Fourie, 11 July 1975 (DFA, 1/178/3, Vol. 5).

553. Letter from Julian Thomas to Brand Fourie, 26 June, p.1; 'Re: supply of jet fuel to Franceville', from Pi Pienaar to Jean-Pierre Daniël, 30 June, p.2; letter from Brand Fourie to Pi Pienaar, 2 July 1975, p.2 (DFA, 1/178/3, Vol. 5).

554. 'I.s. Gabon aangeleenthede', from Jan Boyazoglu to Brand Fourie, 11 July, p.2 (translated from Afrikaans); hand-written note from Jean-Pierre Daniël to Brand Fourie, 24 July 1975 (translated from French) (DFA, 1/178/3, Vol. 5).

555. Letter from Jean-Pierre Daniël to Pi Pienaar, 19 July, p.1; hand-written note from Jean-Pierre Daniël to Brand Fourie, 24 July (translated from French); 'I/s Gaboen besoek', from Jan Boyazoglu to Brand Fourie, 26 July 1975 (DFA, 1/178/3, Vol. 5).

556. 'Use of Franceville airport: discussion at S.A.A. headquarters on 13 August 1975 between Mr. J.P. Daniël and Captain Pienaar and Mr. F. Swarts', August 1975 (DFA, 1/178/3, Vol. 6).

557. 'Visit of Jean-Pierre Daniël on Wednesday 13 August to South Africa', from Jan Boyazoglu to Brand Fourie, 18 August 1975, p.1-2 (DFA, 1/178/3, Vol. 6).

558. 're: Gabon arrangement with special reference to AFFRETAIR', from Jan Boyazoglu to Brand Fourie (to be opened by Rae Killen in Fourie's absence), 25 August 1975 (DFA, 1/178/3, Vol. 7).

559. 'Second draft of the 'loan agreement entered into by and between the Government of the Republic of South Africa and the Government of the Gabonese Republic', October; 'Pouvoirs', from Omar Bongo, 12 September 1975 (DFA, 1/178/3, Vols. 5, 7); 'Gabon: relations with South Africa and technical aid', from Anton Loubser, 2 October 1978, p.1 (DFA, 1/178/4, Vol. 16).

560. 'Questions to be raised during Mr. J.P. Daniel's visit during July 1979', from Jim Williams (CGIC), 28 June 1979, p.1-2 (DFA, 1/178/3, Vol. 9).

561. Interview with Jan Boyazoglou and Julian Thomas, 1 April 2004.

562. Interview with Frans Swarts, 7 December 2002.

563. Péan. 1983. *Affaires africaines*, p.245 (translated from French).

564. Gleijeses. 2001. *Conflicting Missions*, p.276-7, 291; Geldenhuys. 1984. *The Diplomacy of Isolation*, p.80.

565. Crockatt. 1995. *The Fifty Years War*, p.282.

566. Hamann. 2001. *Days of the Generals*, p.18-9; Gleijeses. 2001. *Conflicting Missions*, p.282-3; Kissinger. 1999. *Years of Renewal*, p.802.

567. Gleijeses. 2001. *Conflicting Missions*, p.259-61.

568. Geldenhuys. 1984. *The Diplomacy of Isolation*, p.80; Gleijeses. 2001. *Conflicting Missions*, p.298.

569. Geldenhuys. 1984. *The Diplomacy of Isolation*, p.82; Gleijeses. 2001. *Conflicting Missions*, p.340-1; Hamann. 2001. *Days of the Generals*, p.41.

570. Gleijeses. 2001. *Conflicting Missions*, p.341.

571. Kissinger. 1999. *Years of Renewal*, p.869, 875.

572. Gleijeses. 2001. *Conflicting Missions*, p.330-1.

573. Legum. 1976. 'The Soviet Union, China and the West in southern Africa'.

574. Gleijeses. 2001. *Conflicting Missions*, p.330-1.

575. *South Africa (Republic). Parliament. House of Assembly. Debates* 73, 28 March-3 May 1978, Cols. 4851-2.

576. Sole. 1994. 'South African foreign policy assumptions and objectives from Hertzog to de Klerk', p.110.

Chapter 5: The Military in Command

1. *White Paper on Defence and Armament Production.* 1975. p.7; *White Paper on Defence.* 1977. p.6-10; *White Paper on Defence and Armaments Supply.* 1979. p.1; 1982. p.iii, 4; 1984. p.1.
2. Malan. 1980. 'Die aanslag teen Suid-Afrika'.
3. Selfe. 1987. 'The Total Onslaught and the Total Strategy'.
4. For example Hanlon. 1986. *Apartheid's Second Front.*
5. McCarthy. 1996. 'Challenges for the South African intelligence community', p.65.
6. Baker. 1989. *The United States and South Africa;* Holland. 1988. *The European Community and South Africa.*
7. Karns. 1987. 'Ad hoc multilateral diplomacy'.
8. Crocker. 1981. 'Namibia/Angola Linkages'.
9. Culverson. 1999. *Contesting Apartheid;* Holland. 1988. *The European Community and South Africa.*
10. 'Relations with Francophone Africa', from Glenn Babb to Rae Killen, 16 February 1985, p.1; report from Paul Runge to Glenn Babb, 6 January 1988 (DFA, 1/101/3, Vol. 3A).
11. Jaster. 1988. *The Defence of White Power,* p.31.
12. 'Verhoudinge tussen RSA en Somalië: beleidsbepaling t.o.v. die res van Afrika', from Rae Killen to Pik Botha and Hans van Dalsen, 26 May 1983, p.4 (DFA, 1/99/19, Vol. 2) (translated from Afrikaans).
13. 'Intercontinental Hotel – Bangui, C.A.R.', November 1979, p.1-3 (DFA, 1/183/3, Vol. 10).
14. 'Visit to Bangui, Central African Republic, 3 December, 1979', from Jan Bouwer, December 1979, p.1-3 (DFA, 1/183/3, Vol. 10).
15. <http://www.centrafrique.com/imagesBG.htm>
16. Correspondence with Spencer Whiting, 21 April 2004.
17. 'Record of discussions held at C.G.I.C., Johannesburg, on Wednesday, 24 January, 1979', p.1 (DFA, 1/183/3, Vol. 9).
18. Correspondence with Spencer Whiting, 21 April 2004.
19. 'Visit to Bangui, Central African Republic, 3 December, 1979', from Jan Bouwer, December 1979, p.2-4 (DFA, 1/183/3, Vol. 10).
20. *Rand Daily Mail* 13 October 1979.
21. 'Sentraal-Afrikaanse Republiek: politieke ontwikkeling en verhoudinge met Suid-Afrika', from Pik Botha, October 1979, p.3-4 (DFA, 1/183/3, Vol. 10).
22. Interview with Neil van Heerden and Paul Runge, 7 April 1999.
23. 'Verhoudinge tussen RSA en Somalië: beleidsbepaling t.o.v. die res van Afrika', from Peter Killen to Pik Botha and Johannes van Dalsen, 26 May 1983, p.2 (DFA, 1/99/19, Vol. 2) (translated from Afrikaans).
24. Ingpen & le Roux. 1996. *Safmarine 50,* p.19, 29-30.
25. Hengeveld & Rodenburg. 1995. *Embargo,* p.189; Klinghoffer. 1989. *Oiling the Wheels of Apartheid,* p.46-7; Wilmot. 1989. *Nigeria's Southern Africa Policy, 1960-1988,* p.8; *ARB: Economic, Financial and Technical Series* 16, 3, 1979: 5048.
26. *Nigeria: Bulletin on Foreign Affairs* 9, 5, May 1979: 3.
27. 'Aanhouding 'Tanker Kulu' in Nigerië', from the Department of National Security, 23 May 1979 (DFA, 1/129/3, Vol. 6).

28.   'Meeting between the Minister and Messrs Hersov and Sorour of the South Africa Foundation', from Carl von Hirschberg, June 1979, p.1-2 (DFA, 1/135/3, Vol. 8).

29.   Correspondence with Peter Sorour, 31 January 2004.

30.   'Meeting between the Minister and Messrs Hersov and Sorour of the South Africa Foundation', from Carl von Hirschberg, June 1979, p.3-5 (DFA, 1/135/3, Vol. 8).

31.   Hansard, vol. 60, col. 104, 27 January 1976.

32.   Hansard, vol. 79, col. 460, 9 February 1979.

33.   Geldenhuys. 1984. The Diplomacy of Isolation, p.55.

34.   Correspondence with Colin Eglin, 13 and 15 January 2003.

35.   Cooke. 1983. 'Strategic considerations', p.256.

36.   Terrill. 1986. 'The Comoro Islands in South African regional strategy', p.62-4; Venter, T.D. 1990. 'The Comorian comitragedy', p.142-3; Newsletter on the Oil Embargo against South Africa 23, Second Quarter 1991: 3; Weinberg. 1994. Last of the Pirates, p.9-10.

37.   'Proposed invitation of Comoros Head of State to visit South Africa', from Carl von Hirschberg, 29 April 1979, p.1 (DFA, 1/203/3, Vol. 3).

38.   'Visit to the Comoros Islands, 4-7 December 1979', from Carl von Hirschberg to Brand Fourie, 1 May 1980, p.3 (DFA, 1/203/3, Vol. 4).

39.   'Meeting between Mr von Hirschberg and Colonel Denard', from Carl von Hirschberg, 30 October 1979 (DFA, 1/203/3, Vol. 4).

40.   Lunel. 1991. Bob Denard, p.567, 587; Weinberg. 1994. Last of the Pirates, p.107.

41.   'Comoros: discussion with Mr Denard', from Rae Killen to Hennie Geldenhuys, 18 November 1980, p.1-2 (DFA, 1/203/3, Vol. 4).

42.   'Supply of petroleum products to the Comoros', from Glenn Babb to Rae Killen, 20 November 1980 (DFA, 1/203/3, Vol. 4).

43.   'Visit to the Comoros Islands, 4-7 December 1979', from Carl von Hirschberg to Brand Fourie, 1 May 1980, p.2-3 (DFA, 1/203/3, Vol. 4).

44.   Denard. 1998. Corsaire de la république, p.340-2; Lunel. 1991. Bob Denard, p.566, 592.

45.   Denard. 1998. Corsaire de la république, p.356-7.

46.   Telephone interview with Marie Jacobs (Treaty Section, DFA Legal Department), 18 November 2002.

47.   Denard. 1998. Corsaire de la république, p.371; Lunel. 1991. Bob Denard, p.600.

48.   'Meeting between Mr von Hirschberg and Colonel Denard', from Carl von Hirschberg, 30 October 1979, p.2 (DFA, 1/203/3, Vol. 4).

49.   'Mission to Comoros 4-7 December 1979', to Carl von Hirschberg, November 1979 (DFA, 1/203/3, Vol. 4).

50.   'Visit to the Comoros Islands, 4-7 December 1979', from Carl von Hirschberg to Brand Fourie, 1 May 1980, p.3-5 (DFA, 1/203/3, Vol. 4).

51.   Péan. 1983. Affaires africaines, p.172 (translated from French).

52.   Lunel. 1991. Bob Denard, p.591; Weinberg. 1994. Last of the Pirates, p.112.

53.   Crush & Wellings. 1983. 'The southern African pleasure periphery', p.693, 697; Rogerson. 1990. 'Sun International', p.346, 349-50; Sun International. 1985. p.13, 16-7; Business Day 9 February 1989.

54.   Denard. 1998. Corsaire de la république, p.382; Lunel. 1991. Bob Denard, p.588-9; Weinberg. 1994. Last of the Pirates, p.187; ARB: Economic Series 27, 9, 1990: 10107.

55.   Rogerson. 1990. 'Sun International', p.347-8; <http://www.semdex.com/company_profile/sun.htm>

56. Correspondence with Frans Swarts and Gert van der Veer, 11 February 2003.

57. *Sun International*. 1985. p.17; <http://www.sunresort.com>; Bowman. 1991. *Mauritius*, p.96

58. Lunel. 1991. *Bob Denard*, p.613 (translated from French), 567, 583-7, 608-9, 616-20; Denard. 1998. *Corsaire de la république*, p.356-7, 379, 389-90; Weinberg. 1994. *Last of the Pirates*, p.111-2, 136-7, 186-7.

59. Wilkins & Strydom. 1980. *The Super-Afrikaners*, p.A252.

60. Letter from Pieter van der Westhuizen, 14 June 1979 (DFA, 1/115/3, Vol. 1PL).

61. Cooke. 1983. 'Strategic considerations', p.251, 274-80.

62. 'Seychelles', February 1980, p.2 (DFA, 1/194/4, Vol. 1); 'Beplande staatsgrep in Seychelle', from the Secretary, Department of National Security, to Brand Fourie, 19 April; 'Beplande staatsgrep in Seychelle', from Carl von Hirschberg to Brand Fourie, 2 May; 'Beplande staatsgrep in Seychelle', from Hennie Geldenhuys to Carl von Hirschberg, 15 May 1979 (DFA, 1/194/3, Vol. 3).

63. Reuters and Associated Press news reports, 16-18 November 1979 (DFA, 1/194/3, Vol. 3); Cooke. 1983. 'Seychelles', p.220.

64. Telex to Carl von Hirschberg, 19 November 1979 (DFA, 1/194/3, Vol. 3).

65. Hoare. 1989. *The Road to Kalamata*, back cover; Blum. 1995. *Killing Hope*, p.267.

66. Correspondence with Daan Hamman, 14 March 2004.

67. Weinberg. 1994. *Last of the Pirates*, p.206.

68. Such as Jeremiah 'Jerry' Puren: Puren & Pottinger. 1986. *Mercenary Commander*.

69. Hoare, M. 1986. *The Seychelles Affair*, p.59-91; Mancham. 1983. *Paradise Raped*, p.228-30; <http://www.contrast.org/truth/html/seychelles.html> lists the names of all men involved; Rogers. 2000. *Someone Else's War*, p.155-73.

70. *TRC Report. Vol. 2*. 1999. p.161-3; Hoare, M. 1986. *The Seychelles Affair*, p.22-3, 26, 125; Ellis. 1996. 'Africa and international corruption', p.172-3.

71. Correspondence with Daan Hamman, 14 March 2004.

72. *TRC Report. Vol. 2*. 1999. p.163; Hoare. 1986. *The Seychelles Affair*, p.22-6, 125.

73. *TRC Report. Vol. 2*. 1999. p.161-3.

74. Frankel. 1984. *Pretoria's Praetorians*, p.130; Jaster. 1986. *The Defence of White Power*, p.136-7; Rogers. 2000. *Someone Else's War*, p.179; *TRC Report. Vol. 2*. 1999. p.160.

75. Botha, C.B. 1993. 'Soldiers of fortune or whores of war?', p.86.

76. Hoare. 1986. *The Seychelles Affair*, p.190-5.

77. *TRC Report. Vol. 2*. 1999. p.160, 162; Ellis. 1996. 'Africa and international corruption', p.173; *ARB: Political, Social and Cultural Series* 20, 7, 1983: 6909.

78. Blum. 1995. *Killing Hope*, p.267; Franda. 1982. *The Seychelles*, p.1, 51, 75, 111-2, 117-8.

79. *New York Times* 10 May 1982, p.2.

80. Hamann. 2001. *Days of the Generals*, p.161.

81. <http://www.cia.gov/nic/PDF_GIF_research/defensemkts/south_africa.pdf >, p.6.

82. Patterson. 1985. 'Somalia and the United States, 1977-83', p.202.

83. 'Besoek Somaliëse afvaardiging: samesprekings met Minister van Verdediging en Adj Minister van Buitelandse Sake op 19 mei 1984', 21 May 1984, p.4 (DFA, 1/144/3, Vol. 4) (translated from Afrikaans).

84. Letter from Hassan Wehelie to the Director-General, Department of Home Affairs, 27 June 1984 (DFA, 1/144/3, Vol. 4).

85.   'Somalia: discussion with Mr Hassan Wehelie', from Rae Killen to Brand Fourie, 14 February 1980, p.2 (DFA, 1/144/3, Vol. 1PL).

86.   'Contacts with Somalia', from Rae Killen to Pik Botha, 4 September 1980 (DFA, 1/144/3, Vol. 2).

87.   'Verhoudinge tussen RSA en Somalië: beleidsbepaling t.o.v. die res van Afrika', from Rae Killen to Pik Botha and Hans van Dalsen, 26 May 1983, p.4 (DFA, 1/99/19, Vol. 2) (translated from Afrikaans).

88.   'Somalia', from Glenn Babb to Rae Killen and Jan Wentzel, 31 August 1982, p.2; 'Aid to Somalia', from Rae Killen to Hans van Dalsen, 11 March 1983, p.2 (DFA, 1/144/3, Vol. 2).

89.   Correspondence with Glenn Babb, 20 January 2003.

90.   Draft letter from Pik Botha to Siad Barre, February 1984 (DFA, 1/144/3, Vol. 3).

91.   'Report on visit of a delegation to Somalia, 11-15 February 1984', from Glenn Babb, 21 February, p.11; 'Verhoudings met Somalië', from Rae Killen to Hans van Dalsen and Pik Botha, April 1984, p.2 (DFA, 1/144/3, Vol. 3).

92.   'Meeting with Anglo-American: Somalia' and 'Meeting with Gold Fields, both from Glenn Babb to Rae Killen, 24 and 25 April 1984 (DFA, 1/144/3, Vol. 4).

93.   Whyte. 1997. 'Taking a chance on Zaire'.

94.   Interview with Stefan Landsberg, 4 December 2002.

95.   Interview with Michael Spicer, 7 April 1999; interview with Stefan Landsberg, 4 December 2002.

96.   'Report on visit of a delegation to Somalia, 11-15 February 1984', from Glenn Babb, 21 February 1984, p.12 (DFA, 1/144/3, Vol. 3).

97.   'Verhoudings met Somalië', from Rae Killen to Hans van Dalsen and Pik Botha, April 1984, p.3-5 (DFA, 1/144/3, Vol. 3).

98.   De Beer, J.H. 1998. 'Integration of the Departments of Foreign Affairs and Information in 1980 and adjustments up to 1993', p.119.

99.   Correspondence with Glenn Babb, 20 January 2003.

100.   Landgren 1989. Embargo Disimplemented, p.182-3.

101.   'Programme', 16 May 1984 (DFA, 1/144/3, Vol. 4).

102.   'Besoek Somaliëse afvaardiging: samesprekings met Minister van Verd- ediging en Adj Minister van Buitelandse Sake op 19 mei 1984', 21 May, p.5-6; 'Visit of Lt.-Gen. Ali Samatar, First Vice-President of Somalia', from Glenn Babb to Rae Killen, 22 May 1984, p.4-6, 8-9 (DFA, 1/144/3, Vol. 4).

103.   'Somalia: visit by the Deputy Minister of Foreign Affairs', from Glenn Babb to Rae Killen, 25 June 1984, p.1 (DFA, 1/144/3, Vol. 4).

104.   'Verslag van besoek aan Somalië, 4-5 julie 1984', from Glenn Babb, 10 July 1984, p.2-3, 6 (DFA, 1/144/3, Vol. 4) (translated from Afrikaans).

105.   'Verhoudings met Somalië', from Glenn Babb to Magnus Malan, 12 July 1984, p.2-3 (DFA, 1/144/3, Vol. 4).

106.   'Vergaadering oor toekomstige optrede: samewerking met Somalië', from Glenn Babb, 28 August 1984 (DFA, 1/144/3, Vol. 4).

107.   Interview with Gert van der Veer, 7 December 2002.

108.   Correspondence with Glenn Babb, 20 January 2003.

109.   'Hoofman F.A. Nzeribe', 18 January 1985, p.1-2 (DFA, 1/129/3, Vol. 12) (translated from Afrikaans); West Africa 3014, 23 February 1987: 354-6.

110.   'Background document: Republic of the Sudan', 1992, p.17 (DFA, 1/163/3, Vol. 8).

111.   Correspondence with Glenn Babb, 20 January 2003.

112. Letter from Gert van der Veer, July 1984 (DFA, 1/163/3, Vol. 4).
113. DFA, 1/163/3, Vol. 1PL.
114. 'Hoofman F.A. Nzeribe',. from Aubrey Morton (DFA) to Rae Killen and Magnus Malan, 9 January 1985 (DFA, 1/129/3, Vol. 11).
115. Correspondence with Glenn Babb, 20 January 2003.
116. Report from Johan Marx (Director, Africa Directorate), 30 October 1985 (DFA, 1/129/3, Vol. 12).
117. 'Toenadering tot Soedan: Hoofman Nzeribe', from Glenn Babb, 1 January 1985, p.2 (DFA, 1/163/3, Vol. 4).
118. 'Visit of Chief F.A. Nzeribe of Nigeria from 2 February 1985 to 8 February 1985', 12 February 1985, p.2-3 (DFA, 1/163/3, Vol. 2PL).
119. 'Chief Nzeribe', from Glenn Babb to Rae Killen, 12 February 1985 (DFA, 1/163/3, Vol. 4).
120. 'Visit of Chief F.A. Nzeribe of Nigeria from 2 February 1985 to 8 February 1985', 12 February 1985, p.3-5 (DFA, 1/163/3, Vol. 2PL).
121. 'Emergency aid: drought in Sudan', from Glenn Babb to Hans van Dalsen, 7 February 1984 (DFA, 1/163/3, Vol. 4).
122. 'Donation to Sudan: report back by Chief Nzeribe', from Rusty Evans to Hans van Dalsen, to the attention of Glenn Babb, 7 March 1985, p.1-2 (DFA, 1/163/3, Vol. 2PL).
123. 'Sudan: Chief Nzeribe', from Glenn Babb to Rae Killen and Magnus Malan, 27 March 1985, p.2 (DFA, 1/163/3, Vol. 2PL).
124. Péan. 1983. Affaires africaines, p.137-8, 262; Faligot & Krop. 1985. La piscine, p.231.
125. Péan. 1983. Affaires africaines, p.115.
126. 'Proposed help to Colonel Kamougué via President Bongo', from Rae Killen, 28 November 1980 (DFA, 1/184/3, Vol. 1PL).
127. 'Military aid to Col Wadal Abdel Kamougé: Chad separatist movement', from Rae Killen to Glenn Babb, 24 November 1980 (DFA, 1/184/3, Vol. 1PL); correspondence with Daan Hamman, 14 March 2004.
128. 'Proposed help to Colonel Kamougué via President Bongo', from Rae Killen, 28 November 1980; 'Col Kamougué: Chad', from Glenn Babb to Rae Killen and Jan Wentzel, 23 June 1981, p.1 (DFA, 1/184/3, Vol. 1PL).
129. 'Military aid to Col Wadal Abdel Kamougé: Chad separatist movement', from Rae Killen to Glenn Babb, 24 November 1980, and other documents in DFA, 1/184/3, Vol. 1PL.
130. Correspondence with Daan Hamman, 14 March 2004.
131. 'Col Kamougué: Chad', from Glenn Babb to Rae Killen and Jan Wentzel, 23 June 1981 (DFA, 1/184/3, 1PL).
132. 'Gabon and Chad', from Glenn Babb to Rae Killen and Jan Wentzel, 27 April, p.2; 'Col Kamougué: Chad', from Glenn Babb to Rae Killen and Jan Wentzel, 23 June 1981, p.1-2 (DFA, 1/184/3, 1PL).
133. 'Chad: relations with Pres. Hissène Habré', from Rae Killen and Jan Wentzel to Glenn Babb, 24 September 1982; 'Balansstaat: verhoudings met Tsjaad', 8 November 1982, p.3 (DFA, 1/184/3, Vol. 1PL).
134. Lemarchand. 1985. 'The crisis in Chad', p.248; Nolutshungu. 1996. Limits of Anarchy, p.156.
135. Letter from Pik Botha to Hissène Habré, October 1982 (DFA, 1/184/3, Vol. 1PL).

136. 'Chad: relations with Pres. Hissène Habré', from Rae Killen and Jan Wentzel to Glenn Babb, 24 September; 'Balansstaat: verhoudings met Tsjaad', 2 August 1982 (DFA, 1/184/3, Vol. 1PL).

137. Faligot & Krop. 1985. *La piscine*, p.343; Péan. 1983. *Affaires africaines*, p.12, 287; Weinberg. 1994. *Last of the Pirates*, p.58-60.

138. 'Chad: relations with Pres. Hissène Habré', from Rae Killen and Jan Wentzel to Glenn Babb, 24 September 1982 (DFA, 1/184/3, Vol. 1PL).

139. DFA, 1/184/3, Vol. 1PL.

140. 'Chad', from Glenn Babb to Rae Killen and Jan Wentzel, 25 February 1983 (DFA, 1/184/3, Vol. 2PL).

141. Correspondence with Daan Hamman, 14 March 2004.

142. Lunel. 1991. *Bob Denard*, p.579; Denard. 1998. *Corsaire de la république*, p.353.

143. 'Chad', from Glenn Babb to Rae Killen and Jan Wentzel, 25 February 1983 (DFA, 1/184/3, Vol. 2PL).

144. 'Report', from Glenn Babb, 18 June 1982 (DFA, 1/207/3, Vol. 1).

145. 'EG: meeting with Security Adviser to President Bongo', from Rae Killen, 3 November 1983 (DFA, 1/207/3, Vol. 1).

146. DFA, 1/207/3, Vol. 1.

147. <http://www.bioko.org/island/hist.asp>; Kerdellonton. 1989. 'Afrique', p.54.

148. Interview with Neil van Heerden and Paul Runge, 7 April 1999.

149. For example Ogba. 1989. 'An intelligence model of national security assessment for Nigeria'; *ANC News Briefing* 11, 42, October 1987: 19; 12, 5, February 1988: 19.

150. *ARB: Economic Series* 24, 5, 1987: 9095.

151. Interview with Neil van Heerden and Paul Runge, 7 April 1999.

152. 'Ekwatoriaal-Guinee: Nigeriëse beheptheid met RSA betrokkenheid', from Johan Marx (Director, Africa Directorate) to Neil van Heerden, 26 March, p.2; telex from Hilton Lack (DFA Liaison Officer for the project) to Johan Marx, 24 September 1987 (DFA, 1/129/3, Vols. 3PL, 14A).

153. *ARB: Economic Series* 25, 3, 1988: 9063.

154. *ARB: Economic Series* 25, 5, 1988: 9132.

155. Correspondence with Glenn Babb, 20 January 2003.

156. Interview with Frans Swarts, 7 December 2002.

157. Barber. 2000. 'South Africa's political miracle'; Guelke. 1996. 'The impact of the end of the Cold War on the South African transition',

158. Crocker. 1993. *High Noon in Southern Africa*, p.362.

159. Crocker. 1993. *High Noon in Southern Africa*.

160. *Namibian Independence and Cuban Troop Withdrawal.* 1989.

161. Jaster. 1990. *The 1988 Peace Accords and the Future of South-Western Africa.*

162. Geldenhuys. 1994. 'The head of government and South Africa's foreign relations', p.284.

163. Crocker. 1993. *High Noon in Southern Africa*, p.348, 438.

164. Kaela. 1993. 'Behind Linkage diplomacy', p.122-41.

165. Smit. 1989. 'South Africa and Black Africa', p.127-8.

166. Yao. 1992. 'Le dialogue Yamassoukro – Prétoria', p.7; Yao. 1991. 'Côte d'Ivoire – Afrique du Sud', p.146.

167. This became official during 1991 (*Foreign Affairs List*).

168. Seekings. 2000. *The UDF.*

169. Pfister. 2003. 'Gateway to international victory', p.59-60.

170. Waldmeir. 1997. *Anatomy of a Miracle*, p.39-106.

171. Slabbert. 1989. *The System and the Struggle*, p.181-94; Boraine. 1987. *Dakar Report Back.*
172. Correspondence with Frederik van Zyl Slabbert, 10 February 2003.
173. Pfister. 2003. 'Gateway to international victory', p.60.

Chapter 6: New Diplomacy

1. Bacharach & Lawler. 1981. *Bargaining.*
2. Cited in Geldenhuys & Kotzé. 1991. 'FW de Klerk', p.35.
3. Sarakinsky. 1992. 'South Africa', p.151.
4. De Klerk, F.W. 1998. *The Last Trek*, p.48.
5. *Keesing's Archiv der Gegenwart, 1989*, p.33713.
6. *ARB: Political Series* 26, 12, 1990: 9507-9; *Jeune Afrique* 1509, 4 December 1989: 18-21.
7. Lunel. 1991. *Bob Denard*, p.633, 638-9; Denard. 1998. *Corsaire de la république*, p.406-12, 420; Weinberg. 1994. *Last of the Pirates*, p. 2, 144, 148, 244-9.
8. Van Heerden. 1989. *South Africa and Africa*, Vale. 1992. 'South Africa's New Diplomacy".
9. Ake. 1996. *The Marginalization of Africa*, Collier. 1997. *The Marginalisation of Africa in the World Economy.*
10. Letter from F.W. de Klerk, 23 May 1991, p.3-4 (DFA, 1/101/3, Vol. 4; 1/13/3, Vol. 6; 1/129/3, Vol. 19). The 'Background document: Republic of the Sudan', 1992, p.19 (DFA, 1/163/3, Vol. 8) reveals the letter was sent to 30 African heads of state and government.
11. For example Esterhuysen, Fair & Leistner. 1994. *South Africa in Sub-Equatorial Africa*, p.66; Owoeye. 1994. 'What can Africa expect from a post-Apartheid South Africa?', p.44.
12. Thomas. 1996. *The Diplomacy of Liberation.*
13. Reprinted in Legum. 1989. 'Republic South Africa', p.B671-3.
14. *Southern Africa Political and Economic Monthly* 3, 3, 1989/90: 19-20; 'Declaration on Apartheid and the Destructive Consequences in Southern Africa' (UN document A/S-16/1989).
15. For example Friedman. 1993. *The Long Journey*; Friedman & Atkinson. 1994. *The Small Miracle.*
16. Schoeman & Schoeman. 1993. *South Africa's Foreign Relations in Transition*, p.366, 387; *Keesing's Archiv der Gegenwart, 1991*, p.35618, 35892, 36223.
17. Cited in Clark. 1993. *Nelson Mandela Speaks*, p.23-8.
18. Cited in Clark. 1993. *Nelson Mandela Speaks*, p.90.
19. Cited in Mkhondo. 1993. *Reporting South Africa*, p.101.
20. Pfister. 1997. 'Violence during South Africa's political transition (1990-1994)'.
21. Schoeman & Schoeman. 1993. *South Africa's Foreign Relations in Transition*, p.310-459.
22. Friedman. 1993. *The Long Journey*, p.61-9.
23. Friedman. 1993. *The Long Journey*, p.84.
24. *SouthScan* 7, 15/16, 17 April 1992: 120.
25. Geldenhuys. 1992. 'The foreign factor in South Africa's 1992 referendum'.
26. Hamill. 1992. 'President de Klerk's options', p.291.
27. Clark. 1993. *Nelson Mandela Speaks*, p.179.
28. Uys, S. 1992. 'The ANC's international standing', p.2; Waldmeir. 1997. *Anatomy of a Miracle*, p.194-218.

29.   Pfister. 1997. 'Violence during South Africa's political transition (1990-1994)'.
30.   Kalley. 2001. *South Africa's Treaties in Theory and Practice*, p.587.
31.   *ARB: Economic Series* 27, 8, 1990: 10075; *Political Series* 28, 4, 1991: 10074; Kalley. 2001. *South Africa's Treaties in Theory and Practice*, p.587, 590. *Foreign Affairs List.* 1991-92.
32.   *ARB: Political Series* 27, 12, 1990: 9928-9; Schoeman & Schoeman. 1993. *South Africa's Foreign Relations in Transition*, p.337.
33.   Schoeman & Schoeman. 1993. *South Africa's Foreign Relations in Transition*, p.341.
34.   Correspondence with Hermann Hanekom, 24 January 2003.
35.   *Newsletter on the Oil Embargo against South Africa* 23, Second Quarter 1991: 1-2; Lowe Morna. 1991. 'The pariah's new pals', p.29.
36.   *ARB: Economic Series* 27, 11, 1990: 9890; *Political Series* 27, 11, 1990: 10180.
37.   Schoeman & Schoeman. 1993. *South Africa's Foreign Relations in Transition*, p.358, 369.
38.   *ARB: Economic Series* 27, 11, 1990: 9889; *Political Series* 27, 11, 1990: 10195; Lowe Morna. 1991. 'The pariah's new pals', p.29.
39.   *ARB: Economic Series* 28, 5, 1991: 10398; *Political Series* 28, 6, 1991: 10157; Geldenhuys. 1994. 'The head of government and South Africa's foreign relations', p.287.
40.   Schoeman & Schoeman. 1993. *South Africa's Foreign Relations in Transition*, p. 401-3, 458.
41.   'Background document: Republic of the Sudan', 1992, p.17 (DFA, 1/163/3, Vol. 8).
42.   Letter from Gert van der Veer to the Director General of Sudan's Department of Civil Aviation, 8 February 1991 (DFA, 1/163/3, Vol. 6).
43.   Correspondence with Frans Swarts and Gert van der Veer, 11 February 2003; Smit. 1989. 'South Africa and black Africa', p.128.
44.   Letter from F.W. de Klerk to Omar Bashir, 12 August 1991, p.1 (DFA, 1/163/3, Vol. 6).
45.   'Invoice', from the Director General of Sudan's Department of Civil Aviation to SAA, 18 January 1992; fax from Elfatih Erwa to Uys Viljoen (Deputy Director, North and East Africa), 4 April 1992 (DFA, 1/163/3, Vol. 8).
46.   'Background document: Republic of the Sudan', 1992, p.18 (DFA, 1/163/3, Vol. 8).
47.   'Programme for visiting Sudan Minister of Energy Affairs and Natural Resources', September 1991 (DFA, 1/163/3, Vol. 7).
48.   Letter from F.W. de Klerk to Omar Bashir, 12 August 1991, p.1 (DFA, 1/163/3, Vol. 6).
49.   Landgren. 1989. *Embargo Disimplemented*, p.53, 63-78, 95, 128-9, 215.
50.   'Background document: Republic of the Sudan', 1992, p.18 (DFA, 1/163/3, Vol. 8).
51.   Letter from Derek Auret to Elfatih Erwa, 18 October, p.1, and of 6 November 1991: 'Besprekingspunte: gesprek met Minister Elfatih Erwa, Staatsminister in die Presidensie van Soedan', from Uys Viljoen to Derek Auret, 5 November 1992, p.4 (DFA, 1/163/3, Vols. 7-8).
52.   'Background document: Republic of the Sudan', 1992, p.18; 'Besprekingspunte: gesprek met Minister Elfatih Erwa, Staatsminister in die Presidensie van Soedan', from Uys Viljoen to Derek Auret, 5 November 1992, p.2 (DFA, 1/163/3, Vol. 8).
53.   DFA, 1/101/3, Vols. 4-5.

54. Letter from Hans-Werner Welsch (Bayerische Vereinsbank) to F.W. de Klerk, 18 January 1991 (DFA, 1/101/3, Vol. 4).

55. Letter from F.W. de Klerk to Paul Biya, 20 February 1991, p.1 (DFA, 1/101/3, Vol. 4).

56. 'Cameroon Hydro-Electric Project Nachtigal', from W.A. Niemann (Eskom Engineering Proposals Manager, Johannesburg) to Eric Hirsch (Representative Office for Southern Africa, Bayerische Vereinsbank, Parklands), 20 August; 'Cameroon: internal political situation', from Catherina Gertruda van der Walt (DFA) to Justus de Goede, 6 August 1991, p.3 (DFA, 1/101/3, Vol. 5).

57. 'Cameroon Hydro-Electric Project Nachtigal', from W.A. Niemann to Eric Hirsch, 20 August 1991, p.1 (DFA, 1/101/3, Vol. 5).

58. 'Report on a visit by The Hon René Owona, Minister of Industrial and Trade Development of the Republic of Cameroon to South Africa from 11 to 13 August 1991', from the Programmer (Africa) of VIP Visits, p.2-3 (DFA, 1/101/3, Vol. 5).

59. DFA, 1/101/3, Vol. 5; Schneider. 1991. 'Outlook for trade'.

60. 'Visit by the Deputy Director-General to West Africa: 26 October to 2 November 1991', p.3-5 (DFA, 1/103/3, Vol. 5).

61. 'The outcome of South Africa's application for readmission to FAO', from Jeremy Shearar to all Heads of Mission, 13 November 1991, p.2-4 (DFA, 1/101/3, Vol. 6).

62. Letter from Niël Barnard to Neil van Heerden and F.W. de Klerk, 18 July 1990 (DFA, 1/120/3, Vol. 6).

63. Letter from Justus de Goede to Neil van Heerden, 29 January 1992 (DFA, 1/120/3, Vol. 7).

64. Frankel. 2000. *Soldiers in a Storm*, p.57; Mugyenyi & Swatuk. 1997. 'Of "growth poles" and "backwaters"', p.160.

65. Letter from Niël Barnard to Neil van Heerden and F.W. de Klerk, 18 July 1990 (DFA, 1/120/3, Vol. 6).

66. Letter from Pieter Schabort (First Secretary, Embassy, London) to Rusty Evans, 28 September 1990 (DFA, 1/120/3, Vol. 7).

67. Letter from Herbert Beukes (Deputy Director-General) to Pik Botha, 9 October 1990 (DFA, 1/120/3, Vol. 7).

68. *The Citizen* 13 March 1991.

69. Sinclair. 1981. 'Nigeria'; Aluko. 1982. 'Nigeria and southern Africa'; Agbogu. 1983. 'Nigeria's South African policy since 1960'; Akinyemi. 1994. 'Origins, articulations and continuities in foreign policy and foreign policy formulation'.

70. Akinyemi. 1994. 'Origins, articulations and continuities in foreign policy and foreign policy formulation', p.211-217; Dare. 1991. 'Pretoria-Abuja-Cairo axis'; Shaw & Adibe. 1994. 'South Africa, Nigeria and the prospects for complementary regionalism after Apartheid'.

71. Telex from Lusaka to Lagos on the visit of ANC President Oliver Tambo to Lagos, 10 April 1984 (DFA, 1/129/3, Vol. 2PL); DFA, 1/129/3, Vols. 3PL, 15.

72. Telex No. 1022, 16 November 1984 (DFA, 1/129/3, Vol. 3PL) (translated from Afrikaans).

73. Letter from Niël Barnard to F.W. de Klerk, 6 July 1990 (DFA, 1/129/3, Vol. 6).

74. Letter from F.W. de Klerk to Ibrahim Babangida, 26 September 1991, p.1 (DFA, 1/129/3, Vol. 20).

75. Interview with Pik Botha, 20 April 1999; Botha, R.F. 1995. 'His South African connection'.

76. 'General Obasanjo visit to the RSA', from Colin Paterson (Director, Africa Branch) to Christo Prins, 9 August 1990, p.2-3, 5, 7-9 (DFA, 1/129/3, Vol. 16).

77. Letter from F.W. de Klerk to Ibrahim Babangida, August 1990, p.1-2 (DFA, 1/129/3, Vol. 16).

78. Letter from Olusegun Obasanjo to F.W. de Klerk, 12 December 1990 (DFA, 1/129/3, Vol. 16).

79. DFA, 1/129/3, Vol. 20.

80. Schoeman & Schoeman. 1993. *South Africa's Foreign Relations in Transition*, p.403.

81. Interview with Jeremy Shearar, 8 January 2003.

82. Letter from Jeremy Shearar to Ibrahim Gambari, 18 April 1991 (DFA, 1/129/3, Vol. 18).

83. DFA, 1/129/3, Vol. 18.

84. DFA, 1/129/3, Vol. 19.

85. Letter from F.W. de Klerk, 23 May 1991, p.4 (DFA, 1/101/3, Vol. 4; 1/13/3, Vol. 6; 1/129/3, Vol. 19).

86. Schoeman & Schoeman. 1993. *South Africa's Foreign Relations in Transition*, p.375.

87. Letter from Niël Barnard to F.W. de Klerk, 19 June 1991 (DFA, 1/129/3, Vol. 4PL).

88. Letter from Ibrahim Babangida to F.W. de Klerk, 17 September (DFA, 1/129/3, Vol. 21).

89. Letter from F.W. de Klerk to Ibrahim Babangida, 26 September 1991, p.1 (DFA, 1/129/3, Vol. 20).

90. Schoeman & Schoeman. 1993. *South Africa's Foreign Relations in Transition*, p.393.

91. 'UN: discussion with Ambassador Gambari (Nigeria)', from Jim Steward, 24 February 1992, p.2 (DFA, 1/129/3, Vol. 4PL).

92. Letter from F.W. de Klerk to Ibrahim Babangida, 11 February 1992 (DFA, 1/129/3, Vol. 4PL).

93. 'UN: discussion with Ambassador Gambari (Nigeria)', from Jim Steward, 24 February 1992, p.2 (DFA, 1/129/3, Vol. 4PL).

94. Letter from F.W. de Klerk to Ibrahim Babangida, 3 March 1992, p.1 (DFA, 1/129/3, Vol. 4PL).

95. 'Amptelike besoek aan Nigerië', from Derek Auret to Neil van Heerden, 11 March 1992, p.1 (DFA, 1/129/3, Vol. 21).

96. Interview with Derek Auret, 20 March 2002.

97. Letter from Pik Botha to F.W. de Klerk, 3 March 1992 (DFA, 1/129/3, Vol. 4PL).

98. 'Amptelike besoek aan Nigerië', from Derek Auret to Neil van Heerden, 11 March 1992, p.4-5 (DFA, 1/129/3, Vol. 21) (translated from Afrikaans).

99. Letter from Pik Botha to F.W. de Klerk, 27 February; letter from Derek Auret to Johannes Petru Roux (Director-General, State President's Office), 2 March; letter from F.W. de Klerk to Ibrahim Babangida, 3 March 1992 (DFA, 1/129/3, Vol. 4PL).

100. 'Statement of the Affirmative Result of the Negotiating Process in South Africa', Ministry of Foreign Affairs, Abuja, 18 March 1992 (DFA, 1/129/3, Vol. 21).

101. Letter from Alaba Ogunsanwo to Derek Auret, 23 March 1992 (DFA, 1/129/3, Vol. 21).

102. Van Wyk, A. 1992. 'Significant breakthrough in Nigeria', p.38.

103. Correspondence with Attie du Plessis, 24 January 2003; interview with Hennie Viljoen, 26 January 2003.

104. 'Ghana: prospects for economic and political relations with South Africa', from Carel Wessels (Chief Director, Africa Branch) to Derek Auret, 17 November 1992 (DFA, 1/106/3, Vol. 13).

105. *SAFTO & the State of SA Trade.* 1984. p.9; *Finance Week* 20-26 June 1991: 21-4.

106. Interview with Wim Holtes, 31 March 1999.

107. *SAFTO: annual report, 1991/2,* p.6.

108. Interview with Derek Auret, 8 January 2003.

109. 'Discussion items for Nigeria', March; 'Proposed list of items for bilateral discussions with Nigeria', from Paul Runge to Wim Holtes, 7 April 1992 (DFA, 1/129/3, Vol. 21).

110. *SAFTO: annual report, 1991/2,* p.6; *SAFTO Exporter* 29, 4, April 1992: 1, 10-1.

111. 'Note verbale', to Alaba Ogunsanwo, 16 April 1992 (DFA, 1/129/3, Vol. 22).

112. 'Relations with Nigeria', from Justus de Goede to Derek Auret, 12 August 1992, p.2 (DFA, 1/129/3, Vol. 24).

113. 'Points for discussion' (DFA, 1/129/3, Vol. 21).

114. 'Notas oor samesprekings tussen Staatspresident de Klerk en President Babangida van Nigerië: 10 April 1992, State House, Abuja' (DFA, 1/129/3, Vol. 21).

115. *Newsletter on the Oil Embargo against South Africa,* 27, Second Quarter 1992: 327; *Africa Confidential* 33, 10, 17 April 1992.

116. 'Joint communiqué', Abuja, 10 April 1992, p.2 (DFA, 1/129/3, Vol. 21).

117. Qunta. 1992. 'De Klerk in Abuja', p.13; *SouthScan* 7, 22, 5 June 1992: 167; *West Africa* 3892, 20-26 April 1992: 664.

118. Van Wyk, A. 1992. 'Pillars of co-operation in Africa', p.32; van Wyk, A. 1992. Significant Breakthrough in Nigeria, p.37-8.

119. *Keesing's Archiv der Gegenwart, 1991,* p.36223, 36668; *ARB: Political Series* 29, 3, 1992: 10518; *Sowetan* 2 June 1992.

120. Interview with Neil van Heerden and Paul Runge, 7 April 1999.

121. *Keesing's Archiv der Gegenwart, 1991,* p. 36223, 36572.

122. *SouthScan* 7, 22, 5 June 1992: 162.

123. Cited in *West Africa* 3900, 15-21 June 1992: 1025.

124. Pfister. 2003. 'Gateway to international victory', p.52, 54-5, 63, 68.

125. *ARB: Political Series* 29, 4, 1992: 10527.

126. Cited in *West Africa* 3903, 6-12 July 1992: 1134; Pfister. 2003. 'Gateway to international victory', p.67.

127. Letter from Pik Botha to Ike Nwachukwu, 26 June 1992, p.2, 7 (DFA, 1/129/3, Vol. 23).

128. 'Subject – meeting on 27 June 1992 in Abuja, Nigeria, between the Minister of Foreign Affairs, Mr RF Botha, the Minister of Constitutional Development, Mr RP Meyer and the President of Nigeria, General Ibrahim Babangida and the Nigerian Minister of Foreign Affairs, Maj-Gen Ike Nwachukwu', from Anton van Dalsen to Pik Botha, 30 June 1992, p.1-2 (DFA, 1/129/3, Vol. 23).

129. 'Subject – meetings on 27 June 1992 in Abuja, Nigeria, between the Minister of Foreign Affairs, Mr RF Botha, the Minister of Constitutional Development, Mr RP Meyer and the Secretary-General of the United Nations, Mr Boutros Boutros-Ghali', from Anton van Dalsen to Pik Botha, 29 June 1992, p.1-6 (DFA, 1/129/3, Vol. 23).

130. 'Subject – meeting on 27 June 1992 in Abuja, Nigeria, between the Minister of Foreign Affairs, Mr RF Botha, the Minister of Constitutional Development, Mr RP Meyer and the President of Nigeria, General Ibrahim Babangida and the

Nigerian Minister of Foreign Affairs, Maj-Gen Ike Nwachukwu', from Anton van Dalsen to Pik Botha, 30 June 1992, p.3 (DFA, 1/129/3, Vol. 23).
131.   Chabbra. 1997. *South African Foreign Policy*, p.47-8; Shabazz. 1992. 'Report on the OAU Dakar, Senegal Summit conference', p.21; *West Africa* 3903, 6-12 July 1992: 1134.
132.   UN document S/24232.
133.   OAU draft resolution (S/24232, p.2-3) and S/RES/765 (16 July 1992).
134.   *Africa Confidential* 33, 10, 19 June 1992: 2-4; 33, 14, 17 July 1992: 1; *South-Scan* 7, 22, 5 June 1992: 162; 7, 28, 17 July 1992: 209.
135.   UN documents S/RES/765 (16 July), S/24314 (20 July 1992).
136.   UN documents S/PV.3107 and S/RES/772 (17 August), S/24541 (10 September 1992); Cassette. 1993. 'United Nations Observer Mission in South Africa'.
137.   *ARB: Political Series* 29, 5, 1992: 10564; *Facts and Reports* 22, J, 15 May 1992: 2; *West Africa* 3896, 18-24 May 1992: 853.
138.   *The Guardian* 24 April 1992.
139.   Waldmeir. 1997. *Anatomy of a Miracle*, p.207-18.

Chapter 7: Conclusion

1.   Pfister. 1992. 'United Nations sanctions against Apartheid', p.46-52.
2.   Interview with Neil van Heerden and Paul Runge, 7 April 1999.
3.   Guelke. 1972. 'South African foreign policy in Africa', p.271-2.
4.   Van der Westhuizen. 2001. 'Marketing the 'rainbow nation'', p.70.
5.   Geldenhuys. 1984. *The Diplomacy of Isolation*, p.105.
6.   Williams. 2001. *Intellectuals and the End of Apartheid*, p.113.
7.   De Klerk, F.W. 1998. *The Last Trek*, p.42-3.
8.   Interview with Neil van Heerden and Paul Runge, 7 April 1999; *SAFTO: annual report, 1987/8*, p.6.
9.   Interview with Wim Holtes, 31 March 1999; his interview in *SAFTO & the State of SA Trade*. 1984. p.9.
10.   Correspondence with Peter Sorour, 31 January 2004.
11.   Hocking. 1973. *Oppenheimer and Son*, p.107, 284-8, 338-9, 407-8; Meinardus. 1980. *Die Afrikapolitik der Republik Südafrika*, p.360-6; Newbury. 1989. *The Diamond Ring*, p.317-8, 325, 331, 358.
12.   Hocking. 1973. *Oppenheimer and Son*, p.219-2, 255, 339; Knight & Stevenson. 1986. 'Williamson diamond mine, De Beers, and the Colonial Office'.
13.   Interview with Michael Spicer, 7 April 1999.
14.   *TRC Report. Vol. 4*. 1999. p.18-58; Nattrass. 1999. 'The Truth and Reconciliation Commission on business and Apartheid'.
15.   *TRC Report. Vol. 4*. 1999. p.24-6.
16.   Correspondence with Klaus Oppenheimer, 26 March 2002.
17.   Interview with Denis Venter, 10 March 1999.
18.   Cooper. 1997. 'Niche diplomacy'.
19.   Barber. 2004. *Mandela's World*, p.152-4; Schoeman, M.M.E. 2003. 'South Africa as an emerging middle power'; Solomon. 1997. 'South African foreign policy and middle power leadership'; Vale. 1997. 'Understanding the upstairs and the downstairs'; van der Westhuizen. 1998. 'South Africa's emergence as a middle power'. Also Pfister. 2000. *South Africa's Post-Apartheid Foreign Policy Towards Africa*.
20.   Schraeder. 2001. 'South Africa's foreign policy'.

Appendixes

Appendix A

Biographies of Department of Foreign Affairs Officials

AURET, Derek William
1973-1977 First Secretary, Permanent Mission to the UN, New York
1978-1982 Special Assistant to the Secretary of Foreign Affairs
1982-1985 Minister Plenipotentiary, Embassy, Bonn
1985-1987 Deputy Director, Africa Directorate (S.W.A./Namibia)
1987-1991 Chief Director, Overseas Countries Branch
1991-1995 Deputy Director-General, Africa Branch

BABB, Glenn Robin Ware
1967   Cadet
1967-1969 S.W.A./Namibia Division
1969-1970 Third Secretary, Embassy, Paris
1971   Second Secretary, Embassy, Paris
1972-1973 Head, East, West and Central Africa Section
1974-1975 Training Officer
1975-1977 Counsellor, Embassy, Paris
1978-1980 Counsellor, Embassy, Rome
1980-1983 Deputy Director, Africa Division
1984-1985 Director, Africa Division
1985-1987 Ambassador to Canada, Ottawa
1987-1989 Deputy Director-General, Africa Directorate/Branch
1989-1991 Member of Parliament (NP)
1991-1995 Ambassador to Italy, Rome, accredited to Albania, Malta and San
           Marino, and Permanent Representative to the FAO, Rome

BEST, Norman John
1946-1951 Third Secretary, High Commission, Ottawa
1951-1955 Third Secretary, Embassy, Paris
1955-1958 Deputy Chief, Protocol
1958-1960 Head, Political Division (West)
1960-1965 First Secretary/Counsellor, Embassy, Cologne
1966-1968 Counsellor, Embassy, Brussels
1968-1970 Minister Plenipotentiary, Embassy, Paris
1970-1973 Under-Secretary, Africa Division (Rest of Africa)
1973-1978 Ambassador to Canada, Ottawa
1978-1980 Ambassador to Argentina, Buenos Aires

BOTHA, Roelof Frederik 'Pik'
1953-1956 Cadet
1956-1960 Legation, Stockholm
1960-1963 Embassy, Cologne
1963-1966 Legal team, S.W.A./Namibia case at the ICJ
1967-1968 Under-Secretary
1968-1969 Head, S.W.A./Namibia and UN Section
1970-1974 Member of Parliament (NP) for Wonderboom, Pretoria
1974-1977 Permanent Representative to the UN, New York

1975-1977 Ambassador to the United States, Washington
1977-1994 Minister of Foreign Affairs

BURGER, Albertus Beyers Fourie 'Albie'
1948-1950 Consul, Consulate, Frankfurt
1953-1954 Chargé d'Affaires, Embassy, Bonn
1957-1958 Assistant Secretary, Politics and Economics Division
1958 Consul, Consulate, Antananarivo
1961-1965 Ambassador to Belgium, Brussels
1966-1969 Under-Secretary, Africa Division
1969-1974 Ambassador to France, Paris
1975-1979 Ambassador to the European Commission, Brussels

DE GOEDE, Justus
1967 Cadet
1969-1973 Vice Consul, Consulate-General, Beirut
1973-1975 Counsellor, Middle East Division
1976-1977 Parliamentary Office, DFA, Cape Town
1977-1981 Vice Consul-General, Embassy, Tokyo
1981-1983 Counsellor, Embassy, The Hague
1983-1986 Head, Training Division
1987-1990 Minister Plenipotentiary, Embassy, London
1990-1992 Director, Africa Branch
1993-1995 Head of Mission, Cairo
1995-1998 Ambassador to Egypt, Cairo

EVANS, Leo Henry 'Rusty'
1969 Third Secretary, Embassy, Lisbon
1972 Consul, Consulate-General, Rio de Janeiro
1974-1977 Consul-General, Consulate-General, Sao Paulo
1979 Counsellor, Departmental Administration
1981-1982 Minister Plenipotentiary, Embassy, Washington
1983-1986 Minister Plenipotentiary, Embassy, London
1986-1990 Head, West Africa Section
1990-1991 Deputy Director-General, Africa Branch
1992-1997 Director-General, DFA

FOURIE, Bernardus Gerhardus 'Brand'
1934-1939 Office of the Controller and Auditor General
1939 Legation, Berlin
1940-1946 High Commission, London
1947-1952 Permanent Mission to the UN, New York
1952-1958 Africa, Political, International Organisations Division
1958-1962 Permanent Representative to the UN, New York
1962-1963 Under-Secretary, Africa Division
1963-1966 Secretary, Department of Information
1966-1982 Secretary/Director-General, DFA
1982-1985 Ambassador to the United States, Washington
1985-1989 Chairman, South African Broadcasting Corporation

HANEKOM, Hermann Albert
1965 Cadet
1966-1970 Third Secretary, Embassy, Bern

1970-1972 Under-Secretary, Africa Division (Botswana, Lesotho, Swaziland, Indian
Ocean Islands)
1972-1978 Counsellor, Permanent Mission to the UN, New York
1978-1980 Under-Secretary, Information Division, Head Office
1980-1981 Counsellor, Embassy, Rome
1981-1985 Counsellor, Embassy, Paris
1985-1989 Deputy Director, South Africa Desk
1989-1993 Ambassador to Zaire, Kinshasa, accredited to the Congolese Republic,
and Consul to Rwanda
1994-1996 Deputy Director, Africa Division (OAU, Security)

JAQUET, André
1971-1972 Press Attaché, Embassy, London
1973-1976 Press and Cultural Affairs Attaché, Embassy, Paris
1977-1978 Francophone Africa Desk
1978-1982 Consul, Consulate, Montreal
1983-1984 Counsellor, Embassy, Washington
1986   Director, Overseas Countries Directorate
1987-1990 Director, Africa Directorate (Angola, S.W.A./Namibia)
1990-1994 Ambassador to Switzerland, Bern
1995-1999 Chief Director, Americas and the Caribbean
1999-2003 High Commissioner to Canada, Ottawa
2003-   Chief Director, Training Section (Advisor, Foreign Service Institute)

JOOSTE, Gerhardus Petrus 'Gerhardt'
1929-1934 Private Secretary to the Minister of Finance
1935-1936 Counsellor, Economic Section
1937-1941 Chargé d'Affaires, Legation, Brussels and High Commission, London
1941-1949 Counsellor/Deputy Secretary, Economic Section
1949-1954 Ambassador to the United States, Washington, and Permanent
Representative to the UN, New York
1954-1956 High Commissioner to the United Kingdom, London
1956-1966 Secretary, DFA
1966-1969 Special Advisor to the Prime Minister and the Minister of Foreign Affairs

KILLEN, Peter Rae
1959   Vice-Consul, Consulate, Elizabethville
1961-1962 Second Secretary, Embassy, Ottawa
1963-1964 First Secretary, Embassy, Ottawa
1966   Counsellor, Embassy, London
1970-1972 Minister Plenipotentiary, Embassy, London
1974-1978 Deputy Secretary, Africa Division
1979-1980 Deputy Secretary, Southern Africa Division
1980-1984 Deputy Director-General, Africa Directorate
1985-1987 Director-General, DFA
1987-1990 Ambassador to the United Kingdom, London

LOUBSER, Antonie Eduard 'Anton'
1958-1960 Cadet
1961-1964 Third Secretary, Embassy, Paris
1965-1969 Second Secretary, Embassy, Paris
1970-1975 Counsellor to Belgium, Luxembourg and the European Economic

Community, Embassy, Brussels
1976-1979 Counsellor, Africa Division (French-Speaking and North Africa)
1980-1983 Minister Plenipotentiary, Embassy, Paris
1984-1985 Chief of Protocol
1986-1988 Ambassador to Israel, Tel Aviv
1988-1989 Consul-General, Consulate-General, Copenhagen
1990-1991 Ambassador to Denmark, Copenhagen
1991-2000 Director (Marketing)

LOUW, Eric Hendrik
1924-1925 Member of Parliament (NP) for Beaufort West
1925-1928 Trade Commissioner, Washington
1929   High Commissioner to the United Kingdom, London
1930-1934 Ambassador Extraordinary and Minister Plenipotentiary, Washington
1934   Ambassador, Rome
1934   Ambassador, Lisbon
1934-1937 Ambassador, Paris, accredited to Portugal
1938-1963 Member of Parliament (NP) for Beaufort West
1948-1949 Minister of Mining and Economic Development
1949-1954 Minister of Economics
1954-1956 Minister of Finance
1955-1963 Minister of External/Foreign Affairs

MULLER, Hilgard
1941-1947 Lecturer in Latin, University of Pretoria
1947-1950 Lawyer's firm Dyason, Douglas, Muller and Meyer
1951-1957 Member, Pretoria City Council
1953-1955 Mayor of Pretoria
1958-1960 Member of Parliament (NP) for Pretoria East
1961-1964 Ambassador to the United Kingdom, London
1964-1977 Member of Parliament (NP) for Beaufort West
1964-1977 Minister of Foreign Affairs

PRETORIUS, Johan Frederick
1955-1959 Vice-Counsel, Consulate General, Lourenço Marques
1959-1962 Third/Second Secretary, Embassy, Lisbon
1962-1966 First Secretary, Africa Division
1966-1971 Counsellor, Embassy, Paris
1972-1976 Counsellor, Africa Division (French-Speaking and North Africa)
1976-1981 Ambassador, Embassy, Brasilia
1981-1986 Under-Secretary, Pretoria
1986-1991 Ambassador to Switzerland, Bern

RUNGE, Paul Gustav
1980   Cadet
1981-1985 Third Secretary, Embassy, Paris
1985-1986 Project Liaison Officer in Gabon, Libreville
1987   Far East Section
1988-1989 Senior Officer, West Africa
1989-1991 Manager, Africa Business Development Group, SAFTO
1992-1997 Senior Manager, Africa and Europe, SAFTO
1997-2000 Director, South Africa Foundation

SHEARAR, Jeremy Brown
1958-1961   Third Secretary, Embassy, Paris
1961-1964   Second Secretary, Embassy, Paris
1964-1966   First Secretary, Embassy, Paris
1966-1968   Consular Division
1969-1970   Counsellor, Africa Division (Rest of Africa)
1971-1974   Consul-General/Counsellor, Embassy, London
1975-1978   Minister Plenipotentiary, Embassy, Washington
1978-1980   Minister Plenipotentiary, Embassy, Paris
1980-1984   Deputy Director, Overseas Countries Directorate
1985-1987   Permanent Representative to the UN, Geneva
1988-1991   Permanent Representative to the UN, New York
1991-1994   Deputy Director-General, Multilateral Relations

VAN DALSEN, Johannes 'Hans'
1963-1964   Counsellor, Africa Division (Politics, Economics)
1966-1969   Minister Plenipotentiary, Embassy, London
1969-1970   Ambassador to Belgium, Brussels
1971-1979   Deputy Secretary, Overseas Countries Division
1980-1981   Ambassador to France, Paris
1982   Deputy Director-General, DFA
1982-1985   Director-General, DFA

VAN HEERDEN, Neil Peter
1964-1966   Vice-Consul, Consulate-General, Tokyo
1971-1975   Counsellor, Embassy, Washington
1975-1980   Under-Secretary, Planning Division (Namibia)
1980-1985   Ambassador to Germany, Bonn
1986   Deputy Director-General, Africa Directorate
1987-1992   Director-General, DFA
1992-1995   Ambassador to the European Union, Brussels
1996-2005   Executive Director, South Africa Foundation

VON HIRSCHBERG, Carl Friedrich George
1948-1952   Cadet, Political Division
1952-1957   Third Secretary, Political Division, High Commission, London
1957-1959   Second Secretary, Mission, Vienna
1960-1962   First Secretary, Mission, Vienna
1962-1967   Counsellor, Scientific Liaison and International Organisations Division
1968-1969   Minister, Permanent Mission to the UN, New York
1969-1974   Permanent Representative to the UN, New York
1975-1978   Consul-General, Consulate-General, Tokyo
1979-1980   Deputy Secretary, International Organisations and Central and North Africa
1980-1987   Deputy Director-General, Overseas Countries Directorate
1987-1988   Adviser to the Permanent Representative to the UN, New York
1989-1990   Representative in Windhoek, implementing the Settlement Plan for the
            independence of Namibia
1990-1991   Special Adviser to the Minister of Foreign Affairs
1993-1994   Joint Administrator of Walvis Bay

Appendix B

South African Export to Black Africa, 1961-94
(in million ZAR)

Year	Angola	Benin	Burkina Faso	Burundi	Cameroon	Cape Verde	Central African Federation[5]	Central African Republic	Chad	Comoros	Congo	Total Export
1961	0.97	0.003		0	0.039	0.005	96.279	0.006	0.013	0	0.315	952
1962	0.957	0	0	0.043	0.053	0	85.519	0.001	0.015	0.007	0.329	946
1963	1.971	0	0[1]	0	0.049	0	75.142	0.008	0.014	0.005	0.293	988
1964	2.503	0[3]		0[2]	0	0[2]		0.002[2]	0[2]	0[2]	0.948[2]	954
1965	2.491	0[4]	0[4]	0.001[4]	0.003[4]	0.001[4]		0.002[4]	0.009[4]	0[4]	0.099	974
1966	2.47	0[2]	0[2]	0[2]	0[2]	0[2]		0.004[2]	0.009[2]	0[2]	0.177[2]	1202
1967	2.113[4]	0[4]	0[4]	0[4]	0[4]	0.002[4]		0.003[4]	0.014[4]	0[4]	0.066[3]	1352
1968	4.709	0	0.001	0	0	0.03		0.007	0.014	0	0.202	1389
1969	6.399	0	0	0.008	0	0.075		0.006	0.002	0.004	0.095	1527
1970								0.005		0.013		1525
1971								0.001		0.002		1541
1972								0		0.045		2041
1973	16.308[4]							0.002				2421
1974	35.743				0.001	0.023		0.003	0	0.052	0.217	3350
1975		0	0	0	0				0			3990
1976												4542
1977		0	0	0	0.003	0.736		2.88	0	0.021	1.436	5683
1978		0	0	0	0	0.028		0.646		0.012	0.942	7333
1979		0	0	0.001	0.03			1.179	0.009	0.277	1.611	14811
1980		0	0			1.215		0.276			1.694	12915
1981		1.449	0	0.077	0.041	2.697[2]				1.524	0.669	18207
1982		0.719	0	0.598	0.069	0.025					0.548	19189
1983		0.052	0	0.552[4]	0.025	0.356[1]				4.471	0.438	20620
1984		1.059	0.084	0.266	0.266	0.023					0.566	24868
1985	1.277	1.26	1.1	0.5	8.144	0.499[2]		0.163		5.481	2.149	36312
1986	0.061[2]	1.618	0.1152	0.324[4]	12.956			0.282[2]			2.225	42011
1987		2.212	0.149	1.391[4]	4.528					14.231	0.733[2]	43671
1988	11.045	2.239	0.028	3.927	6.185	0.436		1.005	0.113	20.38	2.598	49724
1989	18.858	3.67		5.227	7.952	2.576		0.285	0	23.717	5.019	58199
1990	52.674			5.208	2.709	0.62		0.648	0	21.213	8.799	60922
1991	137.84	4.134		10.919	5.594	0.256		0.591	0	33.102	13.737	64355
1992	365.17	1.732	0.255	12.003	46.034	0.282		0.704	0	31.738	24.669	68997
1993	263.388	8.021	3.8	13.187	41.082	4.354		0.512	0	36.866	48.744	80671
1994	311.835	2.901	1.483	24.2	15.384	2.969		0.983	0.041	39.752	32.011	90021

Notes: 1: January-March; 2: January-June; 3: January-September; 4: January-October; 5: Malawi, Zambia, Zimbabwe. *Sources:* DFA files; *Foreign Trade Statistics* and *Monthly Abstract of Trade Statistics.* 1992 Pretoria: Department of Customs and Excise; the IDC provided the figures 1988-94. Total export and import figures: *The Europa World Year Book.* London: Europa Publications; *The Statesman's Year-Book: Statistical and Historical Annual of the States of the World.* London: Europa Publications.

Year	Djibouti	Equatorial Guinea	Ethiopia	Gabon	Gambia	Ghana	Guinea	Guinea Bissau	Ivory Coast	Kenya	Liberia	Madagascar	Total Export
1961	0.019	0	0.041	0.017	0.01	0.029	0.009	0	0.029	7.436	0.061	0.401	952
1962	0.012	0.008	0	0.023	0.001	0.006	0	0.003	0.156	5.451	0	0.178	946
1963	0.02	0	0.003	0.018	0.002	0.007	0	0.004	0.112	3.854	0	0.2	988
1964	0.329[3]	0.001[3]	0.001	0.001[3]	0[3]	0.015	0.005		0.09	0.051	0	0.181[3]	954
1965	0.093[3]	0[3]	0.001[3]	0[3]	0[3]	0.019[2]	0.002[4]	0.031[1]	0.089[3]	0.029	0[1]	0.15[1]	974
1966	0.008[2]	0[2]	0[2]	0[2]	0.001[2]	0.002[2]	0[2]	0.002[2]	0.084[2]	0.027[1]	0[1]	0.052	1202
1967	0.238[3]	0[3]	0.001[3]	0.003[3]	0.002	0.054[3]	0.001[1]	0.023[1]	0.096[3]	0[1]	0[1]	0.174[1]	1352
1968		0		0.055	0.002	0.019	0.003	0.038	0.077			0.773	1389
1969		0		0.049	0.001	0.066	0.001	0.057	0.126		0.06	1.357	1527
1970			0.001	0.067						0.05		1.496	1525
1971				0.109								1.711	1541
1972				0.028								1.654	2041
1973				0.292									2421
1974	0.14	0	0.024	0.046		0.547	0.001	0.121[1]	0.129	0.195		2.527	3350
1975					0			0.047					3990
1976													4542
1977	0.037	0	0.075	0.584		2.153	0.002[1]	0	1.433	1.924		0.911	5683
1978	0.125	0	0	0.22	0.001	0.523	0	0	3.308	1.981	0.085	1.292	7333
1979	0			1.599		0.035	0.071	0	3.364	1.778	0.035	1.176	14811
1980	0				0		0.036		2.089			2.713	19915
1981	0	0	0.127	0.147[1]	0	0	0.011	0		6.086	0	0.154	18207
1982	0		0.12		0	0.021	0				0.018		19189
1983	0	0[3]	0.213		0	0.021	0	0.003	6.395	4.111	0.002	1.514	20620
1984	0		0.896		0.005	0.041							24868
1985	0.001	0.396	0.083	5.105	0.246	0.004	0.806	0[1]	12.744	8.46	0	4.97	36312
1986		0.715[2]	0.557	7.748	0.096	0.098	8.44[1]		21.223		0		42011
1987		0.882	0.023	7.574	0.053[2]	1.06				5.83	0	5.444	43671
1988	0	0.677	0.149	8.018		0.122	0.006		26.802	5.402	0.018	7.812	49724
1989	0	0.75	0.001	5.735		0.11	0.08		44.652	11.025	0.144	24.48	58199
1990	0	0	1.155	7.57	0.003	0.247	0.14	0	48.774	24.953	13.3	53.084	60929
1991	0.001	0.336	2.222	9.226	0.319	4.618	0.166	0	66.491	30.452	0.671	42.902	64355
1992	0.423	10.023	0.749	13.989	3.508	21.799	1.241	0	83.462	151.04	2.709	53.498	68997
1993	0.229	4.49	3.863	21.966	1.248	49.477	1.807	0.141	97.892	205.414	0.254	60.958	80671
1994	0.445	0.116	16.411	13.463	1.346	80.922	8.951	0.296	52.833	664.723		68.471	90021

Year	Malawi	Mali	Mauritania	Mauritius	Mozambique	Niger	Nigeria	Reunion	Rwanda	Sao Tome & Principe	Senegal	Total Export
1961		0		3.494	9.775	0	0.14	0.057	0	0.009	0.155	952
1962		0		4.174	12.132	0	0.01	0.221	0.043	0.009	0.425	946
1963		0		3.482	13.734	0[2]	0.03	0.195	0	0.009	0.519	988
1964	0.832	0[1]	0[1]	2.722[1]	11.688[3]	0[4]	0.02	0.592[2]	0[2]	0.012[2]	0.13	954
1965	1.174			5.158	13.104		0.01[4]	0.621[4]	0[4]	0.009[4]	0.089[4]	974
1966	2.2	0[1]	0[1]	4.071	23.934	0[2]	0.06[2]	0.295[2]	0[2]	0.005[2]	0.001[2]	1202
1967	2.157[1]	0[1]	0[1]	3.974	26.406	0[4]	0.03[4]	0.81[4]	0[4]	0.009[4]	0.015[4]	1352
1968	4.105	0	0	4.078	30.199	0	0.04	1.481	0	0.081	0.013	1389
1969	6.919	0	0	3.359	33.674	0	0	1.438	0.001	0.245	0.035	1527
1970	5.171			3.921	36.013			1.992				1525
1971				3.815	44			1.7				1541
1972				5.625	46.7			2.098				2041
1973	8.635[1]			8.081	71.6			4.792				2421
1974	19.314			13.177	61.5		0.42	6.789		0.031	0.263	3350
1975	28.561				56.1			13.6				3990
1976	32.018	0	0	23.441	49.6		1.92	16.94	0	0	0.09[4]	4542
1977		0	0	31.261			0.77	17.59	0.01		0.17	5683
1978		0	0	34.557	78.091		1.89	29.08	0.014		1.066	7333
1979	75.484			45.022	73.349[4]			28.26	0.026	0	0.001	14811
1980	62.6	0		47.288						0	0.01	11915
1981	52.747	0.01	0	35.204	182.512	0	1.98	25.83	0	0	0[1]	18207
1982		0[1]	0.01			0	1.08		0.006	0		19189
1983		0	0.075	33.344		0	0.61	34.22	0.036	0	0.01	20620
1984			0.15			0.848	0		0.127	0		24868
1985	129.81	0.52	0.234	79.163	253.939	1.812	1.21	48.96	0.22	0.356	1.256	36312
1986		0.57	0.367				1.98		0.335[4]		3.007	42011
1987		1.26[1]	0.046[1]	152.24			1.29	71.54	0.562[4]			43671
1988	261.9	0.41	0.042	227.46	293.537	0.189	0.23	82.44	0.253	4.823	1.261	49724
1989	435.36	3.26	0.024	205.29	300.588	0.074	1.02	112.9	0.704	7.543	2.37	58199
1990	420.18	0.43	0.024	316.25	464.663	1.706	1.28	128.7	0.386	29.718	2.768	60929
1991	577.52	1.14	0.944	379.88	690.013	0.973	2.82	208.7	0.575	14.752	3.973	64355
1992	697.98	2	0.538	391.61	678.262	0.047	5.86	181.3	8.17	4.031	0.898	68997
1993	593.053	5.55	0.208	470.932	964.534	0.732	40.658	190.653	4.81	8.671	2.549	80671
1994	622.067	11.054	0.041	541.318	1406.776	2.241	64.641	147.407	11.084	4.952	5.132	90021

Year	Seychelles	Sierra Leone	Somalia	Sudan	Tanzania	Togo	Uganda	Zaire	Zambia	Zimbabwe	Total Export
1961	0.037	0.104	0.01	0.002	1.009	0.019	1.32	6.455			952
1962	0.06	0	0.003	0.002	0.644	0.042	1.003	7.473			946
1963	0.09	0	0	0.008	0.447	0.031	0.001	6.139			988
1964	0.082	0[3]	0.002	0.011	0.003	0.021[3]	0.002	6.783			954
1965	0.148[4]	0.001[4]	0[3]	0[3]	0.003[3]	0[3]	0[3]	3.784[4]			974
1966	0.083[2]	0[2]	0.001[2]	0[2]	0[2]	0[2]	0[2]	3.362[2]	18.461[3]		1202
1967	0.211[4]	0[3]	0[3]	0[3]	0.023[3]	0.008[3]	0.001[3]	2.752[3]	28.033[3]	33.704[3]	1352
1968		0				0		5.106	51.39[3]	42.716[3]	1389
1969	0.485	0				0		6.738	79.191	30.106[2]	1527
1970	0.496	0.001	0	0	0.045		0.077	8.036	67.857	51.392[3]	1525
1971	0.672							8.158	60.322	73.289	1541
1972	1.19				0.181			10.795		72.893	2041
1973								9.962		85.487	2421
1974	1.841		0	0			0.006	24.638	34.906	87.133	3350
1975								26.965	51.379	169.85	3990
1976		0									4542
1977	2.851	0[2]		0[2]		0		40.86			5683
1978	3.978	0.009	0.243	0.005	0.404	0.001		36.051	34.579		7333
1979	6.09	0.021	1.997	0.746	1.717	0.004	0	54.589			14811
1980	6.761	0.061	0.86	0.522	0.025		0.112	8.461	152.7		19915
1981	7.803	0.048	0.005	0.494[3]	0.3	0	0.151		144.59		18207
1982		0.173	0.077	0.341	0.944	0	0.161				19189
1983	7.313	0.002	0.228	1.531	0.497[1]	0	0.028	61.574	220.37	346.89	20620
1984		0.042	0.018	4.351	0.239	0[1]	0.214	85.3			24868
1985	14.512	0.267	0.082	0.561	1.272	0.089	0.01	162.471		403.75	36312
1986	23.132	7.254	0.166	2.375		0.155[2]	0.203	179.432			42011
1987	30.612		0.505	0.805		3.571	0.52	199.809			43671
1988	41.661	0.607	0.433	3.274	1.594	5.988	0.51	273.362		775.92	49724
1989	45.97	0.444	2.769	11.69	3.102	0.519	1.146	214.097	994.96	998.28	58199
1990		0.511	4.606	2.692	11.072	7.331	2.191	466.256	1167.4	1174.5	60929
1991	49.434	0.376	2.233	6.221	9.971	6.445	0.706	307.404	1608.6	1609	64355
1992	61.889	0.148	0	21.33	27.659	11.4	2.949	291.028	1112.2	1553.4	68997
1993	78.469	5.036	1.532	31.037	58.563	14.516	9.19	313.596	1307.156	1747.2	80671
1994	84.151	3.965	4.076	50.506	183.233	11.355	22.728	349.676	1158.676	2459.439	90021

Appendix C

South African Import from Black Africa, 1961-94
(in million ZAR)

Year	Angola	Benin	Burkina Faso	Burundi	Cameroon	Cape Verde	Central African Federation[5]	Central African Republic	Chad	Comoros	Congo	Total Import
1961	0.212		0.001	0.005	0.185	0.001	26.678	0.043				1005
1962	0.857		0	0[1]	0.053	0	7.374[1]	0.002[1]			0.953	1027
1963	1.017		0[3]	0[3]	0.001	0					0.732	1214
1964	0.88		0[2]	0[2]	0[3]	0[3]					0.65[3]	1556
1965	1.371	0.002[3]	0[3]	0[3]	0[2]	0[3]		0.048[3]	0[3]	0[3]	0.631[2]	1758
1966	3.057	0[2]	0	0	0.001[3]	0		0.006[2]	0[2]	0[2]	0.432[2]	1718
1967	1.721[3]	0[3]	0	0	0.006	0		0.093[3]	0[3]	0[3]	0.374[2]	1916
1968	3.418	0	0.002	0	0.003	0.003		0.134	0.346	0	1.363	1878
1969	3.399	0.001	0	0				0.224	0	0	2.125	2128
1970			0	0				0.164	0	0		2543
1971					0.012	0.003		0.084		0.013		2484
1972	4.553[3]	0.003			0.031			0.052				2813
1973	8.745							0.085				3275
1974								0.093		0	5.72	4909
1975										0		5562
1976		0.01			0	0		0.074				5867
1977		0	0		0	0.063		0.136		0	6.298	5141
1978		0			0.771	0.008		0.222		0	3.95	6253
1979		0				0.002[2]		1.536		0	5.606	9904
1980											7.708	14381
1981			0.039		0.025	0.011[1]				0.307	9.849	18430
1982			0	0.175	0.015					0.15	5.336	18374
1983			0	0.704[3]	0.372				5.884		5.81	16204
1984			0	0.001	0.002				0.544		8.592	22075
1985	0.018			0[2]	0.002	0.439		0.007	0	0.834	8.541	22691
1986	0[2]	0.219	0.029	0[3]	0.011	0[2]		0[2]	4.302	0.263	6.975	26864
1987		0	0	0.008	0.133	0.101				0.192	2.985[2]	28673
1988	0	0	0	0.012	0.175	0.077		0.027	1.985	0.194	12.473	39484
1989	9.923	0			0.219	0.102		0.002	0.084	0.243	17.344	44741
1990	0.059				1.667			0.244	1.986		15.379	44125
1991	0.018	0.309	0.959	0.487	7.788	0.948		0.218	2.618	0.984	5.26	48209
1992	0.728	0.455	0.017	0.028	5.653	1.02		0.03	11.21	0.256	4.419	52514
1993	1.13	16.286	3.311	0.146	8.997	0.116		1.285	19.72	0.295	2.218	59018
1994	16.891	9.331	0.034	1.5	7.383	0.132		0.006	6.172	0.322	3.143	79471

Year	Djibouti	Equatorial Guinea	Ethiopia	Gabon	Gambia	Ghana	Guinea	Guinea Bissau	Ivory Coast	Kenya	Liberia	Madagascar	Total Import
1961	0	0	0.014	0.058	0	0.482	0.005	0	1.039	2.749	0	0.136	1005
1962	0[1]	0[1]	0.009	0[1]	0	0.334	0.003	0	2.128	4.161	0	0.134	1027
1963			0.021			0.37	0		1.847	0.943	0	0.059[2]	1214
1964		0[2]	0.021[2]	0.155[2]	0[2]	0.276[2]	0.006[3]	0[3]	3.87	0.769[3]	0[3]	0.114[3]	1556
1965	0[2]	0[2]							2.817[2]				1758
1966	0[2]	0[2]	0.012[2]	0.027[2]	0[2]	0.237[2]	0.004[2]	0[2]	1.17[2]	0.382	0[2]	0.072[2]	1718
1967	0.001[2]	0[2]	0.029[2]	0.121[2]	0	0.171[2]	0.001[3]	0[3]	2.506[2]	1.277[3]	0.001[3]	0.306[3]	1916
1968		0		0.076	0	0.267	0.004	0	4.433		0.002	1.239	1878
1969		0		0.001	0	0.575	0.001	0	3.868		0.001	0.985	2128
1970			0.045	0.069						1.023		1.907	2543
1971				0.051								1.497	2484
1972				0.015									2813
1973				0.084				0[3]					3275
1974	0.003	0	0.344	0.22	0	0.563	0	0	8.934	0.909	0.17	1.56	4909
1975													5562
1976	0.001	0		0.002			0.003	0	26.502			1.414	5867
1977	0	0	0.058	0.246		1.563	0.003	0	21.795	2.765	0.006	0.537	5141
1978	0		0.119	0.482	0.011	0.912	0.019	0	23.275	4.117	0.006	1.766	6253
1979	0			0.114	0.002	1.121	0	0	22.931	4.024		1.809	9904
1980				0.047[1]			0	0					14381
1981	0	0	0.144		0.002	0.86	0.027	0		4.344	0.127	0.998	18430
1982	0.001		0.12		0	0.239	0	0	13.219	12.248	0.027		18374
1983	0	0[2]	0.736		0.003	0.181	0	0			0.012	1.136	16204
1984	0		0.341		0.007	0.001		0	23.582		0.013		22075
1985		0	0.046	4.487		0.311	0.2	0	54.798	5.213	0.002	0.239	22691
1986	0	0[2]	0.108	2.675	0.008	0.004	0[2]	0[2]		16.601	0.012	0.546	26864
1987	0.002	0	0.235	3.108	0.007[2]	0.101			27.382	13.453		0.578	28673
1988	0.001		0.316	5.804	0.101	0.631	0.058	0.011	25.395	19.571	0.474	0.412	39484
1989		0.004	0.467	6.452	0.012	0.651	0.015	0.003	44.153	10.876	0.226	1.346	44741
1990	0	0[2]	0.258	8.263	0	1.249	0.094	0.004	49.801	17.578	0.216		44125
1991	0.015	0.11	0.332	8.888	0.085	2.584	0.169	0.137	46.514	23.729	0.127	2.729	48209
1992	0.003	0	0.108	3.825	0.302	2.869	0.243	0.006	58.9	30.758	0.155	6.594	52514
1993	0.013	0	0.327	4.66	0.125	5.78	0.251	0.038	85.705	28.119	0	4.088	59018
1994		0	0.885	0.416	0.84	22.556	0.133	0.979			0.012	3.692	79471

Year	Malawi	Mali	Mauritania	Mauritius	Mozambique	Niger	Nigeria	Reunion	Rwanda	Sao Tome & Principe	Senegal	Total Import
1961		0		0.013	2.722	0	0.228	0.002	0.004	0.02	0.088	1005
1962		0		0.004[1]	1.328[1]	0	0.219	0.001[1]	0[1]	0.008[1]	0.183	1027
1963		0		0.057			0.27				0.003	1214
1964	1.585											1556
1965	1.951	0.002[3]	0[3]	1.423[3]	6.409[3]	0[3]	0.064[3]	0.001[3]	0[3]	0.003[3]	0.428[3]	1758
1966	1.452	0[2]	0[2]	0.096	8.428	0	0.02[2]	0.07[2]	0[2]	0.007[2]	0.763[2]	1718
1967	0.982	0[3]		1.58	8.748	0[3]	0.07[3]	0.012[3]	0.028[3]	0.031[3]	0.719[3]	1916
1968	1.604	0.001	0.046		9.694		0.074	0.012	0	0.341	0.611	1878
1969	1.583	0	0.094	1.216	9.727		0.181	0.004	0	0.043	0.038	2128
1970	1.823			1.427	10.856			0.002				2543
1971				1.821	10.2			0.024				2484
1972				2.761	10.3			0.004				2813
1973	1.922[3]			2.102	14.4			0.004				3275
1974	5.855	0.011	9.155	4.345	19.5	0	0.208	0.001	0.003	0.047	0.014	4909
1975	6.409				13.1			0.018				5562
1976		0.014	0.006	3.935	9.4	0		0.029	2.16		0[1]	5867
1977	7.204	0	0	5.859		0		0	0.255	0	0.002	5141
1978	8.567	0.042	0.007	5.416	7.221	0	0.042	0.037	0.14	0	0.007	6253
1979	13.61	0.016		1.278	5.83[4]		0.081	0.016	1.407	0	0	9904
1980		0.047	0	2.203		0	0.289	0.13	0.28	0	0.017	14381
1981		0.045		3.846	9.798	0.002	0.108		0	0	0.002[1]	18430
1982		0.025[3]					0.008					18374
1983		0.032	0.071	1.481		0.001	0.012		0.041		0.008	16204
1984		0.397	0.001			0.002	0.116		0			22075
1985	33.6	2.567	0.017	3.7	7.97	0.153	0.441	0.029	0.053	0	0.155	22691
1986			0.005			0.038	0.053	0.155	0[3]	0.001	0.045	26864
1987	66.875	0.153[3]	0.001[3]	3.505			0.122	0.34	0.034[3]			28673
1988	58.539	0.949	0.023	9.28	20.122	0.224	0.246	0.644	0.163	0.166	0.033	39484
1989	81.13	0.37	0.018	10.901	24.386	0.135	2.627	0.298	0.007	0.027	0.029	44741
1990		0.247	0.027	14.279	30.388	0.024	3.425	0.39	0.891	0.023	0.2	44125
1991	91.147	10.671	0.087	14.006	37.673	0.49	1.095	0.44	1.538	0.107	7.16	48209
1992	133.953	7.422	0.203	12.326	50.978	0.432	3.623	0.631	0.134	0.148	0.712	52514
1993	159.606	8.724	0.064	19.224	60.324	0.69	3.684	0.833	0.37	1.656	2.15	59018
1994	185.221	5.821	0.012	15.145	91.931	1.574	21.183	0.904	0.155	0.366	2.9	79471

Year	Seychelles	Sierra Leone	Somalia	Sudan	Tanzania	Togo	Uganda	Zaire	Zambia	Zimbabwe	Total Import
1961	0.03	0.009	0.001	0.192	4.321	0.059	1.221	22.603			1005
1962	0.0011[1]	0.008	0	0.244	3.402	0.037[1]	2.289	3.441			1027
1963		0.054		0.189	2.025		0.323	24.146			1214
1964	0.014[3]	0.027[3]	0.002[2]	0.085[3]	0.57[2]	0[2]	0.124[4]	22.922[4]			1556
1965	0.017[2]	0.042[2]	0[3]	0.041[2]	0.296[2]	0.113[2]	0.333[2]	8.71[2]	17.622[2]	20.047[2]	1758
1966	0.057[3]	0.055[3]	0[2]	0.242[2]	0.429[2]	0	0.097[2]	21.403[2]	12.186[2]	19.817[2]	1718
1967		0.114		0.414		0		6.343	22.59[2]	43.986[2]	1916
1968	0.062	0.111		0.3				1.791	20.592	61.629	1878
1969	0.052							3.375	5.538	73.317	2128
1970	0.018		0.003		1.284		0.045		7.08	85.148	2543
1971								1.778			2484
1972		0.081						2.439			2813
1973		0.023						4.859			3275
1974	0.101		0.232	0.619	0.051	0.003	0.016	9.804	1.733[2]	92.133[3]	4909
1975								7.748	3.61	152.003	5562
1976		0.104		0.014[2]				5.199			5867
1977	0.05	0.416	0.058	0.277	0.307	0.055	3.256	2.245			5141
1978	0.024	0.226	0	0.047	0.073	0.031	1.316	3.115	3.639		6253
1979	0.059	0.467	0.001	0.038	0.126	0.026	1.778	5.744			9904
1980	0.031	0.49				0.189					14381
1981	0.031	0.076	0	0.036[2]	0.097	0.105	0.003	4.535	6.016	218.729	18430
1982		0.262	0	0.054	0.301	0.022	0	3.6			18374
1983	0.064	0.187	0	0.794	0.363[2]	0.14	0	7.855			16204
1984		0.472	0.028	0.195	0.019	0.157[2]	0				22075
1985	0.249	0.024	0.001	0.587	0.194	0.375			19.242	265.039	22691
1986	0.149		0.001	0.705		0.441[2]	0.001	7.093			26864
1987	0.1		0.154	0.218	6.729	19.353	0.029	8.323			28673
1988	0.475	0.058	0.001	0.845	1.637	31.099	0.317	18.034		395.342	39484
1989	0.305	0.038	0.071	0.414	2.58	23.834	0.09	48.147	45.803	469.981	44741
1990		0.067		0.256		10.689		21.79	44.155	452.263	44125
1991	1.06	0.226	0.016	0.628	9.85	21.339	0.158	12.977	47.212	472	48209
1992	0.854	0.982	0.001	0.357	10.29	22.09	0.051	11.37	44.565	762.332	52514
1993	0.975	1.412	0.013	6.278	21.832	29.985	1.101	262.188	76.159	664.292	59018
1994	4.84	0.551	0.001	4.325	15.856	61.607	1.632	353.576	103.89	1021.801	79471

Bibliography

Archives

Archive for Contemporary Affairs (ARCA)

PV.4	E.H. Louw (no relevant files)	PV.395	Department of Information
PV.58	J.D. du P. Basson	PV.451	J.A.M. Hertzog
PV.59	NP Information Service	PV.528	H. Muller (no relevant files)
PV.93	H.F. Verwoerd	PV.532	G.P. Jooste (no relevant files)
PV.118	J.F.W. Haak	PV.546	N. Diederichs
PV.132	B.J. Vorster	PV.734	F.W. de Klerk (no relevant files)
PV.203	P.W. Botha	PV.799	Afrikaanse Handelsinstituut
PV.206	A.E. Rupert	PV.854	B.G. Fourie (no relevant files)
PV.377	J.W. Rall	PV.912	R.P. Meyer (no relevant files)

Department of Defence (DoD)

M.V/ files: Group 1: Ministers of Defence (F.C. Erasmus, 1948-59; J.J. Fouché, 1959-66)
MV/ files: Group 2: Minister of Defence (P.W. Botha, 1966-80)
HS/ or HVS/ files: Group 2, Vol. 1: Chief of Staff (H.V.S.)
KG/ or CGS/ files: Group 5: Commandant General

Department of Foreign Affairs (DFA)

1/13/3	Liberia: relations with	1/115/4/1/1	Nosy Be project: disposal
1/13/4	Liberia: technical assistance		of loan
1/62/3	Mauritius: relations with	1/115/4/2	Narinda Bay project
1/79/3	Ethiopia: relations with	1/116/3	Tanganyika/Tanzania:
1/99/13	Interdepartmental Commit-		relations with
	tee on African Affairs	1/120/3	Uganda: relations with
1/99/19	African states: relations with	1/120/4	Uganda: technical assistance
1/101/3	Cameroon: relations with	1/126/3	Zanzibar: relations with
1/106/3	Ghana: relations with	1/129/3	Nigeria: relations with
1/106/4	Ghana: technical assistance	1/131/3	Sierra Leone: relations with
1/112/3	Zaire: relations with	1/135/3	Kenya: relations with
1/112/4	Zaire: technical assistance	1/135/4	Kenya: technical assistance
1/112/5/1	Zaire: volunteers for Katanga	1/138/3	Reunion: relations with
1/112/5/3	Congo: medical expenses	1/138/4	Reunion: technical assistance
	for SA mercenaries	1/144/3	Somalia: relations with
1/115/3	Madagascar: relations with	1/144/4	Somalia: technical assistance
1/115/3/1	Madagascar: relations with	1/149/3	Gambia: relations with
1/115/4	Madagascar: technical assist.	1/149/4	Gambia: technical assistance
1/115/4/1	Nosy Be project	1/158/3	Malawi: relations with

34/5/188	Mauritania: commercial rel.	34/5/224	Cape Verde: commercial rel.
34/5/192	Rwanda: commercial rel.	34/5/225	Sao Tome and Principe:
34/5/193	Burundi: commercial rel.		commercial relations
34/5/194	Seychelles: commercial rel.	34/18/2	Boycott of South African
34/5/203	Comoros: commercial rel.		products by African states
34/5/207	Equatorial Guinea: commercial relations		

National Archives (NAT.ARC.)

Department of Foreign Affairs (files starting with BTS)
Private Secretary, Minister of Information (1966-78) (files starting with MNL)
Department of Information (1971-80) (files starting with INL)

Interviews and Correspondence

Aliker, Martin Jerome: telephone interview, 24 February 2004
Ambassador Plenipotentiary of Uganda (1963); in Kenyan exile (1971-78); Adviser to Ugandan President Yusufu Lule (April-June 1979); Director, Ugandan Breweries

Auret, Derek William: telephone interview, 20 March 2002; 8 January 2003
See Appendix A

Babb, Glenn Robin Ware: correspondence, January 2003
See Appendix A

Barratt, Charles John Adkinson: correspondence, January 2003
Cadet, DFA (1954-57); Third Secretary, Permanent Mission to the UN, New York (1958-65); Director, South African Institute of International Affairs (1967-94); Member of the Council, Africa Institute (1980-96); DP Representative, Transitional Executive Council, Subcouncil on Foreign Affairs (1993-94)

Botha, Roelof Frederik 'Pik': interview, Pretoria, 20 April 1999
See Appendix A

Boyazoglu, Jan George: telephone interview, 1 April 2004; correspondence, March-April 2004
D.Sc. (Agric), University of Pretoria (1965); Department of ATS (1960-85); Agricultural Counsellor, Embassy, Paris, accredited to the European Communities (1965-82); Board of Trustees, OGAPROV (1971-82); Agricultural Counsellor, Consulate-General, Los Angeles (1982-85); Secretary-General, European Association of Animal Production, World Association of Animal Production and International Committee for Animal Recording, Rome (1986-93); FAO, Rome (1993-97)

Cornwell, Richard John: interview, Pretoria, 19 February 1999
Researcher, Africa Institute (1979-82); Lecturer in Development Administration and African Politics, University of South Africa (1982-87); Head of Information/Director of Current Affairs, Africa Institute (1988-97)

De Villiers, Caspar Francois 'Cas': telephone interview, 18 January 2003
Editor, *Africa Institute Bulletin* (1969-75); Associate, *To the Point* (1972-76); Director, Foreign Affairs Association (1975-78)

Diouf, Bara: interview, Dakar, 8 October 2003
Centre de formation des journalistes, Paris (1955-59); Journalist, *Le monde,* Paris (1958-60); Chairman and Managing Director, Agence de Presse Sénégalaise, Dakar (1960-65); Director of Information, radio and television of Senegal (1965-70); Managing Director, *Le Soleil,* Dakar (1970-88)

Du Plessis, Adriaan Sarel 'Attie': correspondence, January 2003
Executive Director, Sankorp Ltd. & Sanlam (1986-2002); President, AHI (1991-92)

Du Toit, Heinrich de Villefort 'Hein': correspondence, April 2004
Captain (1953); Major (1958); Commandant (1963); Colonel (1966); Brigadier (1968); Major General (1971); Lieutenant General (1974); Staff Officer, General Staff (1953-58); Staff Officer, Adjutant General (1959-63); Chief of Strategic Intelligence (1963-64); Member of Secretariat, Intelligence Co-ordination Committee (South African Police, SADF, DFA) (1964-66); Deputy Director, DMI (1966-71); Chief of Staff: Intelligence (1971-77); Professor, Department of National Strategy, Rand Afrikaans University (1979-93)

Dugard, Christopher John Robert: correspondence, December 2002
Prof. of Law, University of the Witwatersrand, Johannesburg (1969-98)

Eglin, Colin Wells: correspondence, January 2003
Leader, Progressive Party/Progressive Reform Party/Progressive Federal Party (1971-79; 1986-88); Member of Parliament for Sea Point, Cape Town (1974-)

Fourie, Deon François Schönland: interview, Pretoria, 22 April 1999
Lecturer, Department of Political Sciences, University of South Africa (1960-97); Director, Citizen Force Liaison, on the staff of the Chief of the Army (1988-95); consultant for the Department of Defence

Geldenhuys, Deon Johannes: interview, Johannesburg, 1 March 1999
Ph.D., Cambridge University (1977); Research Director, South African Institute of International Affairs (1979-81); Prof., Department of Political Studies, Rand Afrikaans University (1984-)

Hamman, Daniel Smith 'Daan': correspondence, March 2004
Captain (1966); Major (1968); Commandant (1971); Colonel (1978); Brigadier (1980); Major General (1987); Military Attaché, Embassy, London (1975-76); Military Attaché, Embassy, Paris (1977-79); Head, Directorate of Special Tasks, Directorate of Military Intelligence (1980-83)

Hanekom, Hermann Albert: correspondence, January 2003
See Appendix A

Hersov, Basil Edward: correspondence, February 2004
Chairman and Managing Director, Anglovaal (1972-2000); Trustee/Member of the Council/Deputy President/President/Honorary President, South Africa Foundation (1970-96/73-76/76-77/77-79/79-96)

Holtes, Willem Bernard 'Wim': interview, Johannesburg, 31 March 1999
Chief Executive, SAFTO (1963-92); Member of the Council, Africa Institute (1982-92)

Jaquet, André: correspondence, December 2002
See Appendix A

Landsberg, Stefan Adolf Waldemar: telephone interview, 4 December 2002
Metal Studies Consultant, Anglo American Corporation (1980-94)

Leisewitz, Christoph Theodor Lutz: correspondence, May 1999
   Trainee Underwriter/Branch Manager, Natal/Underwriting Manager/Assistant
   General Manager/Manager, Projects Department/Senior General Manager/Executive
   Director/Managing Director, CGIC (1965-68/68-69/69-73/73-78/78-82/82-
   86/86-88/1988-2002)

Leistner, Gerhard Max Erich: telephone interview, 26 February 2003; correspon-
   dence, December 2002-January 2003, January 2004
   Professional Officer, Department of Finance (1957-60); Lecturer/Senior Lec-
   turer, Department of Economics, University of South Africa (1960-64); Researcher,
   Africa Institute (1964-70); Prof., Department of Economics, University of South
   Africa (1970-73); Deputy Director/Director/Senior Research Fellow, Africa
   Institute (1973-77/78-91/92)

Loubser, Antonie Eduard 'Anton': correspondence, February 2004
   See Appendix A

Luyt, Louis: correspondence, February 2003
   Founder and Chairman, Triomf Fertilisers Ltd. (1965-86); D.Com., University
   of Michigan (1980); D.Com. (honoris causa), University of the Orange Free
   State (1983); Honorary Prof. of Law, University of Pretoria (1986-88); LLD,
   University of Pretoria (1988)

Miller, Cecil Jeffries 'Jeff': telephone interview, 17 April 2004
   Roberts Construction (1954-87)

Mills, Gregory John Barrington 'Greg': interview, Johannesburg, 1 March 1999
   Ph.D., Lancaster University (1990); Research Associate, Institute for Defence
   Policy, Johannesburg, and Centre for Defence and International Security Stud-
   ies, Lancaster University (1991-93); Director of Studies/Director, South African
   Institute of International Affairs (1994-96/96-2005); Director, The Brenthurst
   Foundation (2005-)

Munger, Edwin Stanton 'Ned': correspondence, February 2002
   Research Fellow, University of Stellenbosch (1955-56); Prof. in Political Geography,
   California Institute of Technology, Pasadena (1961-88); Founder and President,
   Cape of Good Hope Foundation (1985-97); Board Member, USSALEP (1958-)

Njonjo, Charles Mugane: correspondence, December 2003
   Assistant Registrar General, Attorney General's Chambers, Kenya (1952-53);
   Crown Counsel, Kenya (1955-63); Attorney General, Kenya (1963-80); Member
   of Parliament, Kenya (1979-83); Minister of Constitutional Affairs, Kenya (1980-83)

Oppenheimer, Klaus: correspondence, March 2002
   General Manager, CGIC (1956-65); Member, Export Trade Advisory Committee (1956-65); Managing Director, Imex (1966)

Ridley, Michael Thomas 'Mike': correspondence, May 2004
   Chartered Accountant, James Thompson (1954-64); Financial Director/Chief
   Executive Officer, LTA (1965-71/72-85)

Runge, Paul Gustav: interview, Johannesburg, 7 April 1999; telephone interview,
   18 January 2003
   See Appendix A

Schoeman, Maria Margretha Elizabeth 'Maxi': interview, Johannesburg, 1 March 1999
   Ph.D., University of Wales, Aberystwyth (1998); Prof., Department of Political
   Studies, Rand Afrikaans University (1998-2000); Prof., Department of Political
   Studies, University of Pretoria (2000-)

Shearar, Jeremy Brown: telephone interview, 8 January 2003
    See Appendix A

Slabbert, Frederik van Zyl: correspondence, February 2003
    D.Phil., University of Stellenbosch (1967); Lecturer, University of Stellenbosch
    (1964-68); Senior Lecturer, Rhodes University (1969); Senior Lecturer, Univer-
    sity of Stellenbosch (1969); Senior Lecturer, University of Cape Town (1970-
    71); Prof., Department of Sociology, University of the Witwatersrand (1972-
    74); Member of Parliament, Progressive Party/Progressive Federal Party for
    Rondebosch (1974-86); Leader, Progressive Federal Party (1979-86); Co-
    founder and Director, IDASA (1986-)

Sole, Donald Bell: correspondence, February 2004
    See Appendix A

Sorour, James de Lacy 'Peter': correspondence, January 2004
    Membership Campaign Manager/Deputy Director/Financial Director/Director
    General, South Africa Foundation (1962-65/66-67/68-72/73-87)

Spicer, Michael Wolseley: interview, Johannesburg, 7 April 1999
    Research Associate, Royal Institute of International Affairs, London (Chatham
    House Study Group "Southern Africa in Conflict") (1978-80); Assistant Direc-
    tor, South African Institute of International Affairs (1981-84); Executive Direc-
    tor, Anglo American Corporation (1985-2005); Executive Director, South Af-
    rica Foundation (2005-)

Suzman, Helen: correspondence, November 2002
    Member of Parliament, United Party (1953-59), Progressive Party/Progressive
    Reform Party/Progressive Federal Party (1961-74/74-77/77-89) for Houghton

Swarts, Francois 'Frans': telephone interview, 7 December 2002; correspondence,
    February 2003
    Planning Manager/Commercial Manager/Deputy Chief Executive, SAA (1945-
    81); Chief Executive, SAA (1982-83)

Thomas, Julian Alexis: telephone interview, 1 April 2004; correspondence, April 2004
    D.Phil., Rand Afrikaans University, Johannesburg (1986); Department of ATS
    (1963-86), incl. Agricultural Attaché/Counsellor, Embassy, Paris (1971-79/83-
    86); Manager, Development Bank of Southern Africa, Johannesburg (1987-95)

Tyler, Geoffrey Winston: correspondence, February 2002
    Economist, Association of Chambers of Commerce (1977-82); Chief Execu-
    tive, Durban Chamber of Commerce (1985-99)

Van Aswegen, Jacobus Pieter: interview, Cape Town, 2 November 2001
    Prof. and Head, Department of Business Economics, Rand Afrikaans Univer-
    sity (1978-80); Group Economist, Safmarine (1981-87); Board of Directors,
    Trek Airways, Air Cape, Namib Air (1986); Director/Chairman, Safair (1986-
    87/87-91); Group/Executive Manager, Safmarine (1987-99); Managing Direc-
    tor, Safair (1993-99)

Van der Veer, Gerrit Dirk 'Gert': telephone interview, 7 December 2002; corre-
    spondence, January-February 2003
    Railways and Harbours (1959-77); Chief Superintendent, Railway Operating (1977-
    79); Regional Manger, Railways and Harbours (1979-81); Head, Railway Operating
    (1981-83); Chief Executive, SAA, and Deputy Managing Director, Transnet (1983-93)

Van Heerden, Neil Peter: interview Johannesburg, 7 April 1999
    See Appendix A

Van Tonder, Jacobus Cornelius 'Neels': telephone interview, 19 March 2002
  Brigadier (1983); Major General (1986); Second Secretary, Embassy, Paris
  (1969-70); Head, Special Tasks Directorate (DMI) (1975-84)
Venter, Thomas Denis: interview, Pretoria, 10 March 1999
  D.Litt. et Phil. University of South Africa (1988); Lecturer, Department of Political Science and International Politics, University of Pretoria (1970-74); Assis-
  tant Director, South African Institute of International Affairs (1975-77); Re-
  searcher/Senior Researcher/Chief Researcher/Director, Africa Institute (1978-
  88/89/90-91/92-99)
Viljoen, Jan Hendrik 'Hennie': telephone interview, 26 January 2003
  Director, Coca-Cola South Africa (1975-95); President, Transvaal Chamber of
  Industries (1987-88); President, Witwatersrand Chamber of Commerce and In-
  dustry (1989); Member, Executive Committee, SACOB (1990-94); Deputy
  President/President, SACOB (1991/92)
Whiting, Spencer Roland: correspondence, April 2004
  LTA (1965-83), *inter alia* Deputy Managing (1977-83)

Literature

Abi-Saab, G. 1978. *The United Nations Operation in the Congo, 1960-1964*. Oxford:
  Oxford University Press.
Adams, J. 1984. *The Unnatural Alliance: Israel and South Africa*. London: Quartet.
Agbogu, A.E. 1983. 'Nigeria's South African policy since 1960: an assessment'.
  Ph.D. thesis, University of Pittsburgh.
Ake, C. 1996. *The Marginalization of Africa: notes on a productive confusion*. Lagos:
  Malthouse Press.
Akinyemi, M.C. 1994. 'Origins, articulations and continuities in foreign policy and
  foreign policy formulation: the case of civilian and military governments in Ni-
  geria, 1960-1990, with special reference to South Africa'. Ph.D. thesis, Kent
  University.
Albright, D.E. 1991. 'South Africa in southern Africa', in D.J. Myers, ed., *Regional
  Hegemons: threat perception and strategic response*. Boulder, CO: Westview Press, 97-159.
Alden, C. & J.-P. Daloz. 1996. 'Introduction', in C. Alden & J.-P. Daloz, eds.,
  *Paris, Pretoria and the African Continent: the International Relations of states and societies
  in transition*. Basingstoke: Macmillan, 1-5.
Alden, C. 1996. 'From policy autonomy to policy integration: the evolution of
  France's role in Africa', in C. Alden & J.-P. Daloz, eds., *Paris, Pretoria and the
  African Continent: the International Relations of states and societies in transition*. Basing-
  stoke: Macmillan, 11-25.
Aluko, O. 1977. 'The determinants of the foreign policies of African states', in O.
  Aluko, ed., *The Foreign Policies of African States*. London: Hodder & Stoughton, 1-23.
Aluko, O. 1982. 'Nigeria and southern Africa', in G.M. Carter & P. O'Meara, eds.,
  International Politics in Southern Africa. Bloomington, IN: Indiana University Press, 128-47.
Andemicael, B. 1976. *The OAU and the UN: relations between the Organization of
  African Unity and the United Nations*. New York: Africana Publishing.
Andereggen, A. 1994. *France's Relationship with Subsaharan Africa*. Westport, CT: Praeger.
Arnold, G. 1992. *South Africa: crossing the Rubicon*. Basingstoke: Macmillan.
Art, R.J. 1993. 'Bureaucratic Politics', in J. Krieger, ed., *The Oxford Companion to
  Politics of the World*. New York: Oxford University Press, 99-100.

Bach, D.C. 1980. 'Le Général de Gaulle et la guerre civile au Nigeria', *Canadian Journal of African Studies* 14, 2: 259-72.

Bach, D.C. 1982. 'L'insertion ivoirienne dans les rapports internationaux', in Y.A. Faure & J.F. Médard, eds., *Etat et bourgeoisie en Côte d'Ivoire*. Paris: Karthala, 89-121.

Bach, D.C. 1990. 'Les initiatives franco-sud africains de «dialogue» avec l'Afrique francophone', in D.C Bach, ed., *La France et l'Afrique du Sud: histoire, mythes et enjeux contemporains*. Paris: Karthala; Nairobi: CREDU, 203-14.

Bach, D.C. 1990. 'Un système autonome de relations: la France et l'Afrique du Sud, 1963-1977', in D.C Bach, ed., *La France et l'Afrique du Sud: histoire, mythes et enjeux contemporains*. Paris: Karthala; Nairobi: CREDU, 173-202.

Bacharach, S.B. & E.J. Lawler. 1981. *Bargaining: power, tactics and outcomes*. San Francisco, CA: Jossey-Bass.

Baker, P.H. 1989. *The United States and South Africa: the Reagan years*. New York: Ford Foundation.

Barber, J.P. & C.J.A. Barratt. 1990. *South Africa's Foreign Policy: the search for status and security, 1945-1988*. Cambridge: Cambridge University Press; Johannesburg: South African Institute of International Affairs.

Barber, J.P. 2000. 'South Africa's political miracle: the international dimension', *South African Institute of International Affairs* 7, 1: 51-71.

Barber, J.P. 2004. *Mandela's World: the international dimension of South Africa's Political Revolution, 1990-1999*. Oxford: James Currey; Cape Town: David Philip; Athens, OH: Ohio University Press.

Barnard, L.D. 1977. 'Angola in die internasionale magskonstellasie', *Journal for Contemporary History and International Relations* 2, 1: 66-86.

Barratt, C.J.A. 1970. 'South Africa's Outward Movement', *Modern Age* 14, 2: 129-39.

Barratt, C.J.A. 1971. *Dialogue in Africa*. Johannesburg: South African Institute of International Affairs.

Barratt, C.J.A. 1972. 'South Africa's Outward Policy: from isolation to Dialogue', in N.J. Rhoodie, ed., *South African Dialogue: contrasts in South African thinking on basic race issues*. Johannesburg: MacGraw-Hill, 543-61.

Barratt, C.J.A. 1973. *Southern Africa: intra-regional and international relations*. Johannesburg: South African Institute of International Affairs.

Barratt, C.J.A. 1974. 'Report on a visit to Senegal and the Ivory Coast', *Newsletter of the South African Institute of International Affairs* 6, 3: 19-21.

Barratt, C.J.A. 1975. 'The Department of Foreign Affairs', in D. Worrall, ed., *South Africa: Government and Politics*. Pretoria: J.L. van Schaik, 332-47.

Barratt, C.J.A. 1985. 'South African diplomacy at the UN', in G.R. Berridge & A. Jennings, eds. *Diplomacy at the UN*. Basingstoke: Macmillan: 191-203.

Bealey, F. 1999. *The Blackwell Dictionary of Political Science: a user's guide to its terms*. Oxford: Blackwell.

Berridge, G.R. 1992. *South Africa, the Colonial Powers and "African Defence": the rise and fall of the white entente, 1948-60*. London: Macmillan; New York: St. Martin's Press.

Biddlecombe, P. 1966. 'IMEX: international supermarket', *Perspective* 4, 3: 12-3.

Biermann, H.H.H. ed., 1963. *The Case for South Africa, as Put Forth in the Public Statements of Eric H. Louw, Foreign Minister of South Africa*. New York: MacFadden-Bartell.

Blum, W. 1995. *Killing Hope: U.S. military and CIA interventions since World War II*. Monroe, ME: Common Courage Press.

Boraine, A. 1987. *Dakar Report Back*. Cape Town: Institute for a Democratic Alternative for South Africa.

Botha, C.B. 1993. 'Soldiers of fortune or whores of war?' The legal position of mercenaries with specific reference to South Africa', *Strategic Review for Southern Africa* 15, 2: 75-91.

Botha, R.F. 1995. 'His South African connection', in H. d'Orville, ed., *Leadership for Africa: in honor of Olusegun Obasanjo on the occasion of his 60th birthday.* New York: Africa Leadership Foundation, 55-69.

Boutros-Ghali, B. 1994. 'Introduction', in *United Nations and Apartheid, 1948-1994.* New York: United Nations, Department of Public Information: 3-145.

Bouwer, J.J. 1988. 'Trade credit and trade credit insurance', in G.M.E. Leistner & P.W. Esterhuysen, eds., *South Africa in Southern Africa: economic interaction.* Pretoria: Africa Institute, 90-103.

Bowker, M. 1983. *Superpower Détente: a reappraisal.* London: Sage, for the Royal Institute of International Affairs.

Bowman, L.W. 1982. 'African conflict and superpower involvement in the Western Indian Ocean', in L.W. Bowman & I. Clark, eds., *The Indian Ocean in Global Politics.* Boulder, CO: Westview Press, 87-103.

Bowman, L.W. 1991. *Mauritius: democracy and development in the Indian Ocean.* Boulder, CO: Westview Press; London: Dartmouth.

Breitenbach, J.J. 1974. *South Africa in the Modern World (1910-1970): a contemporary history.* Pietermaritzburg: Shuter and Shooter.

Breytenbach, B. 1986. *End Papers: essays, letters, articles of faith, workbook notes.* New York: Farrar, Straus, and Giroux.

Breytenbach, W.J. 1977. *South Africa Looks to Africa.* Sandton: Southern African Freedom Foundation.

Brits, J.P. 1995. 'The historian and the archives: a 1995 South African perspective', *Historia: Official Organ of the Historical Association of South Africa* 40, 1: 65-71.

Buck, R. 1980. 'Chief Nzeribe: tycoon international', *African Business* 21: 71, 73.

Budlender, D, et al., 1976. *Transkei Independence: report of the Transkei study project.* Johannesburg: University of the Witwatersrand, Wages and Economics Commission.

Bull, H. 1977. *The Anarchical Society: a study of order in world politics.* Basingstoke: Macmillan.

Burchill, S. 1996. 'Introduction', in S. Burchill, et al., *Theories of International Relations.* New York: St. Martin's Press, 1-27.

Butts, K.H. & P.R. Thomas. 1986. *The Geopolitics of Southern Africa: South Africa as regional superpower.* Boulder, CO: Westview Press.

Callaghy, T.M. 1985. 'Zaire and southern Africa', in O. Aluko & T.M. Shaw, eds., *Southern Africa in the 1980s.* London: Allen & Unwin, 61-86.

Carlsnaes, W. 2002. 'Foreign policy', in W. Carlsnaes, T. Risse & B.A. Simmons, eds., *Handbook of International Relations.* London: Sage, 337-9.

Carstens, P. 2001. *In the Company of Diamonds: De Beers, Kleinzee, and control of a town.* Athens, OH: Ohio University Press.

Cassette, J. 1993. 'United Nations Observer Mission in South Africa: a significant event', *South African Yearbook of International Law, 1992/93* 18: 1-23.

Chabbra, H.S. 1997. *South African Foreign Policy: principles, options, dilemmas.* New Delhi: Africa Publishing.

Chafer, T. 2001. 'French African policy in historical perspective', *Journal of Contemporary African Studies* 19, 2: 165-82.

Chettle, J.H. 1984. 'Economic relations between South Africa and black Africa', *SAIS Review* 4, 2: 121-33.

Chipman, J. 1985. *French Military Policy and African Security.* London: Institute for Strategic Studies.

Chipman, J. 1989. *French Power in Africa.* Oxford: Basil Blackwell.

Christiansen, R.E. & J.G. Kydd. 1983. 'The return of Malawian labour from South Africa and Zimbabwe', *Journal of Modern African Studies* 21, 2: 311-26.

Cillié, P.J. 1968. 'Outwards: an Afrikaner view of Africa policy', *Perspective* 6, 3: 7-9.

Clapham, C. 1977. 'Sub-Saharan Africa', in C. Clapham, ed., *Foreign Policy Making in Developing States: a comparative approach.* London: Saxon House, 75-109.

Clapham, C. 1988. *Third World Politics: an introduction.* London: Routledge.

Clark, N.L. 1994. *Manufacturing Apartheid: state corporations in South Africa.* New Haven, CT: Yale University Press.

Clark, S., comp., 1993. *Nelson Mandela Speaks: forging a democratic, nonracial South Africa.* New York: Pathfinder.

Cockram, G.-M. 1970. *Vorster's Foreign Policy.* Pretoria: Academica.

Collier, P. 1997. *The Marginalisation of Africa in the World Economy.* Oxford: Centre for the Study of African Economies.

Cooke, M.W. 1983. 'Seychelles', in F.M. Bunge, ed., *Indian Ocean: five island countries.* Washington, DC: The American University, 195-223.

Cooke, M.W. 1983. 'Strategic considerations', in F.M. Bunge, ed., *Indian Ocean: five island countries.* Washington, DC: The American University, 249-86.

Cooper, A.F. 1997. 'Niche diplomacy: a conceptual overview', in A.F. Cooper, ed., *Niche Diplomacy: middle powers after the Cold War.* London. Macmillan, 1-24.

Craig, G.A. 1983. 'The historian and the study of International Relations', *American Historical Review* 88, 1: 1-11.

Credit Guarantee: a corporate report. 1991. Johannesburg: Financial Mail.

Crockatt, R. 1995. *The Fifty Years War: the United States and the Soviet Union in world politics, 1941-1991.* London: Routledge.

Crocker, C.A. 1981. 'Namibia/Angola Linkages', *Africa Report* 26, 6: 10.

Crocker, C.A. 1993. *High Noon in Southern Africa: making peace in a rough neighborhood.* Johannesburg: Jonathan Ball.

Cronjé, S. 1972. *The World and Nigeria: the Diplomatic History of the Biafran War, 1967-1970.* London: Sidgwick and Jackson.

Crush, J. & P. Wellings. 1983. 'The southern African pleasure periphery, 1966-83', *Journal of Modern African Studies* 21, 4: 673-98.

Cuddumbey, C. 1996. 'France and South Africa', in C. Alden & J.-P. Daloz, eds., *Paris, Pretoria and the African Continent: the International Relations of states and societies in transition.* Basingstoke: Macmillan, 67-92.

Culverson, D.R. 1999. *Contesting Apartheid: U.S. activism, 1960-1987.* Boulder, CO: Westview Press.

D'Oliveira, J. 1978. *Vorster: the man.* Johannesburg: Ernest Stanton.

Daddieh, C.K. 1984. 'Ivory Coast', in T.M. Shaw & O. Aluko, eds., *The Political Economy of African Foreign Policy: comparative analysis.* Aldershot: Gower, 122-44.

Daddieh, C.K. 1997. 'South Africa and Francophone African relations', in L.A. Swatuk & D.R. Black, eds., *Bridging the Rift: the new South Africa in Africa.* Boulder, CO: Westview Press, 183-97.

Darbon, D. 1990. 'Les rapports franco-sud africains depuis 1977', in D.C. Bach, ed., *La France et l'Afrique du Sud: histoire, mythes et enjeux contemporains.* Paris: Karthala, 233-58.

Dare, O. 1991. 'Pretoria-Abuja-Cairo axis', *Africa Forum* 1, 2: 50-2.

Davies, R.H. 1986. 'The military and foreign policy in South Africa: review article', *Journal of Southern African Studies* 12, 2: 308-15.

De Beer, J.H. 1998. 'Integration of the Departments of Foreign Affairs and Information in 1980 and adjustments up to 1993', in *History of the Department of Foreign Affairs. Vol. III: Organization and Management of the Department of External/Foreign Affairs*. Pretoria: Department of Foreign Affairs, 116-44. (Unpublished manuscript)

De Beer, K.J. 1981. 'Die diplomatieke strategie van dr. Hilgard Muller teen die totale aanslag op die Republiek van Suid-Afrika'. D.Phil. thesis, University of the Orange Free State.

De Klerk, F.W. 1998. *The Last Trek: a new beginning*. London: Macmillan.

De Klerk, W.J. 1991. *F. W. de Klerk: the man in his time*. Johannesburg: Jonathan Ball.

De St. Jorre, J. 1972. *The Nigerian Civil War*. London: Hodder and Stoughton.

De St. Jorre, J. 1977. 'South Africa: up against the world', *Foreign Policy* 28: 53-85.

De Villiers, F. 2003. 'Julian Ogilvie Thompson: a giant departs', *Optima* 49, 1: 40-9.

De Villiers, L.E.S. 1980. *Secret Information*. Cape Town: Tafelberg.

De Witte, L. 2002. *The Assassination of Lumumba*. London: Verso.

Decter, M. 1976. *South Africa and Black Africa: a report on growing trade relations*. New York: American Jewish Congress.

Delauney, M. 1982. *De la casquette à la jaquette, ou de l'administration coloniale à la diplomatie africaine*. Paris: La Pensée Universelle.

Delauney, M. 1986. *"Kala-kala": de la grande à la petite histoire*. Paris: Robert Laffont.

Denard, R.P. 1998. *Corsaire de la république*. Paris: Robert Laffont.

Dodgen, S. 1991. 'The sky is open', *Prisma* 6, 4: 12-3.

Dollery, B.E. 1989. 'Capital, labour and state: a general equilibrium perspective on liberal and revisionist approaches to South African Political Economy', *South African Journal of Economics* 57, 2: 124-36.

Domhoff, G.W. 1967. *Who Rules America?* Englewood Cliffs, NJ: Prentice-Hall.

Du Preez, M. 2001. *Louis Luyt: unauthorised*. Cape Town: Zebra Press.

Dugard, C.J.R. 1972. 'Namibia (South West Africa): the Court's opinion, South Africa's response and prospects for the future', *Columbia Journal of Transnational Law* 11, 1: 14-49.

Dugard, C.J.R. 1973. *The South West Africa/Namibia Dispute: documents and scholarly writings on the controversy between South Africa and the United Nations*. Berkeley, CA: University of California Press.

Eglin, C.W. 1971. *Africa: a prospect of reconciliation*. Cape Town: Progressive Party.

Ellis, S. 1996. 'Africa and international corruption: the strange case of South Africa and Seychelles', *African Affairs* 95, 379: 165-96.

Ellis, S. 1998. 'The historical significance of South Africa's Third Force', *Journal of Southern African Studies* 24, 2: 261-99.

Elman, C. & M.F. Elman, eds. 2001., *Bridges and Boundaries: historians, political scientists, and the study of International Relations*. Cambridge, MA: MIT Press.

Elman, C. & M.F. Elman. 1997. 'Diplomatic History and International Relations theory: respecting differences and crossing boundaries', *International Security* 22, 1: 5-21.

Esterhuyse, W.P. 1986. *Anton Rupert: advocate of hope*. Cape Town: Tafelberg.

Esterhuysen, P.W., ed., 1998. *Africa A-Z: continental and country profiles*. Pretoria: Africa Institute.

Esterhuysen, P.W., ed., T.J.D. Fair & G.M.E. Leistner. 1994. *South Africa in Sub-Equatorial Africa: economic interaction*. Pretoria: Africa Institute.

Evans, G. & J. Newnham. 1998. *The Penguin Dictionary of International Relations*. London: Penguin.

Export Project Insurance. c1998. Johannesburg: Credit Guarantee Insurance Corporation.

Faligot, R. & P. Krop. 1985. *La piscine: les services secrets français, 1944-1984.* Paris: Editions du Seuil.

Falk, P.S. 1986. *The Geopolitics of Southern Africa: South Africa as regional superpower.* Boulder, CO: Westview Press.

Fine, B. & Z. Rustomjee. 1996. *The Political Economy of South Africa: from minerals-energy complex to industrialisation.* London: Hurst.

Foccart, J. 1995/1997. *Foccart parle: entretiens avec Philipe Gaillard. Vol. I & II.* Paris: Fayard; Jeune Afrique.

Foreign Affairs List. Pretoria: Department of External/Foreign Affairs. (1955, 1957, 1958, 1961, 1963-64, 1971-72, 1974-75, 1977, 1979, 1982, 1986-92)

Fourie, B.G. 1991. *Brandpunte: agter die skerme met Suid-Afrika se bekendste diplomaat.* Cape Town: Tafelberg.

Fourie, B.G. c1986. *Buitelandse woelinge om Suid-Afrika, 1939-1985.* Pretoria. (Unpublished manuscript)

Franda, M.F. 1982. *The Seychelles: unquiet islands.* Boulder, CO: Westview Press.

Frank, A. 1975. 'Is Pretoria on the point of break-through to Africa?', *African Development* 9, 4: 59.

Frankel, P.H. 1984. *Pretoria's Praetorians: civil-military relations in South Africa.* Cambridge: Cambridge University Press.

Frankel, P.H. 2000. *Soldiers in a Storm: the armed forces in South Africa's democratic transition.* Boulder CO: Westview Press.

Frankel, P.H. 2001. *An Ordinary Atrocity: Sharpeville and its massacre.* New Haven, CT: Yale University Press.

Frederikse, J. 1987. 'South Africa's media: the commercial press and the seedlings of the future', *Third World Quarterly* 9, 2: 638-56.

Friedman, S. & D. Atkinson, eds., 1994. *The Small Miracle: South Africa's negotiated settlement.* Johannesburg: Ravan Press.

Friedman, S., ed., 1993. *The Long Journey: South Africa's quest for a negotiated settlement.* Johannesburg: Ravan Press.

Gaddis, J.L. 1990. 'New conceptual approaches to the study of American foreign relations: interdisciplinary approaches', *Diplomatic History* 14, 3: 403-25.

Gallo, M. 1998. *De Gaulle. Vol. II: La solitude du combattant.* Paris: Robert Laffont.

Gastrow, S. 1985/1987/1992. *Who's Who in South African Politics.* Johannesburg: Ravan Press. (First, Second and Fourth Edition)

Geldenhuys, D.J. & H.J. Kotzé. 1991. 'FW de Klerk: a study in political leadership', *Politikon: South African Journal of Political Studies* 19, 1: 20-44.

Geldenhuys, D.J. 1984. *The Diplomacy of Isolation: South African foreign policy making.* Johannesburg: Macmillan South Africa for the South African Institute of International Affairs.

Geldenhuys, D.J. 1992. 'The foreign factor in South Africa's 1992 referendum', *Politikon: South African Journal of Political Science* 19, 3: 45-63.

Geldenhuys, D.J. 1994. 'The head of government and South Africa's foreign relations', in R.A. Schrire, ed., *Malan to de Klerk: leadership in the Apartheid state.* New York: St. Martin's Press; London: Hurst, 245-90.

The Giants: who owns them, who they own. 1991. Johannesburg: Financial Mail.

Gibbs, D.N. 1991. *The Political Economy of Third World Intervention: mines, money, and U.S. policy in the Congo crisis.* Chicago, IL: University of Chicago Press.

Gibour, J. 1985. 'A closer look at Operation Manta', *African Defence Journal* 62: 58-69.

Gifford, P. & W.R. Louis, eds., 1971. *France and Britain in Africa: imperial rivalry and colonial rule.* New Haven, CT: Yale University Press.

Gill, S. 2001. 'Hegemony', in J. Krieger, ed., *The Oxford Companion to Politics of the World.* New York: Oxford University Press, 354-5.

Gilpin, R. 1981. *War and Change in World Politics.* Cambridge: Cambridge University Press.

Gleijeses, P. 2001. *Conflicting Missions: Havana, Washington, and Africa, 1959-1976.* Chapel Hill, NC: University of North Carolina Press.

Gourevitch, P.A. 1993. 'Political Economy', in J. Krieger, ed., *The Oxford Companion to Politics of the World.* New York: Oxford University Press, 716-7.

Griffiths, I.L. 1989. 'Airways sanctions against South Africa', *Area* 21, 3: 249-59.

Gross, S.R. 1973. 'The United Nations, self-determination and the Namibia opinions', *Yale Law Journal* 82, 3: 535-58.

Grundy, K.W. 1973. *Confrontation and Accommodation in Southern Africa: the limits of independence.* Berkeley, CA: University of California Press.

Guelke, A.B. 1972. 'South African foreign policy in Africa'. M.A. thesis, University of Cape Town.

Guelke, A.B. 1974. 'Africa as a market for South African goods', *Journal of Modern African Studies* 12, 1: 69-88.

Guelke, A.B. 1996. 'The impact of the end of the Cold War on the South African transition', *Journal of Contemporary African Studies* 14, 1: 87-100.

Hackland, B.A. 1984. 'The Progressive Party of South Africa, 1959-1981: political responses to structural changes and class struggle'. D.Phil. thesis, University of Oxford.

Hall, M. 1995. 'The legend of the Lost City: or, the man with golden balls', *Journal of Southern African Studies* 21, 2: 179-99.

Hamann, H. 2001. *Days of the Generals.* Cape Town: Zebra Press.

Hamill, James. 1992. 'President de Klerk's options', *Contemporary Review* 260, 1517: 291-8.

Hanlon, J. 1986. *Apartheid's Second Front: South Africa's war against its neighbours.* Harmondsworth: Penguin.

Harber, A. & B. Ludmann, eds., 1994. *A-Z of South African Politics: the essential handbook, 1994.* Harmondsworth: Penguin.

Harris, V.S. 2000. '"They should have destroyed more': the destruction of public records by the South African state in the final years of Apartheid, 1990-94', *Transformation* 42: 29-56.

Harris, V.S. 2002. 'The archival sliver: a perspective on the construction of social memory in archives and the transition from Apartheid to democracy', in C. Hamilton, et al., *Refiguring the Archive.* Dordrecht: Kluwer, 135-60.

Harshe, R. 1983. 'France, Francophone African states and South Africa: the complex triangle and Apartheid', *Alternatives* 9, 1: 51-72.

Hengeveld, R. & J. Rodenburg, eds., 1995. *Embargo: Apartheid's oil secrets revealed.* Amsterdam: Amsterdam University Press.

Hill, C.R. 2001. 'Foreign policy', in J. Krieger, ed., *The Oxford Companion to Politics of the World.* New York: Oxford University Press, 290-2.

Hoare, C. 1986. 'Mad Mike's own story: Col. Hoare on war and peace', *Soldier of Fortune* January: 44-7, 144.

Hoare, M. 1967. *Congo Mercenary.* London: Robert Hale.

Hoare, M. 1986. *The Seychelles Affair.* New York: Bantam Press.

Hoare, M. 1989. *The Road to Kalamata: a Congo mercenary's personal memoir.* London: Cooper.

Hocking, A. 1973. *Oppenheimer and Son.* Johannesburg: McGraw-Hill.

Holbo, P.S. 1977. 'Editor's note', *Diplomatic History* 1, 1: v-i.

Holden, M. 1989. 'Trade policy debate: import/export trends, 1957-1987', *Indicator SA* 6, 3: 31-6.

Holden, M. 1990. 'The growth of exports and manufacturing in South Africa from 1947 to 1987', *Development Southern Africa* 7, 3: 363-6.

Holland, M. 1988. *The European Community and South Africa: European political co-operation under strain.* London: Frances Pinter.

Holsti, O.R. 1991. 'International Relations models', in M.J. Hogan & T.G. Paterson, eds., *Explaining the History of American Foreign Relations.* Cambridge: Cambridge University Press, 57-88.

Holtes, W.B. 1983. *The Future of Trade Between the Republic of South Africa and Black Africa.* Pretoria: University of Pretoria, Institute for Strategic Studies.

Horrell, M. 1973. *The African Homelands of South Africa.* Johannesburg: South African Institute of Race Relations.

Houghton, D.H. 1976. *The South African Economy.* Cape Town: Oxford University Press. (Fourth Edition).

Hudson, M. 1999. 'Christian Neethling Barnard', in *They Shaped Our Century: the most influential South Africans of the twentieth century.* Cape Town: Human and Rousseau, 27-31.

Hughes, A. 1973. 'Malawi and South Africa's co-prosperity sphere', in Z. Cervenka, ed., *Land-Locked Countries of Africa.* Uppsala: Scandinavian Institute of African Studies. 212-32.

Industrial Development Corporation of South Africa Ltd. 1992. 'The Industrial Development Corporation of South Africa Ltd', in H.B. Falkena, W.J. Kok & E.J. van der Merwe, eds., *Financial Institutions.* Halfway House: Southern Book Publishers, 150-3.

Ingpen, B.D. & W. le Roux. 1996. *Safmarine 50, 1946-1996.* Vlaeberg, Cape Town: Fernwood Press.

Innes, D. 1984. *Anglo American and the Rise of Modern South Africa.* Johannesburg: Ravan Press.

Jaster, R.S. 1988. *The Defence of White Power: South African foreign policy under pressure.* Basingstoke: Macmillan; London: International Institute for Strategic Studies.

Jaster, R.S. 1990. *The 1988 Peace Accords and the Future of South-Western Africa.* London: Brassey's for the International Institute for Strategic Studies.

Jessup, E. 1979. *Ernest Oppenheimer: a study in power.* London: Rex Collings.

Johns, S.W. 1971. 'South Africa's diplomatic opening to the north', *Europa Archiv* 26, 22: 783-94.

Jones, S. & A. Müller. 1992. *The South African Economy, 1910-90.* New York: St Martin's Press.

Jones, S. 1992. 'Union Acceptances: the first merchant bank, 1955-73', in S. Jones, ed., *Financial Enterprise in South Africa since 1950.* Basingstoke: Macmillan, 166-81.

Jooste, G.P. 1977. *Diensherinneringe.* Johannesburg: Perskor.

Kaela, L.C.W. 1993. 'Behind Linkage diplomacy: the Brazzaville Accord revisited', *Transafrican Journal of History* 22: 122-41.

Kalley, J.A. 2001. *South Africa's Treaties in Theory and Practice, 1806-1998.* Lanham, MD: Scarecrow Press.

Kanfer, S. 1993. *The Last Empire: De Beers, diamonds, and the world.* London: Hodder & Stoughton

Karns, M.P. 1987. 'Ad hoc multilateral diplomacy: the Contact Group and Namibia', *International Organization* 41, 1: 93-123.

Kay, D.A. 1970. *The New Nations in the United Nations, 1960-1967*. New York: Columbia University Press.

Kelly, S. 1993. *America's Tyrant: the CIA and Mobutu of Zaire*. Washington, DC: American University Press.

Kerdellonton, C. 1989. 'Afrique: les bonnes affaires de Pretoria', *Jeune Afrique* 1465, 1 February: 47-58.

Kissinger, H.A. 1982. *Years of Upheaval*. Boston, MA: Little and Brown.

Kissinger, H.A. 1994. *Diplomacy*. New York: Simon and Schuster.

Kissinger, H.A. 1999. *Years of Renewal*. New York: Simon and Schuster.

Klare, M.T. 1977. *U.S. Arms Deliveries to South Africa: the Italian connection*. Washington, DC: Transnational Institute.

Klinghoffer, A.J. 1989. *Oiling the Wheels of Apartheid: exposing South Africa's secret oil trade*. Boulder, CO: Lynne Rienner.

Klotz, A.J. 1995. *Norms in International Relations: the struggle against Apartheid*. Ithaca, NY: Cornell University Press.

Knight, J. & H. Stevenson. 1986. 'Williamson Diamond Mine, De Beers, and the Colonial Office: a case-study of the quest for control', *Journal of Modern African Studies* 24, 3: 423-46.

Kotzé, H.J. & A. Greyling. 1994. *Political Organisations in South Africa*. Cape Town: Tafelberg. (Second Edition)

Kwitny, J. 1986. *Endless Enemies: the making of an unfriendly world*. New York: Penguin Books.

Landgren, S. 1989. *Embargo Disimplemented: South Africa's military industry*. Oxford: Oxford University Press for the Stockholm International Peace Research Institute.

Le Pere, G. & A. van Nieuwkerk. 2001. 'Facing the new millennium: South Africa's foreign policy in a globalising world', in K.G. Adar & R. Ajulu, eds., *Globalisation and Emerging Trends in African States' Foreign Policy-Making Processes: a comparative perspective of southern Africa*. Aldershot: Ashgate, 173-210.

Legum, C. 1972. 'Dialogue: the great debate', *Africa Contemporary Record, 1971-72*: A66-A82.

Legum, C. 1976. 'Southern Africa: the politics of Detente', *Year Book of World Affairs* 30: 14-29.

Legum, C. 1976. 'The Soviet Union, China and the West in southern Africa', *Foreign Affairs* 54, 4: 745-62.

Legum, C. 1976. *Vorster's Gamble for Africa: how the search for peace failed*. London: Rex Collings.

Legum, C. 1980. 'South Africa in the contemporary World', in R.M. Price & C.G. Rosberg, eds., *The Apartheid Regime: political power and racial domination*. Cape Town: David Philip; Berkeley, CA: University of California, Institute of International Studies, 281-96.

Legum, C. 1989. 'Republic South Africa: end of President Botha's rule, beginning of the de Klerk era', *Africa Contemporary Record, 1988-89*: B645-B727.

Leistner, G.M.E. & J.H. Moolman. 1974. *Bophuthatswana hulpbronne en ontwikkeling*. Pretoria: Africa Institute.

Leistner, G.M.E. 1976. '"Dialogue and tolerance": report on a recent visit to the Ivory Coast and Senegal', *Africa Institute Bulletin* 14, 3: 93.

Lemarchand, R. 1985. 'The crisis in Chad', in G.J. Bender, J.S. Coleman & R.L. Sklar, eds., *African Crisis Areas and U.S. Foreign Policy*. Berkeley, CA: University of California Press, 239-56.

Litwak, R.S. 2001. 'Détente', in J. Krieger, ed., *The Oxford Companion to Politics of the World*. New York: Oxford University Press, 214-5.

Louw, E.H. 1957. *Union's Africa Policy*. Pretoria: State Information Office.

Louw, E.H. 1959. *The Union and the Emergent States of Africa. Speech at the opening of the South African Bureau of Racial Affairs SABRA, Durban, 31 March*. Johannesburg: SABRA.

Louw, R.H. 2000. 'The legacy of Barend van Niekerk: a challenge to the on-going abuse of prisoners' rights', *South African Journal of Criminal Justice* 13, 1: 83-98.

Lowe Morna, C. 1991. 'The pariah's new pals', *Africa Report* 36, 3: 28-30.

LTA Limited: centenary review, 1889-1989. 1989. Johannesburg: LTA Limited.

Lunel, P. 1991. *Bob Denard: le roi de fortune*. Paris: Edition °1.

Mahoney, R.D. 1983. *JFK: ordeal in Africa*. New York: Oxford University Press.

Makinda, S.M. 1992. 'South Africa as a regional great power', in I.B. Neumann, ed., *Regional Great Powers in International Politics*. Basingstoke: Macmillan, 151-78.

Malan, M.A. de M. 1980. 'Die aanslag teen Suid-Afrika', *ISSUP Strategic Review* November: 3-16.

Mancham, J.R. 1983. *Paradise Raped: life, love and power in the Seychelles*. London: Methuen.

Manoim, I, ed., 1996. *"You Have Been Warned": the first ten years of the Mail & Guardian*. London: Viking.

Marais, J.S. 1975. 'South Africa: a country with great challenges and golden opportunities', in F.R. Metrowich, ed., *Towards Dialogue and Détente*. Sandton: Valiant Publishers, 85-93.

Marx, C. 1994. 'The Ossewabrandwag as a mass movement, 1939-1941', *Journal of Southern African Studies* 20, 2: 195-219.

Mathews, K. 1988. 'The African Group at the UN as an instrument of African diplomacy', *Nigerian Journal of International Affairs* 14, 1: 227-36.

Mathews, K. 1989. 'The Organisation of African Unity in world politics', in R.I. Onwuka & T.M. Shaw, eds., *Africa in World Politics: Into the 1990s*. Basingstoke: Macmillan, 32-63.

Mays, T.M. 2002. *Africa's First Peacekeeping Operation: the OAU in Chad, 1981-1982*. New York: Praeger.

McCarthy, S. 1996. 'Challenges for the South African intelligence community', in W.F. Gutteridge, ed., *South Africa's Defence and Security Into the 21st Century*. Aldershot: Dartmouth, 61-85.

McGowan, P.J. & P. Nel. 1999. 'The study of International Relations', in P. Nel & P.J. McGowan, eds., *Power, Wealth and Global Order: An International Relations Textbook for Africa*. Cape Town: University of Cape Town Press, 1-18.

McMahon, R.J. 1991. 'The study of American foreign relations: national history or international history?', in M.J. Hogan & T.G. Paterson, eds., *Explaining the History of American Foreign Relations*. Cambridge: Cambridge University Press, 11-23.

McNamara, F.T. 1989. *France in Black Africa*. Washington, DC: National Defense University.

McWilliams, J.P. 1989. *Armscor: South Africa's arms merchant*. London: Brassey's.

Médard, J.-F. 1997. 'Njonjo: portrait d'un "Big Man" au Kenya', in E. Terray, ed., *L'Etat contemporain en Afrique*. Paris: L'Harmattan, 49-87.

Meinardus, R. 1980. *Die Afrikapolitik der Republik Südafrika: von der Outward-Looking Policy bis zur Gegenwart*. Bonn: Informationsstelle Südliches Afrika.

Meiring, P. 1973. *Inside Information*. Cape Town: Howard Timmins.

Meiring, P. c1985. *Die lewe van Hilgard Muller*. Silverton: Promedia Publikaries.

Meredith, T. 1995. *Sky Trek: pioneering days of low-fare, air travel between South Africa and Europe*. Johannesburg: Tom Meredith.

Merrett, C. & C.C. Saunders. 2000. 'The Weekly Mail', in L. Switzer & M. Adhikari, eds., *South Africa's Resistance Press: alternative voices in the last generation under Apartheid*. Athens, OH: Ohio University Press, 458-86.

Metrowich, F.R. & C.F. de Villiers. 1975. *The Communist Strategy*. Pretoria: Department of Information.

Metrowich, F.R., ed., 1975. *Towards Dialogue and Détente*. Johannesburg: Valiant Publishers.

Mkhondo, R. 1993. *Reporting South Africa*. London: James Currey; Portsmouth, NH: Heinemann.

Moll, T. 1990. 'From booster to brake? Apartheid and economic growth in comparative perspective', in N.J. Nattrass & E. Ardington, eds., *The Political Economy of South Africa*. Cape Town: Oxford University Press, 74-87.

Molteno, R. 1971. 'South Africa's forward policy in Africa: milestones on the great north road', *The Round Table* 61, 243: 329-45.

Moolman, J.H. 1974. 'South Africans visit West Africa', *Newsletter of the South African Institute of International Affairs* 6, 3: 15-6.

Mugyenyi, J.B. & L.A. Swatuk. 1997. 'Of "growth poles" and "backwaters": emerging Uganda-South Africa relations', in L.A. Swatuk & D.R. Black, eds., *Bridging the Rift: the new South Africa in Africa*. Boulder CO: Westview Press, 153-70.

Muller, C.F.J. 1998. 'The creation of the Department of External Affairs in 1927', in *History of the Department of Foreign Affairs. Vol. I: 1927-1948*. Pretoria: Department of Foreign Affairs, 1-12. (Unpublished manuscript)

Muller, H. 1967. 'South Africa in today's Africa', *Africa Institute Bulletin* 5, 10: 303-6.

Muller, M.E. 1976. *Suid-Afrika se buitelandse verteenwoordiging (1910-1972)*. Pretoria: J.L. van Schaik.

Muller, M.E. 1989. 'The Department of Foreign Affairs', in A.J. Venter, ed., *South African Government and Politics: an introduction to its institutions, Processes and Policies*. Johannesburg: Southern Book Publishers, 241-71.

Muller, M.E. 1996. 'South Africa's changing external relations', in M. Faure & J.-E. Lane, eds., *South Africa: designing new political institutions*. London: Sage, 121-50.

Munger, E.S. 1965. *Notes on the Formation of South African Foreign Policy*. Pasadena, CA: Dahlstrom.

Munger, E.S. 1968. *South Africa's Prime Minister, John Vorster: new impressions of his evolving political commitment*. Hanover, NH: American Universities Field Staff.

Munger, E.S. 1979. *The Afrikaners*. Cape Town: Tafelberg.

Munger, E.S. 1983. *Touched by Africa*. Pasadena, CA: Castle Press.

Murray & Roberts: people & performers. 1976. Johannesburg: Financial Mail.

Murray, H. 1986. 'Anton Rupert', *Leadership South Africa* 5, 4: 10-2, 14.

Murray, H. 1989. 'The quiet South African: an interview', *Leadership South Africa* 8, 1: 7-10.

Namibian Independence and Cuban Troop Withdrawal. 1989. Pretoria: Department of Foreign Affairs.

Nattrass, N.J. 1991. 'Controversies about capitalism and Apartheid in South Africa: an economic perspective', *Journal of Southern African Studies* 17, 4: 654-77.

Nattrass, N.J. 1999. 'The Truth and Reconciliation Commission on business and Apartheid: a critical evaluation', *African Affairs* 98, 392: 373-91.

Neack, L., J.A.K. Hey & P.J. Haney. 1995. *Foreign Policy Analysis: continuity and change in its second generation.* Englewood Cliffs, NJ: Prentice Hall.

The New Encyclopaedia Britannica, Vol. 8. 1986. Chicago, IL: Encyclopaedia Britannica. (Fifteenth Edition)

Newbury, C. 1989. *The Diamond Ring: business, politics, and precious stones in South Africa, 1867-1947.* Oxford: Calendon Press.

Nolutshungu, S.C. 1975. *South Africa in Africa: a study of ideology and foreign policy.* New York: Africana Publishing; Manchester: Manchester University Press.

Nolutshungu, S.C. 1996. *Limits of Anarchy: intervention and state formation in Chad.* Charlottesville, VA: University Press of Virginia.

Nöthling, F.J. 1998. 'South Africa and Africa', in *History of the Department of Foreign Affairs. Vol. II: 1948-1966.* Pretoria: Department of Foreign Affairs, 38-51. (Unpublished manuscript)

Nweke, G.A. 1976. *External Intervention in African Conflicts: France and French-speaking West Africa in the Nigerian Civil War, 1967-1970.* Boston, MA: Boston University, African Studies Center.

Nwokedi, E. 1989. 'France's Africa: a struggle between exclusivity and interdependence', in R.I. Onwuka & T.M. Shaw, eds., *Africa in World Politics: into the 1990s.* Basingstoke: Macmillan, 180-97.

O'Meara, D. 1983. *Volkskapitalisme: class, capital and ideology in the development of Afrikaner nationalism, 1934-1948.* Johannesburg: Ravan Press.

O'Meara, D. 1996. *Forty Lost Years: the Apartheid state and the politics of the National Party, 1948-1994.* Johannesburg: Ravan Press; Athens, OH: Ohio University Press.

Ogba, L.O. 1989. 'An intelligence model of national security assessment for Nigeria: reflections from the South African entente with Equatorial Guinea', *Nigerian Journal of International Affairs* 15, 1: 31-46.

Olivier, G.C. 1973. 'Die grondslae van Suid-Afrika se buitelandse beleid'. Ph.D. thesis, University of Pretoria.

Olivier, G.C. 1975. 'South African foreign policy', in Denis Worrall, ed., *South Africa: Government and Politics.* Pretoria: J.L. van Schaik, 285-331. (Second Edition)

Olivier, G.C. 1977. *Suid-Afrika se buitelandse beleid.* Pretoria: Academica.

Olivier, G.C. 1982. 'South Africa's relations with Africa', in Robert Arthur Schrire, ed., *South Africa: Public Policy Perspectives.* Cape Town: Juta, 269-98.

Olivier, G.C. 1988. 'South Africa as a regional power', in D.J. van Vuuren, et al., eds., *South Africa: the challenge of reform.* Pinetown: Burgess, 551-65.

Oppenheimer, K. & S. Mynhardt. 1996. *Make the World Your Market: an account of the early history of Credit Guarantee Insurance Corporation of Africa Limited, 1956-1965.* Randburg: Credit Guarantee Insurance Corporation.

Owoeye, J. 1994. 'What can Africa expect from a post-Apartheid South Africa?', *Africa Insight* 24, 1: 44-6.

Pallister, D., S. Stewart & I. Lepper. 1987. *South Africa Inc.: the Oppenheimer empire.* London: Simon and Schuster.

Panter-Brick, S.K. 1988. 'Independence, French style', in P. Gifford & W.R. Louis, eds., *Decolonization and African Independence: the transfers of power, 1960-1980.* New Haven, CT: Yale University Press, 73-104.

Parliamentary Register, 1910-1984. 1991. Cape Town: Government Printer.

Patterson, D.K. 1985. 'Somalia and the United States, 1977-83: the new relationship', in G.J. Bender, J.S. Coleman & R.L. Sklar, eds., *African Crisis Areas and U.S. Foreign Policy.* Berkeley, CA: University of California Press, 194-204.

Péan, P. 1983. *Affaires africaines.* Paris: Fayard.

Pelzer, A.N. 1970. *Die Afrikaner-Broederbond: eerste 50 jaar.* Cape Town: Tafelberg.

Penn, J. 1974. *The Right to Look Human: an autobiography.* Johannesburg: McGraw Hill.

Pfister, R. 1992. 'United Nations sanctions against Apartheid: a legal, historical and political approach'. Unpublished seminar paper, University of Bern.

Pfister, R. 1997. 'Violence during South Africa's political transition (1990-1994): perceptions and their instrumentalisation'. Paper presented at the 16th Biennial Conference of the South African Historical Society, University of Pretoria, 6-9 July.

Pfister, R. 2000. *South Africa's Post-Apartheid Foreign Policy Towards Africa.* Iowa City, IO: University of Iowa Libraries. <http://sdrc.lib.uiowa.edu/ejab>

Pfister, R. 2003. 'Gateway to international victory: the diplomacy of the African National Congress in Africa, 1960-1994', *Journal of Modern African Studies* 41, 1: 51-73.

Philipps, E.H. 1969. 'South West Africa, South Africa's fifth province', *Revue militaire générale* 7: 181-98.

Pirie, G.H. 1990. 'Aviation, Apartheid and sanctions: air transport to and from South Africa, 1945-1989', *GeoJournal* 22, 3: 231-40.

Pityana, N.B., ed., 1991. *Bounds of Possibility: the legacy of Steve Biko and Black Consciousness.* Cape Town: David Philip.

Plano, J.C. & R. Olton. 1988. *The International Relations Dictionary.* Santa Barbara, CA: ABC-CLIO. (Fourth Edition)

Pogrund, B. 2000. *War of Words: memoirs of a South African journalist.* New York: Seven Stories Press.

Potgieter, H. & W. Steenkamp. 1981. *Aircraft of the South African Air Force.* Cape Town: C. Struik. (Second Edition)

Potgieter, H. 1986. *Aviation in South Africa.* Cape Town: C. Struik.

Pottinger, B. 1988. *The Imperial Presidency: P.W. Botha, the first 10 years.* Johannesburg: Southern Book Publishers.

Potts, D. 1985. 'Capital relocation in Africa: the case of Lilongwe in Malawi', *Geographical Journal* 151, 2: 182-96.

Prados, J. 1988. *Presidents' Secret Wars: CIA and Pentagon covert operations from World War II through Iranscam.* New York: William Morrow (Quill).

Pretorius, L. 1994. 'The head of government and organised business', in R.A. Schrire, ed., *Malan to de Klerk: leadership in the Apartheid state.* New York: St. Martin's Press; London: Hurst, 209-44.

Price, R.M. 1984. 'Pretoria's southern African strategy', *African Affairs* 83, 330: 11-32.

Prinsloo, D.S. 1997. *Stem uit die Wilderness: 'n biografie oor oud-pres. PW Botha.* Mosselbaai: Vaandel.

'Profile: John Barratt', *Optima* 33, 3, 1985: 141-3.

Puren, J. & B. Pottinger. 1986. *Mercenary Commander.* Alberton: Galago Books.

Qunta, V. 1992. 'De Klerk in Abuja: new hero or new morality?', *Southern Africa Political and Economic Monthly* 5, 9: 12-3.

Rees, M. & C. Day. 1980. *Muldergate: the story of the info scandal.* Johannesburg: Macmillan.

Report of the 1968 Business & Goodwill Mission to Malawi. 1968. Durban: Durban Chamber of Commerce.

Report of the 1973 Trade Mission to Malawi. 1973. Durban: Durban Chamber of Commerce.

Reunion, Mauritius, Malawi . . . report of 1979 trade mission. 1979. Durban: Durban Chamber of Commerce.

Reuvid, J. 1995. 'The petroleum industry', in J. Reuvid, ed., *Doing Business in South Africa.* London: Cogan Page, 232-5.

Rhoodie, E.M. 1983. *The Real Information Scandal.* Pretoria: Orbis SA.

Roberts, J. 2003. *Glitter and Greed: the secret world of the diamond empire.* New York: Disinformation.

Rogers, A. 2000. *Someone Else's War: mercenaries from 1960 to the present.* London: HarperCollins.

Rogerson, C.M. 1990. 'Sun International: the making of a South African tourismus multinational', *GeoJournal* 22, 3: 346, 349-50.

Rosenau, J.N. 1987. 'New directions and recurrent questions in the comparative study of foreign policy', in C.F. Herman, C.W. Kegley Jr. & J.N. Rosenau, eds., *New Directions in the Study of Foreign Policy.* London: Allen & Unwin, 1-10.

Rosenau, J.N. 2001. 'International Relations', in J. Krieger, ed., *The Oxford Companion to Politics of the World.* New York: Oxford University Press, 424-7. (Second Edition)

Ruggie, J.G. 1996. *Winning the Peace: America and world order in the new era.* New York: Columbia University Press.

Rutherford, D. 1992. *Dictionary of Economics.* London: Routledge.

Ryan, C. 1991. 'Trade roots', *Leadership South Africa* 10, 5: 54-9.

'Safair: African to its roots', in *Products of Southern Africa: a visual guide on the products, raw materials, minerals and services available from southern Africa.* Pretoria: New World International, 1993, 7.

Safmarine: 30 years of service. 1976. Johannesburg: Thomson Publishers.

Safren: corporate report. 1991. Johannesburg: Financial Mail.

SAFTO & the State of SA Trade: a corporate report. 1984. Johannesburg: Financial Mail.

Said, A.A., C.O. Lerche Jr. & C.O. Lerche III. 1995. *Concepts of International Politics in Global Perspective.* Englewood Cliffs, NJ: Prentice Hall. (Fourth Edition)

Sampson, A. 1987. *Black and Gold: tycoons, revolutionaries and Apartheid.* London: Hodder and Stoughton.

Samuel, P. 1999. *Michel Debré: l'architecte du Général.* Paris: Arnaud Franel.

Sarakinsky, I.H. 1992. 'South Africa: changing politics and the politics of change', in L. Benjamin & C. Gregory, eds., *Southern Africa at the Crossroads? Prospects for stability and development in the 1990s.* Rivonia: Justified Press, 125-59.

Schneider, M. 1991. 'Outlook for trade', *Leadership South Africa* 10, 6: 46-51.

Schoeman, B.M. 1974. *Vorster se 100 dae.* Cape Town: Human & Rousseau.

Schoeman, E. & C. Schoeman. 1993. *South Africa's Foreign Relations in Transition, 1985-1992: a chronology.* Johannesburg: South African Institute of International Affairs.

Schoeman, M.M.E. 2003. 'South Africa as an emerging middle power: 1994-2003', in J. Daniel, A. Habib & R.J. Southall, eds. *State of the Nation: South Africa 2003-2004.* Pretoria: Human Sciences Research Council, 349-67.

Schraeder, P.J. 1996. 'African International Relations', in A.A. Gordon & D.L. Gordon, eds., *Understanding Contemporary Africa.* Boulder, CO: Lynne Rienner, 129-65. (Second Edition)

Schraeder, P.J. 2001. 'South Africa's foreign policy: from international pariah to leader of the African Renaissance', *The Round Table* 90, 359: 229-43.

Schrire, R.A. & D. Silke. 1997. 'Foreign policy: the domestic context', in W. Carlsnaes & M.E. Muller, eds., *Change and South African External Relations.* Halfway House: International Thomson Publishing (Southern Africa), 3-15.

Seegers, A. 1996. *The Military in the Making of Modern South Africa*. London: I.B. Tauris.

Seekings, J. 2000. *The UDF: a history of the United Democratic Front in South Africa, 1983-1991*. Cape Town: David Philip.

Seidman, A. & N. Makgetla. 1979. 'Transnational corporate involvement in South Africa's military build-up', *Journal of Southern African Affairs* 4, 2: 153-73.

Selfe, J. 1987. 'The Total Onslaught and the Total Strategy: adaptations to the security intelligence decision-making structures under the P.W. Botha administration'. M.A. thesis, University of Cape Town.

Serfontein, J.H.P. 1970. *Die verkrampte aanslag*. Cape Town: Human & Rousseau.

Serfontein, J.H.P. 1979. *Brotherhood of Power: an exposé of the secret Afrikaner Broederbond*. London: Rex Collings.

Shabazz, M. 1992. 'Report on the OAU Dakar, Senegal Summit conference', *Southern Africa Political and Economy Monthly* 5, 10: 20-2, 27.

Shaw, T.M. 1977. 'Kenya and South Africa: "subimperialist" states', *Orbis* 21, 2: 375-94.

Shaw, T.M. 1979. 'The actors in African international politics', in T.M. Shaw & K.A. Heard, eds., *The Politics of Africa: dependence and development*. London: Longman, 357-96.

Shaw, T.M. 1987. 'Foreword', in O. Aluko, ed., *Africa and the Great Powers in the 1980s*. Lanham, MD: University Press of America, i-xi.

Shaw, T.M. & C.E. Adibe. 1994. 'South Africa, Nigeria and the prospects for complementary regionalism after Apartheid', *South African Journal of International Affairs* 1, 2: 1-18.

Shelton, G.L. 1986. 'Theoretical perspectives on South African foreign policy making', *Politikon: South African Journal of Political Studies* 13, 1: 3-21.

Shennan, A. 1993. *De Gaulle*. London: Longman.

Silber, G. 1999. 'Solomon Kerzner', in *They Shaped Our Century: the most influential South Africans of the twentieth century*. Cape Town: Human and Rousseau, 275-8.

Sinclair, M.R. 1981. 'Nigeria: from isolation to African leadership', *International Affairs Bulletin* 5, 3: 2-14.

Sindima, H.J. 2002. *Malawi's First Republic: an economic and political analysis*. Lanham, MD: University Press of America.

Slabbert, F. van Zyl. 1987. *The Last White Parliament: the struggle for South Africa by the leader of the white opposition*. New York: St. Martin's Press.

Slabbert, F. van Zyl. 1989. *The System and the Struggle: reform, revolt and reaction in South Africa*. Johannesburg: Jonathan Ball.

Smit, P. 1989. 'South Africa and black Africa', *Africa Insight* 19, 3: 125-9.

Sole, D.B. 1984. 'Review of "The Diplomacy of Isolation", by Deon Johannes Geldenhuys', *International Affairs Bulletin* 8, 1: 71-2.

Sole, D.B. 1989. *'This Above All'': reminiscences of a South African diplomat*. Cape Town. (Unpublished manuscript)

Sole, D.B. 1994. 'South African foreign policy assumptions and objectives from Hertzog to de Klerk', *South African Journal of International Affairs* 2, 1: 104-13.

Solomon, H. 1997. 'South African foreign policy and middle power leadership', in H. Solomon, ed., *Fairy Godmother, Hegemon or Partner? In search of a South African foreign policy*. Halfway House: Institute for Strategic Studies, 53-64.

South African Airways: thirty years of progress, 1934-1964. 1964. Johannesburg: Da Gama.

The South African Institute of International Affairs: past, present and future. 1984. Johannesburg: South African Institute of International Affairs.

Southall, R.J. 1984. 'South Africa', in T.M. Shaw & O. Aluko, eds., *The Political Economy of African Foreign Policy: comparative analysis*. Aldershot: Gower, 221-62.

Southall, R.J. 1999. *South Africa in Africa: foreign policy-making during the Apartheid era.* Johannesburg: Institute for Global Dialogue.

Sparks, D.L. 2001. 'Indian Ocean region', in J. Krieger, ed., *The Oxford Companion to Politics of the World.* New York: Oxford University Press, 388-90. (Second Edition)

Spence, J.E. 1965. *Republic Under Pressure: a study of South African foreign policy.* London: Oxford University Press.

Starcke, A. 1978. *Survival: taped interviews with South Africa's power élite.* Cape Town: Tafelberg.

Stevens, R.P. 1970. 'South Africa and independent black Africa', *Africa Today* 17, 3: 23-52.

Steyn, J.C. 2002. *Penvegter: Piet Cillié van Die Burger.* Cape Town: Tafelberg.

Stockholm International Peace Research Institute. 1976. *Southern Africa: the escalation of the conflict. A politico-military study.* New York: Praeger.

Stockwell, J. 1978. *In Search of Enemies: a CIA story.* London: John Deutsch.

Stone, D. 2001. 'Think tanks', in N.J. Smelser & P.B. Bates, eds., *International Encyclopedia of the Social and Behavioral Sciences. Vol. 23.* Amsterdam: Elsevier, 15668-71.

Strangwayes-Booth, J. 1976. *A Cricket in the Thorn Tree: Helen Suzman and the Progressive Party.* Johannesburg: Hutchinson.

Stremlau, J.J. 1977. *The International Politics of the Nigerian Civil War, 1967-1970.* Princeton, NJ: Princeton University Press.

Stuttaford, M. 1986. *Safmarine, 1946-1986.* Cape Town: Bowford Publications.

Sun International: a corporate report. 1985. Johannesburg: Financial Mail.

Suzman, H. 1993. *In No Uncertain Terms: memoirs.* London: Sinclair-Stevenson.

Swanepoel, J.J. 1982. 'Die diplomasie van adv. B.J. Vorster'. Ph.D. thesis, University of the Orange Free State.

Swart, S.P.C., J. Adendorff & M.H.H. Louw, eds., 1966. *The Economic and Administrative Development in Bantu Territories.* Sovenga: University College of the North.

Terblanche, H.O. 1983. *John Vorster: OB-generaal en afrikanervegter.* Roodepoort: CUM-Boeke.

Terreblanche, S. & N.J. Nattrass. 1990. 'A periodization of the Political Economy from 1910', in N.J. Nattrass & E. Ardington, eds., *The Political Economy of South Africa.* Cape Town: Oxford University Press, 6-23.

Terrill, W.A. 1986. 'The Comoro Islands in South African regional strategy', *Africa Today* 33, 2/3: 59-70.

Thomas, S. 1996. *The Diplomacy of Liberation: the foreign relations of the African National Congress since 1960.* London: I.B. Tauris.

Thomas, W.H. 1979. 'South Africa and black Africa: the future economic interaction', *Politikon: South African Journal of Political Studies* 6, 2: 103-18.

Tordoff, W. 1984. *Government and Politics in Africa.* Basingstoke: Macmillan.

Truth and Reconciliation Commission of South Africa Report. Vol. 1: The Commission; Vol. 2: Repression and Resistance; Vol. 4: Institutional and Special Hearings. 1999. Basingstoke: Macmillan.

Uys, F. 1993. 'Airlines of Africa: SAFAIR', *World Airnews* 21, 5: 22-3.

Uys, I. 1992. *South African Military Who's Who, 1452-1992.* Germiston: Fortress Publishers.

Uys, S. 1992. 'The ANC's international standing', *SA Foundation Review* 18, 7: 1-2.

Vale, P.C.J. & C.J.J. Mphaisha. 1999. 'Analysing and evaluating foreign policy', in P. Nel & P.J. McGowan, eds., *Power, Wealth and Global Order: an International Relations textbook for Africa.* Cape Town: University of Cape Town Press, 88-102.

Vale, P.C.J. 1992. 'South Africa's 'New Diplomacy'', in G. Moss & I. Obery, eds., *From 'Red Friday' to CODESA.* Johannesburg: Ravan Press, 424-35.

Vale, P.C.J. 1997. 'Understanding the upstairs and the downstairs: prospects for a post-Apartheid foreign policy', in A.F. Cooper, ed., *Niche Diplomacy: Middle Powers after the Cold War*. London. Macmillan, 197-214.

Vallée, O. 2000. 'Une Afrique sous influence: Elf au service de l'Etat français', *Le monde diplomatique* 553, 1 avril: 24.

Van der Westhuizen, J. 1998. 'South Africa's emergence as a middle power', *Third World Quarterly* 19, 3: 435-55.

Van der Westhuizen, J. 2001. 'Marketing the 'rainbow nation': the power of the South African music, film and sport industry', in K.C. Dunn & T.M. Shaw, eds., *Africa's Challenge to International Relations Theory*. New York: Palgrave, 64-81.

Van Heerden, N.P. 1989. *South Africa and Africa: the New Diplomacy*. Pretoria: University of Pretoria, Institute for Strategic Studies.

Van Meter, K. 1980. 'The French role in Africa', in E. Ray, et al., eds., *Dirty Work 2: the CIA in Africa*. London: Zed Books; Secaucus, NJ: Lyle Stuart, 24-35.

Van Niekerk, B. 1970. *The African Image (Negritude) in the Work of Leopold Sedar Senghor*. Cape Town: A A Balkema.

Van Nieuwkerk, A. & K. van Wyk. 1989. 'The operational code of PW Botha: Apartheid, realism and misperception, *International Affairs Bulletin* 13, 3: 70-88.

Van Wyk, A. 1992. 'Pillars of co-operation in Africa: interview with R.F. Botha', *RSA Policy Review* 5, 4: 28-35.

Van Wyk, A. 1992. 'Significant breakthrough in Nigeria', *RSA Policy Review* 5, 4: 36-41.

Van Wyk, A.J. 1998. 'Eric Louw: pioneer diplomat, 1925-1937', in *History of the Department of Foreign Affairs. Vol. I: 1927-1948*. Pretoria: Department of Foreign Affairs, 13-32. (Unpublished manuscript)

Van Wyk, K. 1991. 'Foreign policy orientations of the P.W. Botha regime: changing perceptions of state elites in South Africa', *Journal of Contemporary African Studies* 10, 1: 45-65.

Venter, A.J. 1977. *Vorster's Africa: friendship and frustration*. Johannesburg: Ernest Stanton.

Venter, T.D. 1980. 'Black Africa and the Apartheid issue: a South African response', *Journal of Contemporary African Studies* 1, 1: 81-103.

Venter, T.D. 1980. *South Africa and Black Africa: some problem areas and prospects for rapprochement*. Pretoria: Africa Institute.

Venter, T.D. 1990. 'The Comorian comitragedy: final curtain on Abdallahism?', *Africa Insight* 20, 3: 141-50.

Verhoef, G. 1992. 'Afrikaner nationalism in South African banking: the case of Volkskas and Trust Bank', in S. Jones, ed., *Financial Enterprise in South Africa since 1950*. London: Macmillan, 115-53.

Verwoerd, H.F. 1964. *I. Crisis in World Conscience; II. The Road to Freedom for Basutoland, Bechuanaland, Swaziland*. Pretoria: Department of Information.

Vincent, L. 1999. 'Non-state actors in International Relations', in P. Nel & P.J. McGowan, eds., *Power, Wealth and Global Order: an International Relations textbook for Africa*. Cape Town: University of Cape Town Press, 121-32.

Von der Ropp, K. 1971. 'Chancen eines Dialoges zwischen der Republik Südafrika und dem schwarzen Afrika', *Internationales Afrikaforum* 7, 12: 731-6.

Vorster, B.J. 1970. *South Africa's Outward Policy. One of a series of lectures delivered at annual general meeting of the Suid-Afrikaanse Akademie vir Westenskap en Kuns on the Subject "South Africa in the World", Pretoria, July 1969*. Cape Town: Tafelberg.

Waldmeir, P. 1997. *Anatomy of a Miracle: the end of Apartheid and the birth of the new South Africa*. New York: W.W. Norton.

Walker, M. 1982. *Powers of the Press: the world's great newspapers*. London: Quartet Books.

Weinberg, S. 1994. *Last of the Pirates: the search for Bob Denard.* London: Jonathan Cape.

Weissman, S.R. 1980. 'The CIA and U.S. policy in Zaire and Angola', in E. Ray, et al., eds., *Dirty Work 2: the CIA in Africa.* London: Zed Books; Secaucus, NJ: Lyle Stuart, 157-81.

Whann, C.A. 1998. 'The Political Economy of Cape Verde's foreign policy', *Africana Journal: A Bibliographical and Review Quarterly,* 17: 40-50.

White Paper on Defence and Armament Production. 1975. Pretoria: Department of Defence.

White Paper on Defence and Armaments Supply. 1979, 1982, 1984. Pretoria: Department of Defence.

White Paper on Defence. 1977. Pretoria: Department of Defence.

Whitehill, R. 1986. 'The sanctions that never were: Arab and Iranian oil sales to South Africa', *Middle East Review* 19, 1: 38-46.

Whyte, J. 1997. 'Taking a chance on Zaire: Tenke mining set for feasibility at Tenke-Fungurume', *Northern Miner* 83, 2, 10 March.

Wickman, S.B. 1982. 'Mauritius', in Frederica M. Bunge, ed., *Indian Ocean: five island countries.* Washington, DC: The American University, 127-66.

Wilkins, I. & H. Strydom. 1980. *The Super-Afrikaners: inside the Afrikaner Broederbond.* Johannesburg: Jonathan Ball.

Williams, G. & B. Hackland. 1988. *The Dictionary of Contemporary Politics of Southern Africa.* London: Routledge.

Williams, P.D. 2001. 'Intellectuals and the end of Apartheid: critical security studies and the South African transition'. Ph.D. thesis, University of Wales, Aberystwyth.

Wilmot, P.F. 1989. *Nigeria's Southern Africa Policy, 1960-1988.* Uppsala: Nordic Africa Institute.

Winter, G. 1981. *Inside BOSS: South Africa's secret police.* Harmondsworth: Penguin.

Woldring, K. 1975. 'South Africa's Africa policy reconsidered', *African Review: A Journal of African Politics, Development and International Affairs* 5, 1: 77-93.

Yao, B.K. 1991. 'Côte d'Ivoire – Afrique du Sud: l'aboutissement du dialogue', *Revue juridique et politique: indépendance et coopération* 45, 2: 145-50.

Yao, B.K. 1992. 'Le dialogue Yamassoukro – Prétoria: un aperçu', *Afrique 2000* 9: 5-13.

Yao, B.K. 1996. 'Jacques Foccart: homme d'influence, acteur incontournable de la politique africaine de la France', *Revue juridique et politique: indépendance et coopération* 50, 1: 60-76.

Zartman, I.W. 1967. 'Africa as a subordinate state system in International Relations', *International Organization* 21, 3: 545-64.

Index

Names

Themes

Note: It should be understood that South Africa is the main focus of this work and is therefore party to all entries.